BARRON'S REVIEW COURSE SERIES

Let's Review: Sequential Mathematics, Course I

Lawrence S. Leff

Assistant Principal,
Mathematics Supervision
Franklin D. Roosevelt High School
Brooklyn, New York

BARRON'S

BARRON'S EDUCATIONAL SERIES

All inquiries should be addressed to:
Barron's Educational Series, Inc.
250 Wireless Boulevard
Hauppauge, New York 11788

Library of Congress Catalog Card No. 87-27868

International Standard Book No. 0-8120-3843-6

Library of Congress Cataloging in Publication Data

Leff, Lawrence S.
    Sequential mathematics course I : review text / Lawrence S. Leff.
      p.   cm.
    Includes index.
    ISBN 0-8120-3843-6
    1. Mathematics--1961–   2. Mathematics--Study and teaching
(Secondary)--New York (State)   I. Title.
    [QA39.2.L42 1988]
    510--dc19   87-27868
                                       CIP
                                       AC

PRINTED IN THE UNITED STATES OF AMERICA

3   800   987654

PREFACE

● *For which course can this book be used?*

This book reflects the newly revised syllabus of study for Course I of the New York State Three-Year Sequence in High School Mathematics (1987 revision). It includes the topics that the current revision has introduced: applications of logic, expanded coverage of algebraic fractions and operations, and elements of transformations in geometry.

Teachers of traditional high school level courses in elementary algebra can use the material on logic, geometry, and probability and statistics as a source of possible enrichment activities for their students.

● *What special features does this book have?*

Each chapter closes with a set of summary exercises that provides . comprehensive review of the chapter. Except for Chapters 1 and 7, these exercises include many actual test questions selected from past New York State Course I Regents Examination. Thus the end-of-chapter reviews provide the student with the opportunity to get an early headstart in preparing for this important examination. In addition, several full-length Course I Regents Examinations given in previous years have been reprinted at the end of the book.

The book uses an easy-to-follow writing style that is enhanced by numerous demonstration examples designed to build skill and confidence. The examples and their solutions try to anticipate and then to answer the "why" types of questions that the student may have.

For easy reference, the major topics of the book are grouped by branch of mathematics (Logic, Algebra, Geometry, Coordinate Geometry and Transformations, Probability and Statistics). The clarity of this organization is of great assistance, particularly if the student is using this book as a study aide with another textbook.

The answers to Chapter Review exercises are provided at the back of the book so that the student may obtain additional feedback and guidance in progressing from one chapter to the next.

● *Who should use this book?*

Students who wish to improve their grades will find the concise explanations and numerous demonstration examples and practice exercises especially helpful.

Teachers and school systems who desire an additional teaching and planning resource will find this book an ideal companion to any of the Course I textbooks. Indeed, the depth of coverage and the wealth of practice exercises make this book a possible choice as the primary textbook for the course.

> Note that this symbol (■■■■) signals the beginning of an example and where its solution ends.

LAWRENCE S. LEFF

TABLE OF CONTENTS

CHAPTER 1

Numbers and Variables— Basic Concepts

1.1   USING SYMBOLS AND SETS

_____ KEY IDEAS _____

Numerals, variables, arithmetic operation symbols, and other special symbols are used as a type of mathematical shorthand to make it easier for us to do work in mathematics.

NUMERALS AND VARIABLES.   Numbers are mental concepts, while symbols such as 1, 2, and 3 are **numerals** that are used to help represent these ideas. **Variables** are symbols that represent quantities whose values are not currently known or that may change. Letters of the alphabet are frequently chosen as variables.

REPRESENTING MULTIPLICATION.   The product of two numbers, say 2 and 3, can be represented in a variety of ways. The symbols $\times$ and $\cdot$ (a raised dot) can be used to represent multiplication, as in 2×3 or $2 \cdot 3$. Parentheses can also indicate multiplication, as in $(2)(3)$, $2(3)$, and $(2)3$.

When a number and a variable, or two variables, are written consecutively without an operation symbol between them, the operation of multiplication is implied. The expression $5n$ means "5 multiplied by n." The number 5 is called the **coefficient** of n. The coefficient of $7y$ is 7, and the coefficient of y is 1 since $y = 1 \cdot y$.

If $n = 3$, then $5n = 5 \times 3 = 15$. The expression mn means "m multiplied by n." If $m = 4$ and $n = 6$, then $mn = 4 \times 6 = 24$.

1

COMPARISON SYMBOLS.   In the expression $1 + 1 = 2$, the symbol $=$ is read as "is equal to" and indicates that whatever appears on the left side of the symbol is equal in value to whatever appears on the right side of the symbol. An expression of this type is an **equation**.

A statement that two quantities are not equal is called an **inequality**, as in $1 + 1 \neq 3$. The symbol $\neq$ is read as "is not equal to." If two numbers are not equal, then there are various possibilities, which are summarized in Table 1.1. Keep in mind that statements such as $8 > 7$ ("8 is greater than 7") and $7 < 8$ ("7 is less than 8") are equivalent.

TABLE 1.1   Comparison Symbols

Example	Symbol	Read as . . .
$8 > 7$	$>$	8 *is greater than* 7.
$5 \geq 2$	$\geq$	5 *is greater than* or *equal to* 2.
$1 < 4$	$<$	1 *is less than* 4.
$2 \leq 3$	$\leq$	2 *is less than* or *equal to* 3.

SETS AND SET NOTATION.   A **set** is a collection of things. A description of a set usually includes some rule or guideline that can be used to determine whether an object belongs to a particular set. Some examples of sets are the books on a shelf, the subjects you are taking in school, the letters of the English alphabet, the boys and girls in your mathematics class, and the numbers between 1 and 2.

Some sets can be described by listing all of their members within a pair of braces. Thus the set of vowels in the English alphabet can be written as $\{a, e, i, o, u\}$. Each member of a set is called an **element** of the set. The set of vowels has five elements: a, e, i, o, and u.

FACTS ABOUT SETS.   You should be familiar with the following facts about sets:

● Set $A = $ set B if sets A and B have exactly the same elements regardless of the order in which the elements appear.

Example: If $A = \{-1, 0, 1\}$ and $B = \{1, -1, 0\}$, then set $A = $ set B.

● A set may contain *no* elements. A set that contains no elements is called an **empty set** (*or* **null set**) and is symbolized by $\{ \}$ (*or* $\varnothing$).

Example: If $C = \{$set of cows that can speak French$\}$, then set $C = \{ \}$ or $\varnothing$.

● A set may contain an *infinite* number of elements.

Example: The set of counting numbers is $\{1, 2, 3, 4, 5, \ldots\}$, where the three dots indicate that the pattern continues without ever ending.

● The elements of two sets may be combined to form a new set. The **union** of sets A and B is symbolized as $A \cup B$ and is the set that contains all the elements found in either or both of the sets.

Example: If $A = \{11, 13, 15\}$ and $B = \{11, 12, 14\}$, then $A \cup B = \{11, 12, 13, 14, 15\}$.

● The set that contains only the elements that are common to both sets is called the **intersection** of two sets and is symbolized by an inverted $\cup$.

Example: If $A = \{11, 13, 15\}$ and $B = \{11, 12, 14\}$, then $A \cap B = \{11\}$ since 11 is the only number that is found in both sets.

● If each element of a set A is also a member of a second set B, then set A is a **subset** of set B. The empty set is a subset of *every* set. Also, every set is considered to be a subset of itself.

Example: If $A = \{1, 3, 5\}$ and $B = \{1, 2, 3, 4, 5, 6\}$, then set A is a subset of set B. If $C = \{6, 7, 8\}$, then set C is *not* a subset of set B since every element of set C is not contained in set B.

EXERCISE SET 1.1

1. If $A = \{1, 2, 3, 4, 5, 6, 7, 8\}$, $B = \{7, 9, 10\}$, and $C = \{1, 3, 8, x, y, z\}$, then write the members of each of the following sets:
   (a) $A \cup B$ (b) $A \cap B$ (c) $A \cap C$ (d) $B \cap C$ (e) $B \cup (A \cap C)$

2. Replace $\square$ with a comparison symbol (other than $\neq$) so that the resulting statement is true.
   (a) $3 + 9 \;\square\; 15 - 1$ (d) $0 \;\square\; 3$ (g) $x + 1 \;\square\; x - 1$

   (b) $19.10 \;\square\; 19.01$ (e) $3.14 \;\square\; \dfrac{22}{7}$ (h) $(2.8)(0.7) \;\square\; (0.9)(2.4)$

   (c) $\dfrac{1}{4} \;\square\; \dfrac{1}{3}$ (f) $\dfrac{16}{20} \;\square\; \dfrac{7}{10}$ (i) $x + y \;\square\; y + x$

3. If $A = \{4, 5, 6, 7\}$, then which set is not a subset of A?
   (1) $\{4, 5\}$ (2) $\{\ \}$ (3) $\{0\}$ (4) $\{4, 5, 6, 7\}$

1.2   CLASSIFYING NUMBERS

─────────────────── KEY IDEAS ───────────────────

You are probably already familiar with different types of numbers, such as whole numbers, fractions, positive and negative numbers, and numbers with decimal parts. Organizing numbers into families or sets provides insight into the structure of our number system.

NATURAL AND WHOLE NUMBERS.   The counting numbers 1, 2, 3, 4, 5, 6, . . . form the set of **natural numbers**, usually represented by **N**. If set **N** is expanded to include 0, then the set is called the set of **whole numbers,** usually represented by **W**. Therefore

$$\mathbf{N} = \{\text{natural numbers}\} = \{1, 2, 3, 4, \ldots\},$$
$$\mathbf{W} = \{\text{whole numbers}\} = \{0, 1, 2, 3, 4, \ldots\}.$$

Numbers greater than 0 are called **positive numbers**. Positive 4 is written either as $+4$ or, more simply, as 4.

SET-BUILDER NOTATION.   The expression "the set of all numbers x such that x is greater than 5" may be concisely written as

$$\{x \mid x > 5\}.$$

The vertical bar within the braces is read as "such that." If x is a whole number, then $\{x \mid x > 5\} = \{6, 7, 8, 9, \ldots\}$. Sometimes a colon (:), also read as "such that," is used instead of a vertical bar, as in $\{x : x > 5\}$.

NUMBER OPPOSITES AND THE INTEGERS.   Every number has an *opposite*. Two numbers are **opposite** in the same sense that depositing 25 dollars (positive) and withdrawing 25 dollars (negative) from a bank savings account are opposite activities. The opposite of 25 is symbolized by a raised minus sign in front of 25, as in $^{-}25$, which is read as "negative 25." The opposite of $^{-}4$ is 4. In general, the opposite of number x is ^{-}x. The opposite of a positive number is always a negative number, while the opposite of a negative number is a positive number. The opposite of 0 is 0.

 The set that includes the whole numbers and the opposite of each whole number is called the set of **integers**:

$$\mathbf{Z} = \{\text{integers}\} = \{\ldots, -4, -3, -2, -1, 0, 1, 2, 3, 4, \ldots\}.$$

THE NEGATIVE SIGN.   The ordinary subtraction sign followed by a number or expression can be interpreted as "take the opposite of . . . ." For example,

$$-(+9) = {}^{-}9 \text{ since the opposite of positive 9 is negative 9,}$$

$$-(^{-}2) = +2 \text{ since the opposite of negative 2 is positive 2.}$$

 Since number pairs such as $^{-}5$ (*negative* 5) and -5 (*the opposite of* 5) are equivalent, we will simplify the notation by using a single symbol, a centered minus sign ($-$), to represent both types of numbers (as well as the operation of subtraction). For example, negative 3 will be written as -3, rather than as $^{-}3$.

NUMBER LINE.   Is $-1 > -2$? It is sometimes helpful to use a diagram to illustrate how positive and negative numbers are ordered. Figure 1.1 represents a **number line**, which is like a ruler that continues without ending in both directions. The markings on the ruler correspond to the points on the number line. The number associated with each point on the number line is called the **coordinate** of the point. The point whose coordinate is 0 is called the **origin** and divides the number line so that points to its right are positive and points to its left are negative. The number line is constructed so that the distance between a number, say 3, and the origin is the same as the distance between the number's opposite, -3 in this case, and the origin.

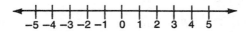

Figure 1.1   A Number Line

The coordinate of every point on the number line is larger than the coordinate of the point to its left. For example, $-2 > -3$, $-1 > -2$, $0 > -1$, $1 > 0$, and so forth. In other words, as we move along the number line from left to right, the coordinates *increase* in value.

RATIONAL, IRRATIONAL, AND REAL NUMBERS.   The set of fractions, where the numerators and denominators are integers (but the denominator cannot be 0), is called the set of **rational numbers**. Examples of rational numbers are $\frac{1}{2}$, $-\frac{6}{13}$ and 0.36 (since $0.36 = \frac{36}{100}$). The set of integers is a subset of the set of rational numbers since integers such as 4 can also be written in fractional form as $\frac{4}{1}$.

Other numbers, called **irrational numbers**, cannot be represented as the quotient of two integers. The value of π (pi) can be *approximated* as $\frac{22}{7}$ or as 3.14, but it cannot be expressed exactly as the quotient of two integers. The number π (pi), therefore, is an example of an irrational number.

The set of rational numbers (which include the whole numbers, natural numbers, and integers) together with the set of irrational numbers forms the set of **real numbers**.

More will be said about these three types of numbers in Chapter 8.

PROPERTIES OF 0 AND 1.   Adding 0 to a number or multiplying a number by 1 always results in the original number. The numbers 0 and 1 are called **identity elements**.

The sum of a number and its *additive inverse* is always 0. The **additive inverse** of a number is the number's opposite. For example, the additive inverse of 5 is -5 since $5 + (-5) = 0$. The additive inverse of -3 is 3 since $-3 + (3) = 0$.

The product of a number and its *multiplicative inverse* is always 1. The **multiplicative inverse** of a nonzero number is the reciprocal of the number. For example, the multiplicative inverse (reciprocal) of 5 is $\frac{1}{5}$ since $5 \times \frac{1}{5} = 1$. The multiplicative inverse of $\frac{2}{3}$ is $\frac{3}{2}$ since $\frac{2}{3} \times \frac{3}{2} = 1$.

Example ▬▬▬▬

1. What value of x makes each of the following true?

$$\text{(a) } x+8=0 \qquad \text{(b) } \left(\frac{3}{4}\right)x=1$$

Solutions: (a) The value of x is -8 since the sum of a number (8) and its opposite (-8) is 0.

(b) The value of x is $\frac{4}{3}$ since the product of a number ($\frac{3}{4}$) and its reciprocal ($\frac{4}{3}$) is 1.

ABSOLUTE VALUE. The **absolute value** of a number x is written as $|x|$ and may be interpreted as the *distance* between the point on the number line whose coordinate is x and the origin. Since distance cannot be negative, $|x|$ is always nonnegative and can be evaluated by writing the number *without* a sign. For example, $|+5|=5$, $|0|=0$, and $|-3|=3$. Here are two more examples:

$$1. \quad |-5|+|-4|=5+4=9$$

$$2. \quad 3|-2|=3(2) \qquad =6$$

Example ▬▬▬▬

2. Which number of the set $\{-2, 5, -8\}$ has the largest absolute value?

Solution: Although -8 is the smallest number, it has the largest absolute value since $|-2|=2$, $|5|=5$, and $|-8|=8$.

EXERCISE SET 1.2

1. Let $A = \{$whole numbers greater than 4$\}$, $B = \{$whole numbers less than 10$\}$, and $C = \{$negative integers$\}$. List the elements of each of the following sets:
   (a) $A \cup B$ (b) $A \cap B$ (c) $A \cap C$ (d) $B \cup C$

2. If $L = \{$whole numbers greater than 5$\}$ and $M = \{$whole numbers less than or equal to 3$\}$, list the elements of $L \cup M$.

3. Find the additive and multiplicative inverses for each of the following numbers:
   (a) 3   (b) -8 (c) $\frac{1}{6}$ (d) $-\frac{3}{4}$ (e) 0.2   (f) $\frac{11}{8}$

4. Which set is a subset of the set of integers?
   (1) Real numbers   (3) Rational numbers
   (2) Irrational numbers   (4) Natural numbers

5. Which of the following sets of numbers is *not* a subset of any of the other sets?
   (1) {Rationals}   (2) {Reals}   (3) {Integers}   (4) {Naturals}

6. Which statement is true for the set of whole numbers?
   (1) The multiplicative identity is 0.
   (2) The additive identity is 1.
   (3) All elements of the set are rational numbers.
   (4) Each whole number has an additive inverse that is also a whole number.

7. Which number is equal to its multiplicative inverse?
   (1) 0   (2) 1   (3) $\dfrac{1}{2}$ (4) -2

8. If $x + y = x$, then what is the value of xy?

9. Find the value of x that makes each of the following statements true:
   (a) $3 + x = 0$ (b) $\dfrac{1}{6}x = 1$ (c) $x - 5 = 0$ (d) $\dfrac{7}{3}x = 1$

10–24. Evaluate each of the following:

10. $|-2| + |1|$

11. $|-5| - 5 + |-5|$

12. $\left|\dfrac{2}{3}\right| - |8|$

13. $|-5||-2|$

14. $\dfrac{|-10|}{10}$

15. $|-3.68| - |-1.79|$

16. $5(|-4| - |-4|)$

17. $|-1.8| + |0.7|$

18. $|-1\frac{3}{4}||-2|$

19. $\dfrac{|-12|}{20}$

20. $\dfrac{|-1.17|}{0.65}$

21. $\left|\dfrac{-3}{5}\right| - \left|\dfrac{-1}{5}\right|$

22. $\left|\dfrac{3}{4}\right|\left|\dfrac{-8}{9}\right|$

23. $\left|\dfrac{-3}{14}\right| + \left|\dfrac{-1}{7}\right|$

24. $1.6(|-2.34| + |1.49|)$

25–33. Replace □ with a comparison symbol ($<$, $>$, or $=$) that makes the resulting statement true.

25. $-5 \;\square\; -1$

26. $|-3| \;\square\; 0$

27. $2 \;\square\; |-4|$

28. $|-5| \;\square\; 5$

29. $|-8| \;\square\; 4(|-2|)$

30. $|-10| \;\square\; -2$

31. $\left|\dfrac{-1}{3}\right| \;\square\; 0.43$

32. $\dfrac{2}{5} \;\square\; \left|\dfrac{-1}{2}\right|$

33. $(1.5)(|-3.2|) \;\square\; 5$

1.3 REVIEWING SOME NUMBER FACTS

--- KEY IDEAS ---

When adding or multiplying numbers, the order of the numbers is not important, whereas in subtraction and division the order of the numbers matters.

When dividing an integer by a smaller integer, if the quotient is an integer having a remainder of 0, then the larger integer is said to be *evenly divisible* by the smaller integer.

SOME LAWS OF ARITHMETIC.   The **commutative law** states that *two* numbers may be added or multiplied in any order. For example,

$$2 + 3 = 3 + 2 \quad \text{and} \quad 2 \cdot 3 = 3 \cdot 2.$$

Three numbers may also be added or multiplied in any order; this is called the **associative law.**

There is no commutative law or associative law for subtraction or division since, if the order of the numbers involved in each of these operations is changed, the answer may be affected. For example, $8 - 2 \neq 2 - 8$, and $\frac{8}{2} \neq \frac{2}{8}$.

DIVISIBILITY.   The number 12 is *divisible by* 4 (or 4 *divides* 12 *evenly*) since the quotient is 3 with a *remainder* of 0. The number 12 is *not* divisible by 5 since, when 12 is divided by 5, there is a remainder of 2. An **even number** is any integer that is divisible by 2, while an **odd number** is any integer that is *not* divisible by 2:

$$\{Even \text{ numbers}\} = \{\ldots, -6, -4, -2, 0, 2, 4, 6, \ldots\},$$

$$\{Odd \text{ numbers}\} = \{\ldots, -5, -3, -1, 1, 3, 5, \ldots\}.$$

The number 0 may be written in different forms as a fraction. For example, $\frac{0}{1} = 0$, $\frac{0}{2} = 0$, and so forth. In other words, 0 divided by any nonzero number is always 0. *Dividing by 0 is not allowed.* An expression such as $\frac{3}{0}$ is said to be "meaningless" or "not defined."

The number 1 may also be represented in different ways as a fraction. For example, $\frac{3}{3} = 1$ and $\frac{x}{x} = 1$ (provided that $x \neq 0$). In general, any nonzero number divided by itself is 1.

Examples ▬▬▬

1.   For what value of x is $\dfrac{1}{x - 4}$ not defined?

Solution: If $x = 4$, then the denominator of the fraction will be equal to 0 since $4 - 4 = 0$. Since division by 0 is not allowed, x cannot have the value of 4.

2.   Express $\dfrac{2}{5}$ as an equivalent fraction having 20 as its denominator.

Solution:

$$\frac{2}{5} \times \frac{4}{4} = \frac{8}{20}. \qquad \blacksquare\blacksquare$$

Since $\frac{4}{4} = 1$, the original fraction is being multiplied by 1, so that the resulting fraction, $\frac{8}{20}$, is equivalent to the original fraction.

A **prime number** is a natural number greater than 1 that is divisible only by itself and 1. The numbers 3, 5, 7, 11, 13, 17, 19, and 23 are examples of prime numbers. The number 2 is the only even number that is also a prime number.

A **composite number** is any natural greater than 1 that is *not* a prime number.

The numbers 5, 10, 15, 20, 25, 30, 35, . . . are *multiples* of 5 since each number is obtained by multiplying 5 by a different positive integer. This means that each multiple of 5 must be divisible by 5. In general, a number m is a **multiple** of a number n if m is divisible by n.

The **least common multiple (LCM)** of two or more numbers is the smallest number that is a multiple of the given numbers. For example, the least common multiple of 8 and 12 is 24 since 24 is the smallest natural number that is divisible by 8 *and* divisible by 12.

Examples ▬▬▬

3. Which of the following is an example of an odd number that is not a prime number?

$$(1)\ 2 \qquad (2)\ 3 \qquad (3)\ 9 \qquad (4)\ 11$$

Solution: The number 9 is an odd number that is divisible by 3. The correct answer is **choice (3)**.

4. Determine the least common multiple of 6 and 15.

Solution: Begin listing the multiples of each number, and select the *smallest* multiple that is common to both.

Multiples of 6:   6, 12, 18, 24, *30*, 36, 42, . . .

Multiples of 15:   15, *30*, 45, . . .

The smallest number common to both series is 30. The LCM of 6 and 15 is **30**. ▬▬▬

EXCERCISE SET 1.3

1. If a and b are any real numbers except 0, which of the following statements is false?

   (1) $b \times 1 = b$ $\qquad$ (2) $\dfrac{0}{a} = \dfrac{0}{b}$ $\qquad$ (3) $\dfrac{a}{b} = \dfrac{b}{a}$ $\qquad$ (4) $0 \times a = b \times 0$

2. How many prime numbers are greater than or equal to 30 and less than or equal to 43?

3. Which of the following numbers is a prime number *and*, when divided by 8, has a remainder of 3?

   (1) 27 $\qquad$ (2) 37 $\qquad$ (3) 24 $\qquad$ (4) 19

4. Change $\dfrac{2}{3}$ to an equivalent fraction whose denominator is 12.

5. Change $\dfrac{1}{5}$ to an equivalent fraction whose denominator is 40.

6. Determine the LCM of each of the following pairs:
   (a) 8 and 28   (b) 3 and 7   (c) 5 and 40   (d) 28 and 44

7. For what value of x is the reciprocal of each of the following not defined?
   (a) $x - 7$ (b) $3 + x$ (c) $4x$ (d) $\dfrac{x}{3}$ (e) $2x - 1$

TABLE 1.2   Rules for Working with Signed Numbers

Operation	Sign of Numbers	Procedure
Multiplication and division	SAME $(+)(+) \;\; = +$ $(-)(-) \;\; = +$ $(+) \div (+) = +$ $(-) \div (-) = +$	Multiply (or divide) numbers while ignoring their signs. Make the sign of the answer *positive*. (a) $(+5)(+8) = +40$ (b) $(-5)(-8) = +40$ (c) $(+40) \div (+8) = +5$ (d) $(-40) \div (-8) = +5$
	DIFFERENT $(+)(-) \;\; = -$ $(-)(+) \;\; = -$ $(+) \div (-) = -$ $(-) \div (+) = -$	Multiply (or divide) numbers while ignoring their signs. Make the sign of the answer *negative*. (a) $(+5)(-8) = -40$ (b) $(-5)(+8) = -40$ (c) $(+40) \div (-8) = -5$ (d) $(-40) \div (+8) = -5$
Addition	SAME $(+) + (+) = +$ $(-) + (-) = -$	Add numbers while ignoring their signs. Write the sum using their *common* sign. (a) $(+5) + (+8) = +13$ (b) $(-5) + (-8) = -13$
	DIFFERENT	Subtract numbers while ignoring their signs. The answer has the same sign as the number having the *larger absolute value*. (a) $(+5) + (-8) = -3$ (b) $(-5) + (+8) = +3$
Subtraction	SAME	(a) $(+5) \underbrace{- (+8)}= (+5) + (-8) = -3$ $\downarrow$ Take the **opposite** and *add*.
	DIFFERENT	(b) $(+5) \underbrace{- (-8)}= (+5) + (+8) = +13$ $\downarrow$ Take the **opposite** and *add*.

1.4 WORKING WITH SIGNED NUMBERS

KEY IDEAS

The rules for multiplying and dividing signed numbers are similar to those for unsigned numbers. The rules for adding signed numbers are influenced by whether the signs of the numbers are the same or different. Subtracting sign numbers involves changing the example into an equivalent addition example.

PARENTHESES.   Parentheses may be used to make an addition or subtraction problem easier to read.

● The sum of $+7$ and -2 is written as $(+7) + (-2)$, rather than as $+7 + -2$.

● The difference between $+5$ and -3 is written as $(+5) - (-3)$, rather than as $+5 - -3$.
Parentheses may also be used in multiplication and division operations.

● The product of $+3$ and -4 may be written in several different ways, including: $(+3)(-4)$ and $3(-4)$.

● The quotient of -6 and $+7$ may be written in several different ways, including: $(-6) \div (+7)$ and $\frac{-6}{+7}$. Also note that the following expressions are equivalent:

$$-\frac{6}{7}, \quad \frac{-6}{7}, \quad \frac{6}{-7}, \quad -\left(\frac{6}{7}\right).$$

OPERATIONS WITH SIGNED NUMBERS.   Review Table 1.2, which summarizes the rules for arithmetic operations with signed numbers.

Examples

1. Find the value of $|-2| + |7| - |-13|$.

Solution: $\begin{aligned} |-2| + |7| - |-13| &= 2 + 7 - 13 \\ &= 9 - 13 \\ &= 9 + (-13) \\ &= -4 \end{aligned}$

2. Subtract -3 from 10.

Solution: The example is written vertically and then rewritten with the subtraction sign changed to addition; the sign of the number being subtracted is circled and replaced by its opposite.

$$+10$$
$$-\,-3$$

Change to addition:

$$\begin{array}{r} +10 \\ + \\ +\ominus3 \\ \hline 13 \end{array}$$

The example may also be written using a horizontal arrangement of terms:

$$10 - (-3) = 10 + (+3) = \mathbf{13}.$$

3. Simplify: $\dfrac{15-50}{-5}$.

Solution: $\dfrac{15-50}{-5} = \dfrac{-35}{-5} = 7$

SIGNED FRACTIONS.   To **add** fractions having the *same* denominator, write the sum of their numerators over the common denominator.

Example: $\dfrac{-1}{5} + \dfrac{3}{5} = \dfrac{(-1+3)}{5} = \dfrac{2}{5}$

To **add** fractions having *different* denominators, first determine the lowest common denominator (LCD) of all the fractions. Then change each fraction to an equivalent fraction having the LCD as its denominator.

Example: $\dfrac{-2}{3} + \dfrac{1}{4} = ?$

The LCD is 12 since 12 is the smallest whole number that is a multiple of 3 and 4. Change each fraction into an equivalent fraction having 12 as its denominator.

$$\left(\frac{-2}{3}\right)\left(\frac{4}{4}\right) + \left(\frac{1}{4}\right)\left(\frac{3}{3}\right) = \frac{(-2)(4)}{12} + \frac{(1)(3)}{12}$$
$$= \frac{-8}{12} + \frac{3}{12}$$
$$= \frac{-8+3}{12}$$
$$= \frac{-5}{12}$$

Multiply by a form of 1 so that an equivalent fraction having the LCD as its denominator results:

To **subtract** fractions, change to an equivalent addition example by taking the opposite of the fraction that follows the subtraction sign.

Example: $\dfrac{-2}{7} - \left(\dfrac{-5}{7}\right) = \dfrac{-2}{7} + \dfrac{(+5)}{7} = \dfrac{3}{7}$

To **multiply** fractions, find the product of the numerators and denominators.

Example: $\left(\dfrac{-3}{11}\right)\left(\dfrac{-2}{5}\right) = \dfrac{(-3)(-2)}{(11)(5)} = \dfrac{6}{55}$

Sometimes, it is convenient to simplify the fractions *before* multiplying.

$$Example: \quad \frac{5}{12}\left(\frac{-3}{10}\right) = \frac{\overset{1}{\cancel{5}}}{\underset{4}{\cancel{12}}}\left(\frac{-\overset{1}{\cancel{3}}}{\underset{2}{\cancel{10}}}\right)$$

$$= \frac{1\cdot(-1)}{4(2)} = \frac{-1}{8}$$

To **divide** fractions, change to an equivalent multiplication example by taking the reciprocal of the second fraction.

$$Example: \quad \frac{4}{21} \div \left(-\frac{2}{7}\right) = \frac{4}{21}\cdot\left(-\frac{7}{2}\right)$$

$$= \frac{\overset{2}{\cancel{4}}}{\underset{3}{\cancel{21}}}\cdot\left(-\frac{\overset{1}{\cancel{7}}}{\underset{1}{\cancel{2}}}\right)$$

$$= \frac{2(-1)}{3(1)} = -\frac{2}{3}$$

EXERCISE SET 1.4

1–40. Perform the indicated operation.

1. $(-7)(-3)$
2. $(-18) \div (+2)$
3. $(-2)^5$
4. $(-5)(+3)(-2)$
5. $(-3) + (-7)$
6. $(-5) + (+12)$
7. $(-9) + (+7)$
8. $-11 + 3$
9. $(-8) - (-5)$
10. $(-14) - (+5)$
11. $(-21) \div -7$
12. $-3 + 4$
13. $-6 + 10 - 7$
14. $-1.6 + (-1.7)$
15. $3.2 \div (-0.8)$
16. $0.2(-4.9)$
17. $(-3)^4$
18. $(-10)^{-2}$
19. $17 + (-9)$

20. $|-10 - (-7)|$
21. $-8 - (-2)$
22. $(-5)^0$
23. $(-1.5)(-0.75)$
24. $\dfrac{-1.05}{-0.35}$
25. $\dfrac{56}{-8}$
26. $(-0.7)^2$
27. $-15 + 7 - 9$
28. $(-2.3)(0.6)$
29. $6 - 13 - 1$
30. $(-4.2) \div (-7)$
31. $(-2)^{-3}$
32. $-8.1 - 1.9$
33. $-8.1 + 1.9$
34. $8.1 - 1.9$
35. $8.1 - (-1.9)$

36. $(-8.1)(-1.9)$

37. $-(8.1 - 1.9)$

38. $-(-8.1 - 1.9)$

39. $|-3 + 1|$

40. $|6 - 15|$

41. Subtract 2 from -18.

42. Subtract -5 from $+3$.

43. From the sum of -4 and $+2$, subtract 6.

44. From the sum of 9 and -7, subtract -4.

45. To the product of -2 and -5, add -3.

46. From the product of -3.2 and 4.1, subtract 1.38.

47. To the quotient of -9.8 and 4.9, add -0.7.

48. If the sum of -3 and an unknown number is 5, what is the unknown number?

49. If the product of some number and -4 is -12, what is the number?

50. When the larger of two numbers is subtracted from the smaller, the difference is -2. If the smaller number is 6, what is the larger number?

51–70.   Perform the indicated operation with the signed fractions.

51. $\left(-\dfrac{3}{5}\right) + \left(-\dfrac{1}{5}\right)$

52. $\left(-\dfrac{8}{9}\right) + \left(\dfrac{7}{9}\right)$

53. $\left(-\dfrac{3}{7}\right)\left(-\dfrac{14}{33}\right)$

54. $\left(+\dfrac{1}{5}\right) \div \left(-\dfrac{3}{10}\right)$

55. $\left(\dfrac{7}{10}\right) - \left(-\dfrac{3}{10}\right)$

56. $\left(-\dfrac{3}{4}\right)(-12)$

57. $\left(-\dfrac{3}{4}\right)^2$

58. $\left(-\dfrac{11}{13}\right) - \left(-\dfrac{2}{13}\right)$

59. $\left(-\dfrac{5}{6}\right) + \left(-\dfrac{1}{2}\right)$

60. $\left(+\dfrac{5}{8}\right)\left(-\dfrac{12}{25}\right)$

61. $\left(-\dfrac{2}{3}\right) + \left(+\dfrac{1}{4}\right)$

62. $\left(-\dfrac{2}{5}\right) + \left(\dfrac{3}{10}\right)$

63. $\left(-\dfrac{3}{4}\right)\left(\dfrac{10}{21}\right)$

64. $-21 \div \left(-\dfrac{1}{3}\right)$

65. $\left(+\dfrac{2}{7}\right) - \left(-\dfrac{1}{9}\right)$

66. $\left(+\dfrac{7}{9}\right) \div \left(-\dfrac{7}{18}\right)$

67. $\left(-\dfrac{5}{6}\right) \div \left(\dfrac{15}{22}\right)$

68. $\dfrac{5}{6} + \left(-\dfrac{1}{10}\right)$

69. $\left(\dfrac{3}{2}\right)^{-3}$

70. $\left(+\dfrac{1}{3}\right) + \left(-\dfrac{1}{4}\right) + \left(\dfrac{1}{5}\right)$

1.5 WORKING WITH EXPONENTS

KEY IDEAS

The numbers 2 and 15 are factors of 30 since $2 \times 15 = 30$. Each of the numbers being multiplied to obtain a product is called a **factor** of the product. A number may be written as the product of more than two factors. For example, $2 \times 3 \times 5 = 30$. If the same number appears as a factor in a product more than once, it may be written using an *exponent*:

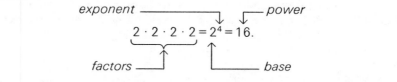

$$\text{exponent} \underline{\qquad\qquad} \qquad \text{power}$$
$$2 \cdot 2 \cdot 2 \cdot 2 = 2^4 = 16.$$
$$\text{factors} \underline{\qquad} \qquad \qquad \text{base}$$

EXPONENTS. Repeated multiplication of the same number may be expressed in a more compact way by writing the number only once with an exponent. The exponent tells the number of times a number is repeated in the multiplication process. For example, $2 \cdot 2 \cdot 2 \cdot 2 = 2^4 = 16$. The number being multiplied (2) is called the base. The number of times the base is used as a factor (4) is called the **exponent**. The product of the repeated factors (16) is called the **power**.

If the exponent is 1, it is usually omitted. For example, $5^1 = 5$. When the exponent is 2, we sometimes refer to the base as being *squared*. For example, 5^2 is usually read as "5 squared" or "the square of 5." Also, 5^3 is usually read as "5 cubed" or "the cube of 5."

Example

1. Evaluate: $(-2)^3$.

Solution:
$$(-2)^3 = (-2)(-2)(-2)$$
$$= (+4)(-2)$$
$$= -8$$

Note: A negative number raised to an *odd* integer power will always have a negative value. A negative number raised to an *even* integer power (except 0) will always have a positive value.

PRIME FACTORIZATION. The **prime factorization** of a number represents the number as the product of prime factors. The prime factorization of 30 is $2 \times 3 \times 5$.

Consider finding the prime factorization of 315. First determine the *smallest* prime number that divides 315 evenly. Since 315 is an odd number, it cannot be divisible by 2. Try dividing 315 by 3. Write 315 as the product of 3 and 105. Repeat this process with 105 and each succeeding factor that is not a prime number.

$$315 = 3 \cdot 105 \qquad \textit{3 is the smallest prime that divides 315.}$$
$$= 3 \cdot 3 \cdot 35 \qquad \textit{3 is the smallest prime that divides 105.}$$
$$= 3 \cdot 3 \cdot 5 \cdot 7 \qquad \textit{5 is the smallest prime that divides 35.}$$

The prime factorization of 315 is $3 \cdot 3 \cdot 5 \cdot 7$, which may also be written as $\mathbf{3^2 \cdot 5 \cdot 7}$.

MULTIPLYING AND DIVIDING POWERS.   Simple rules can be discovered for multiplying and dividing powers having the *same* base. The product of 3^6 and 3^2 can be obtained by writing each power in expanded form:

$$6 + 2 = 8$$
$$3^6 \cdot 3^2 = (3 \cdot 3 \cdot 3 \cdot 3 \cdot 3 \cdot 3)(3 \cdot 3) = 3^8.$$
eight factors of 3

This example suggests the following rule:

MULTIPLICATION RULE FOR EXPONENTS

To **multiply** powers with *like* bases, keep the base and *add* the exponents:

$$a^x a^y = a^{x+y}.$$

A shortcut method for dividing powers having the same base may also be developed:

$$6 - 2 = 4$$
$$\frac{3^6}{3^2} = \frac{3 \cdot 3 \cdot 3 \cdot 3 \cdot 3 \cdot 3}{3 \cdot 3} = 3 \cdot 3 \cdot 3 \cdot 3 = 3^4.$$
four factors of 3

This example suggests the following rule:

QUOTIENT RULE FOR EXPONENTS

To **divide** powers with *like* bases, keep the base and *subtract* the exponents:

$$a^x \div a^y = a^{x-y}.$$

Examples ▬▬▬

2. Multiply: $5^3 \cdot 5^8$.

Solution: $5^3 \cdot 5^8 = 5^{3+8} = \mathbf{5^{11}}$

3. Multiply: $n^4 \cdot n^2$.

Solution: $n^4 \cdot n^2 = n^{4+2} = \mathbf{n^6}$

4. Multiply: $a^2 \cdot b^4$.

Solution: Since the bases are *not* the same, the multiplication rule cannot be used.

5. Divide: $b^7 \div b^2$.

Solution: $b^7 \div b^2 = b^{7-2} = \mathbf{b^5}$ ▬▬

ZERO EXPONENT.   Notice that there are two ways to evaluate $2^3 \div 2^3$:

1. Apply the quotient rule: $2^3 \div 2^3 = 2^{3-3} = 2^0$.

2. Substitute 8 for 2^3: $2^3 \div 2^3 = 8 \div 8 = 1$.

Since the left sides of the equations in methods 1 and 2 are the same, the right sides must be equivalent. Therefore $2^0 = 1$. In general, *any nonzero number or variable raised to the zero power is equal to 1.*

Example ▬▬▬

6. Simplify: (a) $2x^0$ (b) $(2x)^0$.

Solution: (a) $2x^0 = 2(x^0) = 2 \cdot 1 = \mathbf{2}$
            (b) $(2x)^0 = \mathbf{1}$ ▬▬

NEGATIVE EXPONENTS.   Using the quotient rule gives us $3^2 \div 3^6 = 3^{2-6} = 3^{-4}$. By writing the quotient in fraction form and simplifying, we obtain

$$\frac{3^2}{3^6} = \frac{\overset{1}{\cancel{3}} \cdot \overset{1}{\cancel{3}}}{\cancel{3} \cdot \cancel{3} \cdot 3 \cdot 3 \cdot 3 \cdot 3} = \frac{1}{3 \cdot 3 \cdot 3 \cdot 3} = \frac{1}{3^4}.$$

Since the answers must be the same, $3^{-4} = \frac{1}{3^4}$. Similarly, $\frac{1}{3^{-4}} = 3^4$. In general, *any nonzero number (or variable) raised to a negative power may be written with a positive exponent by taking its reciprocal:*

$$x^a = \frac{1}{x^{-a}} \quad \text{and} \quad x^{-a} = \frac{1}{x^a}.$$

Examples ▬▬▬

7. Simplify: $\dfrac{3}{10^{-2}}$.

Solution: $\dfrac{3}{10^{-2}} = 3(10^2) = 3(100) = \mathbf{300}$

8. Write: $\dfrac{9}{2m^{-4}}$ with a positive exponent.

Solution: $\dfrac{9}{2m^{-4}} = \dfrac{9m^4}{2}$

9. Evaluate: $(2+3)^{-1}$.

Solution: $(2+3)^{-1} = 5^{-1} = \dfrac{1}{5}$ *or* **0.2**

10. Evaluate: $2^{-3} + 3(8^{-1})$.

Solution: $2^{-3} + 3(8^{-1}) = \dfrac{1}{2^3} + 3\left(\dfrac{1}{8}\right) = \dfrac{1}{8} + \dfrac{3}{8}$

$$= \dfrac{4}{8} = \dfrac{1}{2} \ or \ \mathbf{0.5}$$

SCIENTIFIC NOTATION. Sometimes it is easier to work with very small and very large numbers if the numbers are written in *scientific notation*. A number N is in **scientific notation** when it is written in the form

$$N = a \times 10^b,$$

where a is a number greater than or equal to 1 but less than 10. For example,

$$123{,}000 = 1.23 \times 10^5, \quad \text{and} \quad 0.000000987 = 9.87 \times 10^{-7}.$$

When a number N is expressed in the form $a \times 10^b$, the value of a represents the significant digits of the original number N. The exponent b is an integer that reflects the direction and number of places the decimal point in the original number must be moved for conversion into scientific notation. If b is a positive integer, then 10^b moves the decimal point of any nonzero number that it multiplies b decimal places to the *right*. If b is a negative integer, then 10^b moves the decimal point of any nonzero number that it multiplies b decimal places to the *left*.

Standard Decimal Form	Changing to Scientific Notation
5 6 0 0 0 0 0 0	$5\,6\,0\,0\,0\,0\,0\,0. = 5.6 \times 10^7$ 7 places
0.0 0 0 0 0 0 0 4 0 3	$.0\,0\,0\,0\,0\,0\,4\,0\,3 = 4.03 \times 10^{-8}$ 8 places

EXERCISE SET 1.5

1. Write each of the following expressions using exponents:

   (a) $4 \cdot 4 \cdot 4 \cdot 4 \cdot 4 \cdot 3 \cdot 3 \cdot 3$ (b) $r \cdot r \cdot s \cdot s \cdot s \cdot s$ (c) $\dfrac{2 \cdot 2 \cdot 2}{y \cdot y \cdot y \cdot y \cdot y}$

2. Evaluate each of the following:

   (a) $2^{-1} + 4^{-1}$ (e) $8^0 + 4^{-2}$ (i) $\left(\dfrac{3}{4}\right)^2 + 4^{-2}$

   (b) $\left(\dfrac{1}{3}\right)^{-1}$ (f) $(-1)^{13} + (-1)^{15}$ (j) $4(10^{-1}) - 2^3(5^{-2})$

   (c) $(-3)^2$ (g) $25(10^{-2})$ (k) $(-2)^2 + (-2)^5$

   (d) $(-5)^3$ (h) $(-99)^1$ (l) $(-1)^{-97}$

3. Write the prime factorization of each of the following expressions:
   (a) 200 (b) 98 (c) 170 (d) $108x$ (e) $441a^2$ (f) $101y^3$

4. Replace the $\square$ with the symbol ($<$, $>$, or $=$) that makes the resulting statement true.

   (a) $3^4 \; \square \; 4^3$ (f) $(-1)^{99} \; \square \; 0$ (k) $4^6 \div 4^2 \; \square \; 4^3$

   (b) $1^0 \; \square \; 1^9$

   (g) $(-2)^3 \; \square \; (2)^{-3}$ (l) $6^0 - 3^{-1} \; \square \; \dfrac{7}{12}$

   (c) $2^{-3} \; \square \; 2^{-2}$ (h) $(2+3)^3 \; \square \; 2^3 + 3^3$

   (d) $5^2 5^3 \; \square \; 5^6$ (i) $10^{-4} \; \square \; 0.001$ (m) $\left(\dfrac{2}{3}\right)^{-1} \; \square \; (-5)^0$

   (e) $5^{-1} + 2^{-1} \; \square \; \dfrac{3}{5}$ (j) $3^{-2} + 3^{-1} \; \square \; \dfrac{5}{9}$ (n) $\left(\dfrac{4}{5}\right)^{-1} \; \square \; 1.25$

5. Find the product or quotient of each of the following:
   (a) $2 \cdot 2^2 \cdot 2^3$ (d) $w \cdot w^3$ (g) $y^4 \div y^5$ (j) $a^3 \cdot a^2 \cdot a^5$
   (b) $4^0 \cdot 4^{-1}$ (e) $n^7 \cdot n$ (h) $z^3 \cdot z^2 \cdot z$ (k) $(d^2)^4$
   (c) $c^8 \cdot c^3$ (f) $t^5 \div t$ (i) $x^{10} \div x^{10}$ (l) $r^2 \cdot s^3$

6. Find the value of x that makes each of the following statements true:
   (a) $5^2 \cdot 5^x = 5^7$ (e) $y^6 \cdot y^x = 1$ (i) $2^x = 0.25$

   (b) $s^4 \cdot s^x = s^9$ (f) $b^8 \div b^x = \dfrac{1}{b^2}$ (j) $3^x = 1$

   (c) $t^x \div t = t^4$ (g) $a^2 \cdot a^x \cdot a^4 = a^{12}$ (k) $10^x = 0.001$

   (d) $w^3 \cdot w^x = w^3$ (h) $n^5 \cdot n^x = \dfrac{1}{n^3}$ (l) $10^x = 4(5)^2$

7. Find the value of n for converting to scientific notation.
   (a) $63{,}000{,}000 = 6.3 \times 10^n$ (c) $10{,}000 = 1.0 \times 10^n$
   (b) $0.000000071 = 7.1 \times 10^n$ (d) $0.00000106 = 1.06 \times 10^n$

8. Express in standard decimal form.
   (a) 3.1×10^9 (b) 6.08×10^4 (c) 8.7×10^{-5} (d) 4.3×10^{11}

9. Express each number in scientific notation.
   (a) 0.000000014 (b) $91{,}000$ (c) $165{,}000$ (d) 0.00000104

1.6   SIMPLIFYING EXPRESSIONS

_____ KEY IDEAS _____

When an arithmetic expression such as $32 - (10 \div 2)2^3 \div 10$ is evaluated, arithmetic operations are *not* necessarily performed in the order in which they are encountered. Expressions inside parentheses are evaluated first. Powers are evaluated next. Products and quotients are evaluated as they are encountered in working from left to right. Lastly, any remaining sums and differences are evaluated, again working from left to right.

Replacing the variables of an algebraic expression with their assigned numerical values results in an arithmetic expression that can be evaluated using these rules.

ILLUSTRATING THE ORDER OF OPERATIONS.   Evaluate expressions within parentheses first:

$$32 - (10 \div 2)2^3 \div 10 = 32 - 5 \cdot 2^3 \div 10.$$

Then, working from left to right, proceed as follows:

Evaluate powers:	$= 32 - 5 \cdot 8 \div 10$
Multiply and divide:	$= 32 - 40 \div 10$
	$= 32 - 4$
Find any sums or differences:	$= \mathbf{28}$

Examples 1–3 illustrate the effect of parentheses.

Examples

1.   Evaluate: $36 \div (18 - 3^2)$.

Solution: $36 \div (18 - 3^2) = 36 \div (18 - 9)$
$= 36 \div 9 = 4$

2.   Evaluate: $36 \div 18 - 3^2$.

Solution: $36 \div 18 - 3^2 = 36 \div 18 - 9$
$= 2 - 9 = -7$

Sometimes an expression enclosed by parentheses will be found inside another pair of parentheses. When parentheses are nested one within another, work "inside to outside" by evaluating the expression found in the *innermost* parentheses first. Notice that the solution to Example 3 replaces the outermost parentheses with brackets. This makes the expression easier to read.

Example ▬▬▬

3. Evaluate: $[50 \div (1 + 8 \div 2)^2]^3$.

Solution:
$$
\begin{aligned}
[50 \div (1 + 8 \div 2)^2]^3 &= [50 \div (1 + 4)^2]^3 \\
&= [50 \div (5)^2]^3 \\
&= [50 \div 25]^3 \\
&= [2]^3 = 8
\end{aligned}
$$

THE DISTRIBUTIVE PROPERTY. We know that $3(2 + 4) = 3(6) = 18$. The **distributive property** of multiplication over addition tells us that an expression of this form can be evaluated in another way:

$$
\begin{array}{ll}
& \text{Distributive Property} \\
3(2 + 4) = 3 \cdot 2 + 3 \cdot 4 & \boldsymbol{a(b + c) = ab + ac} \\
\quad\quad = 6 + 12 & \quad\quad \boldsymbol{and} \\
\quad\quad = 18 & \boldsymbol{(b + c)a = ba + ca}
\end{array}
$$

The following example demonstrates that the distributive property of multiplication works also for subtraction:

$$
\begin{array}{ll}
& \text{Distributive Property} \\
4(5 - 3) = 4(5) - 4(3) & \boldsymbol{a(b - c) = ab - ac} \\
4(2) = 20 - 12 & \quad\quad \boldsymbol{and} \\
8 = 8 & \boldsymbol{(b - c)a = bc - ca}
\end{array}
$$

Example ▬▬▬

4. Remove the parentheses by applying the distributive property:
- (a) $5(x - 1)$ (c) $-(4 - 3x)$
- (b) $6(3y + 2)$ (d) $7 - 2(3 - 2x)$

Solutions: (a) $5(x - 1) = \boldsymbol{5x - 5}$
(b) $6(3y + 2) = 6(3y) + 6(2) = \boldsymbol{18y + 12}$
(c) $-(4 - 3x) = -1(4 - 3x) = -4 + (-1)(-3x) = \boldsymbol{-4 + 3x}$
(d) $7 - 2(3 - 2x) = 7 + (-2)(3) + (-2)(-2x)$
$\quad\quad\quad\quad\quad\quad = 7 - 6 + 4x = \boldsymbol{1 + 4x}$

LIKE TERMS. Terms such as $4x$ and $5x$ are called **like terms** since they have the same variable factor (x) and differ only in their numerical coefficients (4 and 5, respectively). Applying the distributive property in "reverse" provides a way of combining like terms. Here are some examples.

1. $81x + 19x = (81 + 19)x = \boldsymbol{100x}$

2. $7y - y = 7y - 1y = (7 - 1)y = \boldsymbol{6y}$

3. $-2(x + 5) + x = -2x - 10 + x$
$\quad\quad\quad\quad\quad = (-2x + x) - 10$
$\quad\quad\quad\quad\quad = \boldsymbol{-x - 10}$

4. $8x - 3(2x + 7) = 8x + (-3)(2x) + (-3)(7)$
$\quad\quad\quad\quad\quad\quad = 8x - 6x - 21 = \boldsymbol{2x - 21}$

EVALUATING ALGEBRAIC EXPRESSIONS.   To evaluate an algebraic expression, replace each variable with its assigned value. Then evaluate the resulting arithmetic expression, following the rules for order of operations.

Examples ▰▰▰

5. If $r = 24$ and $s = -2$, find the value of each of the following:
   (a) $r \div 3s^3$ (b) $r \div (3s)^3$ (c) $(r \div 3)s^3$

Solutions:
   (a) $r \div 3s^3 = 24 \div 3(-2)^3 = 24 \div 3(-8)$
$$= 24 \div (-24)$$
$$= -1$$
   (b) $r \div (3s)^3 = 24 \div [3(-2)]^3$
$$= 24 \div (-6)^3 = 24 \div (-216)$$
$$= -\frac{1}{9}$$
   (c) $(r \div 3)s^3 = (24 \div 3)(-2)^3$
$$= 8(-8)$$
$$= -64$$

6. If $y = -x^2 + 3$:
   (a) what is the value of y when $x = -4$?
   (b) what is the largest possible value of y for any replacement of x?

Solutions: (a) $y = -x^2 + 3 = -(-4)^2 + 3$
$$= -16 + 3 = -13$$
   (b) For any nonzero value of x, the value of y is less than 3 since the term $-x^2$ produces a negative number. Therefore, when $x = 0$, y has its largest value, **3**.   ▰▰▰

EXERCISE SET 1.6

1. Simplify.
   (a) $(+2)(-5) + (-3)(-7)$ (f) $(-4)(-7) \div (2 - 9)$
   (b) $12 + 16 \div 4$ (g) $-0.6(-5.1 + 3.7)$
   (c) $(12 + 16) \div 4$ (h) $[3 + 2(3^2)]2 \div 7$
   (d) $-27 \div 3^2$ (i) $[6 + 3(4^2) - 2] \div (10^2 \div 5^2)$
   (e) $-0.3(-2.4 - 1.6)$ (j) $[5^2 - (8 - 21 \div 3)] \div 2^3$

2. If $x = -2$ and $y = 3$, find the value of each of the following:
   (a) xy^2 (c) $y + xy$ (e) $x^2 - xy$
   (b) $(xy)^2$ (d) $y(1 + x)$ (f) $x(x - y)$

3. If $y = x^4 + 5$, what is the smallest possible value of y for any replacement value of x?

4. Find the value of each of the following when $a = 2$, $b = 3$, and $c = -5$:

（a）$(b + c)^a$ (d) $a + \dfrac{b}{c}$ (g) $b - c^a$ (j) $\dfrac{b}{c(bc + a^b)}$

（b）$ab + c$ (e) $(ac)^b$ (h) $ac - (b + 1)c$ (k) $c^a + (ac)^{c/5}$

（c）$\dfrac{a + b}{c}$ (f) ac^b (i) ba^{c+a} (l) $c^b a - (ac)^a$

5. Evaluate to a single number by applying the distributive property of multiplication over addition.

（a）$-5(-17 + 4)$ (c) $\dfrac{1}{4}\left(\dfrac{-2}{3} + \dfrac{1}{6}\right)$ (e) $83(3) + 17(3)$

（b）$0.3(-2.7 + 1.4)$ (d) $-0.4(3.8 - 2.1)$ (f) $14(39) - 4(39)$

6. Remove the parentheses by applying the distributive property.
    (a) $3(4x + 3)$ (c) $-3(2x - 5)$ (e) $(3x - 1)(-3)$
    (b) $2(3x - 4)$ (d) $2 - (5 - x)$ (f) $3m - 2(1 - m)$

7. Combine like terms.
    (a) $4x + 7x$ (g) $s - 1.5s$ (m) $9y - y - y$
    (b) $2x - 8x$ (h) $0.7w + 2 - w$ (n) $3(x - 1) + 2x$
    (c) $1.6x + 2.1x$ (i) $2(3x) + 5x$ (o) $2(5x + 3) - 3x$
    (d) $-0.31x + 0.27x$ (j) $3x - 5(2x)$ (p) $-3(1 - x) - 4x$
    (e) $5y + y - 4y$ (k) $5(7x) - x$
    (f) $7t - 2t + 3t$ (l) $3y - 5 + 2y$

CHAPTER 1 REVIEW EXERCISES

1–24. Find the value of each of the following:

1. $3 - 7$

2. $|-5| - |-9|$

3. $\dfrac{-32}{8}$

4. $-9 + 13$

5. $(-5)(-7)(-2)$

6. $(-2)^{-5}$
7. $-6 - (+8)$
8. $-10 - (-5)$
9. $-3 + (-8)$

10. $-4 - (-7)$

11. $-\left(\dfrac{-8}{-4}\right)$

12. $\dfrac{3}{8} - \dfrac{5}{4}$

13. $(-3)^2$

14. $3(-5)^0$

15. $(-5)(-7) + (-6)(+8)$
16. $(-4)^{-1}$
17. $2 - (-24 \div 2 + 6)$
18. $27 \div (1 + 2^3) - 3^2$

19. $\dfrac{1}{5} + \left(-\dfrac{3}{5}\right)$

20. $\dfrac{2}{7} - \left(-\dfrac{1}{14}\right)$

21. $-\dfrac{1}{2} + \dfrac{3}{8}$

22. $\left(-\dfrac{4}{9}\right)\left(-\dfrac{3}{8}\right)$

23. $\left(-\dfrac{5}{12}\right) \div \left(\dfrac{15}{8}\right)$

24. $\left(-\dfrac{10}{21}\right) \div \left(-\dfrac{2}{3}\right)$

25–32. Evaluate each expression when $x = 2$.

25. $4x^0$ **27.** 2^x **29.** $(3x)^2$ **31.** x^{x+5}

26. $(4x)^0$ **28.** $2^{-x} + x^2$ **30.** $3x^2$ **32.** $\dfrac{x^0 - 2x^2}{7}$

33. What is the value of $c \cup \perp xy$ when $c = 3$, $x = 4$, and $y = -5$?

34–38. Simplify by finding the product or quotient.

34. $v^6 v^7$ **35.** $e^4 \div e^r$ **36.** $q^4 q^3 q$ **37.** $r^9 \div r$ **38.** $(x^5 x^8) \div x^3$

39. When $x = -4$ and $y = 3$, what is the value of each of the following expressions?

(a) $x^2 y$ (c) $(xy)^2$ (e) y^x (g) $\dfrac{12}{x} + y$

(b) xy^2 (d) $x^2 y^2$ (f) x^y (h) $\dfrac{12}{x + y}$

40. Find the value of the given expression when $r = -2$ and $s = 10$.

(a) sr^2 (c) $\left(\dfrac{s}{r}\right)^2$ (e) $r + 3s$ (g) $r + \dfrac{s}{2}$ (i) $-3r^2 + \dfrac{s}{r}$

(b) $(sr)^2$ (d) $\left(\dfrac{s}{r}\right)^{-2}$ (f) $(r + 3)s$ (h) $\dfrac{r + s}{2}$ (j) $-3\left(r^2 + \dfrac{s}{r}\right)$

41. Simplify by combining like terms.

(a) $8x - 2x$ (c) $3(x + 2) - x$ (e) $4 - (3x + 7)$

(b) $9y - y$ (d) $5 - 2(x - 1)$ (f) $6x - 3(2 - x)$

42. State the value of x that makes each of the following statements true:

(a) $4 + x = 0$ (d) $u^6 \div u^x = u^3$ (g) $\dfrac{2}{3} x = 1$

(b) $y^8 y^x = y$ (e) $x + \left(-\dfrac{1}{5}\right) = 0$ (h) $m^x = m^{2x} \div m^6$

(c) $7x = 1$ (f) $e^5 e^x = e^2$

43. Which of the following number systems lacks an additive inverse for each of its elements?

(1) Integers   (2) Rationals   (3) Whole numbers   (4) Reals

CHAPTER 2

Logic and Truth Tables

2.1 FINDING TRUTH VALUES OF SENTENCES

KEY IDEAS

Some sentences reflect opinions and cannot be judged to be true or false. Other sentences involve facts and can be evaluated as being true or false. These sentences are called **statements** or **closed sentences**. A statement has a *truth value* of either TRUE (T) or FALSE (F). An **open sentence** is a sentence that cannot be assigned a truth value until more information is known.

OPEN SENTENCES. "He was a president of the United States" is an *open sentence* since its truth value cannot be determined until the pronoun "He" is replaced by the name of a particular person. If "He" is replaced by "George Washington," then the sentence has a truth value of true. If "Bruce Springsteen" replaces "He," then the truth value of the sentence is false.

REPLACEMENT AND SOLUTION SETS. The mathematical sentence $x + 1 = 6$ is an *open sentence* where the letter x is a placeholder for some number. If the possible substitutions for x are limited to 1, 2, 3, 4, or 5, then the set $\{1, 2, 3, 4, 5\}$ is called the *replacement set* for x or the *domain* of x. The **replacement set** for a variable is the set of all possible substitutions for the variable (or pronoun) in an open sentence. The number 5 when substituted for x makes the open sentence $x + 1 = 6$ true since $5 + 1 = 6$. The set $\{5\}$ is called the *solution set*. The **solution set** consists of the subset of all members of the replacement set that make the open sentence true.

The solution set is a subset of the replacement set and may have one member, more than one member, an infinite number of members, or no members. This is illustrated in Table 2.1.

TABLE 2.1   Finding Solution Sets

Replacement Set	Open Sentence	Solution Set
1. {Whole numbers}	$x < 1$	$\{0\}$
2. $\{-2, -1, 0, 1, 2\}$	$x < 1$	$\{-2, -1, 0\}$
3. {Integers}	$x < 1$	$\{\ldots, -4, -3, -2, -1, 0\}$
4. $\{2, 4, 6\}$	$x < 1$	$\{\ \}$ or $\varnothing$

EXERCISE SET 2.1

1–9. Determine the solution set.

Replacement Set	Open Sentence	Solution Set
1. {Whole numbers}	n is between 2 and 7.	?
2. {Integers}	$\dfrac{1}{x+2}$ is undefined.	?
3. {Natural numbers}	n is between 3 and 5, inclusive.	?
4. {Whole numbers ≤ 13}	x is divisible by 3.	?
5. {Real numbers}	$x + 1 > 4.$	?
6. {Rationals}	x is the average of $\dfrac{1}{2}$ and $\dfrac{1}{4}$.	?
7. {Real numbers}	$x = x + 1$	?
8. {Integers}	n is a prime number between 50 and 70.	?
9. $\{1, 3, 5\}$	$x + 1 = 3.$	?

10–17. The replacement set for each of the following open sentences is $\{-2, -1, 0, 1, 2\}$. Write the solution set for each open sentence.

10. $|x| = 2$ **12.** $|x| = x$ **14.** $|x| + x = 0$ **16.** $x^2 = 1$

11. $|x - 1| = 1$ **13.** $|x| = -1$ **15.** $|x| \leq 1$ **17.** $|x| = x^2$

2.2 NEGATING STATEMENTS

────────── KEY IDEAS ──────────

A new statement, called the **negation** of a statement, is formed by inserting the word *not* so that the resulting statement has the opposite truth value of the original statement.

FORMING A NEGATION OF A STATEMENT

Original statement: Monday is the day after Sunday.   (True)
     Negation: Monday is *not* the day after Sunday.   (False)
             or
             It is *not* true that Monday is the day after Sunday.

NOTATION.   Sometimes it is convenient to use letters to represent statements. For example,

        p: Monday is the day after Sunday.   (True)

is read as "Let p represent the statement 'Monday is the day after Sunday'." If p represents a statement, then $\sim p$ (read as "not p") represents the negation of statement p:

        $\sim p$: Monday is *not* the day after Sunday.   (False)

TRUTH TABLES AND NEGATIONS.   If $\sim p$ represents the negation of statement p, then $\sim(\sim p)$ represents the negation of the negation of p (or "double" negation of p). Statements p and $\sim p$ have opposite truth values, whereas p and $\sim(\sim p)$ have the same truth value. For example,

        p: $2+3=5$.   (True)
      $\sim p$: It is not true that $2+3=5$, *or, simply*, $2+3 \neq 5$.   (False)
  $\sim(\sim p)$: It is not true that $2+3 \neq 5$.   (True)

The set of possible truth values of statements can be organized into **truth tables**. The truth table for statement p and its negations is given in Table 2.2. Notice that the first vertical column lists the possible truth values for statement p (T or F). The second column lists the corresponding truth values for $\sim p$, while the last column negates (takes the opposite of) the truth values found in the second column.

TABLE 2.2 Truth Table for Negations of Statement p

p	$\sim p$	$\sim(\sim p)$
T	F	T
F	T	F

NEGATING INEQUALITIES. Table 2.3 shows how to negate inequalities.

TABLE 2.3 Negating Inequalities

Inequality	Negation
$>$	$\ngtr$ *or* $\leq$
$\geq$	$\ngeq$ *or* $<$
$<$	$\nless$ *or* $\geq$
$\leq$	$\nleq$ *or* $>$

Example

Write the negation of p when:
(a) p: $7 < 10$ (b) p: 2 is not a prime number

Solutions:
(a) p: $7 < 10$ (True)
$\sim p$: $7 \geq 10$ (False)
(b) p: 2 is not a prime number. (False)
$\sim p$: It is not true that 2 is not a prime number (True) or, simply, 2 is a prime number. (True)

EXERCISE SET 2.2

1–10. Form the negation of each of the given statements. Determine the truth value of the original statement and of its negation.

1. $3 + 4 = 4 + 3$.

2. $5 < 9$.

3. A week has 7 days.

4. $3 \geq 1$.

5. A prime number is not divisible by 3.

6. The sum of two even numbers is an odd number.

7. A triangle has three sides.

8. Parallel lines do not intersect.

9. Cows cannot talk.

10. The lowest common multiple of two prime numbers is their product.

11–13. Fill in the blank with true *or* false *so that the resulting sentence is true.*

11. If p is false, then $\sim(\sim p)$ is _____ .

12. If $\sim p$ is true, then p is _____ .

13. If p represents the statement "13 is a prime number," then the truth value of $\sim p$ is _____ .

14. Let q represent the statement "$x > 3$." If the domain of x is the set of whole numbers, for what value(s) of x is $\sim q$ true?

15. Let p represent the statement "$x - 1 = 5$." If the domain of x is the set of integers, for what value(s) of x is $\sim p$ false?

16–20. Write the negation of each of the following inequalities without using the $\neq$ symbol:

16. $x > 3$ 17. $x \leq 5$ 18. $x \geq 1$ 19. $x < 4$ 20. $2 \leq x$

2.3 CONNECTING STATEMENTS WITH *AND* AND *OR*

—————— KEY IDEAS ——————

A **compound statement** is a statement formed by combining two or more simple statements, using a connective word or words. The words AND and OR are **logical connectives**.

Much of our study of logic concerns forming compound statements, and then analyzing their truth values.

CONJUNCTION. A new statement can be formed by taking two given statements and connecting them by placing the word AND between them. The resulting compound statement is called a **conjunction**. The conjunction of p and q is written symbolically as $p \wedge q$ (read as "p and q"), and is true only when p and q are true at the same time. As an illustration, consider these statements:

p: x is divisible by 2.
q: x is divisible by 3.
$p \wedge q$: x is divisible by 2, and x is divisible by 3.

In this example, the truth value of $p \wedge q$ depends on the value of x. If $x = 6$, then p is true since 6 is divisible by 2, and q is true since 6 is divisible by 3. Hence $p \wedge q$ is true. If $x = 8$, however, p is true but q is false, so that $p \wedge q$ is false.

TABLE 2.4   Truth Table for Conjunction $p \wedge q$

p	q	$p \wedge q$
T	T	T
T	F	F
F	T	F
F	F	F

The truth table given in Table 2.4 summarizes the different possible combinations of truth values of p and q. In the first row, p and q are both true so that the conjunction is true. In the remaining rows, at least one of the statements, p or q, that make up the conjunction is false, so that the conjunction is also false.

Example ▬▬▬

1. Let p represent "A square has three sides" and q represent "2 is a prime number." Determine the truth of each of the following:

(a) $p \wedge q$ (b) $\sim(p \wedge q)$ (c) $\sim p \wedge q$

Solutions: (a) **False** (since p is false and q is true, $p \wedge q$ is false).

(b) **True** (since the conjunction is false, its negation is true).

(c) **True** (since $\sim p$ is true and q is true, their conjunction is true).

▬▬▬

DISJUNCTION.   When two statements are joined with the word OR, a new statement that is called the **disjunction** of the original statements is formed. The disjunction of statements p and q is written as $p \vee q$ and read as "p or q." The disjunction $p \vee q$ is true when p is true or q is true or both p and q are true. As an example, consider these statements:

p: x is an even number.
q: x is a prime number.
$p \vee q$: x is an even number, or x is a prime number.

In this example the truth value of $p \vee q$ depends on the value of x. If $x = 8$, p is true, q is false, and $p \vee q$ is true. If $x = 9$, however, p and q are each false, so that $p \vee q$ is false.

Table 2.5 gives a truth table for the disjunction $p \vee q$. In the first three rows of this truth table, at least one of the component statements is true, so that the disjunction is true. In the last row of the table both p and q are false, so that the disjunction of p and q is false.

TABLE 2.5 Truth Table for Disjunction *p* ∨ *q*

p	*q*	*p* ∨ *q*
T	T	T
T	F	T
F	T	T
F	F	F

Examples ▰▰▰▰

2. If *p* represents "Math is fun," and *q* represents "Math is difficult," write in symbolic form, using *p* and *q*:
(a) Math is fun or math is difficult.
(b) Math is fun and math is not difficult.
(c) It is not true that math is not fun or math is difficult.

Solutions: (a) *p* ∨ *q*   (b) *p* ∧ ~*q*   (c) ~(~*p* ∨ *q*)

3. If *p* represents "*x* is divisible by 3" and *q* represents "*x* is the LCM (least common multiple) of 4 and 6," then what is the truth value of each of the following statements when *x* = 24?
(a) *p* ∧ *q*   (b) *p* ∨ *q*   (c) ~*p* ∨ ~*q*   (d) ~(*p* ∧ *q*)

Solutions: The LCM of 4 and 6 is 12 since 12 is the smallest positive number that is divisible by both 4 and 6. If *x* = 24, then *p* is true (since 12 is divisible by 3) and *q* is false.
(a) *p* ∧ *q* is **false** since *q* is false.
(b) *p* ∨ *q* is **true** since *p* is true.
(c) ~*p* ∨ ~*q* is **true** since ~*q* is true.
(d) ~(*p* ∧ *q*) is **true** since the conjunction is false, so that its negation is true.

4. Fill in the missing truth values.

(a)

p	*q*	*p* ∨ *q*	*p* ∧ *q*
?	F	T	?

(c)

p	*q*	*p* ∨ *q*	~(*p* ∨ *q*)
F	?	?	T

(b)

p	*q*	~*p*	~*p* ∨ *q*
?	F	?	T

(d)

p	*q*	~*q*	*p* ∧ ~*q*
?	?	?	T

Solutions:

(a) Since the disjunction is true and q is false, p must be **true**. The conjunction $p \wedge q$ is **false** since q is false.

(b) Since the disjunction is true and q is false, $\sim p$ must be **true**, so that p is **false.**

(c) In order for the statement in the last column to be true, the disjunction $p \vee q$ must be **false**. This implies that both p and q must be **false.**

(d) Since the conjunction is true, each of its members must also be true, so that p is **true** and $\sim q$ is **true**; therefore q is **false.** ▰▰▰▰

CONSTRUCTING A TRUTH TABLE FOR A COMPOUND STATE-MENT. The truth value of a compound statement can be determined, for each possible combination of truth values of its component statements, by developing a truth table. To construct a truth table that analyzes the truth value of the compound statement

$$(q \wedge \sim p) \vee \sim q$$

proceed as follows:

Step 1. Label the first two columns of the truth table as p and q, and label the last column as $(q \wedge \sim p) \vee \sim q$. Then, working from left to right, label the columns in between with the component parts of the compound statement. Be sure to provide separate column headings for negations and statements involving a connective. For example,

(1)	(2)	(3)	(4)	(5)	(6)
p	q	$\sim p$	$q \wedge \sim p$	$\sim q$	$(q \wedge \sim p) \vee \sim q$

Step 2. Complete columns (1) and (2) by listing all possible combinations of truth values for p and q. It is common practice to list these combinations in the following order:

	(1)	(2)
	p	q
row 1	T	T
row 2	T	F
row 3	F	T
row 4	F	F

Step 3. In each row of column (3) enter the opposite (negation) of the corresponding truth value in column (1). (*Note: corresponding* means "in the same row.")

Step 4. In each row of column (4) enter the truth value obtained by taking the conjunction of the corresponding truth values in columns (2) and (3).

Step 5. In each row of column (5) enter the opposite (negation) of the corresponding truth value in column (2).

Step 6. In each row of column (6) enter the truth value obtained by taking the disjunction of the corresponding truth values in columns (4) and (5). Here is the completed truth table.

(1)	(2)	(3)	(4)	(5)	(6)
p	q	$\sim p$	$q \wedge \sim p$	$\sim q$	$(q \wedge \sim p) \vee \sim q$
T	T	F	F	F	F
T	F	F	F	T	T
F	T	T	T	F	T
F	F	T	F	T	T

EXERCISE SET 2.3

1–8. Let p *represent the statement "All rectangles are squares,"* q *represent the statement "The product of two odd numbers is an odd number," and* r *represent the statement "The product of two negative numbers is negative." Express each of the following compound statements as an English sentence, and give its truth value:*

1. $p \wedge q$
2. $p \vee q$
3. $\sim r \vee q$
4. $\sim(p \wedge r)$
5. $\sim(r \vee q)$
6. $\sim r \wedge \sim q$
7. $(p \wedge r) \vee \sim p$
8. $(p \wedge q) \vee r$

9–13. Fill in the blank with either true *or* false *so that the resulting statement is correct.*

9. If p is true, then $p \wedge \sim(\sim p)$ is _____.

10. $q \vee \sim q$ is always _____.

11. If $p \vee \sim q$ is true and p is false, then q is _____.

12. $p \wedge q$ and $p \vee q$ have the same truth value when p is false and q is _____.

13. If $\sim(p \wedge q)$ is true and p is true, then q is _____.

14. What is the truth value of $[(-3)(-2) = 6] \wedge [6 - 8 = -2]$?

15. What is the truth value of $(-2 \cdot |-5| = 10) \vee [|-3| = -(-3)]$?

16. What is the truth value of $\left[\left(-\dfrac{18}{9}\right) = x\right] \wedge [x - 2 = 0]$?

17–21. If x *is an integer, what is the smallest value of* x, *if any, that makes the given statement true?*

17. $(x > 32) \wedge (x \text{ is prime})$
18. $(x > 5) \wedge (x < 8)$
19. $(x \text{ is even}) \wedge (x + 2 = 5)$
20. $(x < -4) \wedge (x > -9)$
21. $(x \text{ is divisible by 3}) \wedge (x \text{ is divisible by 5})$

22–23. Find the missing truth values.

22.

p	**q**	**~q**	**p ∧ ~q**	**~(p ∧ ~q)**
?	F	?	?	F

23.

p	**q**	**~p**	**~p ∧ q**	**~q**	**p ∨ ~q**
?	?	?	?	?	F

24. If p represents the statement "n is divisible by 4," and q represents the statement "n is divisible by 3," what is the truth value of the compound statement $p \vee {\sim}q$ for each of the following values of n?
(a) $n = 6$ (b) $n = 12$ (c) $n = 7$ (d) $n = 8$

25. If p represents the statement "x is the largest integer that divides y," and q represents the statement "$y - x > 0$," what is the truth value of the compound statement $p \wedge q$ for each of the following values of x and y?
(a) $x = 10, y = 20$ (c) $x = 8, y = 4$
(b) $x = 17, y = 17$ (d) $x = 12, y = 3$

26. Let p represent the statement "The quotient of x and 4 has a remainder of 1," and q represent the statement "x is divisible only by itself and 1." Which statement is true when $x = 17$?
(1) ${\sim}(p \vee q)$ (2) ${\sim}(p \wedge q)$ (3) $p \wedge q$ (4) ${\sim}p \wedge q$

27–32. In each case construct a truth table for all possible combinations of truth values of p *and* q.

27. ${\sim}(p \wedge {\sim}q)$ **29.** $(p \wedge q) \vee {\sim}q$ **31.** $(p \vee {\sim}q) \wedge {\sim}p$
28. ${\sim}p \vee {\sim}q$ **30.** $p \wedge (p \vee q)$ **32.** ${\sim}[(p \vee q) \vee {\sim}p]$

2.4 ANALYZING A CONDITIONAL STATEMENT

KEY IDEAS

A new statement called a **conditional** is formed from statements p and q by writing, "If p, then q." A conditional is false in the single instance when p is true and q is false.

TRUTH VALUE OF A CONDITIONAL. The shorthand notation $p \rightarrow q$ (read as "p implies q") is used to represent the conditional, "If p, then q." The statement in the "If" clause is called the **hypothesis** (or **antecedent**), while the statement in the "then" clause is called the **conclusion** (or **consequent**). For example, consider these statements:

$$p: \quad \text{I study.}$$
$$q: \quad \text{Mr. Euclid will pass me.}$$
$$p \rightarrow q: \quad \text{If I study, then Mr. Euclid will pass me.}$$

$$\underbrace{}_{hypothesis} \qquad \underbrace{}_{conclusion}$$

A conditional may be thought of as being true provided that whatever "promise" is made in the conclusion part of the statement is not broken when the hypothesis is true. This is illustrated in the truth table given in Table 2.6. The truth table demonstrates that a conditional is always true except in the single case in which the hypothesis p is true, and the conclusion q is false (see row 2 of the truth table).

TABLE 2.6 Truth Table for Conditional $p \rightarrow q$

	p	q	$p \rightarrow q$	Explanation
row 1	T	T	T	I study, and Mr. Euclid passes me.
row 2	T	F	Ⓕ	Mr. Euclid fails to keep his promise.
row 3	F	T	T	No broken promise since I still pass.
row 4	F	F	T	No broken promise since I did not study.

Examples

1. Let p represent "x is divisible by 2," and q represent "The fraction $\dfrac{1}{x-9}$ is undefined." Which of the following statements is true when $x = 9$?

    (1) $p \wedge q$ (2) $p \vee \sim q$ (3) $p \rightarrow \sim q$ (4) $q \rightarrow p$

Solution: When $x = 9$, p is false and q is true. In **choice (3)** the conditional is true since both the hypothesis and the conclusion are false.

2. Consider these statements:

p: 9 is a prime number.

a: 12 is divisible by 2.

r: A square has four equal sides.

Write in words and determine the truth value of each of the following:

(a) $q \rightarrow p$ (b) $p \rightarrow \sim r$ (c) $\sim (p \rightarrow q)$

Solutions:

(a) $q \rightarrow p$: If 12 is divisible by 2, then 9 is a prime number. **False**, since the hypothesis (q) is true and the conclusion (p) is false.

(b) $p \rightarrow \sim r$: If 9 is a prime number, then a square does not have four equal sides. **True**, since the hypothesis (p) is false and the conclusion ($\sim r$) is false.

(c) $\sim (p \rightarrow q)$: It is not true that, if 9 is a prime number, then 12 is divisible by 2. **False**. The truth value of $p \rightarrow q$ is true since p is false and q is true. Therefore, the negation of $p \rightarrow q$ is false.

CONSTRUCTING A TRUTH TABLE FOR A CONDITIONAL STATEMENT.

To construct a truth table for

$$[(p \wedge q) \vee \sim p] \rightarrow (p \vee q),$$

begin by labeling the first two columns as p and q. The statement enclosed by the brackets is the hypothesis, and the expression inside the parentheses, to the right of the arrow, is the conclusion. The first set of columns of the truth table is devoted to analyzing the truth values of the hypothesis and its component statements [see columns (1) through (5) in the accompanying truth table]. The truth value of the conclusion is given in column (6) of the accompanying truth table. The last column of the truth table is labeled with the original conditional. The columns of the truth table are completed as follows:

Columns (1) and (2): The truth values are entered, as usual, for p and q.

Column (3): The conjunction of statements in columns (1) and (2) is true only when both p and q are true. This happens in the first row.

Column (4): In each row the negation of the truth value found in the corresponding row of column (1) is entered.

Column (5): The disjunction is true except in the case in which corresponding rows of columns (3) and (4) are both false. This happens in the second row. This column represents the hypothesis of the given conditional.

Column (6): The disjunction is true except in the case in which corresponding rows of columns (1) and (2) are both false. This is the case in the last row. This column represents the conclusion of the given conditional.

Column (7): The conditional is false only when the hypothesis in column (5) is true and the conclusion in column (6) is false. This situation occurs in the last row of the truth table.

(1)	(2)	(3)	(4)	(5)	(6)	(7)
p	q	$p \wedge q$	$\sim p$	$[(p \wedge q) \vee \sim p]$	$p \vee q$	$[(p \wedge q) \vee \sim p] \rightarrow (p \vee q)$
T	T	T	F	T	T	T
T	F	F	F	F	T	T
F	T	F	T	T	T	T
F	F	F	T	T	F	F

FORMS OF A CONDITIONAL.   *Implication* is another name for a conditional. The "If p, then q" form of the conditional may be expressed in any one of several equivalent forms.

Equivalent Forms	Example
If p, then q.	If I am tired, then I will rest.
p implies q.	I am tired implies I will rest.
q if p.	I will rest if I am tired.
p only if q.	I am tired only if I will rest.

EXERCISE SET 2.4

1–5. Fill in each blank with either true *or* false *so that the resulting statement is correct.*

1. $p \rightarrow q$ is false when p is _____ and q is _____ .

2. If $p \wedge q$ is **true**, then $p \rightarrow q$ is _____ .

3. If $p \rightarrow q$ is false, then $p \vee q$ is _____ .

4. $q \rightarrow \sim p$ is false when q is true and p is _____ .

5. If $p \rightarrow q$ is true and q is false, then p is _____ .

6–10. Determine the truth value.

6. $(|7 - 9| = -2) \rightarrow (|9 - 7| = +2)$

7. $[(-4)^3 < 0] \rightarrow [(-3)^4 > 0]$

8. $[10^{-2} < 10^{-1}] \rightarrow [10^2 < 10^1]$

9. $[5 - 8 = -3] \rightarrow [8 + (-3) = 5]$

10. $[(-2)^{-2} = 0.25] \rightarrow [(-4)^{-4} = 0.50]$

11. Let p represent "x is a prime number," and q represent "x is not divisible by 2." Write each of the following as an English sentence, and state its truth value when x is 23:
   (a) $p \rightarrow q$ (b) $q \rightarrow p$ (c) $\sim p \rightarrow \sim q$ (d) $\sim q \rightarrow \sim p$

12. Let p represent "x is a multiple of 3," and q represent "$x + 1 > 10$." Which of the following statements is true when $x = 9$?
   (1) $p \rightarrow q$ (3) $\sim(p \wedge q) \rightarrow p$
   (2) $\sim p \rightarrow \sim q$ (4) $(p \vee q) \rightarrow (p \wedge q)$

13. Let p represent "A square is a rectangle," and q represent "A circle has three sides." Which of the following statements is true?
   (1) $p \rightarrow (p \vee q)$ (3) $(p \vee q) \rightarrow (p \wedge q)$
   (2) $\sim q \rightarrow q$ (4) $\sim q \rightarrow \sim(p \vee q)$

14. Which of the following statements is true for all possible truth values of p and q?
   (1) $p \rightarrow \sim q$ (3) $p \rightarrow (q \vee \sim q)$
   (2) $(p \vee \sim p) \rightarrow q$ (4) $\sim(p \wedge \sim p) \rightarrow q$

15. Let p represent the statement "x is divisible by a prime number that is less than x," and q represent the statement "x can be written as the product of two identical numbers." Which of the following statements are true when $x = 15$?
   (1) $p \rightarrow q$ (2) $p \rightarrow \sim q$ (3) $p \wedge q$ (4) $\sim q \rightarrow \sim p$

16–21. Construct a truth table for each of the following statements:

16. $(p \wedge q) \rightarrow \sim p$
17. $(p \wedge \sim q) \rightarrow (p \vee q)$
18. $[(p \rightarrow q) \wedge \sim q] \rightarrow \sim p$

19. $\sim(p \vee \sim q) \rightarrow \sim p \wedge q$
20. $[(p \vee q) \wedge \sim q] \rightarrow \sim(p \wedge q)$
21. $(p \rightarrow q) \vee (q \rightarrow p)$

2.5 FORMING THE CONVERSE, INVERSE, AND CONTRAPOSITIVE

KEY IDEAS

By interchanging or negating both parts of a conditional, or by doing both, three conditionals of special interest—the *converse*, the *inverse*, and the *contrapositive*—can be formed. The relationships between certain pairs of these derived conditionals illustrate that it is possible for pairs of statements to look different, yet always agree in their truth values.

RELATED CONDITIONALS.   Starting with the conditional $p \to q$, we can form three related conditionals.

Statement	Symbolic Form	To Obtain from Original . . .
Original	$p \to q$	
Converse	$q \to p$	Switch p with q.
Inverse	$\sim p \to \sim q$	Negate both p and q.
Contrapositive	$\sim q \to \sim p$	Switch and negate p and q.

As an example, let p represent "$x = 2$," and q represent "x is even." Then:

Original:	If $x = 2$, then x is even.	(True)
Converse:	If x is even, then $x = 2$.	(False)
Inverse:	If $x \neq 2$, then x is not even.	(False)
Contrapositive:	If x is not even, then $x \neq 2$.	(True)

As the preceding example indicates, the truth value of the converse *may* be different from the truth value of the original statement. The inverse and the converse will always have the same truth value. The contrapositive may be interpreted as the inverse of the converse or, equivalently, as the converse of the inverse. The original statement and its contrapositive will always have the same truth value.

Examples

1.   What is the inverse of $\sim p \to q$?

Solution: Forming the inverse requires negating both parts of the conditional: $\sim(\sim p) \to \sim(q)$. The hypothesis of this conditional may be simplified by keeping in mind that consecutive negations cancel out since one undoes the effect of the other. The correct answer is $p \to \sim q$.

2.   Let p represent "It is raining," and q represent "I have my umbrella." Express in words the contrapositive of $q \to p$.

Solution: The contrapositive of $q \to p$ is $\sim p \to \sim q$, so that:

$q \to p$:   If I have my umbrella, then it is raining.

negation   negation

$\sim p \to \sim q$:   If it is not raining, then I do not have my umbrella.

LOGICAL EQUIVALENCE.   A pair of statements are *logically equivalent* if they always have the same truth value. Table 2.7 compares the truth values of the related forms of a conditional. Columns (1) and (4) show that a statement and its contrapositive will always have the same truth value. Therefore a statement and its contrapositive are logically equivalent. Columns (2) and (3) establish that the converse and the inverse also are logically equivalent since their truth values are always in agreement.

TABLE 2.7   Truth Table for Related Conditionals

		(1) Original	(2) Converse	(3) Negations		(4) Inverse	Contrapositive
p	q	$p \to q$	$q \to p$	$\sim p$	$\sim q$	$\sim p \to \sim q$	$\sim q \to \sim p$
T	T	T	T	F	F	T	T
T	F	F	T	F	T	T	F
F	T	T	F	T	F	F	T
F	F	T	T	T	T	T	T

logically equivalent statements

Examples

3. Which statement is logically equivalent to $r \to \sim s$?
(1) $\sim s \to r$ (2) $r \to s$ (3) $\sim s \to \sim r$ (4) $s \to \sim r$

Solution: A conditional and its contrapositive are logically equivalent. Choice (1) represents the converse. Negating both parts of the converse leads to the statement in choice (4), which is the contrapositive. The correct answer is **choice (4)**.

4. Given the true statement "If a figure is a square, then the figure is a rectangle," which statement is also true?
(1) If a figure is a not a rectangle, then it is a square.
(2) If a figure is a rectangle, then it is a square.
(3) If a figure is not a rectangle, then it is not a square.
(4) If a figure is not a square, then the figure is not a rectangle.

Solution: A conditional and its contrapositive always have the same truth value. Since the original statement is true, the contrapositive must also be true. The correct answer is **choice (3)**.

5. Construct a truth table to show that the statements

$$q \to (p \wedge q) \quad \text{and} \quad (p \vee q) \to p$$

are logically equivalent

Solution:

(1)	(2)	(3)	(4)	(5)	(6)
p	q	$p \wedge q$	$q \to (p \wedge q)$	$p \vee q$	$(p \vee q) \to p$
T	T	T	T	T	T
T	F	F	T	T	T
F	T	F	F	T	F
F	F	F	T	F	T

The statement $q \to (p \wedge q)$ is logically equivalent to $(p \vee q) \to p$ since columns (4) and (6) have the same truth value for each row of the truth table.

EXERCISE SET 2.5

1–6. Fill in the blank in each of the following so that the resulting statement is true:

1. A conditional and its ———— are logically equivalent.

2. If the inverse of a statement is true, then the ———— must also be true.

3. If j represents the truth value of a conditional statement and k represents the truth value of the contrapositive, then the truth value of $j \wedge k$ is ————.

4. The inverse of "If $x > 0$, then x is positive" is the statement ————.

5. If the converse of a statement is $p \to {\sim} q$, then the original statement is ————.

6. The truth value of the converse of the statement "If the sum of two numbers is negative, then the two numbers are negative" is ————.

7–11. Form the converse, inverse, and contrapositive of each of the following:

7. If a triangle has two equal sides, then the triangle is isosceles.

8. If n is an odd integer, then $n + 1$ is an even integer.

9. If $a + b = b + a$, then $a - b = b - a$.

10. If $n \geq 9$, then $n > 4$.

11. $p \to \, ^\sim q$.

12. Which statement is logically equivalent to the statement "If it is sunny, then it is hot"?
(1) If it is hot, then it is sunny.
(2) If it is not hot, then it is not sunny.
(3) If it is not sunny, then it is not hot.
(4) If it is not hot, then it is sunny.

13. Which statement is logically equivalent to $^\sim p \to q$?
(1) $p \to \, ^\sim q$ (2) $^\sim q \to p$ (3) $q \to \, ^\sim p$ (4) $^\sim q \to \, ^\sim p$

14. In which of the following pairs of statements are the statements logically equivalent?
(1) $k \to h$ and $^\sim h \to \, ^\sim k$ (3) $k \to h$ and $^\sim k \to \, ^\sim h$
(2) $h \to k$ and $^\sim h \to \, ^\sim k$ (4) $h \to k$ and $k \to h$

15. Which statement is logically equivalent to the statement "If $n \leq 5$, then $n \leq 8$"?
(1) If $n > 8$, then $n > 5$.   (3) If $n > 5$, then $n > 8$.
(2) If $n \leq 5$, then $n \leq 8$.   (4) If $n \leq 8$, then $n \leq 5$.

16. Which statement is logically equivalent to the *inverse* of the statement "If I study hard, then I will pass".
(1) If I do not study hard, then I will pass".
(2) If I do not pass, then I will not study hard.
(3) If I will pass, then I study hard.
(4) If I will pass, then I do not study hard.

17–22. Construct a truth table to determine whether, in each given pair of statements, the statements are logically equivalent.

17. $^\sim(p \wedge q)$ and $(^\sim p \vee \, ^\sim q)$

18. $(p \vee q) \to p$ and $p \vee \, ^\sim q$

19. $^\sim q \to \, ^\sim p$ and $p \wedge \, ^\sim q$

20. $(p \wedge q) \to (p \vee q)$ and $^\sim q \to (p \vee q)$

21. $[(p \to q) \vee \, ^\sim q]$ and $(p \vee q) \to p$

22. $[(p \to q) \wedge (q \to p)]$ and $(q \to \, ^\sim p)$

2.6   PROVING THAT A STATEMENT IS A TAUTOLOGY

————————————— KEY IDEAS —————————————

Sometimes statements are combined in such a way that the resulting compound statement is always true or is always false.

TAUTOLOGIES.   What is the truth value of the compound statement $p \vee \sim p$ when p is true? When p is false? The statement is true regardless of the truth value of p. A **tautology** is a compound statement that is always true regardless of the truth values of its component statements. The statement $p \vee \sim p$ is an example of a tautology. Usually we are interested in determining whether more complicated statements are tautologies, in which case a truth table must be constructed.

Example

Construct a truth table to prove that $[(p \rightarrow q) \wedge p] \rightarrow q$ is a tautology.

Solution:

p	q	$p \rightarrow q$	$(p \rightarrow q) \wedge p$	$[(p \rightarrow q) \wedge p] \rightarrow q$
T	T	T	T	T
T	F	F	F	T
F	T	T	F	T
F	F	T	F	T

Since the last column of the truth table shows that $[(p \rightarrow q) \wedge p] \rightarrow q$ is true for all combinations of truth values of p and q, this compound statement is a tautology.

CONTRADICTIONS.   A compound statement that is always false is called a **contradiction**. The statement $p \wedge \sim p$ is an example of a contradiction. It is always false since a statement and its negation cannot be true at the same time.

EXERCISE SET 2.6

1–5. Fill in the blank in each of the following so that the resulting statement is true:

1.   A statement that is a tautology is _____ *(always, sometimes, never)* true.

2.   The truth value of the statement "$(p \wedge q) \rightarrow q$ is a tautology" is _____ .

3.   The truth value of the statement "If two statements are tautologies, then they are logically equivalent" is _____ .

4.   If two statements are tautologies, then they are _____ *(always, sometimes, never)* logically equivalent.

5. The conjunction of two statements that are tautologies is _____ (*always, sometimes, never*) a tautology.

6. Which of the following statements is a tautology?
   (1) $\sim(p \wedge \sim p)$ (3) $p \vee \sim q$
   (2) $\sim(p \vee q)$ (4) $q \wedge \sim q$

7. Which of the following statements is a tautology?
   (1) $\sim(p \rightarrow \sim p)$ (3) $q \rightarrow \sim q$
   (2) $p \rightarrow q$ (4) $(p \rightarrow q) \vee (q \rightarrow p)$

8–20. In each case, construct a truth table in order to determine whether the statement is a tautology.

8. $(\sim p \wedge \sim q) \rightarrow \sim(p \vee q)$
9. $(p \wedge \sim q) \rightarrow (\sim q \rightarrow \sim p)$
10. $(p \rightarrow \sim q) \rightarrow \sim(p \wedge q)$
11. $\sim(p \vee \sim q) \rightarrow \sim p \wedge q$
12. $[(p \rightarrow q) \wedge \sim p] \rightarrow \sim q$
13. $[p \vee (p \wedge q)] \rightarrow \sim q$
14. $\sim(p \rightarrow q) \rightarrow (p \wedge \sim q)$
15. $\sim(p \vee q) \rightarrow p(\sim p \wedge \sim q)$
16. $[(p \vee q) \wedge (\sim p)] \rightarrow q$
17. $\sim(q \rightarrow p) \vee (\sim p \rightarrow \sim q)$
18. $(p \vee \sim q) \rightarrow (\sim p \rightarrow q)$
19. $[(p \wedge q) \vee \sim(p \rightarrow q)] \rightarrow \sim p \vee q$
20. $[(p \vee q) \rightarrow p] \rightarrow [(p \wedge q) \vee \sim q]$

2.7 UNDERSTANDING THE BICONDITIONAL

————————— KEY IDEAS —————————

Two statements may be combined by inserting the words IF AND ONLY IF between them. The resulting compound statement is called the **biconditional** and is true only when both statements have the same truth value.

BICONDITIONALS.   The biconditional of p and q is symbolized by the notation $p \leftrightarrow q$ and is defined to be true when the statements on either side of the double-headed arrow ($\leftrightarrow$) have the same truth value, and false when the statements on the left and right sides of $\leftrightarrow$ have different truth values.

As an illustration, consider these statements:

$$p: \quad 5 \times n = 0.$$
$$q: \quad n = 0.$$
$$p \leftrightarrow q: \quad 5 \times n = 0 \text{ if and only if } n = 0.$$

If p is true and q is true, $p \leftrightarrow q$ is true. If p is false and q is false, $p \leftrightarrow q$ is also true. However, suppose that p and q have opposite truth values. This contradicts a fundamental law of arithmetic which states that, if the product of two numbers is 0, then at least one of the numbers must be 0. The biconditional is false in this case. Table 2.8 gives the truth table for the biconditional.

TABLE 2.8 Truth Table for Biconditional $p \leftrightarrow q$

p	q	$p \leftrightarrow q$
T	T	T
T	F	F
F	T	F
F	F	T

If two statements are logically equivalent, then the biconditional of these statements must always be true since the two statements always have the same truth value. The biconditional of two logically equivalent statements is, therefore, a tautology. For example, since a conditional and its contrapositive are logically equivalent,

$$(p \rightarrow q) \leftrightarrow (\sim q \rightarrow \sim p)$$

is a tautology.

The biconditional $p \leftrightarrow q$ is logically equivalent to the conjunction of a conditional statement and its converse. In other words,

$$(p \leftrightarrow q) \leftrightarrow (p \rightarrow q) \wedge (q \rightarrow p)$$

is a tautology.

Examples

1. Let p represent the statement "$3 + 7 = 10$," q represent the statement "A triangle has three sides," and r represent the statement "9 is a prime number." Express each of the following biconditionals as an English sentence and determine its truth value:

(a) $p \leftrightarrow q$ (b) $p \leftrightarrow r$ (c) $\sim q \leftrightarrow r$

Solutions:

(a) $3 + 7 = 10$ if and only if a triangle has three sides. **True** since both p and q are true.

(b) $3 + 7 = 10$ if and only if 9 is a prime number. **False** since p (true) and r (false) have different truth values.

(c) A triangle does not have three sides if and only if 9 is a prime number. **True** since both $\sim q$ and r are false.

2. Construct a truth table to show that the statement

$$(p \rightarrow q) \leftrightarrow (\sim p \vee q)$$

is a tautology.

Solution:

(1)   (2)   (3)   (4)   (5)   (6)

p	q	$p \rightarrow q$	$\sim p$	$\sim p \lor q$	$(p \rightarrow q) \leftrightarrow (\sim p \lor q)$
T	T	T	F	T	T
T	F	F	F	F	T
F	T	T	T	T	T
F	F	T	T	T	T

Notice that in each row the truth values of columns (3) and (5) agree, so that T is entered in column (6). Since column (6) shows that the biconditional is true for all combinations of truth values of p and q,

$$(p \rightarrow q) \leftrightarrow (\sim p \lor q)$$

is a tautology.

   3.   In Example 2, let p represent "The machine is a computer," and q represent "The machine cannot make a mistake." What statement is logically equivalent to the statement "If the machine is a computer, then the machine cannot make a mistake"?

   Solution: The statement "If the machine is a computer, then the machine cannot make a mistake" can be represented as $p \rightarrow q$. The truth table shows that $p \rightarrow q$ in column (3) is logically equivalent to $\sim p \lor q$ in column (5). The negation of p is the statement "The machine is not a computer." Therefore the logical equivalent of "If the machine is a computer, then the machine cannot make a mistake" is the statement "**The machine is not a computer or the machine cannot make a mistake.**"

EXERCISE SET 2.7

   1.   Which statement is always true?
   (1) $p \land \sim p$ (2) $\sim(\sim p) \leftrightarrow p$ (3) $p \rightarrow \sim p$ (4) $p \land q$

   2.   If $p \leftrightarrow q$ is false, which statement *must* also be false?
   (1) $\sim p \land q$ (2) $p \land q$ (3) $p \rightarrow q$ (4) $p \lor q$

   3.   If j and k each represent a compound statement and $j \leftrightarrow k$ is always true, then which of the following statements is always true?
   (1) j and k are logically equivalent.   (3) $(j \land k)$ is a tautology.
   (2) j and k are tautologies.   (4) $(j \lor k)$ is a tautology.

4. Let p represent "x is a prime number," q represent "x is an odd number," and r represent "x is a multiple of 7." Express each of the following as an English sentence, and determine its truth value if $x = 21$:

   (a) $p \leftrightarrow q$　　(b) $q \leftrightarrow r$　　(c) $p \leftrightarrow \sim r$　　(d) $\sim p \leftrightarrow (q \wedge r)$

5. Let p represent "He is a snob," and q represent "He likes cavier." Express each of the following as an English sentence:

   (a) $p \vee q$　　　(c) $p \rightarrow q$　　　(e) $q \rightarrow p$　　　　(g) $\sim p \rightarrow \sim q$

   (b) $\sim p \wedge q$　　(d) $p \leftrightarrow q$　　(f) $\sim q \rightarrow \sim p$　　(h) $\sim p \leftrightarrow q$

6. If p represents "$x > 5$" and q represents "x is divisible by 3," which statement is true if $x = 10$?

   (1) $p \rightarrow q$　　(2) $(p \vee q) \rightarrow q$　　(3) $(p \wedge q) \rightarrow p$　　(4) $p \leftrightarrow q$

7. Let p represent the statement "x is a prime number," and q represent the statement "$x + 2$ is a prime number." Which statement is true when $x = 17$?

   (1) $p \leftrightarrow q$　　(2) $p \rightarrow \sim q$　　(3) $\sim p \wedge q$　　(4) $p \leftrightarrow \sim q$

8–16. For each of the following statements, (a) construct a truth table, and (b) determine whether the statement is a tautology:

8. $(p \rightarrow q) \leftrightarrow (p \vee q)$
9. $(p \leftrightarrow q) \vee (q \rightarrow \sim p)$
10. $\sim (p \rightarrow q) \leftrightarrow (p \wedge \sim q)$
11. $[p \vee (\sim p \wedge q)] \leftrightarrow p \vee q$
12. $(\sim p \rightarrow q) \leftrightarrow (p \vee q)$
13. $(\sim q \rightarrow \sim p) \leftrightarrow (q \vee \sim p)$
14. $[(p \rightarrow q) \wedge \sim q] \leftrightarrow \sim p$
15. $[(p \vee q) \rightarrow \sim p] \leftrightarrow (p \vee \sim q)$
16. $[(p \vee q) \wedge (p \wedge q)] \leftrightarrow (p \leftrightarrow q)$

17. Construct a truth table to show that $(p \wedge q) \leftrightarrow p$ and $p \rightarrow q$ are logically equivalent.

18. Construct a truth table to show that $[(p \wedge q) \vee \sim (p \vee q)]$ is logically equivalent to $p \leftrightarrow q$.

19. Construct a truth table to show that the biconditional is logically equivalent to the conjunction of a conditional statement and its converse.

20. (a) Construct a truth table for the statement

$$[q \vee (\sim q \rightarrow \sim p)] \leftrightarrow [(p \leftrightarrow q) \rightarrow p].$$

   (b) Determine whether the statement in part (a) is a tautology, and give a reason for your answer.

21. (a) Construct a truth table for the statement

$$(p \vee \sim q) \rightarrow (\sim p \rightarrow \sim q).$$

(b) Determine whether the statement in part (a) is a tautology, and give a reason for your answer.

(c) Let p represent the statement "Today is a holiday," and q represent the statement "I do not attend school." Using your results from part (a), determine which of the following statements is logically equivalent to the statement "Today is a holiday, or I attend school."

(1) If today is a holiday, then I do not attend school.

(2) If today is not a holiday, then I attend school

(3) If today is not a holiday, then I do not attend school.

(4) If I do not attend school, then today is not a holiday.

2.8 APPLYING LOGIC TO SOLVING PROBLEMS

────────────── KEY IDEAS ──────────────

Knowing the truth value of a compound statement, and of each of its component statements except one, may allow a conclusion to be drawn regarding the truth value of the remaining component statement.

DRAWING CONCLUSIONS. If $p \vee q$ is true and p is false, we may conclude that q must be true. If it is given that p is true and the conditional $p \rightarrow q$ is also true, what can be said about the truth value of q? Since the hypothesis and the conditional are true, the conclusion cannot be false; that is, q must be true.

Next suppose that $\sim p$ is true and $p \rightarrow q$ is true. What conclusion can be drawn about the truth value of q? No conclusion is possible. Since $\sim p$ is true, p is false. If the hypothesis is false, then the conditional is true regardless of the truth value of the conclusion.

Example ▰▰▰▰▰

1. If $p \leftrightarrow q$ is false, draw a conclusion regarding the truth value of each of the following:

(a) $p \wedge q$ (b) $p \vee q$ (c) $p \rightarrow q$

Solutions:

(a) $p \wedge q$ is **false**. Since the biconditional is false, either p or q must be false, so that the conjunction must be false.

(b) $p \vee q$ is **true**. Since the biconditional is false, either p or q must be true, so that the disjunction is true.

(c) No conclusion. Since the biconditional is false, either p is true and q is false ($p \rightarrow q$ is false), or p is false and q is true ($p \rightarrow q$ is true). Therefore no conclusion can be drawn regarding the truth value of $p \rightarrow q$.

REASONING LOGICALLY. Can you draw a conclusion from the following set of statements?

(1) If Peter is a freshman, then he takes Course I.
(2) Peter is a freshman.

The conclusion "Peter takes Course I" can be arrived at by using the following procedure:

Step 1: Represent the statements symbolically:

p: Peter is a freshman.
q. He takes Course I.

Step 2: The given statements, called **premises**, are assumed to be true. Write the set of given statements and the unknown conclusion vertically as shown here:

$$p \rightarrow q \quad \text{is true,}$$
$$\underline{p \qquad \text{is true,}}$$
Conclusion: ?

Step 3: Record the truth values next to the symbols. Reason "backwards": since p is true in the second statement, it must be true in the first (conditional) statement. Since the conditional statement is true and its hypothesis is true, its conclusion q must also be true. This pattern of reasoning may be recorded as follows:

$$p^{\text{T}} \rightarrow q^{\text{T}} \quad \text{is true.}$$
$$\underline{p^{\text{T}} \qquad\qquad \text{is true.}}$$
Conclusion: q

Example

2. In each case below, represent each of the given statements symbolically, and draw a valid conclusion, if any is possible.

(a) (1) Either x is odd or x is even.
(2) x is not odd.

Solution:
p: x is odd.
q: x is even.
$$p^{\text{F}} \vee q^{\text{T}} \quad \text{is true.}$$
$$\underline{\sim p \qquad\qquad \text{is true.}}$$
Conclusion: q

Since $\sim p$ is true, p is false. Therefore q must be true in order for the disjunction to be true. The conclusion is "**x is even.**"

(b) (1) If x is divisible by 9, then x is divisible by 3.
(2) x is not divisible by 3.

Solution: p: x is divisible by 9.

                q: x is divisible by 3.

                $p\,^{\text{Ⓕ}} \to q\,^{\text{Ⓕ}}$ is true.

                $\sim q$ is true.

Conclusion: $\overline{\sim p}$

Since $\sim q$ is true, q is false. The conclusion of the conditional is false. Since the conditional is true, the hypothesis (p) must be false. The conclusion is "**x is *not* divisible by 9.**"

(c) (1) If *ABCD* is a square, then *ABCD* is a parallelogram.

  (2) *ABCD* is not a square.

Solution: p: *ABCD* is a square.

                q: *ABCD* is a parallelogram.

                $P\,^{\text{Ⓕ}} \to q$ is true.

                $\sim p$ is true.

Conclusion: $\overline{?}$

Since $\sim p$ is true, p is false. The hypothesis of the conditional is false. The conditional will be true regardless of the truth value of q. Since it is not possible to determine whether q is true or false, no conclusion is possible. ▬▬▬▬

EXERCISE SET 2.8

1–4. If p $\leftrightarrow$ q *is false, draw a conclusion regarding the truth value of each statement.*

1. $p \wedge q$ **2.** $p \vee q$ **3.** $p \to q$ **4.** $q \leftrightarrow p$

5. Given the statements "If we water the lawn in the morning, then it will rain in the afternoon," and "It didn't rain in the afternoon," which statement logically follows?
(1) We didn't water the lawn in the morning.
(2) We watered the lawn in the morning.
(3) It rained in the morning.
(4) It rained in the afternoon.

6. If $B \to \sim C$ and C are both true statements, then which conclusion must be true?
(1) B (2) $\sim B$ (3) $\sim C$ (4) $B \to C$

7. Given the true statements "Mark goes shopping, or he goes to the movies" and "Mark doesn't go to the movies," which statement *must* also be true?
(1) Mark goes shopping.
(2) Mark doesn't go shopping.
(3) Mark doesn't go shopping, and he doesn't go to the movies.
(4) Mark stays home.

8. If $\sim r \rightarrow s$ and $\sim s$ are true, which statement *must* be true?
   (1) r (2) $\sim r$ (3) $r \rightarrow s$ (4) $s \wedge \sim s$

9. Given the true statement, $[(s \vee t) \wedge \sim s]$, which statement *must* also be true?
   (1) t (2) $\sim t$ (3) s (4) $s \wedge \sim t$

10. If $p \vee \sim q$ is true and $p \leftrightarrow q$ is false, then:
    (1) p is true, q is false.   (3) both p and q are true.
    (2) p is false, q is true.   (4) both p and q are false.

11. If $p \rightarrow q$ is false, which can never be true?
    (1) $q \rightarrow p$ (2) $\sim q \rightarrow p$ (3) $p \vee q$ (4) $p \leftrightarrow q$

12. If $p \rightarrow q$ is true and $p \leftrightarrow q$ is false, then:
    (1) p is true, q is false.
    (2) p is false, q is true.
    (3) both p and q are true.
    (4) both p and q are false.

13–20. (a) *Represent each set of true premises symbolically.*
       (b) *Draw a valid conclusion, and use logical principles to show that the conclusion is true.*

13. If I am unhappy, then I cry.
    I do not cry.

14. Amanda will get an A if she passes this test.
    Amanda passes this test.

15. If x is a prime number, then x is an odd number.
    x is not a prime number.

16. If I play tennis, then I will not have time for dinner.
    Either I will play tennis, or I will watch television.
    I do not watch television.

17. If Jason is smart or is lucky, then he will earn a good income.
    Jason will earn a good income.
    Jason is not lucky.

18. If Bob washes the dishes, then Sue dries the dishes.
    Bob washes the dishes, or Gail mows the lawn.
    Gail does not mow the lawn.

19. If it is hot, then I will go swimming.
    Either I will go swimming, or I will jog.
    It is hot.

20. Today is Saturday or Sunday.
    If today is Sunday, then I will watch the football game.
    Today is not Saturday.

CHAPTER 2 REVIEW EXERCISES

REGENTS REVIEW. *Problems included in this section are similar in form and difficulty to those found on the New York State Regents Examination for Course I of the Three-Year Sequence for High School Mathematics. Questions preceded by an asterisk have actually appeared on a previous Regents examination.*

*1. Let p represent "It is summer" and q represent "I go swimming." Using p and q, write in symbolic form: "If I go swimming, then it is summer."

*2. Let p represent the statement "The base angles are congruent," and let q represent the statement "A triangle is isosceles." Using p and q, write in symbolic form: "A triangle is isosceles if and only if the base angles are congruent."

*3. The inverse of a statement is $p \to \sim q$. What is the statement?

4. Write in symbolic form, using p and q the converse of $\sim p \to \sim q$.

*5. If p represents "Today is Monday" and q represents "I am tired," write in symbolic form, using p and q: "Today is Monday, and I am not tired."

*6. The statement $r \vee s$ is false if and only if:
(1) r is true and s is true.   (3) r is false and s is true.
(2) r is true and s is false.   (4) r is false and s is false.

7. $p \to q$ is false when:
(1) p is true, q is false.   (3) p and q are true.
(2) p is false, q is true.   (4) p and q are false.

8. If $p \leftrightarrow q$ is true, then which of the following statements is always true?
(1) p and q have opposite truth values.
(2) $p \wedge q$ is true.
(3) $p \to q$ is true.
(4) $p \vee q$ is true.

*9. Which represents the inverse of the statement "If the base angles of an isosceles triangle are congruent, then the triangle is isosceles"?
(1) If the base angles of the triangle are not congruent, then the triangle is not isosceles.
(2) If the triangle is isosceles, then the base angles are congruent.
(3) If the triangle is not isosceles, then the base angles are not congruent.
(4) If the base angles of a triangle are not congruent, then the triangle is isosceles.

*10. Given the statement "If a figure is a triangle, then it is a polygon," which statement *must* be true?
(1) If a figure is a polygon, then it is a triangle.
(2) If a figure is not a triangle, then it is not a polygon.
(3) If a figure is not a polygon, then it is not a triangle.
(4) If a figure is not a triangle, then it is a polygon.

*11. What is the inverse of $\sim p \rightarrow q$?
(1) $p \rightarrow \sim q$ (2) $q \rightarrow \sim p$ (3) $\sim p \rightarrow \sim q$ (4) $\sim q \rightarrow \sim p$

12. Given these true premises: (1) If John gets a driver's license, then he will buy a car, and (2) John does not buy a car, which of the following conclusions is true?
(1) John gets a driver's license.
(2) John does not get a driver's license.
(3) John buys a car.
(4) No conclusion is possible.

13. If $p \leftrightarrow q$ is false and $\sim q$ is true, then:
(1) p is true and q is false.
(2) p is false and q is true.
(3) p and q are both true.
(4) p and q are both false.

*14. Let p represent "x is a prime number," and let q represent "x is an odd number." Which is true if $x = 15$?
(1) p (2) $\sim q$ (3) $p \wedge q$ (4) $p \vee q$

15. If $p \wedge q$ is false and $p \leftrightarrow q$ is true, then:
(1) p is true, q is false.
(2) p is false, q is true.
(3) p and q are true.
(4) p and q are false.

16. If $p \rightarrow q$ is false, then which statement must be true?
(1) $p \vee q$ (2) $p \wedge q$ (3) $p \leftrightarrow q$ (4) $\sim q \rightarrow \sim p$

*17. Let p represent "x is odd." Let q represent "$x > 8$." When x is 6, which is true?
(1) p (2) q (3) $p \rightarrow q$ (4) $p \wedge q$

*18. If $p \leftrightarrow q$ is true, which statement *must* also be true?
(1) $p \wedge q$ (2) $p \vee q$ (3) $p \wedge \sim q$ (4) $p \rightarrow q$

19. If the inverse of a statement is true, which statement must also be true?
(1) original   (2) contrapositive   (3) converse   (4) implication

20. Given that $\sim p \vee q$ is true, then if q is false, which statement is true?
(1) $p \vee q$ (2) $p \wedge q$ (3) $p \leftrightarrow q$ (4) $\sim p \rightarrow q$

21. If $p \wedge q$ is true, which statement is also true?
    (1) $p \leftrightarrow q$ (2) $p \rightarrow q$ (3) $p \vee q$ (4) all of these

*22. Let p represent the statement "x is even." Let q represent the statement "$x \leq 12$." Which is true if $x = 20$?
    (1) $p \rightarrow q$ (2) $p \wedge {\sim}q$ (3) ${\sim}p \vee q$ (4) all of these

23. Which is *always* false?
    (1) $p \rightarrow q$ (2) $q \rightarrow p$ (3) ${\sim}p \rightarrow {\sim}q$ (4) $p \wedge {\sim}p$

24. If $p \vee q$ is false, which statement must be true?
    (1) $p \rightarrow q$ (2) ${\sim}p \rightarrow q$ (3) $p \leftrightarrow q$ (4) ${\sim}q \rightarrow p$

25. If the converse of a statement is ${\sim}r \rightarrow s$, which of the following is the statement?
    (1) $r \rightarrow {\sim}s$ (2) $r \rightarrow s$ (3) $s \rightarrow {\sim}r$ (4) ${\sim}s \rightarrow r$

26. Which of the following statements is *not* a tautology?
    (1) $p \vee {\sim}p$ (2) $(p \rightarrow q) \vee p$ (3) $p \leftrightarrow p$ (4) $(p \rightarrow q) \vee q$

27. In which of the following pairs are the statements *not* logically equivalent?
    (1) p and ${\sim}({\sim}p)$
    (2) $p \rightarrow q$ and ${\sim}q \rightarrow {\sim}p$
    (3) $p \leftrightarrow q$ and $p \wedge q$
    (4) $q \rightarrow p$ and ${\sim}p \rightarrow {\sim}q$

*28. (a) construct a truth table for the statement
    $[p \vee ({\sim}p \wedge q)] \leftrightarrow (p \vee q)$.
    (b) On the basis of your results from part (a), is $[p \vee ({\sim}p \wedge q)] \leftrightarrow (p \vee q)$ a tautology?

*29. (a) On your answer paper, copy and complete the truth table for the statement

    $$({\sim}p \rightarrow q) \leftrightarrow (p \vee q).$$

p	q	${\sim}p$	${\sim}p \rightarrow q$	$p \vee q$	$({\sim}p \rightarrow q) \leftrightarrow (p \vee q)$

(b) Is $({\sim}p \rightarrow q) \leftrightarrow (p \vee q)$ a tautology?

(c) Let p represent: "I do my homework."
    Let q represent: "I get into trouble."
    Which sentence is equivalent to $(p \vee q)$?
    (1) If I no not do my homework, I will get into trouble.
    (2) I do my homework or I do not get into trouble.
    (3) If I do my homework, I get into trouble.
    (4) I do my homework and I get into trouble.

*30. (a) Copy and complete the truth table for the statement

$$(p \rightarrow q) \leftrightarrow (q \vee \sim p).$$

p	q	$p \rightarrow q$	$\sim p$	$q \vee \sim p$	$(p \rightarrow q) \leftrightarrow (q \vee \sim p)$

(b) Why is $(p \rightarrow q) \leftrightarrow (q \vee \sim p)$ a tautology?

(c) In $(p \rightarrow q) \leftrightarrow (q \vee \sim p)$, let p represent "We pollute the water," and let q represent "The fish will die." Which statement is logically equivalent to "If we pollute the water, then the fish will die"?

    (1) The fish will die or we do not pollute the water.

    (2) We pollute the water and the fish will die.

    (3) If wo do not pollute the water, then the fish will not die.

    (4) If the fish die, then we pollute the water.

31. In each of the following two true statements are given. Write a conclusion that can be deduced by using both statements.

(a) If I am unhappy, then I cry. I do not cry.

(b) $(x + 2 = 5) \vee (7 - x = 5)$. $x = 2$.

(c) Elaine will get an A if she passes this test. Elaine passes this test.

(d) Either I have money, or I will stay home. I do not have money.

(e) If the winds are above 20 knots, I will not go sailing. I am sailing.

UNIT II: ALGEBRA

CHAPTER   3

Solving Linear Equations

3.1   TRANSLATING ENGLISH TO ALGEBRA

KEY IDEAS

Algebra is used to solve problems, so it is important to be able to represent commonly encountered phrases algebraically. Keep in mind that the terms *plus*, *sum*, *more than*, and *increased* or *exceeded by* involve the operation of **addition**; the words *difference*, *less than*, and *diminished by* involve the operation of **subtraction**; the terms *product*, *two times*, *three times*, and so forth, are related to **multiplication**; the term *quotient* refers to **division**.

INTERPRETING ALGEBRAIC EXPRESSIONS.   If n represents some unknown number, how do expressions such as $n + 5$, $n - 3$, $\frac{n}{2}$, and $3n$ compare to the original number? By identifying the arithmetic operations contained in the expression, we may express the relationship between the variables, numbers, and arithmetic operations in words.

Expression	Interpretation
$n + 5$	5 more than n *or* the sum of n and 5 *or* "... exceeds n by 5"
$n - 3$	3 less than n *or* n diminished by 3 *or* the difference between n and 3
$\dfrac{n}{2}$	One half of n *or* n divided by 2 *or* the quotient of n divided by 2
$3n$	Three times n *or* the product of 3 and n *or* 3 multiplied by n

By expressing the width and the length of a rectangle in terms of the same variable the dimensions of the rectangle can be compared.

RECTANGLE		COMPARING LENGTH TO WIDTH
Width	**Length**	**Interpretation**
x	$x + 4$	The length is 4 more than the width *or* The length exceeds the width by 4.
x	$2x$	The length is twice the width.
x	$2(x + 1)$	The length is twice the sum of the width and 1.
x	$2x + 1$	The length exceeds twice the width by 1.

WRITING ALGEBRAIC EXPRESSIONS.   If y represents John's age, how would you represent John's age 5 years ago? John's age 9 years from now? John's age when he is three times as old as he is now? These situations can be represented algebraically by writing an appropriate expression that adds to y, subtracts from y, or multiplies y.

Expression	**Interpretation**
$y - 5$	John's age 5 years ago
$y + 9$	John's age 9 years from now
$3y$	John's age when he is three times as old as he is now
$2(y - 8)$	Twice John's age 8 years ago

Examples

1. Express, in terms of *n*, each of the following:
(a) a number diminished by 6
(b) a number increased by 7
(c) four times the number
(d) the quotient of a number divided by 3
(e) 8 more than the number
(f) 15 less than the number
(g) the value, in cents, of *n* nickels
(h) the value, in cents, of *n* dimes

Solutions:

(a) $n - 6$

(b) $n + 7$

(c) $4n$

(d) $\dfrac{n}{3}$

(e) $n + 8$

(f) $n - 15$

(g) $5n$ ($= 5$ cents $\cdot$ n nickels)

(h) $10n$ ($= 10$ cents $\cdot$ n dimes)

2.   The length of a certain rectangle is three times its width. If x represents the width of the rectangle, express in terms of x the perimeter of the rectangle.

Solution: Let $x = $ width of the rectangle.

Then $3x = $ length of the rectangle.

The perimeter of a rectangle is the distance around the figure, which is found by finding the sum of the lengths of the four sides.

$$
\begin{aligned}
\text{Perimeter} &= 3x + x + 3x + x \\
&= 4x \qquad + 4x \\
&= 8x
\end{aligned}
$$

EXERCISE SET 3.1

1–10. If x *represents a number, express each of the following in terms of* x*:*

1. The sum of the number and 9.
2. 5 less than twice the number.
3. The difference of twice the number and 5.
4. 4 more than three times the number.
5. Three times the number increased by 4.
6. One-half the number increased by 3.
7. The sum of three times the number and 1.
8. Three times the sum of the number and 1.
9. The difference of twice the number and 8.
10. The quotient of two times the number divided by 3.

11–15. If the length of a certain rectangle is represented by l, *then, for each of the following situations, express the width in terms of* l*:*

11. Width is one half of the length.
12. Width is 7 less than the length.
13. Width is equal to the length.
14. Width exceeds one-third the length by 5.
15. Width is twice the difference of the length and 3.

16–20. If s *represents Susan's age, then represent each of the following situations in terms of* s*:*

16. Susan's age 9 years from now.
17. Susan's age 10 years ago.

18. One fourth of Susan's age.
19. Susan's age when she is twice the age she was 5 years ago.
20. Mary's age if Mary's age exceeds twice Susan's age by 4.

21–24. In a certain rectangle, the width of the rectangle is represented by w:

    (a) Express the length in terms of w.
    (b) Express the perimeter of the rectangle in terms of w.

21. The length exceeds the width by 10.
22. The length is twice the width.
23. The length is equal to the width.
24. The length exceeds three times the width by 1.

25–30. Express in terms of n *the number of cents in each of the following:*

25. n quarters
26. n dimes + 4 pennies
27. n dimes + n nickels
28. n quarters and $(n - 1)$ dimes
29. $(n + 1)$ dimes and $(n - 1)$ nickels
30. n nickels + $2n$ dimes

3.2 SOLVING EQUATIONS USING INVERSE OPERATIONS

_____ KEY IDEAS _____

Equations that have the same solution set are **equivalent**. The equations

$$x + 1 = 4, \qquad 2x = 6, \qquad \text{and} \qquad x = 3$$

are equivalent since $\{3\}$ is the solution set of each equation. When solving an equation, our goal is to try to obtain an equivalent equation in which the variable is "isolated" on one side of the equation, so that the solution set can be read from the opposite side, as in $x = 3$.

An equation in which the greatest exponent of the variable is 1 is called a **first-degree** or **linear equation**. This chapter will illustrate how to solve various types of linear equations.

INVERSE OPERATIONS. You can "undo" an arithmetic operation by performing its *inverse*. Adding a number to a variable may be undone by then subtracting the same number. For example,

$$x + 2 - 2 = x + 0 = x.$$

Multiplying   variable by a number may be undone by then dividing by the same number. For example,

$$\frac{3x}{3} = \frac{\overset{1}{\cancel{3}}}{\cancel{3}}x = 1x = x.$$

Addition and subtraction are inverse operations, as are multiplication and division.

SOLVING EQUATIONS USING ADDITION AND SUBTRACTION.

An equivalent equation is produced whenever the *same* number is added to, or subtracted from, each side of an equation. Examples 1 and 2 use this property to solve equations in which the variable must be isolated by performing the same inverse operation on *each* side of the equation.

Examples

1. Solve: $x - 1 = 4$.

Solution: Add 1 to each side.

$$x - 1 + 1 = 4 + 1$$
$$x + 0 = 5$$
$$x = 5$$

The solution set is $\{5\}$.

2. Solve: $-5 = x + 3$.

Solution: Subtract 3 from each side.

$$-5 - 3 = x + 3 - 3$$
$$-8 = x + 0$$
$$-8 = x \text{ or } x = -8$$

The solution set is $\{-8\}$.

Examples 3 and 4 illustrate the fact that sometimes it is convenient to write the inverse operation vertically on a separate line underneath the original equation.

Examples

3. Solve: $b - 2.3 = 4.8$.

Solution:

Align decimal points, then add:

$$\begin{aligned} b - 2.3 &= 4.8 \\ +2.3 &= 2.3 \\ \hline b + 0 &= 7.1 \\ b &= 7.1 \text{ or } \{7.1\} \end{aligned}$$

4. Solve: $w + \dfrac{1}{8} = 5\dfrac{1}{2}$.

Solution: $w + \dfrac{1}{8} = 5\dfrac{4}{8}$

$\phantom{w + \dfrac{1}{8}}-\dfrac{1}{8} = -\dfrac{1}{8}$

Note: $\dfrac{1}{2} = \dfrac{4}{8}$

$$w + 0 = 5\dfrac{3}{8}$$

$$w = 5\dfrac{3}{8} \ or \ \left\{5\dfrac{3}{8}\right\}$$

SOLVING EQUATIONS USING MULTIPLICATION AND DIVISION.

If each side of an equation is multiplied or divided by the same nonzero number, then an equivalent equation results. Examples 5 and 6 illustrate how this property is used to isolate a variable in an equation in which the variable is connected to a number by either multiplication or division.

Examples

5. Solve: $-2n = 10$

Solution: Divide each side by -2.

$$\frac{-2n}{-2} = \frac{10}{-2}$$

$$n = -5 \ or \ \{-5\}$$

6. Solve: $\dfrac{y}{3} = -7$.

Solution: Multiply each side by 3.

$$\overset{1}{\cancel{3}}\left(\frac{y}{\cancel{3}}\right) = 3(-7)$$

$$y = -21 \ or \ \{-21\}$$

CHECKING ROOTS. A **root** of an equation is any number of the replacement set that makes the equation a true statement. To check that a number is a root of an equation, perform these steps:

Step 1. Return to the original equation and replace the variable with the value(s) obtained as the solution.

Step 2. Compare the values of each side of the equation. If these values are the same, then the number is a root of the equation.

Examples ▰▰▰

7. Determine whether 3 is a root of the equation $2x - 1 = 5$.

Solution: Replace x by 3.

$$\frac{2(3) - 1 = 5}{6 - 1 \Big|}$$
$$5 \overset{?}{=} 5\checkmark$$

8. Solve *and* check: $\frac{2}{5}n = 14$.

Solution: When the coefficient of the variable is a fraction, the variable may be isolated by multiplying each side of the equation by the *reciprocal* of the fraction.

$$\left(\frac{5}{2}\right)\left(\frac{2n}{5}\right) = (14)\left(\frac{5}{2}\right) \quad \Bigg| \quad Check: \ \frac{2n}{5} = 14$$

$$n = \frac{\overset{7}{\cancel{14}}}{1} \cdot \frac{5}{\cancel{2}} \qquad \qquad \frac{2}{5}(35)$$
$$ 1 \qquad \qquad \frac{2}{\cancel{5}}(\cancel{35}) \overset{7}{}$$

$$n = 35 \qquad \qquad 1$$

$$\qquad \qquad \qquad \qquad 14 = 14\checkmark \quad ▰▰▰$$

SOLVING WORD PROBLEMS.   If a certain number is increased by 5, the result is -8. What is the number? To solve this problem:

Think ...	Take This Action ...
1. What must I find?	Represent the unknown with a variable: Let n = unknown number.
2. What are the facts?	Translate the facts into an equation: *A number increased by 5 result is* -8
	$n \qquad \qquad + 5 \qquad = \qquad -8$
3. What is the answer?	Solve the equation:
	$n + 5 - 5 = -8 - 5$
	$n + 0 = -13$
	$n = -13$
4. Is my answer correct?	Check the answer in the statement of the problem:
	$-13 + 5 = -8 \qquad$ True.

EXERCISE SET 3.2

1–36. Solve for the variable and check.

1. $x + 5 = -9$
2. $-3x = 12$
3. $-7 = x - 1$
4. $\dfrac{n}{2} = 8$
5. $-0.5w = -35$
6. $-4 = x + 2$
7. $-10 = \dfrac{t}{-3}$
8. $40 = -8s$
9. $n + 8 = -7$
10. $-7.2 = 3 + x$
11. $x - \dfrac{1}{2} = \dfrac{5}{2}$
12. $4n = -3.2$
13. $y + 0.6 = 3$
14. $\dfrac{a}{-3} = -6$
15. $1.2 = m - 1.3$
16. $t + 2 = \dfrac{4}{3}$
17. $\dfrac{2x}{3} = 16$
18. $2 = y + 0.6$
19. $-21 = \dfrac{7x}{8}$
20. $\dfrac{x}{5} = 1.7$

21. $\dfrac{3x}{4} = -12$
22. $y - \dfrac{1}{3} = -2$
23. $\dfrac{r}{3} = -8.4$
24. $-10 = \dfrac{-5a}{3}$
25. $3x = 1\frac{1}{8}$
26. $\dfrac{x}{4} = 2\frac{1}{3}$
27. $-2x = 1\frac{1}{5}$
28. $x + 1.9 = -7.6$
29. $\dfrac{a}{-4} = 1.6$
30. $b + \dfrac{1}{3} = 2\frac{1}{6}$
31. $\dfrac{-3h}{5} = -15$
32. $8k = -\dfrac{7}{2}$
33. $1\frac{1}{3}y = 8$
34. $0.7t = 4.9$
35. $2\frac{1}{4}p = -18$
36. $-1.08w = 0.36$

37. A number diminished by 7 is -3. What is the number?
38. The quotient of a number divided by -4 is 5. What is the number?
39. 19 exceeds a number by 25. What is the number?
40. -14 is less than a number. What is the number?
41. Two thirds of a number is 15. What is the number?
42. 8 exceeds a number by $3\frac{5}{6}$. What is the number?
43. A number decreased by $1\frac{5}{8}$ is $4\frac{1}{2}$. What is the number?
44. The product of $1\frac{1}{4}$ and a number is 10. What is the number?
45. What number when divided by 0.3 has a quotient of 0.75?
46. Which of the following equations is *not* equivalent to $2x = -8$?

(1) $x + 4 = -8$ (2) $x - 2 = -6$ (3) $\dfrac{x}{2} = -2$ (4) $\dfrac{-3x}{2} = 6$

3.3   SOLVING EQUATIONS USING MORE THAN ONE OPERATION

_____ KEY IDEAS _____

To solve an equation in which the variable is involved in two or more arithmetic operations, perform inverse operations one at a time, starting with addition (or subtraction). If the equation contains parentheses, remove these first.

SOLVING EQUATIONS WITH TWO ARITHMETIC OPERATIONS.
In the equation $2n + 5 = -11$ the variable is involved in two operations: multiplication $(2n)$ and addition $(2n + 5)$. In solving this equation, undo the addition before the multiplication.

Examples ▰▰▰

1. Solve and check: $2n + 5 = -11$.

Solution:

$$2n + 5 - 5 = -11 - 5$$
$$2n + \ \ 0 \ = -16$$
$$\frac{2n}{2} = \frac{-16}{2}$$
$$n = -8$$

Check:
$$\underline{2n + 5 = -11}$$
$$2(-8) + 5 \ |$$
$$-16 + 5 \ |$$
$$-11 = -11\checkmark$$

2. Solve and check: $\dfrac{x}{3} - 2 = 13$.

Solution:

$$\frac{x}{3} - 2 + 2 = 13 + 2$$
$$\frac{x}{3} + 0 \quad = 15$$
$$\overset{1}{\cancel{3}}\left(\frac{x}{\cancel{3}}\right) = 3(15)$$
$$x = 45$$

Check:
$$\underline{\frac{x}{3} - 2 = 13}$$
$$\frac{45}{3} - 2 \ |$$
$$15 - 2 \ |$$
$$13 = 13\checkmark$$

3. The EZ-Car Rental Agency charges $35 for the first day, and $22 for each additional day. If John's car rental bill was $167, for how many days did John rent the car?

Solution: Let d = number of additional days after the first day that John rented the car.

Charge for first day		Charge for each additional day		Total charge
35	+	22d	=	167

$$35 + 22d - 35 = 167 - 35$$
$$22d = 132$$
$$\frac{22d}{22} = \frac{132}{22}$$
$$d = 6$$

John rented the car for a total of $1 + 6$ or **7 days**.

Check: $\$35 + 6(\$22) = \$35 + \$132 = \$167.$

SOLVING PROBLEMS INVOLVING AVERAGES.   The average of a set of values is found by dividing the sum of the values by the number of values in the set.

Examples ▬▬▬▬▬

4. Bonnie receives grades of 79, 83, and 86 on her first three mathematics exams. What grade must she receive on her next exam in order to have an average grade of 85 for the four exams?

Solution: Let $x =$ Bonnie's next exam grade.

$$\frac{79 + 83 + 86 + x}{4} = 85$$

$$\frac{248 + x}{4} = 85$$

Multiply each side by 4: $\cancel{4}\left(\dfrac{248 + x}{\cancel{4}}\right) = 4(85)$

$$248 + x = 340$$
$$x = 340 - 248 = 92$$

Bonnie must receive **92** on her next exam.

5. Bill drives at 55 m.p.h. for 2 hours. At what rate of speed must he drive for the next hour so that his average speed for the trip is 50 m.p.h.?

Solution: Let $x =$ Bill's average rate of driving during the third hour.

	Average rate	×	Time	=	Distance
First 2 hours	55 m.p.h.		2		110
Next hour	x		1		x

The table shows that in 3 hours of driving Bill travels a *total* of $110 + x$ miles.

$$\text{Average rate} = \frac{\text{Total distance}}{\text{Total time}}$$

$$50 = \frac{110 + x}{3}$$

$$150 = 110 + x$$

$$150 - 110 = x$$

$$40 = x \; or \; x = \mathbf{40} \text{ m.p.h.}$$

SOLVING EQUATIONS WITH DECIMALS. An equation that contains decimals can be solved by writing an equivalent equation that has been cleared of decimals. To clear an equation of one or more decimal terms, multiply each member of the equation by the power of 10 that will change the decimal number having the greatest number of decimal places to an integer.

Example

6. Solve: $0.03x - 0.7 = 0.8$.

Solution:

Method 1	Method 2
The coefficient of x contains two decimal places, which is the greatest number of decimal positions in the equation. Multiply each member of the equation by 10^2, or 100. $$100(0.03x) - 100(0.7) = 100(0.8)$$ $$3x - 70 = 80$$ $$3x = 80 + 70$$ $$\frac{3x}{3} = \frac{150}{3}$$ $$x = \mathbf{50}$$	$$0.03x - 0.7 = 0.8$$ $$0.03x - 0.7 + 0.7 = 0.8 + 0.7$$ $$0.03x = 1.5$$ $$\frac{0.03x}{0.03} = \frac{1.5}{0.03}$$ $$x = \frac{1.50}{0.03}$$ $$= \frac{150}{3}$$ $$x = \mathbf{50}$$

SOLVING EQUATIONS WITH PARENTHESES. If an equation contains parentheses, remove them by applying the distributive property of multiplication over addition (or subtraction).

Example ▄▄▄▄▄▄

7. Solve and check: $3(1-2x)=-15$.

Solution:

$$3(1-2x)=-15$$
$$3-6x=-15$$
$$3-6x-3=-15-3$$
$$\frac{-6x}{-6}=\frac{-18}{-6}$$

$$x=3 \text{ or } \{3\}$$

Check:
$$3(1-2x)=-15$$
$$3(1-2\cdot 3)$$
$$3(1-6)$$
$$3(-5)$$
$$-15=-15$$

▄▄▄▄▄

SOLVING COMPOUND SENTENCES. Two equations combined by using a logical connective form a **compound sentence**. The solution set of a compound sentence is found by solving each equation independently and then combining the two solution sets using the logical connective.

Examples ▄▄▄▄▄▄

8. Find the solution set of $(2x-1=9) \lor (3x+2=-7)$.

Solution: The solution set of a disjunction of two equations consists of all numbers that are members of the solution set of *either* equation.

$$2x-1=9$$
$$2x-1+1=9+1$$
$$2x=10$$
$$\frac{2x}{2}=\frac{10}{2}$$
$$x=5$$

$\lor$

$$3x+2=-7$$
$$3x+2-2=-7-2$$
$$3x=-9$$
$$\frac{3x}{3}=\frac{-9}{3}$$
$$x=-3$$

The solution set is $\{-3, 5\}$

9. Find the solution set of $(4x=8) \land (3-x=1)$.

Solution: The solution set of a conjunction of two equations consists of all numbers that are members of the solution sets of *both* equations.

$$4x=8$$
$$\frac{4x}{4}=\frac{8}{4}$$
$$x=2$$

$\land$

$$3-x=1$$
$$-3+3-x=1-3$$
$$-x=-2$$
$$\frac{-x}{-1}=\frac{-2}{-1}$$
$$x=2$$

Since the solution set of each equation contains 2, the solution set of the compound sentence is $\{2\}$. ▄▄▄▄▄

EXERCISE SET 3.3

1–42. Solve for the the variable and check.

1. $0.3x = 1.2$
2. $0.4x + 2 = 12$
3. $0.03c = 6$
4. $0.02x = 15$
5. $0.4x = 2.4$
6. $x - 0.4 = 1.6$
7. $3x - 1 = -16$
8. $32 = 3w + 5$
9. $\dfrac{x}{5} + 8 = 10$
10. $3\left(\dfrac{x}{2} - 1\right) = -21$
11. $3(2x - 5) = 9$
12. $4(5 - 2x) = -28$
13. $\dfrac{x}{2} + 5 = -17$
14. $-2(1 - x) = 16$
15. $0.2x + 0.3 = 8.1$
16. $\dfrac{2t}{3} + 5 = 17$
17. $3n - 7 = 14$
18. $\dfrac{2x}{3} - 4 = 12$
19. $0.3x - 2 = 4$
20. $-(8x - 3) = 19$
21. $8 - 5r = -7$
22. $-12 + 3k = -6$

23. $-3(9 - 7p) = -13$
24. $2(3x - 5) - 12 = 0$
25. $4(2x + 3) = -4$
26. $-3\left(8 - \dfrac{x}{2}\right) = 3$
27. $\dfrac{2n - 5}{-3} = -7$
28. $1.04x + 8 = 60$
29. $13 - \dfrac{3x}{4} = -8$
30. $3 = 4x + 19$
31. $-17 = 2(5 + m)$
32. $7 - 3(x - 1) = -17$
33. $\dfrac{2y}{3} - \dfrac{1}{2} = 7\frac{1}{2}$
34. $\dfrac{3x}{4} - 2 = -17$
35. $5(-2p - 6) + 3 = -12$
36. $-3(1 - 4t) - 3 = -24$
37. $0.4(x - 10) = 5.6$
38. $19 - (1 - x) = 18$
39. $18 - 2(h + 1) = 0$
40. $6\left(\dfrac{x}{2} + 1\right) = -9$
41. $0.8(0.4r + 1) = 0.16$
42. $0.25(3x - 5) = \dfrac{5}{2}$

43. Find the solution set: $(3x - 8 = 13) \vee (17 = 1 - 4x)$.

44. Find the solution set: $(2x + 1 = -3) \wedge (1 - 2x = 5)$.

45. Find the solution set: $(3x - 18 = -9) \wedge [2(1 - 6x) = 38]$.

46. The sum of three times a number and 5 is 32. What is the number?

47. When 2 is subtracted from one third of a number, the result is 3. What is the number?

48. 37 exceeds three times the sum of a number and 5 by 1. What is the number?

49. 45 is 9 greater than twice the difference obtained by subtracting 7 from a number. What is the number?

50. A video store rents video tapes at the following rate: $3 for the first day and $2 for each additional day the tape is out. If Bill returns a video tape and is charged $13, for how many days is he being charged?

51. If the length of a side of a square is represented by $2x - 1$, find x if the perimeter of the square is 36. (The perimeter of a square is equal to four times the length of a side.)

52. The length of a certain rectangle is represented by $3x + 5$. If its width is 11 and its perimeter is 80, find the value of x and the length of the rectangle. (The perimeter of a rectangle is twice the sum of its length and width.)

53. If the average of the set of numbers $\{45, 67, 54, 51, x\}$ is 60, find x.

54. Carol's average driving speed for a 4-hour trip was 48 m.p.h. During the first 3 hours her average rate was 50 m.p.h. What was her average rate for the last hour of the trip?

55. A car travels at an average rate of 40 m.p.h. for the first 5 hours and at a uniform rate of speed for the next 3 hours. If the average rate of travel during the 8-hour trip is 43 m.p.h., what is the average rate for the last 3 hours of the trip?

56. The sum of a number and one half of its additive inverse is 12. What is the number?

3.4 SOLVING EQUATIONS INVOLVING MORE THAN ONE VARIABLE TERM

_____ KEY IDEAS _____

An equation in which the variable appears in more than one term can be solved by first collecting and then combining like terms. If the variable appears on both sides of the equation, rearrange terms so that like terms involving the variable are on the same side of the equation and constant terms (numbers without variable factors) are on the opposite side.

VARIABLE TERMS ON THE SAME SIDE. To solve an equation in which the variable appears in more than one term on the same side of the equation, first combine like terms. Then solve the resulting equation as usual.

Examples ▄▄▄▄

1. Solve and check: $5x + 3x = -24$.

Solution: Begin by combining like terms.

$$8x = -24$$

$$\frac{8x}{8} = \frac{-24}{8}$$

$$x = -3$$

Check: $5x + 3x = -24$
$$5(-3) + 3(-3)$$
$$-15 + (-9)$$
$$-24 = -24 \checkmark$$

2.   The sum of two numbers is 25. When twice the larger number is subtracted from three times the smaller, the difference is 5. Find the numbers.

Solution: Let $x = $ smaller of the two numbers.
Then $25 - x =$ larger of the two numbers.

$$3x - 2(25 - x) = 5$$

Remove parentheses: $3x - 50 + 2x = 5$
Combine like terms: $(3x + 2x) - 50 = 5$
$$5x - 50 = 5$$
$$5x - 50 + 50 = 5 + 50$$
$$5x = 55$$
$$\frac{5x}{5} = \frac{55}{5}$$

$$x = 11, \text{ so that } 25 - x = 25 - 11 = 14.$$

The smaller number is **11**, and the larger number is **14**. The check is left for you.

3.   A soda machine contains 20 coins. Some of the coins are nickels, and the rest are quarters. If the value of the coins is $4.40, find the number of coins of each kind.

Solution: Let $x = $ number of nickels.
Then $20 - x = $ number of quarters.

Value of nickels	+	*Value of quarters*	=	*$4.40*
$0.05x$	+	$0.25(20 - x)$	=	4.40

To clear the equation of decimals, multiply each member of each side of the equation by 100.

$$100(0.05x) + 100[0.25(20 - x)] = 100(4.40)$$
$$5x + 25(20 - x) = 440$$
$$5x + 500 - 25x = 440$$
$$-20x + 500 = 440$$
$$-20x = 440 - 500$$
$$\frac{-20x}{-20} = \frac{-60}{-20}$$

$$x = 3 \text{ and } 20 - x = 17$$

There are **3 nickels** and **17 quarters**. The check is left for you.

VARIABLE TERMS ON DIFFERENT SIDES.   If variable terms appear on opposite sides of an equation, work toward collecting variables on the same side of the equal sign and constant terms (numbers) on the other side.

Examples ▬▬▬

4.   Solve and check: $5w + 14 = 3(w - 8)$.

Solution:
Apply the distributive property:
Subtract $3w$ from each side:
Simplify:
Subtract 14 from each side:

Divide each side by 2:

$$5w + 14 = 3(w - 8)$$
$$5w + 14 = 3w - 24$$
$$-3w + 5w + 14 = -3w + 3w - 24$$
$$2w + 14 = -24$$
$$2w + 14 - 14 = -24 - 14$$
$$\frac{2w}{2} = \frac{-38}{2}$$
$$w = -19 \text{ or } \{-19\}$$

$$\begin{array}{r|l} Check: & 5w + 14 = 3(w - 8) \\ & 5(-19) + 14 \,\big|\, 3(-19 - 8) \\ & -95 + 14 \,\big|\, 3(-27) \\ & -81 = -81 \checkmark \end{array}$$

▬▬▬

5.   Solve: $3x + 0.9 = 1.3 - 7x$.

Solution:

Method 1	Method 2
$10(3x) + 10(0.9) = 10(1.3) - 10(7x)$	$3x + 0.9 = 1.3 - 7x$
$30x + 9 = 13 - 70x$	$7x + 3x + 0.9 = 1.3 - 7x + 7x$
$70x + 30x + 9 = 13 - 70x + 70x$	$10x + 0.9 = 1.3$
$100x + 9 = 13$	$10x + 0.9 - 0.9 = 1.3 - 0.9$
$100x + 9 - 9 = 13 - 9$	$10x = 0.4$
$\dfrac{100x}{100} = \dfrac{4}{100}$	$\dfrac{10x}{10} = \dfrac{0.4}{10} = 0.04$
$x = \dfrac{1}{25} \text{ or } 0.04$	$x = 0.04$

The check is left for you.

6.   In 7 years Maria will be twice as old as she was 3 years ago. What is Maria's present age?

Solution: Let $x =$ Maria's present age.
        Then $x + 7 =$ Maria's age 7 years from now,
        and $x - 3 =$ Maria's age 3 years ago.

$$x + 7 = 2(x - 3)$$
$$x + 7 = 2x - 6$$
$$x + 7 - 7 = 2x - 6 - 7$$
$$x = 2x - 13$$
$$x - 2x = 2x - 13 - 2x$$
$$-x = -13$$
$$\frac{-x}{-1} = \frac{-13}{-1}$$
$$x = 13$$

Maria's present age is **13 years**. The check is left for you.   ▆▆▆

EXERCISE SET 3.4

1–40.   Solve for the variable and check.

1. $3x + 4x = -28$

2. $5x - 2x = -27$

3. $0.8x + 0.1x = -36$

4 $7t = t - 42$

5. $w - 0.4w = -4.2$

6. $0.54 - 0.07y = 0.2y$

7. $6h - 14 = 3h + 13$

8. $3(x - 4) - 6 = 0$

9. $2(a - 5) = 4$

10. $3(x , 4) = x$

11 $3 + 2(8 - s) = 3$

12. $7(5 - w) + w = -1$

13. $7 - (3n - 5) = n$

14. $9b = 2b - 3(8 - b)$

15. $3(x - 2) + 2(2 - x) = 0$

16. $1.2x - 0.35 = 0.5x + 5.25$

17. $4(b - 3) = 9 - 3b$

18. $4c - (c + 7) = 5$

19. $5(2x + 1) - (6x - 7) = 0$

20. $1.6(3x - 1) + 0.2x = 8.4$

21. $3(5 - 2n) = 2n - 9$

22. $0.03t = 0.07 + 0.6t$

23. $-(8 - 3x) = 7x + 12$

24. $1 + 7w = 5(7 - 2w)$

25. $7x + 3(x - 2) = -16$

26. $3(4 - x) = 2(x + 11)$

27. $2(d - 7) = 3(7 - d)$

28. $5(8 + x) = 3(x + 6)$

29. $-(11 + 5m) = 4(7 - 2m)$

30. $\dfrac{a - 2}{3} = a - 6$

31. $\dfrac{n - 5}{2} = 3n - 5$

32. $5(6 - q) = -3(q + 2)$

33. $13 - 2(x - 7) = x$

34. $7(2p - 1) = 4(1 - 2p)$

35. $3(7 - 2n) = 6(n + 2)$

36. $5(n + 2) - 2(n + 2) = -9$

37. $y - 6 = 3(2y + 9) + y$

38. $2(7 - 3x) = 3(x + 1) - 7$

39. $2(x - 1) + 3(x + 7) = 0$

40. $0.7(x - 0.2) + 0.3(x - 0.2) = 0.4$

41. The length of a rectangle exceeds twice its width by 5. If the perimeter of the rectangle is 52, find the dimensions of the rectangle.

42. A 72-inch board is cut into two pieces so that the larger piece is seven times as long as the shorter piece. Find the length of each piece.

43. How old is David if his age 6 years from now will be twice his age 7 years ago?

44. Three years ago Jane was one-half as old as she will be 2 years from now. What is Jane's present age?

45. The product of 3 and 1 less than a number is the same as twice the number increased by 14. What is the number?

46. Allan has nickels, dimes, and quarters in his pocket. The number of nickels is 1 more than twice the number of quarters. The number of dimes is 1 less than the number of quarters. If the value of the change in his pocket is 85 cents, how many of each coin does Allan have?

47. Twice the sum of a number and 9 is the same as four times the difference of the number and 6. What is the number?

48. Howard has 14 coins in his pocket, consisting of nickels and dimes. If the value of the coins is 90 cents, how many of each coin does he have?

49. Allison's pocketbook contains a total of 15 dimes and quarters. If the value of these coins is $2.40, how many of each coin does Allison have?

50. A piggy bank contains only nickels, dimes, and quarters. There are twice as many dimes as quarters, and the number of nickels exceeds the number of dimes by 7. If the piggy bank contains $3.10 in change, how many of each coin does it hold?

51. When three times a number is diminished by 17, the result is the same as taking four times the difference between the number and 9. What is the number?

52. The cost of a high school ring was $45 for the large size and $35 for the regular size. The total receipts from the sale of 240 rings were $10,000. How many rings of each size were sold?

53. Eileen paid $18.55 for 90 postage stamps. If some were 22¢ stamps and the rest were 17¢ stamps, how many of each kind were purchased?

54. The total attendance at a school play was 850. The tickets for senior citizens were $1.50 each, and the regular tickets were $2.00 each. If the total receipts were $1650, how many tickets of each kind were sold?

55. Barbara has pennies, nickels, and dimes in her pocket. She has three pennies and a total of nine nickels and dimes. If the value of all the coins is 58 cents, how many nickels and dimes does she have?

56. Jim has a total of 13 nickels and dimes. The value of the dimes exceeds the value of the nickels by 10 cents. Find the number of nickels and of dimes.

57. Five times the difference of a number and 4 is the same as the sum of twice the number and 10. What is the number?

58. Steve is 1 year less than twice as old as James. If James is 13 years younger than Steve, how old is James?

59. Seven times the sum of a number and 5 is the same as three times the sum of the number and 1. What is the number?

60. The length of a rectangle exceeds three times its width by 2. If the width of the rectangle is doubled and its length is diminished by 3, the new rectangle has the same perimeter as the original rectangle. What are the dimensions of the original rectangle?

61. Six times the sum of a number and 7 is the same as the number diminished by 13. What is the number?

62. The average of four numbers is 32. The largest of the four numbers is 5 more than one of the other numbers, and exceeds twice the smallest number by 10. The remaining number is one-half as great as the largest of the four numbers. Find the four numbers.

63.–65.   In the following problems use the formula $I = P \cdot R$, *where* P = *the amount of money invested,* R = *the annual rate of simple interest (expressed as a decimal), and* I = *the interest or investment income:*

63. Part of $5200 is invested at 6% per year, and the rest is invested at 7% per year. The total yearly income from the investment is $343.00. Find the number of dollars invested at each rate.

64. Ted invested $6500, part at a 7% annual rate of interest and the rest at 6%. The incomes from the two investments were equal. Find the amount invested at each rate.

65. Jennifer invested $5000, part at an annual rate of 6% and the remainder at 8%. The annual income from the 8% investment was $260 greater than the annual income from the 6% investment. Find the amount invested at each rate.

3.5 SOLVING CONSECUTIVE INTEGER PROBLEMS

_____ KEY IDEAS _____

Type of Integers	Examples
Consecutive	8, 9, 10, ... $n, n+1, n+2, ...$
Consecutive *even*	14, 16, 18, ... $n, n+2, n+4, ...$
Consecutive *odd*	11, 13, 15, ... $n, n+2, n+4, ...$

CONSECUTIVE INTEGER PROBLEMS. A set of integers is **consecutive** if each integer in the set is greater by 1 than the integer that precedes it.

Consecutive integers: $\{..., -4, -3, -2, -1, 0, 1, 2, 3, 4, ..., n, n+1, ...\}$

A set of odd integers is consecutive if each integer in the set is greater by 2 than the odd integer that precedes it. Similarly, consecutive even integers also differ by 2.

Consecutive odd integers: $\{..., -5, -3, -1, 1, 3, 5, ..., n, n+2, ...\}$
Consecutive even integers: $\{..., -6, -4, -2, 0, 2, 4, 6, ..., n, n+2, ...\}$

Examples ▬▬▬

1. If *x* represents an *even* integer, express each of the following in terms of *x*:
   (a) the next three consecutive *even* integers
   (b) the next larger *odd* integer
   (c) the next *smaller* even integer

Solutions: (a) Given that *x* is an even integer, then $x+2$, $x+4$, and $x+6$ are the next three consecutive *even* integers.
   (b) Suppose that $x = 6$; then 7 is the next larger odd integer. In general, if *x* is an even integer, then $x+1$ must represent the next larger odd integer.
   (c) Suppose that $x = 6$; then 4 is the next smaller even integer. In general, if *x* is an even integer, then $x-2$ must represent the next smaller even integer.

2. Find three consecutive odd integers such that twice the sum of the second and the third is 43 more than three times the first.

Solution: Let x = first odd integer.
            Then $x + 2$ = second consecutive odd integer,
            and $x + 4$ = third consecutive odd integer.

Twice the sum of the second and third is 43 *more than 3 times the first integer*

$$2[(x + 2) + (x + 4)] \qquad = 43 \qquad + \qquad 3x$$
$$2(2x + 6) = 43 + 3x$$
$$4x + 12 = 43 + 3x$$
$$4x + 12 - 3x = 43 + 3x - 3x$$
$$x + 12 = 43$$
$$x + 12 - 12 = 43 - 12$$
$$x = 31$$
$$\text{Then } x + 2 = 33$$
$$x + 4 = 35$$

The three consecutive odd integers are **31**, **33**, and **35**.

Check: Is $2(33 + 35) = 43 + 3(31)$?
$$2(68) \mid 43 + 93$$
$$136 = 136\checkmark$$

EXERCISE SET 3.5

1. If $n + 2$ represents an odd integer, express each of the following in terms of n:
   (a) the next three consecutive odd integers
   (b) the next larger *even* integer
   (c) the next *smaller* odd integer

2. Find three consecutive integers whose sum is 60.

3. Find four consecutive odd integers whose sum is -72.

4. Find four consecutive even integers whose sum is 124.

5. Find four consecutive integers whose sum is 15 less than 5 times the first.

6. Find four consecutive integers such that the sum of the first and the fourth is 29.

7. Find four consecutive integers such that the sum of the second and the fourth is 26.

8. The lengths of the sides of a triangle are consecutive even integers. Find the length of each side if the perimeter of the triangle is 24.

9. Find four consecutive odd integers such that the sum of three times the second integer and the last integer is 104.

10. Find four consecutive odd integers such that their sum is 1 less than five times the smallest.

11. Find four consecutive odd integers such that the sum of the first integer and three times the third integer is 128.

12. Find four consecutive odd integers such that five times the first exceeds their sum by 5.

13. Find four consecutive even integers such that seven times the first exceeds their sum by 18.

14. The length and the width of a rectangle are consecutive odd integers. If the perimeter of the rectangle is 48, find the dimensions of the rectangle.

15. The lengths of the sides of two squares are consecutive even integers. If the sum of the perimeters of the squares is 72, find the length of the side of each square.

16. The lengths of the sides of a triangle are consecutive even integers. The perimeter of the triangle is the same as the perimeter of a square whose side is 5 less than the shortest side of the triangle. Find the lengths of the sides of the triangle.

17. Seven times the second of four consecutive integers exceeds three times the sum of the first and the last integer by 9. Find the four integers.

18. The last of four consecutive odd integers exceeds twice the sum of the first and the second by 11. Find the four integers.

19. Find the largest of five consecutive even integers if their average is -12.

20. Find the smallest of four consecutive odd integers if their average is 35.

21. Find the largest of four consecutive even integers if their average is -28.

3.6 SOLVING PERCENT PROBLEMS

KEY IDEAS

Before you solve percent problems, here are two facts about percents that you should know:

1. A percent compares a number to 100. For example, 35% means "35 out of 100."

2. A percent may be expressed as an equivalent fraction by writing the amount of percent over 100:

$$35\% = \frac{35}{100} = 0.35.$$

TYPES OF PERCENT PROBLEMS. There are three basic types of percent problems that you should know how to solve.

1. Finding a percent of a given number.

Example: What is 15% of 80?

$$n = 0.15 \times 80$$
$$n = 12$$

2. Finding a number when a percent of it is given.

Example: 30% of what number is 12?

$$0.30 \times n = 12$$
$$0.30n = 12$$
$$10(0.3n) = 10(12)$$
$$3n = 120$$
$$n = \frac{120}{3}$$
$$n = 40$$

3. Finding what percent one number is of another.

Example: What percent of 30 is 9?

$$\frac{p}{100} \times 30 = 9$$
$$\frac{p}{100} \times 30 = 9$$

$$\frac{\overset{3}{\cancel{30}p}}{\underset{10}{\cancel{100}}} = 9$$

$$p = \frac{10 \cdot 9}{3} = 30$$

9 is 30% of 30

Examples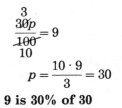

1. If the rate of sales tax is 7.5%, what is the amount of sales tax on a purchase of $40.00?

Solution: Amount of tax $= 7.5\%$ of $40

$$= 0.075 \times 40$$
$$= 3$$

The amount of sales tax is **$3.00.**

2. A pair of sneakers that regularly sells for $35 is on sale for $28. What is the percent amount of the discount?

Solution: The dollar amount of the discount is $35 - $28 = $7.

Think: "What percent of 35 is 7?"

$$\frac{p}{100} \times 35 = 7$$

$$\frac{35p}{100} = 7$$

$$p = \frac{(100)\overset{1}{\cancel{7}}}{\underset{5}{\cancel{35}}} = 20$$

7 is 20% of 35

3. A sum of money was invested for 1 year at an annual rate of simple interest of 8%. If the income from the investment was $46, how much money was invested?

Solution: Let A = amount of money invested at 8%.

$$\underbrace{8\%}_{\substack{\downarrow \ \downarrow \\ 0.08 \times}} \underbrace{\text{of the amount of money invested}}_{\substack{\downarrow \\ A}} \underbrace{\text{is } \$46}_{\substack{\downarrow \\ = 46}}$$

$$0.08A = 46$$

Multiply each side by 100: $8A = 4600$

Divide each side by 8: $A = \dfrac{4600}{8}$

$$A = \$575$$

EXERCISE SET 3.6

1. What is 25% of 44?

2. 6 is what percent of 30?

3. 12 is 15% of what number?

4. 18 is what percent of 24?

5. What is 30% of 18?

6. 21 is 37.5% of what number?

7. A shirt regularly costs $24 but is on sale for 12.5% off the regular price. What is the sale price of the shirt?

8. 18 is what percent of 45?

9. 20 is 62.5% of what number?

10. 4 is what percent of 20?

11. A sweater that regularly costs $32 is on sale for $24. What is the percent of discount?

12. If the sales tax rate is 7%, what is the amount of sales tax on a purchase of $40?

13. The larger of two numbers exceeds three times the smaller by 2. If the smaller number is 30% of the larger, find the two numbers.

14. If the two numbers are in the ratio of 2 : 5, what percent of the larger is the smaller?

15. The larger of two numbers is 2 less than three times the smaller. If the smaller is 37.5% of the larger, find the two numbers.

16. If 50% of a number is 20, then what is 75% of the same number?

17. 30% of 50 is what percent of 60?

18. 40% of 60 is equal to 60% of what number?

19. What is the amount of interest, in dollars, earned in 1 year on an investment of $800 if the annual rate of interest is 6.5%?

20. 128 is what percent of 96?

21. If the yearly income from a $1000 investment is $50, what is the annual rate of interest?

22. A shirt is on sale at 20% off the list price. If the sale price of the shirt if $24, what is the list price?

3.7 WRITING RATIOS AND SOLVING PROPORTIONS

KEY IDEAS

The **ratio** of two numbers a and b ($b \neq 0$) is the quotient of the numbers, and is written as

$$\frac{a}{b} \quad \text{or} \quad a : b \text{ (read as "a is to b").}$$

A **proportion** is an equation that states that two ratios are equal. To *solve* a proportion for an unknown member, set the cross-products equal and solve the resulting equation.

SOLVING PROBLEMS INVOLVING RATIOS. Comparisons of quantities are often expressed in terms of a ratio. If John is 20 years old and Glen is 10 years old, then John is twice as old as Glen. The ratio of John's age to Glen's age is $2:1$ since

$$\frac{\text{John's age}}{\text{Glen's age}} = \frac{20 \text{ years}}{10 \text{ years}} = \frac{2}{1} \text{ or } 2:1.$$

Examples ▬▬▬

1. The length and the width of a rectangle are in the ratio of $3:1$.
(a) What is the ratio of the width to the perimeter?
(b) If the perimeter of the rectangle is 56 cm, find the dimensions of the rectangle.

Solutions: Since the length and the width are in the ratio of $3:1$, the length is three times as great as the width.

Let x = width of the rectangle.
Then $3x$ = length of the rectangle.

$$\begin{aligned}
\text{Perimeter} &= \text{Sum of the lengths of the four sides} \\
&= x + 3x + x + 3x \\
&= 8x
\end{aligned}$$

(a) $\dfrac{\text{Width}}{\text{Perimeter}} = \dfrac{x}{8x} = \dfrac{1}{8}$ *or* **1 : 8.**

(b) Perimeter $= 8x = 56$

$$\frac{8x}{8} = \frac{56}{8}$$

$$x = 7 \text{ and } 3x = 3(7) = 21$$

The width of the rectangle is **7**, and the length is **21**.

Check: Is the perimeter 56?
Yes, since $P = 2(7) + 2(21) = 14 + 42 = 56$.

2. Two numbers are in the ratio of 6 : 1, and their difference is 40. What is the *smaller* number?

Solution: Since the numbers are in a 6 : 1 ratio, the larger number is six times as great as the smaller number.

$$\text{Let } x = \text{smaller number.}$$
$$\text{Then } 6x = \text{larger number.}$$
$$6x - x = 40$$
$$\frac{5x}{5} = \frac{40}{5}$$
$$x = 8.$$

The smaller number is **8.**

Check: The larger number is $6 \times 8 = 48$. Does $48 - 8 = 40$? Yes.

SOLVING PROPORTIONS.   In a proportion, the cross-products are equal. For example,

$$\frac{2}{6} = \frac{4}{12} \quad \text{and} \quad 6 \cdot 4 = 2 \cdot 12$$
$$\checkmark$$
$$24 = 24$$

_____ Equal Cross-Products Rule _____

If $\dfrac{a}{b} = \dfrac{c}{d}$,   then $a \times d = b \times c$,

where b and d cannot be equal to 0. The terms b and c are called **means**, and the terms a and d are the **extremes**.

Examples ▮▮▮▮▮

3. Solve for x and check: $\dfrac{2}{3} = \dfrac{x+9}{21}$.

Solution: Cross-multiply and then simplify.

$$3(x+9) = 2 \cdot 21$$
$$3x + 27 = 42$$
$$3x + 27 - 27 = 42 - 27$$
$$3x = 15$$
$$\frac{3x}{3} = \frac{15}{3}$$
$$x = 5$$

Check: $\dfrac{2}{3} = \dfrac{x+9}{21}$

$$\frac{5+9}{21}$$
$$\frac{14}{21}$$
$$\frac{14 \div 7}{21 \div 7}$$
$$\frac{2}{3} = \frac{2}{3} \checkmark$$

4. The ratio of the number of girls to the number of boys in a certain mathematics class is 3 : 5. If there is a total of 32 students in the class, how many are girls and how many are boys?

Solution:

Method 1	Method 2
Let x = number of girls. Then $32 - x$ = number of boys. $$\frac{\text{Girls}}{\text{Boys}} = \frac{3}{5} = \frac{x}{32 - x}$$ Cross-multiply: $$5x = 3(32 - x)$$ $$5x = 96 - 3x$$ $$5x + 3x = 96 - 3x + 3x$$ $$\frac{8x}{8} = \frac{96}{8}$$ $$x = 12$$ $$32 - x = 32 - 12 = 20$$	Let $3x$ = number of girls. Then $5x$ = number of boys. $$3x + 5x = 32$$ $$8x = 32$$ $$\frac{8x}{8} = \frac{32}{8}$$ $$x = 4$$ Therefore $3x = 3(4) = 12$ and $5x = 5(4) = 20$

There are **12 girls** and **20 boys** in the class.

DIRECT VARIATION. Two variable quantities may be related in such a way that their ratio remains constant when the quantities are changed. This type of relationship is called a **direct variation**. If a change in the value of one variable is known, the corresponding value of the other variable can be calculated by forming a proportion.

Examples

5. If 25 pennies weigh 42 grams, find the weight, in grams, of 75 pennies.

Solution: Let x = weight, in grams, of 75 pennies.

Assuming that each penny weighs exactly the same, the ratio of the number of pennies to their weight (pennies to grams) remains constant.

$$\frac{\text{Pennies}}{\text{Grams}} = \frac{25}{42} = \frac{75}{x}$$

Cross-multiply: $25x = (75)(42)$

$$\frac{25x}{25} = \frac{(75)(42)}{25}$$

$$x = \frac{\overset{3}{(\cancel{75})}(42)}{\underset{1}{\cancel{25}}}$$

$$x = 126 \text{ grams.}$$

The 75 pennies weigh **126 grams.**

Check: Is $\dfrac{75}{126} = \dfrac{25}{42}$? Yes, since $\dfrac{75 \div 3}{126 \div 3} = \dfrac{25}{42}$.

6.   If 2.54 centimeters = 1 inch, how many centimeters are equivalent to 1 foot?

Solution: Let x = number of centimeters in 1 foot.

$$\frac{\text{Centimeters}}{\text{Inches}} = \frac{2.54}{1} = \frac{x}{12} \qquad \text{since 1 foot = 12 inches}$$

Cross-multiply: $x = 12(2.54)$

$x = \textbf{30.48 cm}$

EXERCISE SET 3.7

1–10. Solve each proportion for the variable.

1. $\dfrac{2}{6} = \dfrac{8}{x}$

2. $\dfrac{9}{x} = \dfrac{3}{4}$

3. $\dfrac{x}{2} = \dfrac{50}{4}$

4. $\dfrac{1}{x+1} = \dfrac{10}{5}$

5. $\dfrac{2}{3} = \dfrac{2-x}{12}$

6. $\dfrac{2x-5}{3} = \dfrac{9}{4}$

7. $\dfrac{x+5}{4} = \dfrac{x+2}{3}$

8. $\dfrac{4}{x+3} = \dfrac{1}{x-3}$

9. $\dfrac{10-x}{5} = \dfrac{7-x}{2}$

10. $\dfrac{4}{11} = \dfrac{x+6}{2x}$

11.   Jane's age exceeds Sue's age by 5. If the ratio of Jane's age to Sue's age is $3 : 2$, how old is each girl?

12. Find the number that must be added to both the numerator and the denominator of the fraction $\dfrac{7}{12}$ in order for the resulting fraction to have a value of $\dfrac{3}{4}$.

13. In Jill's purse the ratio of the number of dimes to the number of nickels is $3 : 4$. If the value of these coins is $3.00, how many of each coin does Jill have?

14. If eight jars of jam cost $15.00, what would be the cost of 12 jars of the same jam?

15. On a certain map 1.5 inches represents 100 miles. If two cities on this map are 12 inches apart, what is their distance in miles?

16. A recipe for four servings requires $\frac{2}{3}$ cups of sugar. How many cups of sugar are needed if the same recipe is used to prepare six servings?

17. If 60 miles/hour is equivalent to 88 feet/second, how many feet/second is equivalent to a speed of 12 miles/hour?

18. The lengths of the sides of a triangle are in the ratio of $1 : 3 : 4$. If the perimeter of the triangle is 72, what is the length of the shortest side?

19. Two cities are known to be 256 miles apart. On a certain map they are at a distance of 1.6 inches from each other. If another two cities on the same map are 2.5 inches apart, what is their actual distance in miles?

20. A book shelf 36 inches in length can hold 14 identical books. How many of these books can fit on a shelf that is 54 inches long?

21. A car moving at a constant rate travels 96 miles in 2 hours. If the car maintains this rate, how far will it travel in 3 hours?

22. John is twice as old as Steve, and Jeffrey is three times as old as John. If the sum of their ages is 63 years, how old is Jeffrey?

23. If four pairs of socks cost $10.00, how many pairs of the same socks can be purchased for $15.00?

24. The number of kilograms of corn needed to feed 5000 chickens is 30 less than twice the number of kilograms of corn needed to feed 2800 chickens. How many kilograms of corn are needed to feed 2800 chickens?

25. A class consisted of 14 boys and 19 girls. On a certain day all the boys were present and some girls were absent, so that the girls present made up only 30% of the class attendance. How many girls were absent?

26. Three numbers are in the ratio of $1 : 3 : 5$. If their average is 18, find the smallest number.

CHAPTER 3 REVIEW EXERCISES

REGENTS REVIEW. *Problems included in this section are similar in form and difficulty to those found on the New York State Regents Examination for Course I of the Three-Year Sequence for High School Mathematics. Problems preceded by an asterisk have actually appeared on a previous Course I Regents Examination.*

*1. Solve for x: $4x - 3 = 41$.

*2. Solve for a: $3a + 0.2 = 5$.

*3. Solve for x: $4(2x - 1) = 20$.

4. If three times a certain number is decreased by 7, the result is 20. What is the number?

*5. Solve for x: $0.03x = 36$.

6. Solve for z: $3z + 9 = 1 - z$.

*7. What percent of 200 is 14?

8. Solve for y: $9y + 10 - 5y = 12$.

*9. Solve for x: $2(x + 3) = x + 7$.

10. Two numbers are in the ratio of $5:1$, and their *difference* is 28. What is the smaller number?

*11. Solve for x: $5 + 3(x + 2) = 14$.

12. On a map 1 centimeter equals 50 kilometers. If two cities are 175 kilometers apart, how many centimeters apart are they on the map?

*13. Solve for a: $\dfrac{a + 2}{12} = \dfrac{5}{3}$.

14. If 60% of a number is 144, what is the number?

*15. Solve for y: $0.02y - 1.5 = 8$.

16. Solve for x: $6x - 3(x - 4) = 18$.

17. Solve for y: $\dfrac{5y}{3} - 2 = 38$.

18. Solve for y: $\dfrac{y}{9} = \dfrac{y + 1}{12}$.

*19. The ratio of Tom's shadow to Emily's shadow is 3 to 2. If Tom is 180 centimeters tall, how many centimeters tall is Emily?

*20. The length of a rectangle is 3 more than three times its width. The perimeter of the rectangle is 62. Find the length and the width of the rectangle.

21. Solve for x: $\dfrac{x-3}{4} - 6 = x$.

22. The sum of three consecutive integers is 90. Find the integers.

23. The denominator of a fraction is 5 more than the numerator. If the numerator is decreased by 7 and the denominator is not changed, the new fraction is equal to $\dfrac{1}{3}$. Find the original fraction.

*24. A box of plant food recommends adding $1\frac{1}{2}$ ounces of plant food to every 4 quarts of water. How many ounces of plant food should be added to 16 quarts of water?

25. A test was failed by 15% of a class. If six students failed, how many students were in the class?

26. The difference between two numbers is 1. The sum of three times the larger and twice the smaller is 13. Find the numbers.

*27. What is the value in cents of n nickels and d dimes?
(1) $n+d$ (2) $5n+10d$ (3) $0.05n+0.10d$ (4) $15nd$

*28. A booklet contains 30 pages. If nine pages in the booklet have drawings, what percent of the pages in the booklet have drawings?
(1) 30% (2) 9% (3) 3% (4) $\frac{3}{10}$%

29. If $n+1$ represents an even integer, which expression also represents an even integer?
(1) n (2) $n+2$ (3) $n+3$ (4) $n-2$

30. If 50% of a number is 20, then 75% of the same number is:
(1) $7\frac{1}{2}$ (2) 15 (3) 30 (4) 40

*31. If x represents a number, which expression represents a number that is 5 less than three times x?
(1) $5x-3$ (2) $5-3x$ (3) $3x-5$ (4) $3-5x$

*32. The equation $5x+10=55$ has the same solution set as the equation:
(1) $x=45$ (2) $x+10=11$ (3) $5x=65$ (4) $5x+15=60$

33. What is the solution set of $(3x-1=11) \wedge (5x=7x-8)$?
(1) $\{-4, 4\}$ (2) $\{-4\}$ (3) $\{4\}$ (4) $\{\ \}$

34. In a class of 30 students, the ratio of the number of boys to the number of girls is $2:3$. What is the total number of boys in the class?
(1) 5 (2) 6 (3) 12 (4) 18

*35. In n represents an odd integer, which of the following represents the next larger consecutive odd integer?
(1) $n-1$ (2) $2n$ (3) $n+2$ (4) $n+1$

CHAPTER 4

Solving Literal Equations and Inequalities

4.1 SOLVING LITERAL EQUATIONS

KEY IDEAS

A **formula** is an equation that uses mathematical operations to explain how the value of one variable is related to the value(s) of one or more other variables. A formula is an example of a *literal equation*. A **literal equation** is any equation that contains more than one variable.

EVALUATING FORMULAS. The value of a specified variable in a formula can be found if the values of the other variables that appear in the formula are given. For example, the formula to convert from degrees Fahrenheit to degrees Celsius is the equation $C = \frac{5}{9}(F - 32)$. To find the Celsius temperature that is equivalent to 68 degrees Fahrenheit, write the equation, replace F with 68, and simplify:

Write the equation: $$C = \frac{5}{9}(F - 32)$$

Substitute 68 for F: $$= \frac{5}{9}(68 - 32)$$

Evaluate, following order of operations: $$= \frac{5}{9}(\cancel{36})$$

Divide 36 by 9: $$= \frac{5}{\cancel{9}}(\cancel{36})^{4}$$

$$= 5 \cdot 4$$

$$= 20$$

A temperature of 68 degrees Fahrenheit is equivalent to **20 degrees Celsius.**

SOLVING FOR A GIVEN VARIABLE. Sometimes it is helpful to solve a literal equation for a specified variable, so that it becomes easy to see how this variable depends on the other members of the equation. We solve for a given variable in an equation that contains two or more different variables by *isolating* the specified variable. Isolating a variable so that it stands alone on one side of the equation is accomplished in much the same way that an equation having a single variable is solved.

Examples

1. The perimeter P of a rectangle is given by the formula $P = 2l + 2w$. Solve for the length, l.

Solution:	$P = 2l + 2w$
Subtract $2w$ from each side:	$P - 2w = 2l + 2w - 2w$
Simplify:	$P - 2w = 2l$
Divide each side by the coefficient of l:	$\dfrac{P - 2w}{2} = \dfrac{2l}{2}$
Simplify:	$\dfrac{P - 2w}{2} = l$ or $l = \dfrac{P - 2w}{2}$

2. Solve for x: $ax = bx + c$.

Solution:	$ax = bx + c$
Subtract bx from each side of the equation:	$ax - bx = bx + c - bx$
Apply the distributive property and simplify:	$x(a - b) = c$
Divide by the coefficient of x:	$\dfrac{x(a - b)}{(a - b)} = \dfrac{c}{(a - b)}$
Since division by 0 is undefined, $a \neq b$.	$x = \dfrac{c}{a - b}$

EXERCISE SET 4.1

1. Given the formula $C = \dfrac{5}{9}(F - 32)$, find C for each value of F.

    (a) $F = 32$ (b) $F = -4$ (c) $F = 50$ (d) $F = 0$ (e) $F = 212$

2. In the formula $C = \dfrac{5}{9}(F - 32)$, at what temperature does $F = C$?

    (1) $+40$ (2) -40 (3) $+8$ (4) -8

3. In the formula $C = \pi D$, find C if $\pi = \dfrac{22}{7}$ and $D = 14$.

4. In the formula $V = lwh$, find V if $l = 6$, $w = 4$, and $h = 5$.

5. In the formula $A = \pi r^2$, find A if $\pi = 3.14$ and $r = 10$.

6. In the formula $P = 2(l + w)$, find P if $l = 4.2$ and $w = 3.8$.

7. In the formula $y = mx + b$, find b if $x = 3$, $y = 2$, and $m = 4$.

8. In the formula $z = xy^2$, find z if $x = 4$ and $y = -3$.

9. In the formula $y = 2x - 1$, if the replacement set of x is the set of whole numbers, what is the smallest possible value of y?

10. In the formula $I = PRT$, find I when $P = \$1000$, $R = 6\%$, and $T = 2$.

11–25. Solve for x.

11. $p = 4x$
12. $c = ax + b$
13. $rx + sx = t$
14. $\dfrac{x}{a} = \dfrac{b}{c}$
15. $ax - b = cx$
16. $a(x + b) = c$
17. $c = ax + 2x$
18. $8dx + dx = y$
19. $x(a + b) - c = 0$
20. $ax - c = d - bx$
21. $\dfrac{x}{2} - \dfrac{y}{2} = 1$
22. $0.09x + 0.2y = 0.16$
23. $\dfrac{x}{2} - \dfrac{x}{3} = a$
24. $y(x - 2) = x$
25. $3(x + a) = 5(x - a)$
26. Solve for t: $rt = d$.
27. Solve for L: $V = lwh$.
28. Solve for h: $A = \dfrac{1}{2} bh$.
29. Solve for w: $P = 2(l + w)$.
30. Solve for r: $C = 2\pi r$.
31. Solve for l: $S = \dfrac{n}{2(a + l)}$.
32. Solve for n: $l = a + (n - l)d$.
33. Solve for b: $A = \dfrac{1}{2} h(a + b)$.
34. Solve for F: $C = \dfrac{5}{9}(F - 32)$.
35. Solve for b: $x = \dfrac{a + b + c}{3}$.
36. Solve for h: $A = 2l + 2w + 2h$.
37. Solve for t: $P = A(1 + rt)$.

4.2 SOLVING INEQUALITIES USING INVERSE OPERATIONS

_____ KEY IDEAS _____

> To solve an inequality, isolate the variable, using addition, subtraction, multiplication, and division as is done when solving an equation. Be careful! If both sides of an inequality are multiplied or divided by the same *negative* number, then an equivalent inequality results *only if the direction of the inequality is* **reversed**.

GRAPHING INEQUALITIES. Review Table 4.1 on page 92, which illustrates the graphing of inequalities in which the variable may be any real number. The shaded region of the number line represents the solution set and consists of an infinite number of values.

Examples ▇▇▇▇▇

1. If x is an *integer*, list the elements of $\{x \mid -4 < x < 1\}$.

Solution: The solution set consists of the set of all integers between -4 and 1, but not including -4 and 1.

$$\{x \mid -4 < x < 1\} = \{-3, -2, -1, 0\}.$$

2. Which of the following is a member of the solution set of $-3 < x \le 1$?

$$(1)\ -3 \qquad (2)\ -4 \qquad (3)\ -2 \qquad (4)\ 2$$

Solution: The solution set consists of the set of all integers between -3 and 1, including 1. Since -2 is contained in this interval, the correct answer is **choice (3)**. ▇▇▇▇

SOLVING INEQUALITIES. To solve an inequality algebraically, express the inequality as an equivalent inequality that has the variable on one side of the inequality sign and a constant (number) on the other side. The three properties listed below are useful when working toward isolating a variable in an inequality. Note that each property is true for both the "is greater than (>)" and the "is less than (<)" inequality relation.

1. *Addition/Subtraction Property.* An equivalent inequality results whenever the same number is added to (*or* subtracted from) each side of an inequality. For example, to solve $x - 1 > 2$, proceed as follows:

Add 1 to each side: $\qquad x - 1 + 1 > 2 + 1$
Simplify: $\qquad\qquad\qquad x > 3$

TABLE 4.1 Graphing Inequalities

Solution Set	Graph	Comment
1. $x \geq 2$		The darkened circle around 2 indicates that the solution set includes 2.
2. $x < -1$		The open circle around -1 indicates that the solution set does *not* include -1.
3. $(x < -1) \vee (x \geq 2)$		The logical connective $\vee$ (OR) joins two inequalities that are graphed on the *same* number line.
4. $-2 < x \leq 1$		The inequality is read as "-2 is less than x *and* x is less than or equal to 1" or, more simply, as "x is between -2 and 1, including 1." The inequality $-2 < x \leq 1$ is equivalent to $(x > -2) \wedge (x \leq 1)$.
5. $-3 \leq x \leq 2$		Here x is between -3 and 2, including -3 and 2. The inequality $-3 \leq x \leq 2$ is equivalent to $(x \geq -3) \wedge (x \leq 2)$.

2. *Multiplication/Division Property I.* An equivalent inequality results whenever each side of an inequality is multiplied by (*or* divided by) the same *positive* number. For example to solve $\frac{x}{2} \geq -3$, proceed as follows:

$$\text{Multiply each side by 2:} \quad 2\left(\frac{x}{2}\right) \geq 2(-3)$$
$$\text{Simplify:} \quad x \geq -6$$

3. *Multiplication/Division Property II.* Whenever each side of an inequality is multiplied by (*or* divided by) a negative number, an equivalent inequality results, provided that the direction of the original inequality sign is reversed (from "greater than" to "less than," or vice versa). For example, to solve $-3x > 12$, proceed as follows:

$$\text{Divide each side by } -3: \quad \frac{-3x}{-3} \;\square\; \frac{12}{-3}$$
$$\text{Simplify:} \quad x \;\square\; -4$$
$$\text{Reverse the inequality sign:} \quad x < -4$$

Examples

3. If the replacement set is $\{1, 3, 5, 7\}$, find the solution set of $2x + 4 > 10$.

Solution:
$$2x + 4 > 10$$
$$2x + 4 - 4 > 10 - 4$$
$$2x > 6$$
$$\frac{2x}{2} > \frac{6}{2}$$
$$x > 3$$

The members of the replacement set that satisfy this inequality are 5 and 7. The *solution set is* $\{5, 7\}$.

4. Solve: $4 > 1 - x$.

Solution: $4 > 1 - x$
Subtract 1 from each side: $4 - 1 > -1 + 1 - x$
Simplify: $3 > -x$
*See note below. $-x < 3$
Divide each side by -1: $\dfrac{-x}{-1} \;\square\; \dfrac{3}{-1}$
Reverse the inequality sign: $x > -3$

Note: Switching the left and right sides of an inequality results in an equivalent inequality, provided that the direction of the inequality symbol is reversed. In general, $a > b$ and $b < a$ are equivalent inequalities.

5. Find and graph the solution set: $1 - 2x \le x + 13$.

Solution:	$1 - 2x \le x + 13$
Subtract x from each side:	$1 - 2x - x \le x + 13 - x$
Combine like terms:	$1 - 3x \le 13$
Subtract 1 from each side:	$1 - 3x - 1 \le 13 - 1$
Divide each side by -3:	$\dfrac{-3x}{-3} \,\square\, \dfrac{12}{-3}$
Reverse the inequality sign:	$x \ge -4$

The graph of $x \ge -4$ is

The solution set is $\{x \mid x \ge -4\}$.

Check: Although it is not possible to check each member of the solution set, you should choose at least one representative value of the solution set and verify that this number makes the original inequality a true statement. Since -4 is a member of the solution set, replace x by -4 in the original inequality.

$$
\begin{array}{c|c}
1 - 2x & x + 13 \\
\hline
1 - 2(-4) & -4 + 13 \\
1 + 8 & \\
9 & \le \quad 9 \qquad \text{True}
\end{array}
$$

6. If the replacement set is the set of integers, find the *smallest* value of y that makes the inequality $1 > 3 - 2(y - 4)$ a true statement.

Solution:	$1 > 3 - 2(y - 4)$
Apply the distributive property:	$1 > 3 - 2y + 8$
Simplify:	$1 > -2y + 11$
Subtract 11 from each side:	$1 - 11 > -2y + 11 - 11$
Simplify:	$-10 > -2y$
Divide each side by -2:	$\dfrac{-10}{-2} \,\square\, \dfrac{-2y}{-2}$
Reverse the inequality sign:	$5 < y \text{ or } y > 5$

Since the replacement set is the set of integers, the solution set is $\{6, 7, 8, 9, \ldots\}$. The *smallest* member of the solution set is **6**.

Check: Replace x by 6 in the *original* inequality.

$$
\begin{array}{c|c}
1 > & 3 - 2(y - 4) \\
\hline
& 3 - 2(6 - 4) \\
& 3 - 2(2) \\
& 3 - 4 \\
\end{array}
$$

$$1 > -1 \qquad \text{True}$$

EXERCISE SET 4.2

1–21. Find and graph the solution set for each of the following inequalities:

1. $x + 8 > 5$

2. $y - 1 \leq -3$

3. $9 - 2x > 1$

4. $\dfrac{n}{-3} < 2$

5. $3(x + 1) > -6$

6. $\dfrac{x}{3} - \dfrac{x}{2} < 2$

7. $\dfrac{y}{3} - 1 \leq -2$

8. $2x > 4x - 1$

9. $7 \leq 3x - 2$

10. $1 \geq 3 - \dfrac{x}{5}$

11. $3x + 12 \geq 5x + 4$

12. $1 - 5x < -9$

13. $4 - \dfrac{x}{2} \geq 1$

14. $\dfrac{x}{2} \leq 3 + \dfrac{x}{6}$

15. $7(9 - 2x) > -(x + 2)$

16. $9 > 2(5 - y) - 3$

17. $3(1 - x) + x > 0$

18. $11 \leq 3(1 - 7x) - 6$

19. $\dfrac{x}{6} - 3 > \dfrac{x}{2}$

20. $2 + \dfrac{n}{4} \geq n + \dfrac{3}{4}$

21. $0.1x - 0.02x \geq 8$

22. If the replacement set is the set of integers, what is the largest value of x that makes the inequality $7x - 6 < 8$ a true statement?

23. Which of the following is a member of the solution set of $-2 \leq x < 1$?
(1) 1   (2) 2   (3) 0   (4) -3

24. Which of the following is *not* a member of the solution set of $-4 < x \leq 2$?
(1) -2 (2) -3 (3) 2   (4) -4

25. If the replacement set is $\{-2, -1, 0, 1, 2\}$, find the solution set for each of the following inequalities.
(a) $1 - 3x \geq -5$ (c) $4x + 5 - x \geq 2$ (e) $1 - (3 - x) \leq 2$
(b) $2(x + 1) < x$ (d) $0 > x + 1$ (f) $3(x + 1) > 2(x - 1)$

26. Draw the graphs of each of the following inequalities:
(a) $-2 < x < 5$ (e) $(x > 3) \vee (x < 1)$
(b) $0 < x \leq 4$ (f) $(x \leq -2) \vee (x > 3)$
(c) $-3 < x < 3$ (g) $(2x < 6) \vee (3x + 1 > 10)$
(d) $-1 \leq x < 4$ (h) $(8 + x > 2x) \wedge (1 - x < 5)$

4.3   SOLVING COMPOUND INEQUALITIES

―――――――― KEY IDEAS ――――――――

The logical AND connective ($\wedge$) or the logical OR connective ($\vee$) may be used to combine inequalities. The resulting inequality is called a **compound inequality**. For example, if the replacement set is the set of integers, then the solution set of $(x > 5) \wedge (x < 9)$ consists of the integers 6, 7, and 8 since these are the only integers that are greater than 5 *and*, at the same time, less than 9.

INTERPRETING COMPOUND INEQUALITIES.   The graph of the compound inequality $(x \geq 1) \wedge (x < 4)$ is shown in Figure 4.1.

Figure 4.1   Graph of a Compound Inequality

The darkened region of the number line represents the solution set and consists of the interval on the number line on which the graphs of the two simple inequalities $x \geq 1$ and $x < 4$ overlap. This interval includes all numbers between 1 and 4, including 1, and can be expressed as $1 \leq x < 4$ (read as "1 is less than or equal to x *and* x is less than 4"). Hence

$$(x \geq 1) \wedge (x < 4) \qquad \text{and} \qquad 1 \leq x < 4$$

are equivalent expressions.

The graph of the solution set of $(x \leq -1) \vee (x \geq 3)$ (see Figure 4.2) consists of all values less than or equal to -1 *or* greater than or equal to 3. Hence the graph consists of two nonoverlapping sections since all values *between* -1 and 3 do *not* satisfy this inequality condition.

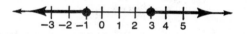

Figure 4.2   Graph of a Solution Set

Examples

1. Express inequality $(x \geq -2) \wedge (x < 3)$ as a single inequality.

Solution: The "boundary" values of the interval that x can range between are -2 and 3, including -2, so that the inequality $-2 \leq x < 3$ is equivalent to $(x \geq -2) \wedge (x < 3)$.

2. Which inequality is represented by the following graph?

(1) $2 < x \leq -3$ (3) $-3 < x \leq 2$
(2) $-3 \leq x < 2$ (4) $-3 \leq x \leq 2$

Solution: The graph includes all values between -3 and 2, including -3. The correct answer is **choice (2)**.

SOLVING COMPOUND INEQUALITIES.   A compound inequality is solved by first solving each inequality that appears on either side of the logical connective. The two solution sets that are obtained are then combined, using the same logical connective to form the solution set of the compound inequality.

Examples ▬▬▬

3. Find and graph the solution set: $(-2x + 8 < 0) \wedge (x < 7)$.

Solution: $-2x + 8 < 0 \qquad \wedge \qquad x < 7$
$$-2x + 8 - 8 < 0 - 8$$
$$-2x < -8$$
$$\frac{-2x}{-2} \;\square\; \frac{-8}{-2}$$
$$x > 4$$
$$(x > 4) \qquad \wedge \qquad (x < 7)$$

The graph of $(x > 4) \wedge (x < 7)$ is

The solution set is $\{x \mid 4 < x < 7\}$.

4. What is the truth value of $(x = 3) \wedge (2x - 1 \geq 5)$?

Solution: First solve the inequality:
$$2x - 1 \geq 5$$
$$2x - 1 + 1 \geq 5 + 1$$
$$2x \geq 6$$
$$\frac{2x}{2} \geq \frac{6}{2}$$
$$x \geq 3$$

Rewrite the compound inequality as $(x = 3) \wedge (x \geq 3)$.

The statement is **true** when $x = 3$ since the inequality is a true statement: $3 \geq 3$.

5. Find and graph the solution set: $(x + 1 < 0) \vee (2x + 5 > 9)$.

Solution: $\quad x + 1 < 0 \qquad \vee \qquad 2x + 5 \qquad > 9$
$$x + 1 - 1 < 0 - 1 \qquad\qquad 2x + 5 - 5 \qquad\qquad > 9 - 5$$
$$x < -1 \qquad\qquad\qquad 2x > 4$$
$$\frac{2x}{2} > \frac{4}{2}$$
$$x < -1 \qquad \vee \qquad x > 2$$

The graph of $(x < -1) \vee (x > 2)$ is

The solution set is $\{x \mid (x < -1) \vee (x > 2)\}$.

SOLVING EXTENDED INEQUALITIES. An inequality such as

$$-2 \le 3x + 1 \le 7$$

may be solved by expressing it as the conjunction of two inequalities:

$$(-2 \le 3x + 1) \wedge (3x + 1 \le 7)$$

and then solving the inequalities on the left and right sides of the conjunction independently.

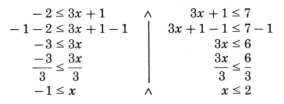

The graph of $(-1 \le x) \wedge (x \le 2)$ is shown in Figure 4.3

Figure 4.3   Graph of an Extended Inequality

The solution set is $\{-1 \le x \le 2\}$.

EXERCISE SET 4.3

1–4. Express each of the following inequalities as an equivalent inequality having the form a ≤ x ≤ b:

1. $(x > -5) \wedge (x < 3)$
2. $(x \le 7) \wedge (x > 2)$
3. $(x > -3) \wedge (x \le 0)$
4. $(-x \le 4) \wedge (x + 1 \le -1)$

5. Which inequality is represented by the accompanying graph?

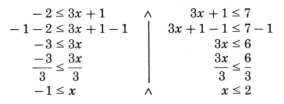

(1) $-2 \le x < 3$ (3) $x > 3$ or $x \le 2$
(2) $-2 < x \le 3$ (4) $x \ge 3$ or $x < -2$

6. The number line below shows the solution set of which inequality?

(1) $-3 < x < 5$ (3) $-3 \le x < 5$
(2) $-3 < x \le 5$ (4) $-3 \le x \le 5$

7. Which inequality is represented by the graph below?

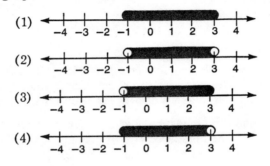

(1) $-2 < x \le 6$ (3) $-2 < x < 6$

(2) $-2 \le x < 6$ (4) $-2 \le x \le 6$

8. Which statement is represented by the graph below?

(1) $x \le 6$ (3) $x > 6$

(2) $x < 6$ (4) $x \ge 6$

9. Which graph shows the solution set of $-1 \le x < 3$?

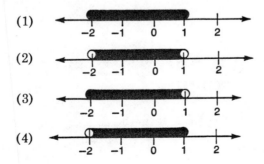

(1)

(2)

(3)

(4)

10. Which graph represents the solution set of $-2 \le x < 1$?

(1)

(2)

(3)

(4)

11–18. Find and graph the solution set.

11. $(x < -2) \wedge (3x + 1 > 16)$

12. $(x + 1 \ge 0) \vee (3 - x > 7)$

13. $(4x + 1 \le 9) \wedge (2x \ge x - 5)$

14. $(5n + 3 > 3n - 17) \wedge (2 - n > 7)$

15. $(2 - n > 0) \vee (19 - 3n < 1)$

16. $(8 < 3x - 4) \wedge (2x - 1 \le 13)$

17. $(x - 5 \ge 2x) \vee \left(\dfrac{x}{3} - 1 \ge 0\right)$

18. $(x - 3x < 10) \wedge (1 - x \le 2)$

19–26. If the replacement set is the set of integers, find elements of the solution set of each of the following inequalities:

19. $-4 \le x \le 0$
20. $-5 < x \le 1$
21. $(x > 1) \wedge (x \le 6)$
22. $(x < -1) \wedge (x \ge -3)$
23. $-5 < x + 1 < 4$
24. $-2 \le 3x - 4 < 5$
25. $(2x - 3 = 1) \wedge (2x \ge x - 1)$
26. $(3x - 2 > x - 6) \wedge (2x + 1 \le x + 5)$

27–32. Find and graph the solution set.

27. $-3 \le x + 1 < 7$
28. $-1 < 2x - 3 \le 5$
29. $0 \le 3 - 6x \le 12$
30. $-2 \le 1 - 3x < 4$
31. $6 \le 6 + 5x \le 21$
32. $5 < 3(2x - 1) \le 29$

33. An angle is acute if its measure is greater than 0 degree and less than 90 degrees. If the measure of an acute angle is represented by $2x - 6$ degrees, what is the set of all possible values of x?

34. An angle is obtuse if its measure is greater than 90 degrees and less than 180 degrees. If the measure of an obtuse angle is represented by $3y + 15$, what is the set of all possible values of y?

35. The perimeter of a rectangle is at most 84 cm. If the length of the rectangle is 17 cm, what is the set of all possible values of the width?

4.4   SOLVING WORD PROBLEMS USING INEQUALITIES

―――――――――――― KEY IDEAS ――――――――――――

Word problems that use phrases such as *is greater than* (>), *is less than* (<), *is at most* (≤), and *is at least* (≥) require that an inequality be used to determine the set of values that satisfy the conditions of the problem.

SOLVING INEQUALITIES.   Word problems that involve inequalities are solved using an approach similar to the one used to solve word problems that lead to equations.

Examples ▬▬▬▬

1. Find all integers such that the integer increased by 6 is greater than one third of itself.

Solution: Let $x =$ an integer.

Integer increased by 6 is greater than one third of the number

$$x \qquad +6 \qquad > \qquad \frac{x}{3}$$

$$x + 6 > \frac{x}{3}$$

Multiply each side by 3: $\qquad\qquad 3(x + 6) > 3\left(\frac{x}{3}\right)$

Remove parentheses: $\qquad\qquad\qquad 3x + 18 > x$

Subtract x from each side: $\qquad 3x - x + 18 > x - x$

Simplify: $\quad 2x + 18 > 0$

Subtract 18 from each side: $\qquad\qquad 2x > -18$

Divide each side by 2: $\qquad\qquad\qquad \dfrac{2x}{2} > \dfrac{-18}{2}$

$$x > -9$$

Since x can be any integer greater than -9, the set $\{-8, -7, -6, -5, \ldots\}$ represents the set of *all* integers having the property that, when they are increased by 6, they are greater than one third of the original number.

Check: When -8 from the solution set is used, $-8 + 6 = -2$. Is $-2 > -\dfrac{8}{3}\left(= -2\dfrac{2}{3}\right)$? Yes.

2. Steve is 5 years older than Peter. If the sum of their ages is at most 37 years, what is the *oldest* that Peter can be?

Solution: Let $x =$ Peter's age.

Then $x + 5 =$ Steve's age.

$$x + (x + 5) \le 37 \qquad \text{(The sum of their ages cannot exceed 37.)}$$
$$2x + 5 \le 37$$
$$2x + 5 - 5 \le 37 - 5$$
$$\frac{2x}{2} \le \frac{32}{2}$$
$$x \le 16$$

The *oldest* that Peter can be is **16 years**.

Check: If Peter is 16, then Steve is $16 + 5 = 21$. Is $16 + 21 \le 37$? Yes.

3. What is the smallest positive integer that can be added to both the numerator and the denominator of the fraction $\frac{2}{7}$ so that the value of the resulting fraction *is at least* $\frac{1}{2}$?

Solution: Let $x =$ a positive integer.

$$\frac{2+x}{7+x} \geq \frac{1}{2}$$

Since the numerator and the denominator of both fractions are positive numbers, an equivalent inequality results from cross-multiplying.

$$2(2+x) \geq 1(7+x)$$

Remove the parentheses:	$4 + 2x \geq 7 + x$
Subtract x from each side:	$4 + 2x - x \geq 7 + x - x$
Simplify:	$4 + x \geq 7$
Subtract 4 from each side:	$4 + x - 4 \geq 7 - 4$
Simplify:	$x \geq 3$

If x is an integer, then the solution set to the inequality is $\{3, 4, 5, 6, \ldots\}$. Therefore **3** is the *smallest* integer value that can be added to both the numerator and the denominator of $\frac{2}{7}$ so that the value of the resulting fraction is at least $\frac{1}{2}$.

Check: $\dfrac{2+3}{7+3} = \dfrac{5}{10} = \dfrac{1}{2}.$ Is $\dfrac{1}{2} \geq \dfrac{1}{2}$? Yes.   ▬▬▬▬

EXERCISE SET 4.4

1. The sum of three consecutive odd integers is at most 75. What are the largest possible integers that may comprise this set of three?

2. One number is five times another number. The sum of the two numbers is greater than 45. Find the smallest possible values for the two numbers if both are integers.

3. A certain classroom has six rows, and each row must have the same number of student desks. What is the minimum number of desks that must be placed in each row so that the classroom can accommodate at least 32 students and each student has his or her own desk?

4. George is twice as old as Edward, and Edward's age exceeds Robert's age by 4 years. If the sum of their ages is at least 56 years, what is the minimum age of each person?

5. The length and the width of a rectangle are in the ratio 4:1. If the perimeter of the rectangle is at most 90, what are the largest possible dimensions of the rectangle?

6. Susan has seven more nickels than dimes in her pocketbook. If the total value of these coins is at least $2.00, what is the least number of nickels that she has?

7. The perimeter of a square is at least 20 cm and at most 44 cm. What is the set of all possible dimensions of this square?

8. Jerry is saving to buy a VCR that costs $345. Jerry has already saved $37. What is the least amount of money Jerry must save each week so that at the end of 11 weeks he has enough money (excluding tax) to buy the VCR?

9. What is the smallest positive integer that, when added to both the numerator and the denominator of the fraction $\frac{3}{11}$, makes the value of the resulting fraction at least $\frac{1}{2}$?

10. The length of each side of a certain triangle is 7 less than twice the length of a side of a certain square, which is a whole number. What are the smallest possible dimensions of the triangle if the perimeter of the triangle is at least as great as the perimeter of the square?

11. What is the greatest positive integer that can be added to both the numerator and the denominator of the fraction $\frac{11}{45}$ so that the value of the resulting fraction does not exceed $\frac{1}{3}$?

12. A portion of a wire 60 inches in length is bent to form a rectangle whose length exceeds twice its width by 1. What are the smallest possible dimensions of the rectangle if no more than 4 inches of the wire is unused?

CHAPTER 4 REVIEW EXERCISES

REGENTS REVIEW. *Problems included in this section are similar in form and difficulty to those found on the New York State Regents Examination for Course I of the Three-Year Sequence for High School Mathematics. Problems preceded by an asterisk have actually appeared on a previous Course I Regents Examination.*

*1. Solve for y in terms of a, b, and x: $ay - bx = 2$.

*2. Solve for E in terms of I and R: $\dfrac{E}{I} = R$.

3. Using the formula $A = \dfrac{h}{2}(b + c)$, find A when $h = 7$, $b = 11$, and $c = 5$.

4. If the replacement set for x is $\{-2, 0, 2, 4, 6\}$, what is the solution set of $x + 3 \le 5$?

*5. Solve for b in terms of V and h: $V = \dfrac{bh}{3}$.

6. Using the relation $A = \dfrac{1}{2}bh$, find A if $b = 4$ and $h = 5$.

*7. Given the inequality $8x \geq 3(x - 5)$.
(a) Solve for x.
(b) Choose one value of x from your solution in part (a), and show that it makes the inequality $8x \geq 3(x - 5)$ true.

*8. One member of the solution set of $-5 < x \leq -1$ is:
(1) -1 (2) -5 (3) 3 (4) -6

*9. An expression equivalent to $3x - 2 < 7$ is:
(1) $x > \dfrac{5}{3}$ (2) $x < \dfrac{5}{3}$ (3) $x > 3$ (4) $x < 3$

*10. The expression $6 \leq x + 4$ is equivalent to:
(1) $x \geq 2$ (2) $x \leq 2$ (3) $x \leq -2$ (4) $x \geq 10$

*11. The largest possible value of x in the solution set of $2x + 1 \leq 7$ is:
(1) 6 (2) 2 (3) 3 (4) 4

12. What are the numbers in the solution set of $4 \leq x < 7$ is x is an integer?
(1) $5, 6$ (2) $5, 6, 7$ (3) $4, 5, 6$ (4) $4, 5, 6, 7$

*13. Which inequality is represented by the graph?

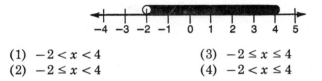

(1) $x < 4$ (3) $-4 \leq x < 4$
(2) $-4 < x \leq 4$ (4) $-4 \leq x \leq 4$

14. If $4x + a = 4a + x$, then $x =$
(1) a (2) $5a$ (3) 0 (4) 4

*15. Patty needs $80 to buy a bicycle. She has already saved $35. If she saves $10 a week from her earnings, what is the least number of weeks she must work to have enough money to buy the bicycle?

(1) 5 (2) 8 (3) 3 (4) 4

*16. Which inequality is the solution set of the graph shown below?

(1) $-2 < x < 4$ (3) $-2 \leq x \leq 4$
(2) $-2 \leq x < 4$ (4) $-2 < x \leq 4$

*17. An architect wants to design a rectangular room so that its length is 8 meters more than its width, and its perimeter is greater than 56 meters. If each of the dimensions of the room must be a whole number of meters, what are the *smallest* possible measures, in meters, of the length and width?

*18. One number is four times another. The sum of the two numbers is less than 12. Find the largest possible values for the two numbers if both are integers.

*19. Find the three largest consecutive integers whose sum is less than 86.

*20. One integer is 3 more than twice another integer. The sum of these integers is greater than 24. Find the *smallest* values for these integers.

21. Find the solution set: $(9 - 4x > 1) \wedge (0 \le 3x + 3)$.

22. If angle H is an obtuse angle whose measure is represented by $\frac{x}{2} + 37$, find the set of all possible values of x.

23. If the domain of x is the set of odd integers, find and graph the solution set of $-1 \le x + 2 < 5$.

24. If n represents a negative even integer, represent in terms of n the *least* positive integer that, when added to n, gives a positive odd integer.

25. Which is the graph of $(-x > 4) \vee (2x - 1 > 7)$?

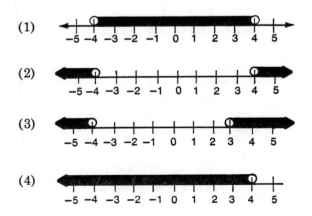

CHAPTER 5

Operations with Polynomials

5.1 CLASSIFYING POLYNOMIALS

_____ KEY IDEAS _____

The algebraic expression $5x^2 - 3x + 13$ is an example of a *trinomial* since it contains *three* terms: $5x^2$, $3x$, and 13. The expression $5x^2 - 3x$ is a *binomial* since it contains *two* terms. The expression $5x^2$ is a *monomial* since it contains *one* term. The general name given to an algebraic expression that contains one monomial or the sum (or difference) of *more than one* monomial term is *polynomial*.

MONOMIALS AND TERMS.   A **monomial** is a single number or variable, or the product of numbers and variables. Although the words *monomial* and *term* are sometimes used interchangeably, a term may involve the quotient as well as the product of variables, whereas a monomial may not have a variable denominator. For example, the terms

$$2a, \qquad 3a^2b, \qquad \frac{5a}{4}, \qquad \text{and} \qquad -a^3$$

are monomials. The term $\dfrac{2}{x}$, however, is *not* a monomial since it involves a quotient in which the variable appears in the denominator.

PARTS OF A MONOMIAL.   The *numerical coefficient* of $3x^2y$ is 3, and the *literal factor* is x^2y. The **numerical coefficient** (*or numerical factor*) of a monomial is the number that multiplies the variable(s) of a monomial. The **literal factor** of a monomial is the part that consists only of a variable or the product of variables. Here are some additional examples.

Monomial	Numerical Coefficient	Literal Factor
$-7x^2y^3$	-7	x^2y^3
y	1 (since $y = 1y$)	y
$-a^2$	-1 (since $-a^2 = -1a^2$)	a^2
$\dfrac{x^3}{2}$	$\dfrac{1}{2}$ $\left(\text{since } \dfrac{x^3}{2} = \dfrac{1}{2} \cdot x^3 \right)$	x^3

Like monomials have the same literal (variable) factors. For example, $2xy$ and $5xy$ are *like* monomials since they differ in only their numerical coefficients. The monomials x^2y and xy^2 are *unlike* terms since the variable bases do *not* have the same exponents.

Like monomials can be added or subtracted by combining their numerical coefficients and using the same literal factor:

$$2xy + 5xy = (2 + 5)xy = 7xy.$$

Examples ▬▬▬

1. Which of the following is a monomial?

(1) $2x + 5y$ (2) $\dfrac{3x}{y^4}$ (3) $7w^{-2}$ (4) $\dfrac{x^3}{2}$

Solution: Choice (1), $2x + 5y$, is not a monomial since it involves the sum of two terms. Choice (2), $\dfrac{3x}{y^4}$, is not a monomial since it contains a variable denominator. Choice (3), $7w^{-2}$, can be written with a positive exponent as $\dfrac{7}{w^2}$; therefore it is not a monomial. However, $\dfrac{x^3}{2}$ is a monomial since it does not contain a *variable* in the denominator and can be rewritten as $\dfrac{1}{2} \cdot x^3$. The correct answer is **choice (4)**.

2. Combine:
  (a) $x^3y^4 + 2x^3y^4$ (b) $4a^2b - 5a^2b$

Solutions:

  (a) $x^3y^4 + 2x^3y^4 = (1 + 2)x^3y^4 = \mathbf{3x^3y^4}$
  (b) $4a^2b - 5a^2b = (4 - 5)a^2b = \mathbf{-a^2b}$ ▬▬▬

POLYNOMIALS. A **polynomial** is a monomial or the sum (or difference) of monomial terms. A **binomial** is a polynomial having *two* monomial terms, while a **trinomial** is a polynomial having *three* monomial terms. The polynomial $3x^2 + x - y$ is a polynomial in *two* variables since it has two different variables, x and y. The polynomial $3x^2 + x - 7$ is a polynomial in *one* variable since x is the only variable that it contains.

A polynomial in one variable is in **standard form** when its terms are arranged so that the exponents decrease in value as the polynomial is read from left to right. To write a polynomial in standard form, it may be necessary to rearrange its terms. For example,

$$\text{Given polynomial:} \qquad 8x^3 + 6x^4 - 2x + 5$$

$$\text{Polynomial in standard form:} \quad 6x^4 + 8x^3 - 2x + 5$$

The **degree** of the polynomial in one variable is the value of the highest power of the variable. If the polynomial consists of a single number, its degree is 0. Here are three more examples.

Polynomial	Standard Form	Degree
1. $4x + 2x^3 - x^2$	$2x^3 - x^2 + 4x$	3
2. $5 - 3x$	$-3x + 5$	$1 \ (3x = 3x^1)$
3. 2	2	$0 \ (2 = 2 \cdot 1 = 2x^0)$

SIMPLIFYING POLYNOMIALS.   A polynomial is in *simplest* form when no two of its terms can be combined. For example, the first and last terms of the polynomial $5c^4d - 3c + c^4d$ are like terms, so that the polynomial can be simplified as follows:

$$5c^4d - 3c + c^4d = (5c^4d + 1c^4d) - 3c$$
$$= 6c^4d - 3c.$$

Examples ▰▰▰

3. Simplify: $3(4a^2b - 2ab + 7) - 2$.

Solution: Remove the parentheses by multiplying each term inside the parentheses by 3. Then combine like terms.

$$3(4a^2b - 2ab + 7) - 2 = 3(4a^2b) + 3(-2ab) + 3(7) - 2$$
$$= 12a^2b - 6ab + 19$$

4. Simplify: $4x - (2x^2 - 5x + 3)$.

Solution: The expression $4x - (2x^2 - 5x + 3)$ is equivalent to $4x - 1(2x^2 - 5x + 3)$. Remove the parentheses by multiplying each term within the parentheses by -1. Then combine like terms.

$$4x - (2x^2 - 5x + 3) = 4x - 1(2x^2 - 5x + 3)$$
$$= 4x + (-1)(2x^2) + (-1)(-5x) + (-1)(+3)$$
$$= 4x - 2x^2 + 5x - 3$$
$$= -2x^2 + (4x + 5x) - 3$$
$$= -2x^2 + 9x - 3$$

In Example 4 the expression $-(2x^2 - 5x + 3)$ could also have been simplified by removing the parentheses and rewriting each term with its *opposite* algebraic sign.

EXERCISE SET 5.1

1. Which of the following can *not* be written as a monomial?

   (1) $3x + 4x$ (2) $\dfrac{x}{7}$ (3) $\dfrac{7}{x}$ (4) $\dfrac{7}{x^{-1}}$

2. For each of the following monomials, write the numerical coefficient and the literal factor:

   (a) $3a^6b$ (b) $-w^3y^2$ (c) n (d) $\dfrac{1}{3}x^4$ (e) $\dfrac{2r^3s^4}{5}$ (f) -3

3. All of the following are like monomials *except:*
   (1) $-4m^3n^2p^5$ (2) $12m^3n^2p^5$ (3) $7m^2n^3p^5$ (4) $n^2m^3p^5$

4. Write each of the following polynomials in standard form, and determine its degree:
   (a) $x^2 - x^3 + x - 12$ (c) $3n - 5n^3 + 13$
   (b) $5y^2 - 3y + y^3 - 2y^4$ (d) $-(6x - x^4 + 3x - 8)$

5. If $3(2x - 1) = 5x$, what is the value of the polynomial $x^3 - 2x^2 + 10$?

6. If $x - 2 = 10 - 3x$ and $2y - 1 = 1$, what is the value of the binomial $3x - 2y$?

7–14. Simplify each of the following expressions:
7. $3(2a^3 - 5a + 1) + 15a$
8. $-(3x^2 - 7x - 9)$
9. $5ax - x^2 + 6ax$
10. $a^2b - 2ab + 3a^2b$
11. $2y - 5(3y - 8y^2 + 1)$
12. $3x^2y^3 - 7x^2y^3 + 5x^2y^3$
13. $-rs^3 + 5rs^3 - r^3s$
14. $x(x^2 - 3x + 4) + x^3$

15. What binomial must be added to $3a - 5b$ in order for the sum to be 0?

16. What trinomial must be added to $2x^2 - 5x + 1$ in order for the sum to be 0?

5.2 MULTIPLYING AND DIVIDING MONOMIALS

KEY IDEAS

Powers of the *same* nonzero base are *multiplied* by *adding* their exponents and keeping the same base. Powers of the *same* nonzero base are *divided* by *subtracting* their exponents and keeping the same base. For example,

$$y^{10}y^3 = y^{10+3} = \mathbf{y^{13}} \qquad \text{and} \qquad \frac{y^{10}}{y^3} = y^{10-3} = \mathbf{y^7}.$$

MULTIPLYING MONOMIALS.   To **multiply** monomials, group and then multiply like factors. For example, to multiply $3x^5$ by $2x^3$, proceed as follows:

Group like factors: $\qquad\qquad\qquad\qquad (3x^5)(2x^3) = (3 \cdot 2)(x^5 x^3)$
Multiply numerical factors: $\qquad\qquad\qquad\qquad\qquad = 6(x^5 x^3)$
Multiply variable factors with the same base: $\qquad\quad = 6x^{5+3} = \mathbf{6x^8}$

Examples ▆▆▆▆

1. Multiply: $(3a^2b)(-4a^3)$.

Solution: $(3a^2b)(-4a^3) = (3)(-4)(a^2a^3)b$
$\qquad\qquad\qquad\qquad = -12(a^2a^3)b$
$\qquad\qquad\qquad\qquad = \mathbf{-12a^5b}$

2. Multiply: $(2x^5y)(4x^3)(-3xy)$.

Solution: $(2x^5y)(4x^3)(-3xy) = [(2)(4)(-3)](x^5x^3x)(yy)$
$\qquad\qquad\qquad\qquad\qquad\quad = \mathbf{-24x^9y^2}$ ▆▆▆▆

POWER LAWS OF EXPONENTS.   The properties of exponents can be used to develop a shortcut method for raising a power to another power. For example,

$$(x^5)^4 = x^5 \cdot x^5 \cdot x^5 \cdot x^5 = x^{\overbrace{5+5+5+5}} = x^{20}.$$

$$\xrightarrow{\quad 5 \cdot 4 = 20 \quad}$$

In general, to raise a power to another power, *multiply* their exponents.

$$(a^m)^p = a^{mp}.$$

Similarly, to raise a product of variables to a power, raise each factor of the product to the power. For example,

$$(ab)^3 = a^3b^3 \quad \text{and} \quad (-4y)^2 = (-4)^2y^2 = 16y^2.$$

In general,

$$(a^m b^n)^p = a^{mp} b^{np}.$$

Examples ████

3. Simplify: $(-2a^4)^3$.

Solution: $(-2a^4)^3 = (-2)^3(a^4)^3 = -8a^{12}$

4. Simplify: $(w^3y^2)^5$.

Solution: $(w^3y^2)^5 = (w^3)^5(y^2)^5 = w^{3 \cdot 5}y^{2 \cdot 5} = w^{15}y^{10}$ ████

DIVIDING MONOMIALS. As the following example illustrates, monomials are **divided** using a procedure similar to that for multiplying monomials. To divide $\dfrac{24a^5b^4c}{8a^2b}$, proceed as follows:

Group the quotients of like variables: $\quad \dfrac{24a^5b^4c}{8a^3b} = \left(\dfrac{24}{8}\right)\left(\dfrac{a^5}{a^3}\right)\left(\dfrac{b^4}{b^1}\right)c$

Divide numerical coefficients: $\qquad\qquad\qquad = 3\left(\dfrac{a^5}{a^3}\right)\left(\dfrac{b^4}{b^1}\right)c$

Divide factors having the same base: $\qquad\quad = 3a^{5-3}b^{4-1}c$

$$= 3a^2b^3c$$

Examples ████

5. Divide: $\dfrac{20y^3}{4y^7}$.

Solution: $\dfrac{20y^3}{4y^7} = \dfrac{5y^3}{y^7} = 5y^{-4} = \dfrac{5}{y^4}$

6. Divide $-15m^2np^4$ by $3m^5p^4$.

Solution: Write the quotient in fractional form and simplify:

$$\frac{-15m^2np^4}{+3m^5p^4} = \left(\frac{-15}{3}\right)\left(\frac{m^2}{m^5}\right)(n)\left(\frac{p^4}{p^4}\right)$$

$$= (-5)(m^{2-5})(n)(p^{4-4})$$

$$= (-5)(m^{-3}(n)(p^0)$$

Replace p^0 by 1: $\qquad = (-5)(m^{-3})n$

Replace m^{-3} by $\dfrac{1}{m^3}$: $\qquad = \dfrac{-5n}{m^3}$ ████

EXERCISE SET 5.2

1–24. Multiply.
1. $(5y^2)(-3y)$
2. $(-p^2q)(-7pq^3)$
3. $(-3ax)(-5ay)$
4. $4y^3(-3y^2)$
5. $y^2 \cdot y^3 \cdot y^4$
6. $(-x^4)(-x^2)(-x)$
7. $(7q^2w^3)(-3qw)$
8. $(x^2y^3)(-2xy^2)$
9. $(-3m^5n^2)(-9mn^3)$
10. $(-0.2ab)(0.35a^3b^2)$
11. $(0.4y^3)(-0.15y^2)$
12. $(rs^2)(r^2s)(r^2s^2)$
13. $(-3x)(7x^2)(-2x)$
14. $(8a^2bc)(-5ab^2c^3)$
15. $(-7w^3)(3w)(2w^4y^2)$
16. $(-6a^2b^3)(-2ac^2)$
17. $(-9w^2y)(-3w^3y^{12})$
18. $(-3a^2b^4)(-2a^3c^2)(-4b^5c^6)$
19. $(5h^3k^2)(-2hk)(h^4k^7)$
20. $(-ab)^3(a^2b^2)$
21. $(-xy)(3x^2)(-4xy^2)$
22. $(s^2t^3)(-4s^3t)(-9st)$
23. $\left(\dfrac{1}{2}x^2y\right)\left(\dfrac{2}{5}x^3y^2\right)$
24. $(-8r^3s^4)(rs)^2$

25–42. Simplify
25. $b^2(-b^3)$
26. $x^4(-x)^3$
27. $(-a)^5(-a^5)$
28. $(x^2y^4)^6$
29. $(-2ab^2)^5$
30. $2(-3w^4)^3$
31. $-a^2(-a)^2$
32. $(-b)(-b)^3$
33. $(4p^2q^5)^3$
34. $(-5r^7s^3)^2$
35. $(-2xy^2z^3)^3$
36. $3y^2 + (3y)^2$
37. $(-2a^3) + (-2a)^3$
38. $[(-p^2)^4]^3$
39. $[(-3ab)^2]^3 + [(-3ab)^3]^2$
40. $(-2x^5y^4)^3 + 7x^{15}y^{12}$
41. $5a^4b^{14} - (-3a^2b^7)^2$
42. $(3n^2)^3 - (5n^2)^3$

43–62. Divide.
43. $\dfrac{21p^8}{3p^5}$
44. $\dfrac{-9b^7}{18b^3}$
45. $\dfrac{y^2}{y^6}$
46. $\dfrac{3x^7}{-27x^7}$
47. $\dfrac{72c^6}{8c^{11}}$
48. $\dfrac{-24a}{-4a^6}$
49. $\dfrac{8a^2b^3}{12ab^2}$
50. $\dfrac{12r^3}{3rs^4}$
51. $\dfrac{15a^2}{-6a^3b}$
52. $(-48x^3y^2)^2 \div (12xy)$
53. $(1.05x^5y^3) \div (0.35x^2y^2)$
54. $\dfrac{36p^8q^2r^3}{-4p^6q^2}$
55. $\dfrac{-32j^5m}{-8j^4m^3p^2}$
56. $\dfrac{108a^3b^2c^9}{36a^5b^2c^6}$
57. $\dfrac{-6w^8y^3z^5}{42w^9y^4z}$
58. $\dfrac{(-5x^2y^7)^{13}}{(-5x^2y^7)^{13}}$
59. $\dfrac{(3x-y)^8}{(3x-y)^7}$
60. $\dfrac{(-2a^3)^2}{8ab}$
61. $(x^2y)^3 \div (x^2y)^3(xy^2)$
62. $(4a^3b^2)(3a^7b) \div (6a^4b^3)$

5.3 ADDING AND SUBTRACTING POLYNOMIALS

ADDING POLYNOMIALS.   To add two polynomials, collect like terms and then simplify. For example,

$$(4x^2 + 3y) + (5x^2 - 2y + 7) = (4x^2 + 5x^2) + (3y - 2y) + 7$$
$$= 9x^2 + y + 7$$

Sometimes it is easier to add polynomials by writing them on separate lines, one underneath the other, so that like terms are aligned in the same vertical columns. The numerical coefficients of like terms can then be added mentally. For example, the sum of $(4x^2 + 3y)$ and $(5x^2 - 2y + 7)$ may be found as follows:

Write the first term, using 0 as a placeholder: $\qquad\qquad 4x^2 + 3y + 0$
Write the second term, placing like terms in the
same columns: $\qquad\qquad\qquad\qquad\qquad\qquad +\ 5x^2 - 2y + 7$
Combine like terms in each column: $\qquad\qquad\qquad 9x^2 + \ \ y + 7$

Example ▬▬▬

1. The lengths of the sides of a triangle are represented by the binomials $3x + 7y$, $2x - 15y$, and $4x + 21y$. Express the perimeter of this triangle as a binomial.

Solution: The perimeter of a triangle is found by adding the lengths of its sides.

$$3x + 7y$$
$$2x - 15y$$
$$4x + 21y$$
$$\text{Perimeter} = 9x + 13y$$

▬▬▬▬

SUBTRACTING POLYNOMIALS.   To subtract a polynomial from another polynomial, add the *opposite* of each term of the polynomial that is being subtracted.

Examples ▮▮▮▮

2. Subtract $3a - 2b - 9c$ from $5a + 7b - 4c$.

Solution:

$$(5a + 7b - 4c) - (3a - 2b - 9c) = (5a + 7b - 4c) + (-3a + 2b + 9c)$$
$$\text{Group like terms:} \quad = (5a - 3a) + (7b + 2b) + (-4c + 9c)$$
$$\text{Combine like terms:} = \mathbf{2a + 9b + 5c}$$

3. How much greater is $29a^2 + 13b + 3c$ than $17a^2 - 6b + 8c$?

Solution: Subtract $(17a^2 - 6b + 8c)$ from $(29a^2 + 13b + 3c)$. It is sometimes convenient to perform the subtraction by writing the polynomials vertically, aligning like terms in the same columns. Write the polynomial being subtracted underneath the other polynomial. Change to an addition example by circling the sign of each term of the bottom polynomial and replacing it with its opposite sign. Then add like terms.

Original Subtraction Example

$$29a^2 + 13b + 3c$$
$$- \quad +17a^2 - 6b + 8c$$

Equivalent Addition Example

$$29a^2 + 13b + 3c$$
$$\ominus\oplus 17a^2 \ominus 6b \oplus 8c$$
$$\mathbf{12a^2 + 19b - 5c} \quad ▮▮▮▮$$

EXERCISE SET 5.3

1–10. Add.

1. $(5y - 8)(3y - 2)$

2. $(4x^2 + 1) + (3x^2 - 7)$

3. $(2x - 5y + 4c) + (-3x + 2y - 3c)$

4. $(2n^2 - 7n + 8) + (8n^2 - 3n - 11)$

5. $(7p^3 - 4p^2 + 9) + (-5p^3 + 6p - 7)$

6. $(-8m^2 - 7m) + (8m^2 + 3m + 2)$

7. $(-x^3 + 7x^2 - 9) + (3x^3 + x^2 - 6x)$

8. $(7t^5 - 8t^3 + 2t) + (5t^3 - 2t^3 + 4)$

9. $(3x^2 - 5x) + (2x^2 + 7) + (9x - 10)$

10. $(5r^2s^2 - 7r^2s + 3rs) + (-8r^2s^2 + 2rs^2 - 3rs + 1)$

11–15. Subtract.

11. $(6x + 5) - (3x - 2)$

12. $(-2y - 9) - (-8y + 6)$

13. $(4n^2 + 11) - (10n^2 + 7)$

14. $(2x^3 - 4x^2 + 9x) - (5x^3 + x^2 - 2x)$

15. $(3y^4 - 2y^3 - 9) - (4y^3 + 3y^2 - 7y)$

16. Subtract $3x - 2$ from $4x + 3$.

17. From $5x^2 - 2x + 3$, subtract $3x^2 + 4x + 3$.

18. From $3x^2 - 4$, subtract $x^2 + 2x - 7$.

19. From $3x^2 - 7x + 12$, subtract $x^2 - 7x - 3$.

20. From the sum of $5x^2 + 8$ and $-2x^2 - 4$, subtract $3x^2 + 7$.

21. From the sum of $2x^3 + 6x^2 - 3$ and $x^3 - 9x + 7$, subtract $8x^3 + x^2 - 5x + 2$.

22. How much greater is $x^4 + 6x^2 + 12$ than $8x^2 - 9$?

23. What polynomial must be added to $4x^3 - 5x^2 + 13$ in order for their sum to be 0?

24–27. Solve for n.

24. $-2(3n - 7) + 3(n + 4) = 5(n + 2)$

25. $(n^2 - 8n + 13) + (3n^2 + 5n - 7) = 4n^2 + n - 14$

26. $(4n^2 - 11n - 8) - (7n^2 + 2n - 1) = -(3n^2 + 2n - 15)$

27. $\dfrac{4n^2 + 2n - 1}{4} = \dfrac{5n^2 - 6n + 3}{5}$

28. Express in simplest form the perimeter of a rectangle having a length of $3x^2 - 5x + 1$ and a width of $4x^2 + 3$.

29. Express in simplest form the width of a rectangle having a perimeter of $8x^2 - 10x + 16$ and a length of $x^2 + 2x - 3$.

30. Find the average of $3x^2 - 9$, $2x^2 + 2$, and $4x^2 + 1$.

5.4 MULTIPLYING AND DIVIDING POLYNOMIALS

KEY IDEAS

The methods used for *multiplying* and *dividing* polynomials are based on the distributive property, as illustrated in the following set of arithmetic examples:

1. $\dfrac{15+9}{3} = \dfrac{15}{3} + \dfrac{9}{3} = 5+3 = \mathbf{8}$

2. $(30+1)(10+2) = $

$$
\begin{array}{r}
30+1 \\
\times\, 10+2 \\
\hline
\end{array}
$$

Multiply 30 and 1 by 10: $\quad 300+10$
Multiply 30 and 1 by 2: $\quad \underline{60+2}$
Add the columns: $\quad 300+70+2 = \mathbf{372}$

MULTIPLYING A POLYNOMIAL BY A MONOMIAL. To **multiply a polynomial by a monomial, multiply *each* term of the polynomial by the monomial.** For example,

$$
\begin{aligned}
4x^2(2x^3 + xy - 3y^2) &= 4x^2(2x^3) + 4x^2(xy) + 4x^2(-3y^2) \\
&= 8x^{2+3} + 4x^{2+1}y - 12x^2y^2 \\
&= \mathbf{8x^5 + 4x^3y - 12x^2y^2}
\end{aligned}
$$

Examples

1. The length of a rectangle is represented by $4x^2 - 5x + 1$, and its width is represented by $3x$. Represent the area of the rectangle as a trinomial.

Solution: Area $= \qquad$ Length $\qquad \times \quad$ Width
$$
\begin{aligned}
&= (4x^2 - 5x + 1) \quad \times \quad (3x) \\
&= (4x^2)3x - 5x(3x) + 1(3x) \\
&= \mathbf{12x^3 - 15x^2 + 3x}
\end{aligned}
$$

2. Multiply: $3ab^2(5a^2 - 2ab + 4a^3)$.

Solution:

$$
\begin{aligned}
3ab^2(5a^2 - 2ab + 4a^3) &= 3ab^2(5a^2) + 3ab^2(-2ab) + 3ab^2(4a^3) \\
&= 15(aa^2)b^2 - 6(aa)(b^2b^1) + 12(aa^3)b^2 \\
&= \mathbf{15a^3b^2 - 6a^2b^3 + 12a^4b^2}
\end{aligned}
$$

3. Multiply: $0.8m(0.7m + 5n^3)$.

Solution:
$$
\begin{aligned}
0.8m(0.7m + 5n^3) &= 0.8m^1(0.7m^1) + 0.8m(5n^3) \\
&= (0.8)(0.7)m^2 + (0.8)(5)mn^3 \\
&= \mathbf{0.56m^2 + 4mn^3}
\end{aligned}
$$

DIVIDING A POLYNOMIAL BY A MONOMIAL. To **divide** a polynomial by a monomial, divide each term of the polynomial by the monomial. For example,

$$\frac{72x^3 - 32x^2}{8x} = \frac{72x^3}{8x} - \frac{32x^2}{8x}$$

$$= \left(\frac{72}{8}\right)\left(\frac{x^3}{x}\right) - \left(\frac{32}{8}\right)\left(\frac{x^2}{x}\right)$$

$$= 9x^{3-1} - 4x^{2-1}$$

$$= 9x^2 - 4x$$

MULTIPLYING A POLYNOMIAL BY A POLYNOMIAL. When **multiplying polynomials**, it is sometimes convenient to write them vertically, one polynomial underneath the other. For example, the product of $(2x + 7)$ and $(x + 3)$ may be found as follows:

$$
\begin{array}{r}
2x + 7 \\
x + 3 \\
\hline
2x^2 + 7x \\
+ 6x + 21 \\
\hline
2x^2 + 13x + 21
\end{array}
$$

$x(2x + 7) =$

$3(2x + 7) =$

Add like terms by column:

The product of $(2x + 7)$ and $(x + 3)$ is $\mathbf{2x^2 + 13x + 21.}$

Example ▬▬▬▬

5. Find the product of $(5a^4 - 6a^2 + 2a - 7)$ and $(3a - 4)$.

Solution: Write the polynomial having the fewer number of terms underneath the other polynomial.

Use $0 \cdot a^3$ as a placeholder:

Polynomial with fewer terms:

$$5a^4 + 0 \cdot a^3 - 6a^2 + 2a - 7$$
$$3a - 4$$

$3a(5a^4 + 0 \cdot a^3 - 6a^2 + 2a - 7) =$

$- 4(5a^4 + 0a^3 - 6a^2 + 2a - 7) =$

Combine like terms:

$$15a^5 + 0a^4 - 18a^3 + 6a^2 - 21a$$
$$- 20a^4 + 0a^3 + 24a^2 - 8a + 28$$
$$\mathbf{15a^5 - 20a^4 - 18a^3 + 30a^2 - 29a + 28}$$

EXERCISE SET 5.4

1–26. Multiply.

1. $3x(x^2 - 5x + 7)$
2. $5y^2(y^3 + 8y - 1)$
3. $-4a(a^3 + 6a - 9)$
4. $(3n^2 - 2n + 1)(7n)$
5. $b^2(-2b^3 + 8b + 4)$
6. $0.06c^3(0.5c^2 - 0.8)$
7. $xy^2(2x^2 - 3y^2 + 8xy)$
8. $pq(3p^2 + 5q^2 - 7pq + 10)$
9. $a^2b(2a^5 + b^2 - 3ab)$
10. $(3x + 7)(2x - 9)$
11. $(11a - 3)(8a + 7)$
12. $(r^2 + 5r + 8)(r + 3)$
13. $(3s^2 - 4s + 7)(5s + 2)$
14. $(x + y)(x^2 - xy + y^2)$

15. $a^2b(2a^3b - 5ab^2 - 3ab)$
16. $(9x^3 - 2x^2 + 7)(4x - 1)$
17. $(3a - 7a^3 + 5)(a^2 - 2)$
18. $(p^3 + 3p^2q + 6pq^2)(p - q)$
19. $(5w + 8)(5w - 8)$
20. $(2c - 7)^2$
21. $(3y^2 - 9)(3y^2 + 9)$
22. $5x(x + 6)(3x - 4)$
23. $(2x^2 - 5x + 1)(x^2 + x + 2)$
24. $(a^2 + ab + b^2)(a - b)$
25. $(x - 2)(3x - 1)(5x + 6)$
26. $(n + 4)^3$

27. Express as a trinomial in terms of x the area of a square whose side has a length represented by $5x - 2$.

28. To the product of $(4x - 1)$ and $(3x - 5)$, add $2x^2 - 8x - 9$.

29. From the product of $(2x + 3)$ and $(x - 6)$, subtract $-3x^2 + 5x + 4$.

30. From the product of $(x^2 - 4)$ and $(2x + 1)$, subtract $4x^3 - 2x^2 + 7x - 2$.

31–38. Divide.

31. $\dfrac{32a^5 - 8a^2}{4a}$

32. $\dfrac{15p^3 - 45p^2 + 9p}{3p}$

33. $\dfrac{t^4 + t^3 + 5t^2}{t^2}$

34. $\dfrac{18r^4 - 27r^3s^2}{9p^2}$

35. $\dfrac{30y^6 + 5y^3 - 10y^2}{-5y^2}$

36. $\dfrac{h^3k^2 + h^2k^3 - 7hk}{hk}$

37. $\dfrac{(a^2b)^2 - (ab)^3}{ab}$

38. $\dfrac{0.14a^3 - 1.05a^2b}{0.7a}$

39–43. In the accompanying table the column headings refer to measurements of a rectangle. Enter the missing expressions in simplest form.

	Length	Width	Perimeter	Area
39.	$3x - 7$	$5x + 2$	?	?
40.	$2x^2 - 7x + 1$	$4x - 1$	?	?
41.	?	$6x$	?	$18x^2 - 24x$
42.	$3x + 4$	?	$2x^2 + 6x + 4$	?
43.	?	$x^2 + 10$	$4x^2 - 6x + 12$	?

44–47. Solve for x.

44. $(x + 6)(x - 6) = x(x + 4)$

45. $(x - 3)^2 = x(x + 12)$

46. $(x + 2)(x - 1)(x + 3) = x^2(x + 4) - 9$

47. $(2x^2 + 7x - 4)(x - 3) = x^2(2x + 1) - 13$

48. A square and a rectangle have the same area. The length of the rectangle is 8 more than a side of the square, and the width of the rectangle is 4 less than a side of the square. Find the length of a side of the square.

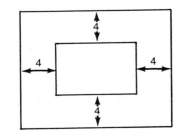

49. In the accompanying figure, a border 4 cm in width surrounds a rectangle whose length exceeds its width by 5. If the area of the rectangular border is 216 cm², what are the dimensions of the inner rectangle?

5.5 MULTIPLYING BINOMIALS USING FOIL

— KEY IDEAS —

When a pair of binomials such as $(3x + 7)$ and $(2x + 5)$ are written next to each other on the same line, special pairs of terms may be identified by their position: $3x$ and $2x$ are the *First* terms of each binomial; $3x$ and 5 are the *Outermost* terms; 7 and $2x$ are the *Innermost* terms; and 7 and 5 are the *Last* terms of each binomial. The first letters of these four words form the word **FOIL.**

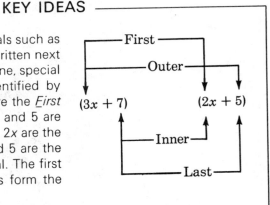

USING FOIL TO MULTIPLY BINOMIALS. A shortcut method for multiplying a pair of binomials is based on FOIL. The letters of FOIL tell us the products that must be formed in order to obtain the product of two binomials: form the product of the First terms, the product of the Outer terms, the product of the Inner terms, and the product of the Last terms. Then write the sum of these products. The following horizontal format can be used:

$$
\begin{array}{cccc}
\text{F} & \text{O} & \text{I} & \text{L}
\end{array}
$$

$$
\begin{aligned}
(3x + 7)(2x + 5) &= \overbrace{(3x \cdot 2x)} + \overbrace{[(3x \cdot 5)} + \overbrace{(7 \cdot 2x)]} + \overbrace{(7 \cdot 5)} \\
&= \quad 6x^2 \quad + \quad [15x \quad + \quad 14x] \quad + \quad 35 \\
&= 6x^2 + 29x + 35
\end{aligned}
$$

Example

Use the FOIL method to find each of the following products:
(a) $(x - 2)(x - 6)$ (c) $(5x - 9)(2x + 3)$
(b) $(y + 3)^2$ (d) $(w - 6)(w + 6)$

Solution:

$$
\begin{array}{cccc}
\text{F} & \text{O} & \text{I} & \text{L}
\end{array}
$$

(a) $(x - 2)(x - 6) = x^2 + [(-6x) + (-2x)] + 12 = x^2 - 8x + 12$

(b) Rewrite the square of the binomial as the product of two identical binomials.

$$
\begin{array}{cccc}
\text{F} & \text{O} & \text{I} & \text{L}
\end{array}
$$

$$(y + 3)^2 = (y + 3)(y + 3) = y^2 + [3y + 3y] + 9 = y^2 + 6y + 9$$

$$
\begin{array}{cccc}
\text{F} & \text{O} & \text{I} & \text{L}
\end{array}
$$

(c) $(5x - 9)(2x + 3) = 10x^2 + [15x + (-18x)] - 27 = 10x^2 - 3x - 27$

$$
\begin{array}{cccc}
\text{F} & \text{O} & \text{I} & \text{L}
\end{array}
$$

(d) $(w - 6)(w + 6) = w^2 + [6w + (-6w)] - 36$
$$= w^2 + 0w - 36 = w^2 - 36.$$

Notice that the product of two binomials is *not* always a trinomial.

EXERCISE SET 5.5

1–30. Use FOIL to find each of the following products:

1. $(x - 4)(x - 7)$
2. $(y + 3)(y + 10)$
3. $(a + 2)(a + 2)$
4. $(t - 8)(t + 8)$
5. $(2x + 1)(x + 4)$
6. $(3x + 1)(2x + 5)$
7. $(2y - 1)(4y - 3)$
8. $(a + 7)(a - 7)$
9. $(n + 9)(n + 9)$
10. $\left(x - \dfrac{1}{4}\right)\left(x + \dfrac{1}{4}\right)$
11. $(8m - 7)(5m + 9)$
12. $(4x - 13)(x + 6)$
13. $(5w - 3)(4x + 7)$
14. $(6t + 7)(3t - 11)$
15. $(2x - 5)(2x + 5)$

16. $(5 - 6p)(8 - 3p)$
17. $10 - x)(10 + x)$
18. $(0.6y - 5)(0.4y + 8)$
19. $(x + y)(x - y)$
20. $(1 - 4x)(9 - 5x)$
21. $(3 - 7z)(7 + 3z)$
22. $(p + 3q)(2p - 7q)$
23. $(a + 0.8)(a - 0.8)$
24. $(4w - 3y)(2w - 5y)$
25. $(2r + 9s)(3r - 11s)$
26. $(r - 0.5t)(r + 0.5t)$
27. $(5n - 4)(5n + 4)$
28. $(7k + 2)(3k - 11)$
29. $(2x^2 - 1)(x + 5)$
30. $(3y^2 + 5z)(2y - 7z^2)$

31–39. Express each of the following products as a trinomial:

31. $(x - 7)^2$ **34.** $(4t + 7)^2$ **37.** $2(3x - 1)^2$
32. $(y + 6)^2$ **35.** $(x + 2y)^2$ **38.** $-3(1 - 4y)^2$
33. $(2n - 3)^2$ **36.** $(0.3n - 5)^2$ **39.** $5p(3p + 2)^2$

40–45. Find the value of p.

40. $(x + p)(x - 9) = x^2 - 81$ **43.** $(x + 3)(x + p) = x^2 + 2x - 3$
41. $(x + p)^2 = x^2 + 4x + 4$ **44.** $(px - 3)(px + 3) = 25x^2 - 9$
42. $(x + 7)(x + p) = x^2 + 11x + 28$ **45.** $(4x + 5)(x + p) = 4x^2 - 7x - 15$

46–50. Simplify by writing each of the following as a trinomial:

46. $-(x - 5)^2$
47. $x^2 - 9 + (x + 3)^2$

48. In the accompanying diagram, the width of the inner rectangle is represented by x and the length by $2x - 1$. The width of the outer rectangle is represented by $x + 3$ and the length by $x + 5$.

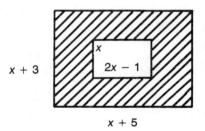

$x + 3$

$x + 5$

a Express the area of the shaded region as a trinomial in terms of x.
b If the perimeter of the outer rectangle is 24, what is the value of x?

49. The length of a rectangle exceeds the width by 3. If the length is increased by 2 and the width is decreased by 1, the area remains the same. What are the original dimensions of the rectangle?

50. The length of a rectangle is twice its width. If the length is decreased by 4 and the width is increased by 3, the area remains the same. What are the original dimensions of the rectangle?

51. The square of the larger of two consecutive integers exceeds the product of the two consecutive integers by 10. Find the smaller of the two integers.

52. In a set of three consecutive odd integers, the product of the first and the third integer exceeds the product of the first and the second integer by 14. Find the smallest integer in the set.

CHAPTER 5 REVIEW EXERCISES

REGENTS REVIEW. *Problems included in this section are similar in form and difficulty to those found on the New York State Regents Examination for Course I of the Three-Year Sequence for High School Mathematics. Problems preceded by an asterisk have actually appeared on a previous Course I Regents Examination.*

*1. Find the sum of $4a + 2b - c$ and $3a - 5b - 2c$.

*2. From $5x^2 - 3x + 2$ subtract $3x^2 - 4x - 1$.

*3. Express $3x^2(2x - 5)$ as a binomial.

*4. Express as a trinomial: $(3x - 1)(x + 2)$.

*5. Express as a trinomial: $(5x^2 + 2x - 3) - (2x^2 - 3x + 7)$.

*6. Subtract $4m - h$ from $4m + h$.

*7. The length of a rectangle is represented by $2x + 3$ and the width by $x + 2$. Express the area of the rectangle as a trinomial in terms of x.

*8. Express $\dfrac{15x^2}{-3x}$ in simplest form.

9. The lengths of the sides of a triangle are represented by $x + 1$, $2x + 3$, and $3x - 5$. Express the perimeter of the triangle as a binomial in terms of x.

10. Express the average of $3x + 5$ and $7x - 5$ in terms of x.

*11. Find the product of $8y^3$ and $3y^6$.

12. The length of a side of a square is represented by $a - 2b$. Express the area of the square as a trinomial.

*13. Perform the indicated operations and express the result as a trinomial: $3x(x + 1) + 4(x - 1)$.

14. If $12x$ is subtracted from $6x$, what is the difference?

*15. If the product $(2x + 3)(x + k)$ is $2x^2 + 13x + 15$, find the value of k.

16. Find the product of $(2x - 1)$ and $(x^3 - 3x + 5)$.

17. The length of a rectangle is $x + 3$, and the width is $x - 5$. Express in terms of x the perimeter of the rectangle.

18. From $5x^2 - 6x + 2$ subtract $3x^2 + 7$.

19. The sum of two polynomials is 0. If one of the polynomials is $3x^2 + 5x - 7$, what is the other polynomial?

20. What is the sum of the quotients obtained by dividing $(14x^3 - 35x^2 + 7x)$ by $7x$ and $(15x^3 - 9x^2 + 3x)$ by $3x$?

*21. The product of $(3x^5)$ and $(4x^2)$ is:
    (1) $7x^7$ (2) $12x^7$ (3) $7x^{10}$ (4) $12x^{10}$

*22. The expression $18x^6 \div 3x^3$ is equivalent to:
    (1) $15x^2$ (2) $15x^3$ (3) $6x^2$ (4) $6x^3$

*23. The product of $9x^3$ and $2x^4$ is:
    (1) $11x^7$ (2) $11x^{12}$ (3) $18x^7$ (4) $18x^1$

*24. The expression $(3x^2y^3)^2$ is equivalent to:
    (1) $9x^4y^6$ (2) $9x^4y^5$ (3) $3x^4y^6$ (4) $6x^4y^6$

*25. The quotient of $\dfrac{-4a^6b^2}{2a^2b}$ is:
    (1) $2a^3b^2$ (2) $-2a^4b^2$ (3) $-2a^4b$ (4) $-6a^3b$

*26. The length of a rectangle is represented by $x - 5$ and the width by $x + 2$. The area of the rectangle is represented by:
    (1) $x^2 + 3x - 10$ (2) $2x - 3$ (3) $x^2 - 3x - 10$ (4) $4x - 6$

27. The quotient of $(4x^3 - 3x^2) \div x^2$ is:
    (1) 1 (2) $2x - 3$ (3) $4x - 3$ (4) $4 - 3x$

28. The expression $(2x)^3(4x^2)$ is equivalent to:
    (1) $33x^5$ (2) $32x^5$ (3) $128x^5$ (4) $128x^6$

29. If $15a^2 - 3a$ is divided by $3a$, the quotient is:
    (1) $5a$ (2) $2a$ (3) $5a - 3$ (4) $5a - 1$

30. The expression of $(x + 2)^2 - 4x - 4$ is equivalent to:
    (1) x^2 (2) $x^2 - 4x$ (3) $x^2 + 4x$ (4) $x^2 - 4x + 8$

31. The expression $(2a^2)^3$ is equivalent to:
    (1) $2a^5$ (2) $2a^6$ (3) $8a^5$ (4) $8a^6$

32. The expression $x(x - y)(x + y)$ is equivalent to:
    (1) $x^2 - y^2$ (2) $x^3 - y^3$ (3) $x^3 - xy^2$ (4) $x^3 - x^2y + y^2$

33. When $12x^4 - 3x^3 + 6x^2$ is divided by $3x^2$, the quotient is:
    (1) $9x^2 - 3$ (2) $5x^2$ (3) $4x^2 - 3x + 2$ (4) $4x^2 - x + 2$

CHAPTER 6

Factoring

6.1 FINDING THE GREATEST COMMON FACTOR (GCF)

_____ KEY IDEAS _____

The prime factorization of a number factors the number as the product of two or more numbers that cannot be factored further. For example, the prime factorizations of 18 and 30 are

$$18 = 2 \cdot 3 \cdot 3 \quad \text{and} \quad 30 = 2 \cdot 3 \cdot 5.$$

The Greatest Common Factor (GCF) of 18 and 30 is **6** ($= 2 \times 3$). The **GCF** of two or more terms is the product of their common prime factors.

FINDING THE GCF. To obtain the GCF (greatest common factor) of two or more terms, compare their prime factorizations and write the product of the prime factors that are common to each term. For example, to find the GCF of $15y^3$ and $10y$, proceed as follows:

Write the prime factorization of $15y^3$: $3 \cdot \mathbf{5} \cdot \mathbf{y} \cdot y \cdot y$

Write the prime factorization of $10y$: $2 \cdot \mathbf{5} \ \mathbf{y}$

Select common factors: The GCF of $15y^3$ and $10y$ is **5y**.

Example

   1. Determine the GCF of $21a^5$ and $-14a^3$.

   Solution: Write the prime factorization of each monomial.

$$21a^5 = \quad 3 \cdot 7 \cdot \mathbf{a} \cdot \mathbf{a} \cdot \mathbf{a} \cdot a$$

$$-14a^3 = -1 \cdot 2 \cdot 7 \cdot \mathbf{a} \cdot \mathbf{a} \cdot \mathbf{a}$$

The GCF of $21a^5$ and $-14a^3$ is **$7a^3$**.

FACTORING POLYNOMIALS. Compare the terms of the polynomial $2xy^2 - 6x^2y + 4xy$. Notice that each term includes similar factors. The GCF of the terms of the polynomial is $2xy$ since

$$2xy^2 = \mathbf{2xyy}$$
$$6x^2y = 3 \cdot \mathbf{2xxy}$$
$$4xy = 2 \cdot \mathbf{2xy}$$

What factor "remains" when $2xy$ is *factored out* of $2xy^2 - 6x^2y + 4xy$?

$$2xy^2 - 6x^2y + 4xy = 2xy(\underline{?})$$

To find this factor, divide the original polynomial by $2xy$. (For example, if 3 is a factor of 21, the corresponding factor may be found by dividing 21 by 3, thereby obtaining 7 as the other factor.)

$$\frac{2xy^2 - 6x^2y + 4xy}{2xy} = \frac{2xy^2}{2xy} - \frac{6x^2y}{2xy} + \frac{4xy}{2xy} = y - 3x + 2$$

Therefore $2xy^2 - 6x^2y + 4xy = \mathbf{2xy(y - 3x + 2)}$.

Example

2. Factor: $24x^3y + 30x^2y^5$.

Solution:

Step 1. Find the GCF of the terms of the polynomial.

$$24x^3y = 2 \cdot 2 \cdot \mathbf{2} \cdot \mathbf{3xx} \cdot x \cdot \mathbf{y}$$
$$30x^2y^5 = 5 \cdot \mathbf{2} \cdot \mathbf{3xx} \cdot \mathbf{y} \cdot yyyy$$

The GCF of $24x^3y$ and $30x^2y^5$ is $2 \cdot 3xxy = 6x^2y$.

Step 2. Find the remaining factor by dividing the polynomial by the GCF.

$$\frac{24x^3y + 30x^2y^5}{6x^2y} = \frac{24x^3y}{6x^2y} + \frac{30x^2y^5}{6x^2y}$$

$$= 4x + 5y^4$$

Therefore $24x^3y + 30x^2y^5 = \mathbf{6x^2y(4x + 5y^4)}$.

You can *check* that the factorization of a polynomial is correct by multiplying the factors on the right side of the equals sign, and then comparing the resulting product with the original polynomial on the left side of the equals sign.

As you gain experience in factoring, you will be able to use shortcut techniques. For example, in many cases the GCF of the terms of a polynomial can be found by making a visual comparison of the terms and thinking:

1. "What is the largest number, if any, that evenly divides the numerical coefficient of each term?"

2. "Which variable bases, if any, are contained in each term? What is the greatest *common* exponent of these variable factors?"

After the GCF is found, the remaining factor of each term can be obtained by mentally applying the reverse of the distributive property. Below are some additional examples that illustrate this idea. For each example, check your answer by multiplying the factors.

Examples

3. Factor: $21x^3 - 28x^5$.

Solution: The GCF of $21x^3$ and $28x^5$ is $7x^3$.

$$21x^3 - 28x^5 = 7x^3(\underline{\ ?\ }) - 7x^3(\underline{\ ?\ })$$

Use the reverse of the distributive property by thinking: "What term when multiplied by $7x^3$ gives $21x^3$? What term when multiplied by $7x^3$ gives $28x^5$?"

$$21x^3 - 28x^5 = 7x^3(3) - 7x^3(4x^2)$$
$$= \boldsymbol{7x^3(3 - 4x^2)}$$

4. Factor: $20a^2c + 32a^3b^2$.

Solution: The GCF of $20a^2c$ and $32a^3b^2$ is $4a^2$.

$$20a^2c + 32a^3b^2 = 4a^2(\underline{\ ?\ }) + 4a^2(\underline{\ ?\ })$$
$$= 4a^2(5c) + 4a^2(8ab^2)$$
$$= \boldsymbol{4a^2(5c + 8ab^2)}$$

5. Factor: $9x^4 - 3x^3 + 12x$.

Solution: The GCF of $9x^4$, $-3x^3$, and $12x$ is $3x$.

$$9x^4 - 3x^3 + 12x = 3x(\underline{\ ?\ }) + 3x(\underline{\ ?\ }) + 3x(\underline{\ ?\ })$$
$$= 3x(3x^3) - 3x(x^2) + 3x(4)$$
$$= \boldsymbol{3x(3x^3 - x^2 + 4)}$$

6. Factor: $-2rs - 2$.

Solution: $-2rs - 2 = -2(rs) - 2(1) = \boldsymbol{-2(rs + 1)}$

7. Factor: $12x + 7y$.

Solution: This cannot be expressed in factored form since the terms have no common factors other than 1.

EXERCISE SET 6.1

1–5. Write the prime factorization of each integer.

1. 11   **2.** 24.   **3.** 128   **4.** 196   **5.** 200

6–14. Find the GCF for each set of terms.

6. 48 and 190
7. 30 and 60
8. $11x$ and $22x^2$
9. a^2b and ab^2
10. $5n^3$ and $-15n^5$
11. $8x^2y^3$ and $20x^3y$
12. $-3x$ and $-3x^4$
13. a^3b, a^2b^3, and a^2b^4
14. $9h^6k^5$, $-27h^3k^2$, and $18h^3k^5$

15–32. Factor each of the following polynomials so that one of the factors is the GCF:

15. $5x^2 + 11x$
16. $6a^3 - 9a^2$
17. $4p^2q + 12p^2q$
18. $7n^2 + 7t^2$
19. $x^3 + x^2 + x$
20. $14x - 7x^2$
21. $n^4 - 2n^3 + 5n^2$
22. $4s^3 - 12s^2 + 8s - 20$
23. $3y^7 - 6y^5 + 12y^3 + 21$
24. $-3a - 3b$
25. $8u^5w^2 - 40u^2w^5$
26. $-14t^3 - 21t^5$
27. $p^2k^4 - p^3k^2 + (pk)^2$
28. $an^3 - 4n^2 + 8n$
29. $(p - q)^3 + (p - q)^2$
30. $(x + a)^2 - a(x + a)$
31. $a^3b^5c^2 - a^4b^2c^3 + a^5b^2c$
32. $18x^3y - 12x^2y^2 + 24x^4y$

33. If the area of a rectangle is $14x^3 - 21x^2$ and the width is $7x^2$, what is the length?

34. If the area of a rectangle is $45h^4 - 18h^2$ and the length is $5h^2 - 2$, what is the width?

6.2 MULTIPLYING CONJUGATE BINOMIALS AND FACTORING THEIR PRODUCTS

───────────── KEY IDEAS ─────────────

Binomial pairs such as $(x + 3)$ and $(x - 3)$, $(m + 7)$ and $(m - 7)$, and $(2y + 5)$ and $(2y - 5)$ are examples of *conjugate binomials*. **Conjugate binomials** are binomials that take the sum and difference of the *same* two terms.

MULTIPLYING CONJUGATE BINOMIALS. Observe the pattern in the following examples, in which pairs of conjugate binomials are multiplied:

$$
\begin{array}{c}
\ \ \text{F}\quad\ \ \text{O}\quad\ \ \text{I}\quad\ \ \text{L} \\
(x + 3)(x - 3) = x^2 - 3x + 3x - 9 = x^2 - 9; \\
(m + 7)(m - 7) = m^2 - 7m + 7m - 49 = m^2 - 49; \\
(2y + 5)(2y - 5) = 4y^2 - 10y + 10y - 25 = 4y^2 - 25.
\end{array}
$$

Notice that the sum of the outer and inner products will always be equal to 0, so that the product always lacks a "middle" term. *The product of a pair of conjugate binomials is a binomial formed by taking the difference of the squares of the first and last terms of each of the original binomials.* In general,

───────────── Multiplying Conjugate Binomials ─────────────

$$(a + b)(a - b) = a^2 - b^2$$

Example

1. Find the product of $(x - 3y)$ and $(x + 3y)$.

Solution: $(x - 3y)(x + 3y) = x^2 - (3y)^2 = x^2 - 9y^2$

FACTORING THE DIFFERENCE OF TWO SQUARES. By reversing the pattern observed in multiplying two conjugate binomials, we acquire a method for factoring a binomial that represents the difference of two squares. To illustrate, since $(x + 5)(x - 5) = x^2 - 25$, then $x^2 - 25$ can be factored by observing that

$$x^2 - 25 = (x)^2 - (5)^2 = (x + 5)(x - 5).$$

To factor a binomial that is the *difference* of two squares, write the product of the corresponding pair of conjugate binomials. In general,

—————— Factoring the Difference of Two Squares ——————

$$p^2 - q^2 = (p+q)(p-q)$$

Examples ▰▰▰▰▰

2. Factor: $n^2 - 100$.

Solution: $n^2 - 100 = (n)^2 - (10)^2 = (n+10)(n-10)$

3. Factor: $4a^2 - 25b^2$.

Solution: $4a^2 - 25b^2 = (2a)^2 - (5b)^2 = (2a+5b)(2a-5b)$

4. Factor: $0.16y^2 - 0.09$.

Solution: $0.16y^2 - 0.09 = (0.4y)^2 - (0.3)^2 = (0.4y+0.3)(0.4y-0.3)$

5. Factor: $p^2 - \dfrac{36}{49}$.

Solution: $p^2 - \dfrac{36}{49} = (p)^2 - \left(\dfrac{6}{7}\right)^2 = \left(p+\dfrac{6}{7}\right)\left(p-\dfrac{6}{7}\right)$ ▰▰▰▰▰

EXERCISE SET 6.2

1–16. Multiply.

1. $(x+2)(x-2)$
2. $(y-10)(y+10)$
3. $(3a-1)(3a+1)$
4. $(-n+6)(-n-6)$
5. $(4-x)(4+x)$
6. $(1-2y)(1+2y)$
7. $(0.8n-7)(0.8n+7)$
8. $\left(x-\dfrac{2}{3}\right)\left(x+\dfrac{2}{3}\right)$
9. $\left(2y-\dfrac{1}{5}\right)\left(2y+\dfrac{2}{10}\right)$
10. $\left(0.2p-\dfrac{3}{8}\right)\left(0.2p+\dfrac{3}{8}\right)$
11. $(0.5n+0.3)(0.5n-0.3)$
12. $(a-7b)(a+7b)$
13. $(x^2-8)(x^2+8)$
14. $(y^3-z)(y^3+z)$
15. $(m^2-n^2)(m^2+n^2)$
16. $(2w-3)^2$

17–31. Factor.

17. $x^2 - 144$
18. $y^2 - 0.49$
19. $25 - a^2$
20. $p^2 - \dfrac{1}{9}$
21. $16a^2 - 36$
22. $64x^2 - 1$
23. $h^2 - k^2$
24. $121w^2 - 25z^2$
25. $\dfrac{4}{9}x^2 - 49$
26. $0.36y^2 - 0.64x^2$
27. $0.09h^2 - 0.04$
28. $\dfrac{1}{4}y^2 - \dfrac{1}{9}$
29. $100a^2 - 81b^2$
30. $n^4 - 49$
31. $x^6 - y^4$

6.3 FACTORING QUADRATIC TRINOMIALS

——————————— KEY IDEAS ———————————

Given two binomials, a polynomial that represents their product can be found using FOIL.

Starting with a polynomial that represents the product of two binomials, the binomial factors of the polynomial can be discovered using methods that are based on applying the *reverse* of FOIL.

TERMS OF A QUADRATIC POLYNOMIAL.   A quadratic polynomial in a single variable takes the general form

$$ax^2 + bx + c,$$

where the coefficients a, b, and c are real numbers, except that a cannot be equal to 0. In this course, we will usually consider only rational values for a, b, and c.

	SPECIAL TERMS		
Quadratic Polynomial	**Quadratic**	**Linear**	**Constant**
$2x^2 + 5x + 3$	$2x^2$	$5x$	3
$x^2 - 2x$	x^2	$-2x$	0
$x^2 - 16$	x^2	$0x$	-16

FACTORING $ax^2 + bx + c$ $(a = 1)$.   FOIL can be used to verify that the product of $(x + 2)$ and $(x + 5)$ is $x^2 + 7x + 10$. The binomial factors of the quadratic trinomial $x^2 + 7x + 10$ may, therefore, be written as follows:

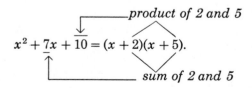

Observe that there is a relationship between the terms of the binomial factors and the values of the coefficients of the terms of the quadratic trinomial. For example, the product of 2 and 5 is 10 (c term), and the sum of 2 and 5 is 7 (coefficient of b term). This suggests a convenient method by which similar types of quadratic trinomials may be expressed in factored form. When attempting to factor a quadratic trinomial of the form

$x^2 + bx + c$, think: "What *two* numbers when multiplied give c *and* when added give b?" If two such numbers exist, say p and q, then write

$$x^2 + bx + c = (x + p)(x + q), \quad \text{where } p + q = b \text{ and } pq = c.$$

Example ▆▆▆▆

1. Factor $x^2 + 11x + 18$ as the product of two binomials.

Solution: *Step 1.* Write $x^2 + 11x + 18 = (x \quad \square)(x \quad \square)$.

Step 2. Think: "What two numbers when multiplied give 18, *and* when added give 11?" Since the product and the sum of these factors are both positive, each factor must be positive. List the set of all possible pairs of positive integers whose product is 18. Then choose the pair of factors that satisfy the additional condition that their sum is 11.

Factors of 18	Sum of Factors = 11?
1 and 18	$1 + 18 = 19$
2 and 9	$2 + 9 = 11$ *Success!*

The desired numbers are 2 and 9, so there is no need to test other pairs of factors of 18.

Step 3. Write the binomial factors.

$$x^2 + 11x + 18 = (x + 2)(x + 9)$$

Step 4. Check by multiplying the factors using FOIL.

$$\begin{aligned} (x + 2)(x + 9) &= x^2 + 9x + 2x + 18 \\ &= x^2 + 11x + 18 \end{aligned} \qquad \blacksquare\blacksquare$$

As you gain more experience, you will able to consolidate this four-step factoring procedure.

Example ▆▆▆▆

2. Factor $n^2 - 5n - 14$ as the product of two binomials.

Solution: The numbers you are seeking have different signs since their product is negative. Write

$$n^2 - 5n - 14 = (n + \square)(n - \square).$$

Think: "What two numbers when multiplied give -14, *and* when added give -5?" The desired numbers are $+2$ and -7.

$$n^2 - 5n - 14 = (n + 2)(n - 7). \qquad \text{The check is left for you.}$$

                                                                         ▆▆▆

FACTORING $ax^2 + bx + c$ **($a \neq 1$).** When factoring a quadratic trinomial in which the coefficient of the quadratic term is *not* 1, you must take into account the effect of the coefficient a in forming the products of the "first" and "outer" terms. For example, to factor $2x^2 - 7x + 6$, proceed as follows:

Step 1. Determine the possible first terms of the binomial factors. The only positive factors of the numerical coefficient of $2x^2$ are 2 and 1. Therefore the first term of the binomial factors must be $2x$ and x:

$$2x^2 - 7x + 6 = (2x \quad \Box)(x \quad \Box).$$

Step 2. Determine the possible last terms of the binomial factors. Since $+6$ is the last term of the quadratic polynomial, the last terms of the binomial factors must be factors of 6, *and* they must have the *same* sign. Since the middle term is negative, the last terms of each binomial factor must be negative. This means that the last terms of the binomial factors are restricted to the following pairs:

$$-1 \text{ and } -6, \quad -2 \text{ and } -3.$$

Step 3. The factors of $+6$ found in step 2 can be used to form the possible binomial factors of $2x^2 - 7x + 6$. For each possible pair, test whether the sum of the outer product and the inner product gives a middle term of $-7x$.

Possible Binomial Factors	Outer + Inner Products $= -7x$?
$(2x - 1)(x - 6)$	$-12x + (-x) = -13x$
$(2x - 6)(x - 1)$	$-2x + (-6x) = -8x$
$(2x - 3)(x - 2)$	$-4x + (-3x) = -7x$ *Success!*

Therefore $2x^2 - 7x + 6 = (2x - 3)(x - 2)$.

Example 3 illustrates that the coefficient of the quadratic term may have more than one pair of possible factors.

Example

3. Factor $4x^2 + 3x - 7$.

Solution:

Step 1. List possible pairs of binomial factors of the quadratic polynomial whose first terms are factors of the quadratic coefficient a. Since the product of the first terms of each factor must be $4x^2$, possible binomial factors must take the form

$$(2x \quad ?)(2x \quad ?) \quad \text{or} \quad (4x \quad ?)(x \quad ?).$$

Step 2. Find all possible pairs of factors. The possible pairs of factors of -7 are 1 and -7, and -1 and 7.

Step 3. Form all possible pairs of binomial factors. Find the pair of factors whose outer and inner products have a sum of $3x$.

Possible Binomial Factors	Outer Product + Inner Product $= 3x$?
$(2x - 7)(2x + 1)$ $(2x + 7)(2x - 1)$	$2x + (-14x) = -12x \neq 3x$ $-2x + 14x \quad = \quad 12x \neq 3x$
$(4x - 1)(x + 7)$ $(4x + 1)(x - 7)$ $(4x - 7)(x + 1)$ $(4x + 7)(x - 1)$	$28x + (-x) \quad = \quad 27x \neq 3x$ $-28x + x \quad = -27x \neq 3x$ $4x + (-7x) = - \ 3x \neq 3x$ $-4x + 7x \quad = \quad 3x \quad$ *Success!*

Therefore $4x^2 + 3x - 7 = (4x + 7)(x - 1)$.

EXERCISE SET 6.3

1–24. Factor.

1. $x^2 + 8x + 15$
2. $x^2 - 10x + 21$
3. $x^2 + 4x - 21$
4. $y^2 + 6y + 9$
5. $n^2 + 3n - 88$
6. $a^2 - 4a - 45$
7. $w^2 - 13w + 42$
8. $b^2 + 3b - 40$

9. $t^2 - 7t - 60$
10. $y^2 - 9y + 8$
11. $s^2 - s - 56$
12. $x^2 - 19x + 90$
13. $y^2 - 2x + 1$
14. $a^2 + a - 20$
15. $2a^2 + 5a - 3$
16. $2q^2 - q - 15$

17. $3x^2 + 2x - 21$
18. $5s^2 + 14s - 3$
19. $5t^2 + 18t - 8$
20. $3n^2 + 29n - 44$
21. $7x^2 + 52x - 32$
22. $-x^2 + x + 12$
23. $-h^2 - h + 30$
24. $x^4 - 3x^2 - 10$

25. If $2x - 3$ is a factor of $4x^2 + 4x - 15$, what is the other binomial factor?

26. If $x + 8$ is a factor of $4x^2 + 27x - 40$, what is the other binomial factor?

27. If $2x + 6$ is a factor of $6x^2 + 4x - 42$, what is the other binomial factor?

28. If $6x + 5$ is a factor of $12x^2 - 14x - 20$, what is the other binomial factor?

29. If $5x - 8$ is a factor of $30x^2 - 38x - 16$, what is the other binomial factor?

30. If the binomial factors of $4x^2 - 36x + 81$ are identical, what is each factor?

31–45. Factor as the product of two binomials.

31. $4x^2 - 10x - 50$	**36.** $12y^2 - 5y - 28$	**41.** $x^2 - (x + 42)$
32. $6m^2 + m - 12$	**37.** $8d^2 - 22d + 15$	**42.** $t - 2(t^2 - 5)$
33. $10p^2 - 33p - 7$	**38.** $6a^2 - 13a + 5$	**43.** $c(c - 4) - 45$
34. $8n^2 + 9n - 14$	**39.** $16x^2 - 24x + 9$	**44.** $y(y + 10) + 4(y + 12)$
35. $3h^2 + 11h - 42$	**40.** $8r^4 - 10r^2 + 3$	**45.** $6x(x + 2) - (x - 4)$

6.4   FACTORING COMPLETELY

KEY IDEAS

A polynomial is *factored completely* when *each* of its factors cannot be factored further. Sometimes it is necessary to apply more than one factoring technique in order to factor a polynomial completely.

A STRATEGY FOR FACTORING COMPLETELY.   To factor a polynomial completely, proceed as follows:

1. Factor out the GCF, if any.

2. If there is a binomial, determine whether it can be factored as the difference of two squares.

3. If there is a quadratic trinomial, determine whether it can be factored as the product of two binomials by using the reverse of FOIL.

Examples

1. Factor completely: $3x^3 - 75x$.

Solution: First factor out the GCF of $3x$.

$$3x^3 - 75x = 3x(x^2 - 25)$$
$$= 3x(x - 5)(x + 5)$$

2. Factor completely: $t^3 + 6t^2 - 16t$.

Solution: First factor out the GCF of t.

$$t^3 + 6t^2 - 16t = t(t^2 + 6t - 16)$$
$$= t(t + 8)(t - 2)$$

3. Factor completely: $x^4 - y^4$.

Solution: Factor as the difference of two squares.

$$x^4 - y^4 = (x^2)^2 - (y^2)^2$$

Factor $(x^2 - y^2)$:
$$= (x^2 - y^2)(x^2 + y^2)$$
$$= (x - y)(x + y)(x^2 + y^2)$$

EXERCISE SET 6.4

1–12. Factor completely.

1. $2y^2 - 50$
2. $b^3 - 49b$
3. $x^3 + x^2 - 56x$
4. $8w^3 - 32w$
5. $-x^2 - 7x - 10$
6. $3y^2 - 9y + 6$

7. $12s^3 - 2s^2 - 4s$
8. $10y^3 + 50y^2 - 500y$
9. $3t^4 + 12t^3 - 15t^2$
10. $p^4 - 1$
11. $9a^2w^2 - 12a^2w + 4a^2$
12. $-5t^2 + 5$

6.5 SOLVING QUADRATIC EQUATIONS BY FACTORING

--- **KEY IDEAS** ---

If a and b are real numbers and $a \cdot b = 0$, then

$$a \vee b = 0.$$

In words, if the product of two numbers equals 0, then the first number equals 0, *or* the second number equals 0, *or* both numbers equal 0. This is sometimes referred to as the *zero product rule*. The zero product rule provides a way of solving equations in which one side of the equation is 0, while the other side can be expressed in factored form.

SOLVING QUADRATIC EQUATIONS BY FACTORING. A quadratic equation is in *standard form* when the equation is written as

$$ax^2 + bx + c = 0,$$

where $a \neq 0$. If $a = 0$, then the equation reduces to

$$bx + c = 0,$$

which is a *linear* (first-degree) *equation*. If the left side of the quadratic equation $ax^2 + bx + c = 0$ can be factored, then the zero product rule allows us to solve the quadratic equation by setting each factor equal to 0. To illustrate, the quadratic equation $x^2 + 4x = 5$ can be solved by factoring, using the following procedure:

Write the quadratic equation in standard form:	$x^2 + 4x - 5 = 0$
Factor the quadratic polynomial:	$(x + 5)(x - 1) = 0$
Set each factor equal to 0:	$(x + 5 = 0) \vee (x - 1 = 0)$
Solve each equation:	$x = -5 \vee \quad x = 1$
Write the solution set:	$\{-5, 1\}$

Each member of the solution set can be checked by substituting for x in the *original* equation.

Let $x = -5$.

$$\frac{x^2 + 4x}{(-5)^2 + 4(-5)} = 5$$
$$25 - 20$$
$$5 = 5$$

Let $x = 1$.

$$\frac{x^2 + 4x}{(1)^2 + 4(1)} = 5$$
$$1 + 4$$
$$5 = 5$$

When solving quadratic equations, keep in mind that:

● The quadratic equation must be expressed in standard form *before* you attempt to factor the quadratic polynomial.

● Every quadratic equation has *two* solutions. Each solution is called a **root** of the equation.

● The solution set of a quadratic equation can be checked by verifying that each different root makes the *original* equation a true statement.

● Not every quadratic equation can be solved by factoring. However, in this course, only quadratic equations that can be solved by factoring will be considered.

Examples ▮▮▮▮

1. Solve for x: $2x^2 - 15 = 7x$.

Solution:

Write the quadratic equation, which must be put into standard form:	$2x^2 - 15 = 7x$
Subtract $7x$ from each side:	$2x^2 - 15 - 7x = 7x - 7x$
Simplify:	$2x^2 - 7x - 15 = 0$
Factor the quadratic polynomial:	$(2x + 3)(x - 5) = 0$
Set each factor equal to 0:	$(2x + 3 = 0) \vee (x - 5) = 0$
Solve each equation:	$2x = -3 \vee \quad x = 5$
	$x = \dfrac{-3}{2}$

The solution set is $\left\{\dfrac{-3}{2}, 5\right\}$. The check is left for you.

2. Solve for p: $p^2 = 3p$.

Solution: $p^2 - 3p = 0$
$$p(p - 3) = 0$$
$$p = 0) \vee (p - 3 = 0)$$
$$p = 3$$

The solution set is $\{0, 3\}$. The check is left for you.

Note: A common error in solving this type of equation is to begin by dividing each side of the original equation by p. This is incorrect since we would then be dividing by 0, one of the solutions of the equation.

3. Solve for a: $a^2 + 6a + 9 = 0$.

Solution: $(a+3)(a+3) = 0$
$$(a+3=0) \lor (a+3=0)$$
$$a = -3 \lor \quad a = -3$$

The two roots are equal, so the root does not have to be written twice in the solution set.

The solution set is $\{-3\}$. The check is left for you.

4. Solve for y: $y^2 - 49 = 0$.

Solution: $(y-7)(y+7) = 0$
$$(y-7=0) \lor (y+7=0)$$
$$y = 7 \lor \quad y = -7$$

The solution set is $\{-7, 7\}$. The check is left for you.

5. Solve for a: $6a^2 + 18a + 12 = 0$.

Solution: Observe that 6 is a common factor of each term of the equation. Therefore the equation may be simplified *before* attempting to factor the quadratic polynomial by dividing each term of the equation by 6.

$$\frac{6a^2}{6} + \frac{18a}{6} + \frac{12}{6} = \frac{0}{6}$$
$$a^2 + 3a + 2 = 0$$
$$(a+2)(a+1) = 0$$
$$(a+2) = 0 \lor (a+1) = 0$$
$$a = -2 \lor \quad a = -1$$

The solution set is $\{-2, -1\}$. The check is left for you.

6. One positive number is 4 more than another. The sum of the squares of the two numbers is 40. Find the numbers.

Solution: Let x = smaller number.

Then $x + 4$ = larger number.
$$x^2 + (x+4)^2 = 40$$
$$x^2 + (x+4)(x+4) = 40$$
$$x^2 + x^2 + 8x + 16 = 40$$
$$2x^2 + 8x + 16 = 40$$
$$2x^2 + 8x + 16 - 40 = 0$$
$$\frac{2x^2}{2} + \frac{8x}{2} - \frac{24}{2} = \frac{0}{2}$$
$$x^2 + 4x - 12 = 0$$
$$(x+6)(x-2) = 0$$
$$(x+6) = 0 \lor (x-2) = 0$$
$$x = -6 \lor x = 2$$

| Reject -6 since numbers must be positive. | $x + 4 = 2 + 4 = 6$ |

The two numbers are **2** and **6**. Check the answer in the statement of the problem. Is the sum of the squares of 2 and 6 equal to 40? Yes, since $2^2 + 6^2 = 4 + 36 = 40$.

7. Solve for n: $\dfrac{n-4}{2} = \dfrac{3n}{n+4}$.

Solution: Cross-multiply. Then write the quadratic equation in standard form.

$$(n-4)(n+4) = 2(3n)$$
$$n^2 - 16 = 6n$$
$$n^2 - 6n - 16 = 0$$
$$(n-8)(n+2) = 0$$
$$(n-8 = 0) \vee (n+2 = 0)$$
$$n = 8 \vee \qquad n = -2$$

The solution set is $\{-2, 8\}$. The check is left for you.   ▬▬▬

SOLVING HIGHER DEGREE EQUATIONS BY FACTORING COMPLETELY. Sometimes more than one factoring technique must be applied in expressing a polynomial in factored form, so that the zero product rule can be used. This is illustrated in the example that follows. The check is left for you.

Examples ▬▬▬

8. Solve for n: $n^3 + 5n^2 - 6n = 0$.

Solution:

Factor out the GCF of n:	$n^3 + 5n^2 - 6n = 0$
Factor the quadratic polynomial:	$n(n^2 + 5n - 6) = 0$
Use the zero product rule:	$n(n+6)(n-1) = 0$
	$(n = 0) \vee (n+6 = 0) \vee (n-1 = 0)$
	$n = 0 \vee \qquad n = -6 \vee n = 1$

The solution set is $\{0, -6, 1\}$.

Note: The solution set has three members since the highest power of the variable in the original equation is 3. The original equation is a cubic equation, called a *third-degree equation*.   ▬▬▬

EXERCISE SET 6.5

1–40. Find the solution set for each of the following equations:

1. $(x+2)(x-8) = 0$
2. $y^2 + 3y + 2 = 0$
3. $x^2 + 14x + 49 = 0$
4. $x^2 - 7x = 0$
5. $x^2 - 5x + 4 = 0$
6. $x^2 - x = 12$
7. $a^2 + a = 56$
8. $3x^2 - x = 0$

9. $q^2 - 6q = 27$
10. $11n - n^2 = 0$
11. $2r^2 - 5r - 3 = 0$
12. $6 = t^2 - t$
13. $y^3 - 9y = 0$
14. $x^2 + 4x = 60$
15. $y^2 + 9y = 36$
16. $2h^2 - 32 = 0$
17. $2a^2 + 10a + 8 = 0$
18. $t^3 - 90t = 10t$
19. $5(x^2 - 2) = -23x$
20. $2x(x + 5) = 6 - x$
21. $x^3 + 2x^2 - 3x = 0$
22. $3n^2 = 3n + 60$
23. $y^3 + 5y^2 = 50y$
24. $8p^2 = 6p - p^2$

25. $0 = -(x^2 + 2x - 63)$
26. $2n^2 + 9n = 5$
27. $2x^2 + 48 = 20x$
28. $9x^2 - 12x + 4 = 0$
29. $2b^2 - 18 = 5b$
30. $3a^3 + a^2 = 2a$
31. $6x = x^2$
32. $n^2 = 10n + 3000$
33. $35 + w^2 = 12w$
34. $b(b - 2) = b$
35. $10x^2 = 3(x + 9)$
36. $(x - 3)(x - 1) = 24$
37. $6t^2 = 7t + 3$
38. $(x - 2)(x + 1) = 10$
39. $8x^2 + 18x = 5$
40. $(t + 2)^2 - 6(t + 2) - 27 = 0$

41–44. Cross-multiply and then solve for x.

41. $\dfrac{x + 5}{x + 1} = \dfrac{x - 1}{4}$

42. $\dfrac{x - 3}{x - 2} = \dfrac{x + 3}{2x}$

43. $\dfrac{x - 2}{x} = \dfrac{x + 4}{3x}$

44. $\dfrac{x - 7}{x + 1} = \dfrac{x - 10}{2x + 1}$

45–51. Solve each of the following algebraically, and check:

45. One positive number is 5 more than another. The sum of their squares is 53. Find both numbers.

46. The square of a certain positive number is 10 more than three times the number. Find the number.

47. One positive number is 8 more than another. The sum of their squares is 130. Find both numbers.

48. The square of a positive number decreased by four times the number is 12. Find the positive number.

49. The sum of the squares of two consecutive positive integers is 52. Find the integers.

50. Find three consecutive positive even integers such that the difference in the squares of the first and the third is 48.

51. Find three consecutive odd integers such that three times the square of the first integer is twelve more than the product of the second and third integers.

6.6 SOLVING WORD PROBLEMS INVOLVING QUADRATIC EQUATIONS

KEY IDEAS

The solutions to many types of word problems lead to quadratic equations. A few representative types will be discussed in this section.

GEOMETRY-RELATED PROBLEMS. It is possible that both roots of a quadratic equation may *not* satisfy the conditions of a word problem. For example, it may be necessary to reject any negative roots that arise in solving a quadratic equation in which the variable represents a physical dimension such as length or width.

Examples

1. The length of a rectangle exceeds the width by 6. If the area is 55, find the dimensions of the rectangle.

Solution: Let x = width of the rectangle.
Then $x + 6$ = length of the rectangle.

$$\text{Length} \times \text{Width} = \text{Area}$$
$$(x + 6)x = 55$$
$$x^2 + 6x = 55$$
$$x^2 + 6x - 55 = 0$$
$$(x - 5)(x + 11) = 0$$
$$(x - 5 = 0) \vee (x + 11 = 0)$$
$$x = 5 \vee x = -11$$

Reject this answer since the width cannot be a negative number.
The width of the rectangle is **5**, and the length is **11**.

Check: The length (11) exceeds the width (5) by 6, and the area is 55 since $11 \times 5 = 55$.

2. The length of a rectangular garden is twice its width. The garden is surrounded by a rectangular concrete walk having a uniform width of 4 feet. If the area of the garden and the walk is 330 square feet, what are the dimensions of the garden?

Solution: Let x = width of the garden.
Then $2x$ = length of the garden.

In the accompanying diagram the innermost rectangle represents the garden. Since the walk has a uniform width, the width of the larger (outer) rectangle is $4 + x + 4 = x + 8$. The length of the larger rectangle is $4 + 2x + 4 = 2x + 8$. The area of the larger rectangle is given as 330. Hence:

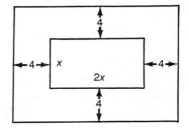

$$\text{Length} \times \text{Width} = \text{Area}$$
$$(2x + 8)(x + 8) = 330$$
$$2x^2 + 24x + 64 = 330$$
$$2x^2 + 24x + 64 - 330 = 0$$
$$2x^2 + 24x - 266 = 0$$
$$\frac{2x^2}{2} + \frac{24x}{2} - \frac{266}{2} = \frac{0}{2}$$
$$x^2 + 12x - 133 = 0$$
$$(x - 7)(x + 19) = 0$$
$$(x - 7) = 0 \vee (x + 19) = 0$$
$$x = 7 \vee \qquad x = -19.$$

Reject -19 since the width must be a positive number.
The width of the garden is **7 feet** and the length is **14 feet**.

NUMBER-RELATED PROBLEMS. In some problems, two or more numbers are related in a way that allows them to be represented using the same variable. Additional information about these unknown numbers is included in the problem so that an equation involving the variable can be written and solved.

Examples

3. The difference between two positive numbers is 5, and the product of the numbers is 36. Find the two numbers.

Solution: Let $x =$ smaller positive number.
Then $x + 5 =$ larger positive number.

$$\overbrace{\text{Product of numbers}}\overbrace{\text{is } 36}$$

$$x(x + 5) = 36$$
$$x^2 + 5x = 36$$
$$x^2 + 5x - 36 = 0$$
$$(x - 4)(x + 9) = 0$$
$$(x - 4 = 0) \vee (x + 9 = 0)$$
$$x = 4 \vee \qquad x = -9$$

Reject -9 since the problem states that the numbers are positive.

The smaller number $= x = 4$ and the larger number $= x + 5 = 9$. The check is left for you.

4. If the second of three positive consecutive integers is added to the product of the first and the third, the result is 71. Find the integers.

Solution: Let $x =$ first positive integer.

Then $x + 1 =$ next larger consecutive positive integer.

and $x + 2 =$ third of three positive consecutive integers.

Second integer + product of first and third is 71

$$x + 1 \quad + \quad x(x + 2) \quad = 71$$
$$x + 1 \quad + \quad x^2 + 2x \quad = 71$$
$$x^2 + 3x + 1 \quad = 71$$
$$x^2 + 3x + 1 - 71 \quad = 0$$
$$x^2 + 3x - 70 \quad = 0$$
$$(x - 7)(x + 10) \quad = 0$$
$$(x - 7 = 0) \lor (x + 10 \quad = 0)$$
$$x = 7 \lor x \quad = -10.$$

Reject -10 since the integers must be positive.

The three consecutive integers are **7, 8**, and **9**. The check is left for you.

EXERCISE SET 6.6

1. Find a positive number that is 42 less than its square.

2. Find two consecutive positive integers such that the square of the first decreased by 25 equals three times the second.

3. Find three consecutive positive odd integers such that the square of the smallest exceeds two times the largest by 7.

4. The sum of two positive integers is 31. If the sum of the squares of these numbers is 625, find the smaller of the numbers.

5. Find three consecutive positive integers such that the square of the first is equal to the third.

6. The sum of a number and the square of its additive inverse is 30. What is the number?

7. When the first of three consecutive positive integers is multiplied by the third, the result is 1 less than six times the second. Find the three integers.

8. Find three positive consecutive odd integers such that the square of the smallest is 9 more than the sum of the other two.

9. Find three consecutive positive integers such that the product of the first and the third integer is 15.

10. The side of a certain square is 3 feet longer than that of another square. The sum of the areas is 117 square feet. Find the length of the *smaller* square.

11. If a side of a square is doubled and an adjacent side is diminished by 3, a rectangle is formed whose area is numerically greater than the area of the square by twice the original side of the square. Find the dimensions of the original square.

12. One positive number exceeds another by 5. The sum of their squares is 193. Find both numbers.

13. The sum of two positive numbers is 12. The sum of their squares is 90. Find both numbers.

14. One positive number is 1 more than twice the other number. The difference of their squares is 40. Find both numbers.

15. A rectangular picture 30 cm wide and 50 cm long is surrounded by a frame having a uniform width. If the combined area of the picture and the frame is 2016 sq. cm, what is the width if the frame?

16. The art staff of a high school is determining the dimensions of paper to be used in a school publication. The area of each sheet is to be 432 sq cm. The staff has agreed on margins of 3 cm on each side and 4 cm on top and bottom. If the printed matter is to occupy 192 cm on each page, what must be the overall length and width of the paper?

17. A rectangular picture 24 inches by 32 inches is surrounded by a border of uniform width. If the area of the border is 528 square inches less than the area of the picture, find the width of the border.

18. The perimeter of a certain rectangle is 24 inches. If the length is doubled and the width is tripled, then the area is increased by 160 square inches. Find the dimensions of the original square.

CHAPTER 6 REVIEW EXERCISES

REGENTS REVIEW. *Problems included in this section are similar in form and difficulty to those found on the New York State Regents Examination for Course I of the Three-Year Sequence for High School Mathematics. Problems preceded by an asterisk have actually appeared on a previous Course I Regents Examination.*

1. One factor of $x^2 - 4x - 21$ is $x + 3$. What is the other factor?

2. Express as the product of two binomials: $x^2 + 2x - 15$.

*3. Factor: $x^2 + x - 30$.

4. Factor: $x^2 - 36$.

*5. The area of a rectangle is represented by $x^2 + 2x$ and the length by $x + 2$. Express the width of the rectangle in terms of x.

6. Find the *positive* root of the equation $2x^2 - 18 = 0$.

*7. Factor: $x^2 - 7x + 10$.

8. Factor completely: $2x^2 - 50$.

*9. Factor: $9x^2 - 1$.

10. Factor completely: $x^3 - 10x^2 - 56x$.

11. Factor completely: $r^3s - rs^3$.

12. Factor: $3x^2 + 2x - 5$.

*13. Factor: $x^2 - y^2$.

*14. Find three consecutive even integers such that the square of the first is 80 less than the square of the third.

*15. A garden is in the shape of a square. The length of one side of the garden is increased by 3 feet, and the length of an adjacent side is increased by 2 feet. The garden now has an area of 72 square feet. What is the length of a side of the original square garden?

*16. Find two consecutive positive integers such that the square of the smaller is 1 more than four times the larger.

17. Solve for x and check: $x(x + 3) - 4(x - 2) = 14$.

*18. One factor of $25x^2 - 9$ is $5x - 3$. The other factor is:
(1) $5x - 3$ (2) $5x + 3$ (3) $-5x - 3$ (4) $-5x + 3$

19. A root of the equation $x^2 - 13x - 48 = 0$ is:
(1) 8   (2) 2   (3) 12   (4) 16

*20. The solution set of $x^2 - 16 = 0$ is:
(1) $\{2, -8\}$ (2) $\{4, -4\}$ (3) $\{-4\}$ (4) $\{4\}$

*21. Which are the factors of $15y^2 - 5y$?
(1) $5y - 1$ and $3y + 5$ (3) $5y$ and $3y$
(2) $5y$ and $3y - 1$ (4) $5y - y$ and $3y + 5$

*22. Which is the solution set of $x^2 - 3x - 10 = 0$?
(1) $\{-5, 2\}$ (2) $\{5, -2\}$ (3) $\{2, 5\}$ (4) $\{-2, -5\}$

23. One positive number is 7 more than another. The sum of their squares is 85. Find both numbers.

CHAPTER 7

Operations with Algebraic Fractions

7.1   SIMPLIFYING ALGEBRAIC FRACTIONS

A fraction may be simplified by dividing the numerator and the denominator by common factors (other than 1). For example,

$$\frac{10}{15} = \frac{\overset{1}{\cancel{5}} \cdot 2}{\cancel{5} \cdot 3} = \frac{\mathbf{2}}{\mathbf{3}}.$$

The factor of 5 appears in the numerator and the denominator, so that the quotient is 1. The fraction $\frac{2}{3}$ is in lowest terms since the numerator and the denominator do not have any common factors greater than 1.

ALGEBRAIC FRACTIONS.   An **algebraic fraction** is the quotient of two polynomials, provided that the denominator is not equal to 0. Here are some examples of algebraic fractions:

$$\frac{-3}{7}, \quad \frac{2x}{5y}, \quad \frac{a^2 b}{bc}, \quad \frac{x+y}{x^2 - xy}.$$

Recall that division by 0 is not permitted. Whenever a fraction with a variable denominator is written, the replacement set for the variable(s) in the denominator will be understood to *exclude* any value(s) that would make the denominator equal to 0. For example, for the fraction $\dfrac{3}{m-1}$, m cannot be equal to 1. If m were equal to 1, the denominator of the fraction would be equal to 0 since $1 - 1 = 0$.

145

CANCELLATION OF COMMON FACTORS. Whenever a fraction contains the same *factor* in both the numerator and the denominator, the quotient of these identical *factors* is 1, so that they can be crossed out. This process is sometimes referred to as **cancellation**. For example, since $3a$ is a *factor* of both $3ab^2$ and $3ay$, then

$$\frac{\overset{1}{\cancel{3a}}b^2}{\underset{1}{\cancel{3a}}y} = \frac{b^2}{y}.$$

On the other hand, it would be incorrect to cancel $3a$ in a fraction in which $3a$ appeared as one of the *terms* of a polynomial. Here is an example of an illegal cancellation:

$$\frac{\cancel{3a} + b^2}{\cancel{3a}}.$$

No cancellation of identical *terms* in the numerator and denominator is permitted since $3a$ is *not* a *factor* of the numerator.

WRITING FRACTIONS IN LOWEST TERMS. Algebraic fractions, like arithmetic fractions, are written in *lowest terms* by factoring out the GCF of the numerator and the denominator and then *canceling* common factors.

Examples ▦

1. Write in lowest terms: $\dfrac{10x^6}{15x^2}$.

Solution: The GCF of $10x^6$ and $15x^2$ is $5x^2$.

$$\frac{10x^6}{15x^2} = \frac{\overset{1}{\cancel{5x^2}} \cdot 2x^4}{\underset{1}{\cancel{5x^2}} \cdot 3} = \frac{2x^4}{3}$$

2. Write in lowest terms: $\dfrac{14a^5b}{35a^4b^3}$.

Solution: The GCF of $14a^5b$ and $35a^4b^3$ is $7a^4b$.

$$\frac{14a^5b}{35a^4b^3} = \frac{\overset{1}{\cancel{7a^4b}} \cdot 2a}{\underset{1}{\cancel{7a^4b}} \cdot 5b^2} = \frac{2a}{5b^2}$$

Notice that the variable part of the answer may be obtained by finding the quotient of the variable factors of the numerator and denominator:

$$\frac{\overset{2}{\cancel{14}}a^5b}{\underset{5}{\cancel{35}}a^4b^3} = \frac{2a^{5-4}b^{1-3}}{5} = \frac{2ab^{-2}}{5} = \frac{2a}{5b^2}$$

3.   Write in lowest terms: $\dfrac{6a^5 - 20a^3}{8a^2}$.

Solution: *Step 1*. Factor out the GCF from the numerator.

$$\frac{6a^5 - 20a^3}{8a^2} = \frac{2a^3(3a^2 - 10)}{8a^2}$$

Step 2. Cancel common factors in the numerator and denominator. Observe that $8 \div 2 = 4$ and $a^3 \div a^2 = a$.

$$\frac{\overset{1a}{\cancel{2a^3}}(3a^2 - 10)}{\underset{4}{\cancel{8a^2}}}$$

Step 3. Write the remaining factors.

$$\frac{a(3a^2 - 10)}{4}$$

4.   Write in lowest terms: $\dfrac{-2x - 10}{x^2 - 25}$.

Solution: First factor the numerator and the denominator.

$$\frac{-2x - 10}{x^2 - 25} = \frac{-2(x + 5)}{(x + 5)(x - 5)}$$

Then cancel common factors: $\dfrac{\overset{1}{-2(\cancel{x + 5})}}{\underset{1}{(\cancel{x + 5})(x - 5)}} = \dfrac{-2}{(x - 5)}$

EXERCISE SET 7.1

1–24.   Write each fraction in lowest terms.

1. $\dfrac{28a^5}{4a^2}$

2. $\dfrac{-52x^3y}{-13xy}$

3. $\dfrac{100c^2}{25c^5}$

4. $\dfrac{32w^7z^6}{18w^2z^9}$

5. $\dfrac{2ab^2 - 2a^2b}{4ab}$

6. $\dfrac{-x - y}{x + y}$

7. $\dfrac{10y^3 - 5y^2}{15y}$

8. $\dfrac{12x^3 - 21x^4}{9x^2}$

9. $\dfrac{0.48xy - 0.16y}{0.8y}$

10. $\dfrac{21r^2s - 7r^3s^2}{14rs}$

11. $\dfrac{-3x - 6}{x + 2}$

12. $\dfrac{y^2 + 4y}{2y + 8}$

13. $\dfrac{3x + 15}{x^2 + 5x}$

14. $\dfrac{x^2 - 4}{x + 2}$

15. $\dfrac{10y + 30}{y^2 - 9}$

16. $\dfrac{-6a + 18}{a^2 - 3a}$

17. $\dfrac{2x - 16}{x^2 - 64}$

18. $\dfrac{x + 1}{x^2 - x - 2}$

19. $\dfrac{x^2 - 9}{x^2 + 3x + 4}$

20. $\dfrac{1 - x^2}{3x + 3}$

21. $\dfrac{2x^2 - 50}{2x^2 + 14x + 20}$

22. $\dfrac{x^2 - x - 42}{x^2 + 7x + 6}$

23. $\dfrac{a^2 - 4b^2}{(a + 2b)^3}$

24. $\dfrac{x^2 - y^2}{(x - y)^2}$

7.2 MULTIPLYING AND DIVIDING FRACTIONS

KEY IDEAS

To **multiply** fractions, write the product of the numerators over the product of the denominators. Then write the resulting fraction in lowest terms.

$$\frac{4}{9} \cdot \frac{3}{10} = \frac{4 \cdot 3}{9 \cdot 10} = \frac{12}{90} = \frac{2}{15}.$$

Sometimes the multiplication process can be made easier by canceling pairs of common factors in the numerator and the denominator *before* multiplying the fractions. For example,

$$\frac{4}{9} \cdot \frac{3}{10} = \frac{\overset{2}{\cancel{4}}}{\underset{3}{\cancel{9}}} \cdot \frac{\overset{1}{\cancel{3}}}{\underset{5}{\cancel{10}}} = \frac{2}{15}.$$

To **divide** one fraction by another fraction, multiply the first fraction by the reciprocal of the second fraction.

MULTIPLYING FRACTIONS. Algebraic fractions are *multiplied* in much the same way that fractions are multiplied in arithmetic.

Examples ▰▰

1. Write the product: $\left(\dfrac{2x^3}{3y^5}\right)\left(\dfrac{4x^2}{7y}\right)$.

Solution: $\left(\dfrac{2x^3}{3y^5}\right)\left(\dfrac{4x^2}{7y}\right) = \dfrac{(2x^3)(4x^2)}{(3y^5)(7y)} = \dfrac{8x^5}{21y^6}$

2. Write the product in lowest terms: $\left(\dfrac{2a^7}{3b^2}\right)\left(\dfrac{12b^5}{5a^3}\right)$.

Solution: Cancel common factors in the numerator and denominator *before* multiplying.

$$\frac{\overset{a^4}{\cancel{2a^7}}}{\underset{1}{\cancel{3b^2}}} \cdot \frac{\overset{4b^3}{\cancel{12b^5}}}{\cancel{5a^3}} = \frac{(2a^4)(4b^3)}{5} = \frac{8a^4b^3}{5}$$

Fractions that contain polynomials should be factored, if possible, and then simplified *before* they are multiplied.

Examples ▰▰▰

3. Write the product in lowest terms: $\dfrac{12y^2}{x^2+7x} \cdot \dfrac{x^2-49}{2y^5}$.

Solution: Factor the binomials, and then cancel pairs of common factors in the numerator and denominator before multiplying.

$$\frac{12y^2}{x^2+7x} \cdot \frac{x^2-49}{2y^5} = \frac{12y^2}{x(x+7)} \cdot \frac{(x+7)(x-7)}{2y^5}$$

$$= \frac{\overset{6}{\cancel{12}}\cancel{y^2}}{x(x+7)} \cdot \frac{(\cancel{x+7})(x-7)}{\underset{1y^3}{\cancel{2y^5}}}$$

Write the products of the remaining factors in the numerator and denominator:

$$= \frac{6(x-7)}{xy^3}$$

4. Write the product in lowest terms: $\dfrac{a^3-a^2b}{20b^3} \cdot \dfrac{5a+5b}{a^2}$.

Solution: Before multiplying, factor the numerators of each fraction. Cancel pairs of common factors in the numerators and denominators. Then multiply.

$$\frac{a^3-a^2b}{20b^3} \cdot \frac{5a+5b}{a^2} = \frac{\cancel{a^2}(a-b)}{\underset{4}{\cancel{20}b^3}} \cdot \frac{\cancel{5}(a+b)}{\cancel{a^2}}$$

$$= \frac{(a-b)(a+b)}{4b^3}$$

$$= \frac{a^2-b^2}{4b^3}$$

DIVIDING FRACTIONS. Algebraic fractions are *divided* in much the same way that fractions are divided in arithmetic.

Examples ▰▰▰

5. Write the quotient in lowest terms: $\dfrac{8m^2}{3} \div \dfrac{6m^3}{3m-12}$.

Solution: To begin, change from division to multiplication by taking the reciprocal of the second fraction: Where possible, factor.

$$\frac{8m^2}{3} \div \frac{6m^3}{3m-12} = \frac{8m^2}{3} \cdot \frac{3m-12}{6m^3}$$

Cancel pairs of common factors in the numerator and denominator:

$$= \frac{\overset{4}{\cancel{8m^2}}}{\underset{1}{\cancel{3}}} \cdot \frac{\overset{1}{\cancel{3}}(m-4)}{\underset{3m}{\cancel{6m^3}}}$$

Multiply the remaining factors:

$$= \frac{4(m-4)}{3m}$$

6. Divide and express in simplest form: $\dfrac{x^2-2x-8}{x^2-25} \div \dfrac{x^2-4}{2x+10}$.

Solution: Change to a multiplication example, and factor the numerators and denominators of each fraction.

$$\frac{x^2-2x-8}{x^2-25} \div \frac{x^2-4}{2x+10} = \frac{x^2-2x-8}{x^2-25} \cdot \frac{2x+10}{x^2-4}$$
$$= \frac{(x+2)(x-4)}{(x-5)(x+5)} \cdot \frac{2(x+5)}{(x-2)(x+2)}$$
$$= \frac{2(x-4)}{(x-5)(x-2)}$$

DIMENSIONAL ANALYSIS.

In converting units of measurement it is sometimes helpful to treat the units of measurement as "factors" which can be canceled in the multiplication process in the same way that common numerical and literal factors are canceled when multiplying fractions. For example, to convert a speed of 18 kilometers (km) per hour (hr) to meters (m) per minute (min), proceed as follows:

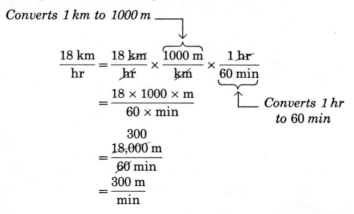

Therefore, a speed of 300 m/min is equivalent to a speed of 18 km/hr.

EXERCISE SET 7.2

1–16. Write the product or quotient in simplest form.

1. $\dfrac{12a^2}{5c} \cdot \dfrac{15c^3}{8a}$

2. $\dfrac{3y}{4x} \cdot \dfrac{8x^2-4x}{9y}$

3. $\dfrac{5y+10}{x^2} \cdot \dfrac{3x^2-x^3}{15}$

4. $\dfrac{8}{rs} \cdot \dfrac{r^2s-rs^2}{12}$

5. $\dfrac{3x}{5y} \div \dfrac{12x^2-15x}{20y^2}$

6. $\dfrac{2b^2-2b}{3a} \cdot \left(\dfrac{2a}{3b}\right)^2$

7. $\dfrac{18}{x^2-y^2} \div \dfrac{9}{x+y}$

8. $\dfrac{(a+b)^2}{4} \div \dfrac{a+b}{2}$

9. $\dfrac{2x+6}{8} \div \dfrac{x+3}{2}$

10. $\left(\dfrac{ay^2}{b^4}\right)^3 \cdot \left(\dfrac{b}{y^3}\right)^5$

11. $\left(\dfrac{ax^2}{b^3}\right)^3 \div \left(\dfrac{a^2x}{b}\right)^2$

12. $\left(\dfrac{3x}{4y}\right)^2 \div \dfrac{9x^2-6x}{8y}$

13. $\dfrac{(x-7)^2}{x^2-6x-7} \cdot \dfrac{5x+5}{x^2-49}$

14. $\dfrac{a^2-b^2}{2ab} \div \dfrac{a-b}{a^2}$

15. $\dfrac{x^2-9}{x^2-8x} \cdot \dfrac{x-8}{x^2-6x+9}$

16. $\dfrac{x^2-3x}{x^2+3x-10} \div \dfrac{x^2-x-6}{x^2-4}$

17. The area of a rectangle is represented by $p^2 - 2p - 35$, and the length is represented by $p + 5$. In terms of p, what is the width of the rectangle?

18–20. Perform the indicated operations, and express the result in simplest form.

18. $\dfrac{7a^2}{12b^2}\left(\dfrac{2a}{5b^2}\right)^3 \div \dfrac{21a^3}{25b^7}$

19. $\dfrac{4x-8ax^2}{3} \div \dfrac{8a^2x^2-2}{3+6ax}$

20. $\dfrac{t^2-4}{t^2-1} \div \dfrac{4t+12}{9t+9} \cdot \dfrac{t^2+2t-3}{2-t}$

21. Convert a speed of 25 m/min so that it is expressed in the following units of measurement.

    a. m/sec   b. m/hr   c. Km/sec   d. Km/hr

22. Convert a speed of 45 m/hr so that it is expressed in

    a. Km/hr   b. Km/sec   c. cm/min   d. cm/sec

7.3   ADDING AND SUBTRACTING FRACTIONS WITH LIKE DENOMINATORS

―――――― KEY IDEAS ――――――

To **add** (or **subtract**) fractions having like denominators, write the sum (*or* difference) of the numerators over the common denominator.

Addition

$$\frac{5}{9}+\frac{2}{9}=\frac{5+2}{9}=\frac{\mathbf{7}}{\mathbf{9}}$$

Subtraction

$$\frac{7}{11}-\frac{4}{11}=\frac{7-4}{11}=\frac{\mathbf{3}}{\mathbf{11}}$$

COMBINING FRACTIONS. In the methods used to add or subtract algebraic fractions are patterned after those used in arithmetic.

Examples ▬▬

1. Write the sum in lowest terms: $\dfrac{5y}{9x^2} + \dfrac{y}{9x^2}$.

Solution: Write the sum of the numerators over the common denominator and simplify.

$$\frac{5y}{9x^2} + \frac{y}{9x^2} = \frac{5y + y}{9x^2}$$

$$= \frac{6y}{9x^2}$$

$$= \frac{\overset{2}{\cancel{6}y}}{\underset{3}{\cancel{9}x^2}} = \frac{2y}{3x^2}$$

2. Write the difference in lowest terms: $\dfrac{5a + b}{10ab} - \dfrac{3a - b}{10ab}$.

Solution: Write the difference of the numerators over the common denominator and simplify.

$$\frac{5a + b}{10ab} - \frac{3a - b}{10ab} = \frac{5a + b - (3a - b)}{10ab}$$

$$= \frac{5a + b - 3a + b}{10ab}$$

$$= \frac{(5a - 3a) + (b + b)}{10ab}$$

$$= \frac{2a + 2b}{10ab}$$

$$= \frac{\overset{1}{\cancel{2}}(a + b)}{\underset{5}{\cancel{10}}ab} = \frac{a + b}{5ab}$$

▬▬

NEGATIVE SIGNS AND FRACTIONS. Notice that $\dfrac{-1}{1}$ and $\dfrac{1}{-1}$ are each equivalent to -1. Similarly, all of the following algebraic fractions are equivalent since they have a coefficient of -1:

$$\frac{-x}{y}, \qquad \frac{x}{-y}, \qquad \text{and} \qquad -\frac{x}{y}.$$

An equivalent fraction results if the signs (that is, the factor of -1) are exchanged between any two of the following: the numerator, the denominator, and the sign of the fraction.

Example ▬▬▬

3. Express as a single fraction in lowest terms: $\dfrac{4x}{x^2-4}+\dfrac{x+6}{4-x^2}$.

Solution: Rewrite $4-x^2$ as $-x^2+4$. Then factor out -1 so that

$$-x^2+4=-(x^2-4).$$

$$\frac{4x}{x^2-4}+\frac{x+6}{4-x^2}=\frac{4x}{x^2-4}+\frac{x+6}{-(x^2-4)}$$

Write the negative sign in front
of the second fraction:

$$=\frac{4x}{x^2-4}-\frac{x+6}{x^2-4}$$

Write the numerators over the
common denominator:

$$=\frac{4x-(x+6)}{x^2-4}$$

Simplify the numerator:

$$=\frac{4x-x-6}{x^2-4}$$

Write the fraction in lowest terms:

$$=\frac{3x-6}{x^2-4}$$

Factor, and cancel common factors:

$$=\frac{\overset{1}{\cancel{3(x-2)}}}{\underset{1}{\cancel{(x-2)}(x+2)}}$$

$$=\frac{3}{x+2}$$

EXERCISE SET 7.3

1–14. Write the sum or difference in lowest terms.

1. $\dfrac{2a}{14}+\dfrac{5a}{14}$

2. $\dfrac{5x+2}{3}-\dfrac{x+1}{3}$

3. $\dfrac{4}{a+b}+\dfrac{1}{-a-b}$

4. $\dfrac{2r+s}{r+2s}+\dfrac{r+5s}{r+2s}$

5. $\dfrac{3(n^2-2n)}{10n}+\dfrac{2n^2+n}{10n}$

6. $\dfrac{3(2b-1)}{4b}-\dfrac{5b+3}{4b}$

7. $\dfrac{2(3y+15)}{9y}-\dfrac{3(4y+8)}{9y}$

8. $\dfrac{7(x+y)}{12xy}-\dfrac{3x-y}{12xy}$

9. $\dfrac{p}{p^2-9}+\dfrac{3}{9-p^2}$

10. $\dfrac{5a-b+c}{2a+b}+\dfrac{a+4b-c}{2a+b}$

11. $\dfrac{x+y}{11}-\dfrac{2x+4y}{22}$

12. $\dfrac{a^2-5}{a-b}-\dfrac{b^2-5}{a-b}$

13. $\dfrac{7t+3}{8rs}-\dfrac{3t+7}{8rs}+\dfrac{2(t+5)}{8rs}$

14. $\dfrac{2xb+b^2}{5b^2}+\dfrac{-4xb}{5b^2}+\dfrac{9b^2-8xb}{5b^2}$

7.4 ADDING AND SUBTRACTING FRACTIONS WITH UNLIKE DENOMINATORS

KEY IDEAS

The *lowest common denominator* (LCD) of $\frac{1}{6}$ and $\frac{7}{45}$ may be found by following these steps:

Step	Example
1. Write the prime factorization of each denominator.	1. $6 = 2 \cdot 3$ $45 = 5 \cdot 9 = 5 \cdot 3^2$
2. Write the product of the highest power of each different prime factor that is contained in at least one of the denominators.	2. $LCD = 2 \cdot 5 \cdot 3^2$ $= 10 \cdot 9$ $= \mathbf{90}$

FINDING THE LCD OF ALGEBRAIC FRACTIONS. The LCD of algebraic fractions can be found by following a procedure similar to the one used to find the LCD of arithmetic fractions.

Examples ■■■

1. Find the LCD of the fractions $\dfrac{3}{4ab}$ and $\dfrac{2}{3ab^2}$.

Solution: *Step 1.* Write the prime factorization of each denominator.

$$4ab = 2^2 \cdot a \cdot b \qquad \text{and} \qquad 3ab^2 = 3 \cdot a \cdot b^2$$

Step 2. Write the product of each of the different prime factors. If the same variable (or numerical) base is contained in more than one denominator, then write the variable (or number) with its greatest exponent.

$$\text{LCD} = 2^2 \cdot 3 \cdot a \cdot b^2 = 4 \cdot 3 \cdot ab^2 = \mathbf{12ab^2}$$

2. Find the LCD of the fractions $\dfrac{3x}{x^2 - 1} + \dfrac{5x - 2}{x^2 + 2x + 1}$.

Solution: Factor, and then compare denominators.

$$x^2 - 1 = (x + 1)(x - 1)$$
$$x^2 + 2x + 1 = (x + 1)(x + 1) = (x + 1)^2$$
$$\text{LCD} = (x - 1)(x + 1)^2$$

3. Find the LCD of the fractions $\dfrac{7y}{2y^2 - 18} + \dfrac{5}{4y^2 - 12y}$.

Solution: Factor, and then compare denominators.

$$2y^2 - 18 = 2(y^2 - 9) = 2(y - 3)(y + 3)$$
$$4y^2 - 12y = 4y(y - 3) = 2^2 y(y - 3)$$
$$\text{LCD} = 4y(y - 3)(y + 3)$$

RAISING A FRACTION TO HIGHER TERMS. If the numerator and the denominator of a fraction are each multiplied by the same nonzero quantity, an equivalent fraction results. For example,

$$\frac{2x}{3y} \cdot \frac{4}{4} = \frac{8x}{12y}.$$

The fraction $\dfrac{8x}{12y}$ is equivalent to $\dfrac{2x}{3y}$ since it was obtained by multiplying $\dfrac{2x}{3y}$ by $\dfrac{4}{4}$, which is another way of writing the number 1.

Example

4. Write $\dfrac{5}{8}$ as an equivalent fraction that has 24 as its denominator.

Solution: Since $24 \div 8 = 3$, 8 must be multiplied by 3 in order to obtain 24 as a denominator. To change $\frac{5}{8}$ into an equivalent fraction having 24 as its denominator, multiply *both* the denominator and the numerator by 3.

$$\frac{5}{8} \cdot \frac{3}{3} = \frac{15}{24}$$

COMBINING FRACTIONS WITH UNLIKE DENOMINATORS. To add or subtract fractions in arithmetic, the denominators must be the same. If the denominators are *different*, each fraction must be changed into an equivalent fraction having the LCD as its denominator. This allows the fractions to be combined by writing the sum (or difference) of the numerators over the LCD. Algebraic fractions are combined in much the same way.

Examples

5. Add: $\dfrac{2x + 1}{6} + \dfrac{3x - 5}{8}$.

Solution: The LCD of 6 and 8 is 24. Observe that $24 \div 6 = 4$. This means that multiplying the first fraction by $\frac{4}{4}$ will produce an equivalent fraction having the LCD of 24 as its denominator. Since $24 \div 8 = 3$, multiplying the second fraction by $\frac{3}{3}$ will also give an equivalent fraction having 24 as its denominator.

$$\frac{2x+1}{6}+\frac{3x-5}{8}=\left(\frac{2x+1}{6}\right)\frac{4}{4}+\left(\frac{3x-5}{8}\right)\frac{3}{3}$$

Write the numerators over the LCD:
$$=\frac{4(2x+1)+3(3x-5)}{24}$$

Combine like terms in the
numerator:
$$=\frac{8x+4+9x-15}{24}$$

$$=\frac{17x-11}{24}$$

6. Write the difference in simplest form: $\dfrac{3}{10xy}-\dfrac{10x-y}{5xy^2}$.

Solution: Write the prime factorizations of each denominator.

$$10xy = 2 \cdot 5xy$$
$$5xy^2 = 5xy^2$$
$$\text{LCD} = 2 \cdot 5xy^2$$

Compare each of the factored denominators to the LCD. Multiply the numerator and denominator of each fraction by the factors contained in the LCD that are missing from the denominator of that fraction.

$$\left(\frac{3}{10xy}\right)\frac{y}{y}-\left(\frac{10x-y}{5xy^2}\right)\frac{2}{2}=\frac{3y}{10xy^2}-\frac{2(10x-y)}{10xy^2}$$
$$=\frac{3y-20x+2y}{10xy^2}$$
$$=\frac{5y-20x}{10xy^2}$$
$$=\frac{\overset{1}{\cancel{5}}(y-4x)}{\underset{2}{\cancel{10}xy^2}}$$
$$=\frac{y-4x}{2xy^2}$$

7. Subtract: $\dfrac{7x-2}{4}-x$.

Solution: Rewrite x as $\frac{x}{1}$. Since the LCD of 4 and 1 is 4, multiply the second fraction by $\frac{4}{4}$.

$$\frac{7x-2}{4} - x = \frac{7x-2}{4} - \left(\frac{x}{1}\right)\left(\frac{4}{4}\right)$$

$$= \frac{7x-2}{4} - \frac{4x}{4}$$

$$= \frac{7x-2-4x}{4}$$

$$= \frac{3x-2}{4}$$

8. Combine and express the result in simplest form:

$$\frac{5}{x^2-9} - \frac{3}{x} + \frac{1}{2x+6}.$$

Solution: Write the prime factorizations of each denominator.

$$x^2 - 9 = (x+3)(x-3)$$
$$x = x$$
$$2x + 6 = 2(x+3)$$
$$\text{LCD} = 2x(x+3)(x-3)$$

Compare each of the factored denominators to the LCD. Multiply the numerator and denominator of each fraction by the factors contained in the LCD that are missing from the denominator of that fraction.

$$\left(\frac{5}{(x+3)(x-3)}\right)\frac{2x}{2x} - \left(\frac{3}{x}\right)\frac{2(x+3)(x-3)}{2(x+3)(x-3)} + \left(\frac{1}{2(x+3)}\right)\frac{x(x-3)}{x(x-3)}$$

$$= \frac{5(2x) - 3(2)(x+3)(x-3) + 1(x)(x-3)}{2x(x+3)(x-3)}$$

$$= \frac{10x - 6(x^2-9) + x^2 - 3x}{2x(x+3)(x-3)}$$

$$= \frac{10x - 6x^2 + 54 + x^2 - 3x}{2x(x+3)(x-3)} = \frac{-5x^2 + 7x + 54}{2x(x+3)(x-3)}$$

EXERCISE SET 7.4

1–36. Write each of the following expressions as a single fraction in simplest form:

1. $\dfrac{5x}{6} + \dfrac{2x}{3}$

2. $\dfrac{a+1}{2} - \dfrac{a}{3}$

3. $\dfrac{x+7}{3} + \dfrac{x-2}{4}$

4. $\dfrac{3b}{8a^2} + \dfrac{5b}{12a^5}$

5. $\dfrac{2w-1}{8} - \dfrac{w+2}{6}$

6. $\dfrac{4a}{5x} - \dfrac{3a}{10x}$

7. $\dfrac{3y-2}{2} + \dfrac{2(y+5)}{9}$

8. $\dfrac{2c-9}{5x} - \dfrac{4c+3}{7x}$

9. $\dfrac{x+2}{-3} + \dfrac{x-3}{2}$

10. $\dfrac{4x}{x-1} + 2$

11. $\dfrac{2x}{3} + \dfrac{3x}{4} - \dfrac{x}{6}$

12. $\dfrac{3}{5a^2b} + \dfrac{1}{3a^2b}$

13. $\dfrac{3a+b}{10c} + \dfrac{5a-2b}{4c}$

14. $\dfrac{5t^2-9}{4t^2} + \dfrac{11}{6t}$

15. $\dfrac{7}{t} - \dfrac{3}{t^3} + \dfrac{5t+2}{t^2}$

16. $\dfrac{3}{8rs} + \dfrac{5}{6r^2} - \dfrac{1}{4s^2}$

17. $\dfrac{x-a^2}{a} + 2a$

18. $\dfrac{x^2}{(x+1)^2} - \dfrac{x-1}{x+1}$

19. $\dfrac{3}{x+2} - \dfrac{2}{x-2}$

20. $\dfrac{5}{b-3} - \dfrac{4}{b}$

21. $\dfrac{y}{y^2-9} - \dfrac{1}{y+3}$

22. $\dfrac{3b}{2a} - \dfrac{2a}{3b} + 1$

23. $\dfrac{6}{7p} - 1 + \dfrac{3}{4p}$

24. $\dfrac{2x-y}{3} + \dfrac{x-2z}{4} - \dfrac{y+3z}{2}$

25. $\dfrac{a}{s} - \dfrac{a}{r}$

26. $\dfrac{2}{x^2-1} + \dfrac{1}{2x+2}$

27. $\dfrac{4x}{a^2bc^3} - \dfrac{2x}{abc^2} + \dfrac{7x}{a^3b^2c}$

28. $\dfrac{2}{3} - \dfrac{x}{x-3}$

29. $\dfrac{a}{a-b} + \dfrac{b}{a+b}$

30. $\dfrac{6}{y^2-9} + \dfrac{4}{(y-3)^2}$

31. $\dfrac{3}{x^2-4} + \dfrac{2}{x^2+5x+6}$

32. $\dfrac{5}{r^2-s^2} - \dfrac{3}{(r+s)^2}$

33. $\dfrac{2x}{x^2+7x} - \dfrac{6x-5}{x^2-49}$

34. $w - y - \dfrac{1}{w+y}$

35. $\dfrac{5}{a^2-3a-10} + \dfrac{3a-2}{a^2-25} - \dfrac{2a}{3a+6}$

36. $\dfrac{2b}{b^3-9b} - \dfrac{6}{b^2-4b-21} + 2$

37–39. Find each of the following products by first simplifying the expressions within the parentheses:

37. $\left(\dfrac{r}{s} - \dfrac{s}{r}\right)\left(\dfrac{r}{s} + \dfrac{s}{r}\right)$

38. $\left(2 + \dfrac{2}{x}\right)\left(\dfrac{1}{x+1} - 1\right)$

39. $\left(\dfrac{1}{x+1} - \dfrac{1}{x-1}\right)^2$

7.5 SOLVING EQUATIONS INVOLVING FRACTIONS

KEY IDEAS

The equation

$$\frac{x+1}{4} - \frac{2}{3} = \frac{1}{12}$$

has *fractional coefficients* since it is equivalent to

$$\frac{1}{4}(x+1) - \frac{2}{3} = \frac{1}{12},$$

but it is not a fractional equation.

The equation

$$\frac{2}{y} - \frac{9}{10} = \frac{1}{5y}$$

is an example of a **fractional equation** since some of the *denominators* contain a variable.

Each of these equations can be solved by first clearing the equation of fractions.

SOLVING EQUATIONS WITH FRACTIONS. To solve an equation that has fractional terms, multiply each member of *both* sides of the equation by the least common multiple (that is, the LCM) of the denominators. This will produce an equivalent equation that does not contain any fractions.

Examples

1. Solve for *x* and check: $\dfrac{x+1}{4} - \dfrac{2}{3} = \dfrac{1}{12}$.

    Solution: The LCM of 4, 3, and 12 is 12.

    Multiply each term by 12: $\overset{3}{\cancel{12}}\left(\dfrac{x+1}{\cancel{4}}\right) - \overset{4}{\cancel{12}}\left(\dfrac{2}{\cancel{3}}\right) = \overset{1}{\cancel{12}}\left(\dfrac{1}{\cancel{12}}\right)$

    $$3(x+1) - 4(2) = 1$$
    $$3x + 3 - 8 \quad = 1$$
    $$3x - 5 = 1$$
    $$3x = 5 + 1$$
    $$\frac{3x}{3} = \frac{6}{3}$$
    $$x = \mathbf{2}$$

Check: $\dfrac{x+1}{4} - \dfrac{2}{3} = \dfrac{1}{12}$

$$\begin{array}{c|c} \dfrac{2+1}{4} - \dfrac{2}{3} & \\[2mm] \dfrac{3}{4} - \dfrac{2}{3} & \\[2mm] \dfrac{9}{12} - \dfrac{8}{12} & \\[2mm] \dfrac{1}{12} & \dfrac{1}{12} \end{array}$$

$$\dfrac{1}{12} = \dfrac{1}{12}$$

2. Solve for y: $\dfrac{2}{y} - \dfrac{9}{10} = \dfrac{1}{5y}$.

Solution: The LCM of y, 10, and $5y$ is $10y$.

Multiply each term by $10y$: $\overset{1}{\cancel{10y}}\left(\dfrac{2}{\cancel{y}}\right) - \overset{1}{\cancel{10y}}\left(\dfrac{9}{10}\right) = \overset{2}{\cancel{10y}}\left(\dfrac{1}{\cancel{5y}}\right)$

$$20 - 9y = 2$$
$$-9y = 2 - 20$$
$$\dfrac{-9y}{-9} = \dfrac{-18}{-9}$$
$$y = 2$$

The check is left for you.

3. Solve for the positive value of n: $\dfrac{3}{5} + \dfrac{n-2}{3} = \dfrac{14}{5n}$.

Solution: The LCM of 5, 3, and $5n$ is $15n$.

Multiply each term by $15n$: $\overset{3}{\cancel{15n}}\left(\dfrac{3}{\cancel{5}}\right) + \overset{5}{\cancel{15n}}\left(\dfrac{n-2}{\cancel{3}}\right) = \overset{3}{\cancel{15n}}\left(\dfrac{14}{\cancel{5n}}\right)$

$$9n + 5n(n-2) = 42$$
$$9n + 5n^2 - 10n = 42$$
$$5n^2 - n = 42$$
$$5n^2 - n - 42 = 0$$
$$(5n + 14)(n - 3) = 0$$
$$5n + 14 = 0 \text{ or } n - 3 = 0$$
$$n = -\dfrac{14}{5} \text{ or } n = 3$$

The check is left for you.

EXERCISE SET 7.5

1–26. Solve for the variable and check.

1. $\dfrac{x}{5} - 12 = 4$

2. $\dfrac{x}{3} - \dfrac{x}{4} = 1$

3. $\dfrac{n}{2} - 3 = \dfrac{n}{5}$

4. $\dfrac{a}{4} - \dfrac{a}{5} = 2$

5. $\dfrac{y}{2} = 2 - \dfrac{y}{6}$

6. $\dfrac{b}{4} = \dfrac{2b}{5} + \dfrac{5}{2}$

7. $\dfrac{2x}{5} - 4 = \dfrac{2x}{3}$

8. $\dfrac{2r}{3} - \dfrac{5r}{12} = \dfrac{5}{4}$

9. $\dfrac{5m}{3} - \dfrac{3m}{2} = 2$

10. $\dfrac{5}{x} + 3x = \dfrac{17}{x}$

11. $\dfrac{5}{3} + \dfrac{y+1}{9} = 1$

12. $\dfrac{x-1}{2} - \dfrac{x-1}{3} = 2$

13. $\dfrac{3}{x} - \dfrac{1}{2x} = \dfrac{1}{2}$

14. $\dfrac{2x+3}{18} - \dfrac{x}{9} = \dfrac{2x-1}{6}$

15. $\dfrac{3}{2a-1} + 2 = \dfrac{9}{2a-1}$

16. $\dfrac{x}{4} - \dfrac{x+2}{12} = \dfrac{x-2}{3}$

17. $n - 4 = \dfrac{n-1}{4}$

18. $\dfrac{x-2}{2} + \dfrac{2x-1}{20} = \dfrac{x}{4}$

19. $\dfrac{2x-4}{4} = 5 + \dfrac{2-x}{3}$

20. $\dfrac{c+2}{2} - 4 = \dfrac{c-1}{3}$

21. $\dfrac{y-3}{6} + \dfrac{y-25}{5} = 0$

22. $\dfrac{2x+1}{12} + \dfrac{x-3}{4} = \dfrac{x-1}{6}$

23. $2 + \dfrac{9}{x} = \dfrac{5}{x^2}$

24. $\dfrac{1}{x} - \dfrac{x-1}{14} = \dfrac{1}{7x}$

25. $\dfrac{x-1}{16} + \dfrac{5}{8x} = \dfrac{1}{x}$

26. $\dfrac{3}{m^2} - \dfrac{1}{3m} = \dfrac{m+5}{6m}$

27–30. Solve each of the following inequalities:

27. $\dfrac{3x-1}{4} > \dfrac{x+3}{2}$

28. $\dfrac{y+5}{8} < \dfrac{y-1}{4}$

29. $\dfrac{n+6}{3} - 2 \le \dfrac{n-2}{2}$

30. $\dfrac{a+1}{4} - \dfrac{3a}{8} \ge \dfrac{1}{2}$

31. Solve for x: $\dfrac{1}{a} - \dfrac{1}{x} = \dfrac{1}{b}$.

32. Solve for r: $\dfrac{1}{r} - \dfrac{2}{s} = \dfrac{1}{2r}$.

33. Solve for y: $\dfrac{y}{a} - \dfrac{a+y}{y-a} = \dfrac{y}{2a}$.

34. Solve for x: $\dfrac{1}{b} + \dfrac{1}{a} = \dfrac{a}{bx} - \dfrac{b}{ax}$.

35. The first of three consecutive odd integers exceeds two thirds of the largest integer by 3. Find the three integers.

36. One half of the largest of three consecutive even integers exceeds one fourth of the second integer by 5. Find the integers.

CHAPTER 7 REVIEW EXERCISES

1–12. Write each of the following expressions as a single fraction in simplest form:

1. $\dfrac{5x+8}{3} - \dfrac{2(x+1)}{3}$

2. $\left(\dfrac{3b-3}{4ab}\right)\left(\dfrac{ab+a}{6}\right)$

3. $\dfrac{2a+6}{8} \cdot \dfrac{2}{a+3}$

4. $\dfrac{x-1}{3} \div \dfrac{4x-8}{9}$

5. $\dfrac{x+2}{4} - \dfrac{x-3}{3}$

6. $\dfrac{a+b}{3} + \dfrac{a-b}{2}$

7. $\dfrac{x^2-1}{x+2} \div \dfrac{x+1}{5x+10}$

8. $\dfrac{4x}{2x+6} + \dfrac{x}{x+3}$

9. $\dfrac{3a+1}{a^2-1} - \dfrac{1}{a+1}$

10. $\left(\dfrac{x^2-y^2}{4}\right) \div \left(\dfrac{y-x}{12}\right)$

11. $\dfrac{6a^2b}{x^2-x-72} \div \dfrac{2ab^3}{x^2-64}$

12. $\dfrac{x^2-9}{x} \cdot \dfrac{x^2+2x}{x^2+5x+6}$

13–20. Solve for the variable and check:

13. $\dfrac{t}{6} - \dfrac{t}{8} = 2$

14. $\dfrac{r}{3} + \dfrac{5r}{12} = \dfrac{9}{4}$

15. $\dfrac{1}{2x} = \dfrac{1}{x} - 2$

16. $\dfrac{3}{y} = 2 + \dfrac{5}{y}$

17. $\dfrac{x+2}{x} - \dfrac{3}{2x} = 5$

18. $\dfrac{a-2}{3} + \dfrac{2a-4}{4} = 5$

19. $\dfrac{3}{x} + \dfrac{1}{2x} = \dfrac{x-6}{2}$

20. $\dfrac{n-1}{6} - \dfrac{1}{n} = \dfrac{n-1}{12}$

CHAPTER 8

Operations with Irrational Numbers

8.1 WRITING RATIONAL NUMBERS AS DECIMALS, AND DECIMAL NUMBERS AS FRACTIONS

—————— KEY IDEAS ——————

A **rational number** is a number that can be written in fractional form as p/q, where p and q are integers, except that q cannot be equal to 0. A rational number can be written as a decimal number by dividing the denominator into the numerator.

TERMINATING VERSUS REPEATING DECIMAL NUMBERS. Every rational number can be represented as either a *terminating decimal* number or as a never-ending *repeating decimal* number.

To change $\dfrac{3}{8}$ to a decimal:

$$
\begin{array}{r}
0.375 \\
8\overline{)3.000} \\
-\ 0 \\
\hline
30 \\
-24 \\
\hline
60 \\
-56 \\
\hline
40 \\
-40 \\
\hline
\end{array}
$$
Remainder is 0. → 0

To change $\dfrac{2}{11}$ to a decimal:

$$
\begin{array}{r}
0.1818\ldots \\
11\overline{)2.000000} \\
-\ 0 \\
\hline
20 \\
-11 \\
\hline
90 \\
-88 \\
\hline
20 \\
-11 \\
\hline
90 \\
-88 \\
\hline
20 \\
\end{array}
$$
← Remainder is never 0.

The decimal representation of 3/8 is **0.375**, which is a terminating decimal.

The decimal representation of 2/11 is **0.1818...**, where the digits 1 and 8 repeat endlessly.

If, when changing 3/8 to decimal form, the division process were continued, the quotient would look like this: 0.375000 .... These additional zeros are *not significant* and may be deleted without affecting the value of the decimal number. Thus 0.375 has three significant decimal digits (3, 7, and 5). A **terminating decimal number** is a decimal number that has a definite number of significant decimal digits. On the other hand, a **repeating decimal number** is a decimal number in which one or more nonzero digits endlessly repeat.

NOTATION.   In a repeating decimal number the digit or group of digits that repeat is called the **repetend**. The repetend is usually indicated by writing a bar over the digits that repeat. For example,

$$0.1818 \ldots = 0.\overline{18}.$$

$$\underset{\text{repetend}}{\underbrace{}}$$

EXPRESSING A DECIMAL NUMBER AS A FRACTION.   Every terminating decimal number and every repeating decimal number can be written in fractional form as the quotient of two integers.

To change a terminating decimal number into its fractional equivalent, multiply the decimal number by a fraction whose numerator and denominator are the smallest power of 10 that changes the decimal number into an integer. For example,

$$0.7 = 0.7 \quad \times \frac{10}{10} \quad = \frac{7}{10};$$

$$0.36 = 0.36 \quad \times \frac{100}{100} \quad = \frac{36}{100};$$

$$2.987 = 2.987 \times \frac{1000}{1000} = \frac{2987}{1000}.$$

To convert a repeating decimal such as $0.\overline{12}$ into fractional form, proceed as follows.

Step 1. Let $N = 0.\overline{12}$.

Step 2. Multiply N by the power of 10 that has as its exponent the number of repeating digits. Since N ($=0.\overline{12}$) has *two* repeating digits, multiply N by 10^2, or 100. To multiply any number by 100, move the decimal point of the number two places to the right. Therefore, before multiplying N by 100, it is helpful to write N with two additional decimal digits.

$$N = 0.\overline{12} = 0.12\overline{12}$$
$$100N = 100(0.12\overline{12})$$
$$= 12.\overline{12}$$

Step 3. Subtract the equation written in step 1 from the equation written in step 2. Then solve for N.

$$100N = 12.\overline{12}$$
$$N = 0.\overline{12}$$
$$\overline{99N = 12.00}$$
$$\frac{99N}{99} = \frac{12}{99}$$

Step 4. Write the answer in simplest form:

$$N = 0.\overline{12} = \frac{12}{99} = \frac{4}{33}.$$

Example ▰▰▰▰

1. Express $0.4\overline{2}$ as a fraction in lowest terms.

Solution:

Step 1. Let $N = 0.4\overline{2}$.
Step 2. Since there is one repeating digit, multiply N by 10. Let $10N = 10(0.4\overline{2}) = 4.\overline{2}$.
Step 3. Subtract equations. In order to align decimal digits, write $4.\overline{2}$ as $4.2\overline{2}$

$$10N = 4.2\overline{2}$$
$$N = 0.4\overline{2}$$
$$\overline{9N = 3.8}$$
$$\frac{9N}{9} = \frac{3.8}{9}$$
$$N = \frac{3.8}{9} = \frac{38}{90}$$

Step 4. Write the answer in simplest form:

$$0.4\overline{2} = \frac{38}{90} = \frac{19}{45}.$$

▰▰▰▰▰

EXERCISE SET 8.1

1–4. Express each of the following rational numbers as a repeating decimal:

1. $\dfrac{8}{11}$ **2.** $\dfrac{23}{90}$ **3.** $\dfrac{109}{300}$ **4.** $\dfrac{67}{33}$

5–28. Express each of the following decimal numbers as a fraction in lowest terms:

5. 0.48	**13.** $0.\overline{629}$	**21.** $-0.5\overline{18}$
6. 0.09	**14.** $0.3\overline{8}$	**22.** $0.4\overline{18}$
7. 0.713	**15.** $0.5\overline{49}$	**23.** $0.28\overline{71}$
8. 1.43	**16.** $1.9\overline{7}$	**24.** $0.985\overline{3}$
9. $0.\overline{36}$	**17.** $0.5\overline{7}$	**25.** $4.13\overline{6}$
10. $1.\overline{2}$	**18.** $0.8\overline{63}$	**26.** $-2.5\overline{1}$
11. $0.4\overline{1}$	**19.** $0.7\overline{441}$	**27.** $2.0\overline{27}$
12. $0.\overline{5}$	**20.** $0.5\overline{27}$	**28.** $1.6\overline{51}$

29–35. Replace □ with the symbol (<, >, or =) that makes the resulting statement true.

29. $5(0.\overline{6})$ □ 3.0

30. $\dfrac{14}{19}$ □ $0.7\overline{2}$

31. $0.\overline{3} + 0.\overline{6}$ □ 1

32. 1.9 □ $1.\overline{90}$

33. $11(1.\overline{90})$ □ 20

34. $(0.\overline{6})^2$ □ $\dfrac{4}{9}$

35. $0.\overline{7} + 0.\overline{5}$ □ $1.\overline{2}$

8.2 EVALUATING RADICALS AND CLASSIFYING REAL NUMBERS

_____ KEY IDEAS _____

What is the area of a square whose side is 5? To find the area of this square, we *square* 5 by writing $5 \times 5 = 25$. The area of the square is 25.

What is the length of a side of a square whose area is 25? To find the length of a side of this square, we find the *square root* of 25 by thinking, "The product of which two identical numbers is 25?" Since $25 = 5 \times 5$, the square root of 25 is 5.

Finding the square of a number and finding the square root of a number are inverse operations in the same sense that adding and subtracting are inverse operations.

SQUARE ROOTS. The **square root** of a nonnegative number N is one of two identical factors whose product is N. The symbol $\sqrt{}$ is called a **radical sign** and is used to indicate that we wish to *extract* the square root of any number, called the **radicand**, that is written underneath the symbol. For example,

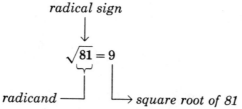

radical sign

$$\sqrt{81} = 9$$

radicand ⎯⎯⎯⎯⎯⎯ ⎯⎯→ square root of 81

The square root of 81 is 9 since $9 \times 9 = 81$. Notice that there is another pair of identical factors whose product is 81, that is, $-9 \times -9 = 81$. However, the expression $\sqrt{N}$ will always be taken to mean the *positive* square root of N. The positive root of a number is sometimes called the *principal square root*. Compare the following notation, and observe the effect of the placement of the negative sign:

$$\sqrt{81} = 9;$$
$$-\sqrt{81} = -9;$$
$$\pm\sqrt{81} = \pm 9 \ (\pm \text{ is read as "positive or negative."})$$

Example ▰▰▰▰

1. Express each of the following as a rational number:

(a) $\sqrt{64}$ (b) $-\sqrt{121}$ (c) $\sqrt{\dfrac{49}{100}}$ (d) $\pm\sqrt{0.16}$

Solutions:

(a) $\sqrt{64} = 8$ (c) $\sqrt{\dfrac{49}{100}} = \dfrac{7}{10}$

(b) $-\sqrt{121} = -11$ (d) $\pm\sqrt{0.16} = \pm 0.4$ ▰▰▰▰

PERFECT SQUARES. The numbers 1, 4, 9, and 16/25 are examples of *perfect squares*. A **perfect square** is any rational number whose square root is also a rational number. The numbers 8 and 5/9 are *not* perfect squares since their square roots are not rational numbers.

RADICALS HAVING INDEXES OTHER THAN 2. If squaring a number and taking the square root of a number are inverse operations, then we should be able to find inverse operations for cubing a number, for raising a number to the fourth power, and so forth. For example, we know that $2^3 = 8$. It follows that the cube root of 8 is 2 since $2 \times 2 \times 2 = 8$. The following notation is used, where 3 is called the index of the radical:

$$\sqrt[3]{8} = 2.$$

The cube root of any number N is one of *three* equal factors whose product is N, so that the index of the radical is 3. In general, the rth root of a number N is defined as one of r equal factors whose product is N, and is denoted by a radical whose index is r:

$$\text{index}$$
$$\downarrow$$
$$\text{radical sign} \rightarrow \sqrt[r]{N}$$
$$\underline{\qquad\qquad} \rightarrow \text{radicand}$$

When a radical is written without an index, it is assumed to represent a square root, so that its index is understood to be 2. Therefore

$$\sqrt[2]{16} = \sqrt{16} = 4.$$

NEGATIVE RADICANDS. Notice that $\sqrt{-25}$ cannot be evaluated since we cannot find two identical factors whose product is *negative* 25. Keep in mind that, if two numbers are identical, then they must have the same sign. If they have the same sign, then their product must be *positive*.

On the other hand, $\sqrt[3]{-8} = -2$ since $-2 \times -2 \times -2 = -8$. We may conclude that, if the radicand is a negative number:

● The radical cannot be evaluated if the index is an *even* number since the product of an even number of factors must be *positive*. In such cases, the radical is *not defined*.

● The radical can be evaluated if the index is an *odd* number since the product of an odd number of negative factors is negative. Therefore $\sqrt{-64}$ is not defined, while $\sqrt[3]{-64} = -4$.

Example ▬▬▬

2. What is the largest possible integer value of x for which the expression $\sqrt{26-x}$ is a positive integer?

Solution: The value of x must be an integer less than or equal to 26; otherwise the radicand would be negative. If $x = 25$, then

$$\sqrt{26-x} = \sqrt{26-25} = \sqrt{1} = 1. \qquad \blacksquare$$

The largest possible integer value of x is **1**.

IRRATIONAL AND REAL NUMBERS.   The square root of a number that is *not* a perfect square is *not* rational. For example, $\sqrt{7}$ is not equal to a rational number since we cannot find two identical rational numbers whose product is 7. We can, however, represent $\sqrt{7}$ by an infinite, *nonrepeating* decimal number: $\sqrt{7} = 2.6457513\ldots$, and $\sqrt{7}$ is an example of an irrational number. An **irrational number** is any number that can be represented by a never-ending decimal that has no pattern of repeating digits.

The square root of any nonnegative number that is *not* a perfect square is irrational. Similarly, the cube root of any number that is not a perfect cube is irrational. However, the set of irrational numbers also includes other types of infinite, nonrepeating decimal numbers such as π ($= 3.1415926\ldots$).

The set of **real numbers** is the union of the sets of rational and irrational numbers. For every real number, there is a point on the number line that has that real number as its coordinate. Similarly, every point on the number line has a coordinate that is either a rational or an irrational number.

Example ▬▬▬

3.   Which of the following is an irrational number?

(1) $\sqrt{49}$ (2) $\sqrt{8}$ (3) $\sqrt{\dfrac{25}{81}}$ (4) 0

Solution: Choice (2), 8, is not a perfect square. Since the square root of a number that is not a perfect square is irrational, **choice (2)** is the correct answer. Also note that choice (1), $\sqrt{49}, = 7 = \frac{7}{1}$; choice (3), $\sqrt{25/81}, = 5/9$; and choice (4), 0, is rational since it can be written as the numerator of any fraction having an integer denominator except 0, for example, 0/2. ▬▬▬

EXERCISE SET 8.2

1–16. Simplify each of the following:

1. $\sqrt{100}$

2. $-\sqrt{36}$

3. $\sqrt{0.49}$

4. $\sqrt{\dfrac{9}{25}}$

5. $\pm\sqrt{144}$

6. $\sqrt{0.09}$

7. $\sqrt{\dfrac{121}{169}}$

8. $\sqrt{\dfrac{1}{64}}$

9. $2\sqrt{\dfrac{9}{4}}$

10. $-3\sqrt{\dfrac{16}{36}}$

11. $\sqrt[5]{-32}$

12. $\sqrt[3]{1000}$

13. $\sqrt[4]{625}$

14. $\sqrt[3]{-216}$

15. $\sqrt[7]{-1}$

16. $\sqrt[3]{\dfrac{8}{27}}$

17. Which of the following is *not* defined?
    (1) $\sqrt{-1000}$ (2) $-\sqrt{1000}$ (3) $\sqrt[3]{-1000}$ (4) $\pm\sqrt{1000}$

18. What is the *smallest* integer value of x for which the expression $\sqrt{x-16}$ is a positive integer?

19. What is the *largest* integer value of x for which the expression $\sqrt{11-x}$ is defined?

20. Which of the following expressions represents an irrational number?

    (1) $\sqrt{\dfrac{1}{16}}$ (2) $-\sqrt{\dfrac{9}{25}}$ (3) $\sqrt{-1}$ (4) $\sqrt{12}$

21–35. Evaluate.

21. $\sqrt{9}+\sqrt{16}$

22. $(\sqrt{4})(\sqrt{100})$

23. $(\sqrt{25})^2$

24. $\dfrac{\sqrt{81}}{\sqrt{9}}$

25. $\dfrac{\sqrt[3]{8}}{\sqrt{4}}$

26. $\dfrac{\sqrt[4]{81}}{\sqrt[5]{-32}}$

27. $2\sqrt{64}$

28. $-6-\sqrt{36}$

29. $-4+\sqrt{9}$

30. $-2+\sqrt{25}-6$

31. $-3-(\sqrt[3]{-8})$

32. $-1-2\sqrt{1}$

33. $\sqrt[4]{16}-\sqrt{16}$

34. $\sqrt[3]{64}-\sqrt{64}$

35. $-\sqrt[3]{-1}+\sqrt[3]{-125}$

36. $3\sqrt{16}+2\sqrt{25}$

8.3 APPROXIMATING SQUARE ROOTS

―――――――――――― KEY IDEAS ――――――――――――

Square roots of perfect squares have *exact* rational number equivalents. Rational number approximations can be calculated for square roots of numbers that are *not* perfect squares. The symbol $\approx$ will be used to mean "is approximately equal to."

FINDING INTEGER ESTIMATES OF SQUARE ROOTS. The square root of a positive number can be approximated to the nearest integer by finding two consecutive perfect squares between which the number lies. Consider, for example, $\sqrt{72}$. Observe that

$$64 < 72 < 81;$$
$$8^2 < 72 < 9^2;$$
$$8 < \sqrt{72} < 9.$$

Since 72 is closer to 8^2 than to 9^2, $\sqrt{72}$, is closer to 8 than it is to 9. To the nearest *integer*, $\sqrt{72} = 8$.

DIVIDE AND AVERAGE METHOD. If we were to offer 8 as an estimate of $\sqrt{72}$, then the corresponding factor of 72 would be 9 since $72 \div 8 = 9$. Since the value of $\sqrt{72}$ lies between 8 and 9, a better estimate of $\sqrt{72}$ may be obtained by taking the average of 8 and 9. The *divide and average* method illustrated in the example that follows uses this principle to find a rational approximation of the square root of a number that is not a perfect square.

Example ▬▬▬

Find an approximation of $\sqrt{40}$ that is correct to the nearest (a) tenth and (b) hundredth.

Solution: *Step 1.* Let $N = \sqrt{40}$. Make a reasonable initial estimate of $\sqrt{N}$.

$$6^2 < 40 < 7^2$$

Since 40 is closer to 36 than to 49, use 6.0 as the first estimate of $\sqrt{40}$.

(a) To find an approximation that is correct to the nearest tenth, proceed as follows.

Step 2. Divide N by the estimate. Carry the quotient to one more decimal place than in the divisor (the estimate).

$$\text{Quotient} = \frac{N}{\text{estimate}} = \frac{40}{6.0} = 6.66$$

Step 3. Obtain an improved estimate by taking the average of the quotient calculated in step 2 and the estimate from step 1.

$$\text{New estimate} = \frac{\text{quotient} + \text{estimate}}{2}$$

$$= \frac{6.66 + 6.0}{2}$$

$$= \frac{12.66}{2}$$

$$= 6.33$$

Therefore $\sqrt{40} \approx 6.33$ so that $\sqrt{40} = $ **6.3** *correct to the nearest tenth.*

(b) To obtain an estimate of $\sqrt{40}$ that is correct to the nearest hundredth, repeat steps 2 and 3.

Step 2. Quotient $= \dfrac{N}{\text{estimate}} = \dfrac{40}{6.33} = 6.319$

Step 3. New estimate $= \dfrac{\text{quotient} + \text{estimate}}{2}$

$$= \frac{6.319 + 6.33}{2}$$

$$= \frac{12.649}{2}$$

$$= 6.324$$

Therefore, $\sqrt{40} \approx 6.324$ so that $\sqrt{40} = $ **6.32** *correct to the nearest hundredth.*

REMARKS ON THE DIVIDE AND AVERAGE METHOD

1. The best initial estimate of $\sqrt{N}$ may *not* be an integer. For example, in estimating $\sqrt{72}$, 72 is approximately midway between 8^2 and 9^2. Therefore a good first estimate of $\sqrt{72}$ is 8.5, rather than 8.0.

2. A variety of other methods can also be used to approximate square roots. A table of square roots is sometimes available, and many pocket calculators have a square root key that automatically displays the square root of any nonnegative number that is entered.

EXERCISE SET 8.3

1–12. Use the divide and average method to approximate the square roots of each of the following numbers correct to the nearest tenth:

1.	78	**5.**	69	**9.**	52.8
2.	47	**6.**	270	**10.**	1.3
3.	21	**7.**	8.6	**11.**	0.58
4.	108	**8.**	31.4	**12.**	0.043

13–20. Use the divide and average method to approximate the square roots of each of the following numbers correct to the nearest hundredth:

13.	60	**17.**	809
14.	12	**18.**	1.3
15.	179	**19.**	0.70
16.	95.6	**20.**	0.08

8.4   SIMPLIFYING RADICALS

KEY IDEAS

A radical may be distributed over each factor of its radicand. In general,
$$\sqrt{ab} = \sqrt{a}\sqrt{b}.$$
For example,
$$\sqrt{12} = \sqrt{4 \cdot 3} = \sqrt{4} \cdot \sqrt{3} = 2\sqrt{3}.$$

SIMPLIFYING RADICALS.   The square root of a whole number is in simplest form when the number does not include any perfect square factors greater than 1. To simplify an irrational square root, factor the radicand, if possible, in such a way that one of its factors is the *largest* perfect square factor. Distribute the radical over each factor. Then evaluate the square root of the perfect square factor. For example, to simplify $\sqrt{80}$ proceed as follows:

Factor the radicand: $\sqrt{80} = \sqrt{16 \cdot 5}$

Write the radical over each factor: $= \sqrt{16} \cdot \sqrt{5}$

Evaluate the square root of the perfect square: $= 4\sqrt{5}$

If the largest perfect square factor of the radicand is not factored out initially, then the procedure must be repeated. For example,

$$\sqrt{80} = \sqrt{4 \cdot 20} = \sqrt{4} \cdot \sqrt{20} = 2 \cdot \sqrt{20}$$
$$= 2\sqrt{4}\sqrt{5} = (2 \cdot 2)\sqrt{5} = 4\sqrt{5}$$

Examples ▬▬▬

   1. Simplify: $\sqrt{45}$.

   Solution: $\sqrt{45} = \sqrt{9 \cdot 5} = \sqrt{9}\sqrt{5} = 3\sqrt{5}$

   2. Simplify: $2\sqrt{48}$.

   Solution: $2\sqrt{48} = 2\sqrt{16 \cdot 3} = 2\sqrt{16} \cdot \sqrt{3} = (2 \cdot 4)\sqrt{3} = 8\sqrt{3}$

   3. Simplify: $\frac{1}{3}\sqrt{108}$.

Solution: $\frac{1}{3}\sqrt{108} = \frac{1}{3}\sqrt{36 \cdot 3} = \frac{1}{3}\sqrt{36} \cdot \sqrt{3}$

$$= \frac{1}{3}(6)\sqrt{3} = \mathbf{2\sqrt{3}}$$

4. Simplify: $\sqrt{x^5}$.

Solution: Observe that $\sqrt{x^2} = x$, $\sqrt{x^4} = x^2$, $\sqrt{x^6} = x^3$ and so forth. The exponent of the greatest perfect square factor of a variable power is the largest even number that is less than or equal to the exponent of the variable radicand:

$$\sqrt{x^5} = \sqrt{x^4 \cdot x} = \sqrt{x^4} \cdot \sqrt{x} = \mathbf{x^2 \cdot \sqrt{x}.}$$ ▬▬

SIMPLIFYING $\sqrt[a]{N}(a \neq 2)$. A radical having an index other than 2 is simplified in a manner that is similar to the one used to simplify square root radicals.

Examples ▬▬▬

5. Simplify: $5\sqrt[3]{16}$.

Solution: $5\sqrt[3]{16} = 5\sqrt[3]{8} \cdot \sqrt[3]{2} = (5 \cdot 2)\sqrt[3]{2} = \mathbf{10\sqrt[3]{2}}$

6. Simplify: $\sqrt[3]{108a^3}$.

Solution: $\sqrt[3]{108a} = \sqrt[3]{27a^3(4)} = \sqrt[3]{27}\sqrt[3]{a^3}\sqrt[3]{4} = \mathbf{3a\sqrt[3]{4}}$ ▬▬

SOLVING $ax^2 + c = 0$. A quadratic equation that is missing the first-degree (middle) term may be solved by writing an equivalent equation that isolates the square of the variable on one side of the equation. The variable can be then be found by taking the square root of both sides of the equation.

Examples ▬▬▬

7. Solve for x: $2x^2 - 50 = 0$.

Solution:

Method 1: Extracting Roots	Method 2: Factoring
$2x^2 = 50$	$2(x^2 - 25) = 0$
$x^2 = \dfrac{50}{2}$	$2(x - 5)(x + 5) = 0$
	$x - 5 = 0$ or $x + 5 = 0$
$x^2 = 25$	$x = 5 \qquad x = -5$
$\sqrt{x^2} = \pm\sqrt{25}$	$\{-5, 5\}$
$x = \pm 5$ or $\{-5, 5\}$	

8. Solve for n: $n^2 - 17 = 0$.

Solution:

Method 1: Extracting Roots	Method 2: Factoring
$n^2 - 17 = 0$ $n^2 = 17$ $\sqrt{n^2} = \pm\sqrt{17}$ $n = \pm\sqrt{17}$	Since $n^2 - 17$ cannot be factored using rational numbers, this method cannot be used.

EXERCISE SET 8.4

1–33. Write each of the following radicals in simplest form:

1. $\sqrt{28}$

2. $\sqrt{40}$

3. $-\sqrt{63}$

4. $-\sqrt{98}$

5. $2\sqrt{75}$

6. $\sqrt{192}$

7. $\dfrac{\sqrt{48}}{4}$

8. $\dfrac{1}{2}\sqrt{72}$

9. $4\sqrt{90}$

10. $-\sqrt{112}$

11. $\sqrt{500}$

12. $\sqrt[3]{216}$

13. $\sqrt[4]{128}$

14. $\sqrt[3]{-16}$

15. $\sqrt[3]{54}$

16. $\sqrt[5]{64}$

17. $\sqrt{a^8}$

18. $\sqrt[3]{x^6}$

19. $\sqrt{0.16x^2}$

20. $\sqrt{0.09b^4}$

21. $\sqrt{a^7}$

22. $\sqrt{x^5}$

23. $\sqrt{a^4b^2}$

24. $\sqrt[3]{x^2z^9}$

25. $\sqrt{r^2s^3}$

26. $\sqrt{p^5q^4}$

27. $\sqrt{8c^4}$

28. $\sqrt{99t^3}$

29. $\sqrt{180x^4y}$

30. $\sqrt[3]{125m^6}$

31. $\sqrt{17n^8}$

32. $\sqrt{44a^2b^6c^4}$

33. $\sqrt[3]{128x^4}$

34–40. Solve for x.

34. $3x^2 - 12 = 0$

35. $2x^2 - 28 = 0$

36. $\dfrac{x^2}{2} - 16 = 0$

37. $2x^2 = x^2 + 48$

38. $3x^2 = 28 - x^2$

39. $(x - 5)^2 = 16$

40. $(x + 3)^2 = 6x + 25$

8.5   MULTIPLYING AND DIVIDING RADICALS

―――――――― **KEY IDEAS** ――――――――

In general,

$$(p\sqrt{a})(q\sqrt{b}) = (pq)\sqrt{ab},$$

and, provided that q and b are not 0,

$$(p\sqrt{a}) \div (q\sqrt{b}) = \frac{p\sqrt{a}}{q\sqrt{b}} = \frac{p}{q}\sqrt{\frac{a}{b}}.$$

MULTIPLYING AND DIVIDING RADICALS.   To **multiply** (*or* **divide**) radicals *having the same index, proceed as follows*:

Step 1. Multiply (*or* divide) their rational coefficients, if any.
Step 2. Multiply (*or* divide) their radicands.
Step 3. Write the resulting product (*or* quotient) in simplest form.

Examples ▬▬

1. Multiply: $(2\sqrt{6})(4\sqrt{8})$.

Solution: $(2\sqrt{6})(4\sqrt{8}) = (2 \cdot 4)(\sqrt{6} \cdot \sqrt{8}) = 8\sqrt{48}$
$$= 8\sqrt{16} \cdot \sqrt{3}$$
$$= 8 \cdot 4\sqrt{3}$$
$$= \mathbf{32\sqrt{3}}$$

2. Divide: $18\sqrt{120} \div 6\sqrt{3}$.

Solution: $18\sqrt{120} \div 6\sqrt{3} = \dfrac{18\sqrt{120}}{6\sqrt{3}}$
$$= 3\sqrt{40}$$
$$= 3\sqrt{4} \cdot \sqrt{10} = (3 \cdot 2)\sqrt{10}$$
$$= \mathbf{6\sqrt{10}}$$

SQUARING RADICALS.   Notice in the following examples:

$$(\sqrt{4})^2 = \sqrt{4} \cdot \sqrt{4} = \sqrt{16} = 4$$

that the product of the square roots of two identical numbers is equal to the number (radicand) itself. In general,

$$\sqrt{N} \cdot \sqrt{N} = N.$$

Examples ▬▬

3. Evaluate: $(5\sqrt{3})^2$.

Solution: $(5\sqrt{3})^2 = (5\sqrt{3})(5\sqrt{3}) = (5.5)(\sqrt{3} \cdot \sqrt{3}) = 25 \cdot 3 = \mathbf{75}$

4. Simplify by using the distributive property: $\sqrt{6}(\sqrt{15} - \sqrt{6})$.

Solution:
$$\sqrt{6}(\sqrt{15} - \sqrt{6}) = (\sqrt{6} \cdot \sqrt{15}) - (\sqrt{6} \cdot \sqrt{6})$$
$$= \sqrt{90} - 6$$
$$= \sqrt{9} \cdot \sqrt{10} - 6$$
$$= \mathbf{3\sqrt{10} - 6}$$

WRITING RADICALS IN SIMPLEST FORM. The square root of a term is in simplest form if each of the following statements is true:

1. The radical does *not* contain a perfect square factor greater than 1.

Example: $\sqrt{18}$ is not in simplest form.
$\sqrt{18} = \sqrt{9 \cdot 2} = \sqrt{9} \cdot \sqrt{2} = 3\sqrt{2}$ is in simplest form.

2. The radical does *not* contain a fraction.

Example: $\sqrt{\dfrac{3}{4}}$ is *not* in simplest form.

$\sqrt{\dfrac{3}{4}} = \dfrac{\sqrt{3}}{\sqrt{4}} = \dfrac{\sqrt{3}}{2}$ is in simplest form.

3. The radical does *not* appear in the denominator. If it does, rationalize the denominator by multiplying the numerator and the denominator by the radical denominator.

Example: $\dfrac{5}{\sqrt{7}}$ is *not* in simplest form.

$\dfrac{5}{\sqrt{7}} \cdot \left(\dfrac{\sqrt{7}}{\sqrt{7}}\right) = \dfrac{5\sqrt{7}}{7}$ is in simplest form.

Use the multiplication property of 1.

Example ▬▬

5. Express $\sqrt{\dfrac{9}{40}}$ in simplest form.

Solution:
$$\sqrt{\dfrac{9}{40}} = \dfrac{\sqrt{9}}{\sqrt{40}}$$

Rationalize the denominator: $= \dfrac{3}{\sqrt{40}} \cdot \dfrac{\sqrt{40}}{\sqrt{40}}$

Simplify the numerator:
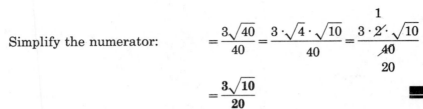

$$= \frac{3\sqrt{10}}{20}$$

EXERCISE SET 8.5

1–33. Multiply, and write the product in simplest form.

1. $\sqrt{7} \cdot \sqrt{11}$

2. $\sqrt{12} \cdot \sqrt{3}$

3. $3\sqrt{5} \cdot 2\sqrt{7}$

4. $2\sqrt{6} \cdot 5\sqrt{6}$

5. $(\sqrt{13})^2$

6. $(-\sqrt{8})^2$

7. $-(\sqrt{5})^2$

8. $-(-\sqrt{7})^2$

9. $(3\sqrt{2})^2$

10. $(-4\sqrt{3})^2$

11. $-(2\sqrt{5})^2$

12. $-(-2\sqrt{3})^2$

13. $-\sqrt{15} \cdot 2\sqrt{5}$

14. $(2\sqrt{8})(-3\sqrt{12})$

15. $(5\sqrt{14}) \cdot \left(\frac{1}{2}\sqrt{10}\right)$

16. $\sqrt{5} \cdot \sqrt{2} \cdot \sqrt{10}$

17. $\sqrt{3} \cdot \sqrt{5} \cdot \sqrt{6}$

18. $(\sqrt{2})^3$

19. $(\sqrt{3})^4$

20. $(-\sqrt{5})^3$

21. $(-\sqrt{6})^4$

22. $2(\sqrt{8})^3$

23. $\sqrt[3]{2} \cdot \sqrt[3]{4}$

24. $\sqrt[3]{3} \cdot \sqrt[3]{9}$

25. $\sqrt[4]{2} \cdot \sqrt[4]{32}$

26. $\sqrt[3]{5} \cdot \sqrt[3]{16}$

27. $\sqrt{x} \cdot \sqrt{x^3}$

28. $\sqrt{10a} \cdot \sqrt{8a}$

29. $\sqrt{y^5} \cdot \sqrt{y^4}$

30. $\sqrt{b^4} \cdot \sqrt{b^3}$

31. $-2\sqrt{ab} \cdot 3\sqrt{a^3b}$

32. $(2\sqrt{5b})^2$

33. $\sqrt{r^2s^3} \cdot \sqrt{st}$

34–47. Divide, and write the quotient in simplest form

34. $\dfrac{\sqrt{18}}{\sqrt{2}}$

35. $\dfrac{\sqrt{60}}{\sqrt{15}}$

36. $\dfrac{12\sqrt{54}}{4\sqrt{3}}$

37. $\dfrac{21\sqrt{96}}{7\sqrt{2}}$

38. $\dfrac{\sqrt{252}}{3\sqrt{7}}$

39. $\dfrac{-5\sqrt{88}}{-2\sqrt{2}}$

40. $\dfrac{\sqrt{0.8}}{\sqrt{5}}$

41. $\dfrac{\sqrt{0.018}}{\sqrt{0.2}}$

42. $\dfrac{\sqrt{x^5}}{\sqrt{x}}$

43. $\dfrac{\sqrt{a}}{\sqrt{a^3}}$

44. $\dfrac{\sqrt{y^8}}{\sqrt{y^3}}$

45. $\dfrac{\sqrt{90x^4}}{\sqrt{2x^2}}$

46. $\dfrac{\sqrt{a^7b}}{\sqrt{a^3b}}$

47. $\dfrac{(\sqrt{x^3y^4})^2}{x^2y^3}$

48–59. Simplify.

48. $\dfrac{10}{\sqrt{5}}$

49. $\dfrac{8}{3\sqrt{2}}$

50. $\sqrt{\dfrac{7}{25}}$

51. $\dfrac{\sqrt{6}}{\sqrt{8}}$

52. $\sqrt{\dfrac{63}{16}}$

53. $\sqrt{\dfrac{20}{9}}$

54. $\dfrac{2\sqrt{32}}{6\sqrt{18}}$

55. $-\sqrt{\dfrac{5}{140}}$

56. $\sqrt{\dfrac{64}{13}}$

57. $-\sqrt{\dfrac{49}{27}}$

58. $\sqrt{\dfrac{20}{45}}$

59. $\dfrac{1}{\sqrt{4/3}}$

60. Solve for x: $\dfrac{2x}{3\sqrt{2}} = \dfrac{3\sqrt{2}}{x}$.

8.6   COMBINING LIKE RADICALS

─────────────── KEY IDEAS ───────────────

Like radicals are radicals that have the same index and the same radicand; $3\sqrt{5}$ and $-2\sqrt{5}$ are examples of like radicals. However, $4\sqrt{11}$ and $4\sqrt{6}$ are not like radicals since they have different radicands, and $\sqrt{7}$ and $\sqrt[3]{7}$ are not like radicals since they do not have the same index.

ADDING AND SUBTRACTING RADICALS.   To **add** or **subtract** like radicals, combine their rational coefficients and use the same radical factor. For example,

$$2\sqrt{6} + 3\sqrt{6} = (2+3)\sqrt{6} = \mathbf{5\sqrt{6}}.$$

Sometimes a radical must be simplified before it can be combined with another radical. This is illustrated in Examples 1–6 below.

Examples ▬▬▬

1. Find the sum of $4\sqrt{3}$ and $\sqrt{75}$.

Solution: $4\sqrt{3} + \sqrt{75} = 4\sqrt{3} + \sqrt{25} \cdot \sqrt{3}$

$$= 4\sqrt{3} + 5\sqrt{3}$$

$$= (4+5)\sqrt{3} = \mathbf{9\sqrt{3}}$$

2. Subtract: $\sqrt{2} - \sqrt{32}$.

Solution: $\sqrt{2} - \sqrt{32} = \sqrt{2} - \sqrt{16} \cdot \sqrt{2}$

$$= \sqrt{2} - 4\sqrt{2}$$

$$= (1-4)\sqrt{2} = \mathbf{-3\sqrt{2}}$$

3. Combine: $3\sqrt{20} - \sqrt{5} + \dfrac{1}{2}\sqrt{80}$.

Solution: $3\sqrt{20} - \sqrt{5} + \dfrac{1}{2}\sqrt{80} = 3\sqrt{4} \cdot \sqrt{5} - \sqrt{5} + \dfrac{1}{2}\sqrt{16}\ \sqrt{5}$

$$= (3 \cdot 2)\sqrt{5} - \sqrt{5} + \frac{1}{2}(4)(\sqrt{5})$$

$$= 6\sqrt{5} - \sqrt{5} + 2\sqrt{5}$$

$$= 5\sqrt{5} + 2\sqrt{5} = \mathbf{7\sqrt{5}}$$

4. Simplify: $\sqrt{3}(\sqrt{6} + 2\sqrt{24})$.

Solution: $\sqrt{3}(\sqrt{6} + 2\sqrt{24}) = (\sqrt{3} \cdot \sqrt{6}) + 2(\sqrt{3} \cdot \sqrt{24})$

$$= \sqrt{18} + 2\sqrt{72}$$

$$= \sqrt{9 \cdot 2} + 2\sqrt{36 \cdot 2}$$

$$= \sqrt{9} \cdot \sqrt{2} + 2\sqrt{36} \cdot \sqrt{2}$$

$$= 3\sqrt{2} + (2 \cdot 6)\sqrt{2}$$

$$= 3\sqrt{2} + 12\sqrt{2} = \mathbf{15\sqrt{2}}$$

5. Add: $\sqrt[3]{16} + \sqrt[3]{2}$.

Solution: $\sqrt[3]{16} + \sqrt[3]{2} = \sqrt[3]{8 \cdot 2} + \sqrt[3]{2}$

$$= \sqrt[3]{8} \cdot \sqrt[3]{2} + \sqrt[3]{2}$$

$$= 2\sqrt[3]{2} + \sqrt[3]{2} = \mathbf{3\sqrt[3]{2}}$$

6. Express in simplest form: $\dfrac{9}{\sqrt{27}} + \sqrt{12}$.

Solution: $\dfrac{9}{\sqrt{27}} + \sqrt{12} = \dfrac{9}{\sqrt{9} \cdot \sqrt{3}} + \sqrt{4} \cdot \sqrt{3}$

$$= \dfrac{\overset{3}{\cancel{9}}}{\cancel{3}\sqrt{3}} + 2\sqrt{3}$$

$$= \dfrac{3}{\sqrt{3}} + 2\sqrt{3}$$

$$= \dfrac{3}{\sqrt{3}} \dfrac{\sqrt{3}}{\sqrt{3}} + 2\sqrt{3}$$

$$= \dfrac{3\sqrt{3}}{3} + 2\sqrt{3}$$

$$= \sqrt{3} + 2\sqrt{3} = \mathbf{3\sqrt{3}}$$

EXERCISE SET 8.6

1–40. Simplify.

1. $8\sqrt{11} + \sqrt{11}$

2. $3\sqrt{5} - 7\sqrt{5}$

3. $2\sqrt[3]{6} + 3\sqrt[3]{6}$

4. $\dfrac{\sqrt{7}}{5} + \dfrac{\sqrt{7}}{3}$

5. $\dfrac{1}{3}\sqrt{13} + \dfrac{1}{2}\sqrt{13}$

6. $\sqrt{8} + \sqrt{2}$

7. $2\sqrt{54} - 4\sqrt{3}$

8. $\sqrt{32} + \sqrt{50}$

9. $2\sqrt{48} - \sqrt{27}$

10. $\sqrt{28} + 3\sqrt{2}$

11. $3\sqrt{p} - \sqrt{p} + 4\sqrt{p}$

12. $\sqrt{16x} + \sqrt{9x}$

13. $x\sqrt{12} - x\sqrt{3}$

14. $\sqrt{5x^2} + \sqrt{5x^2}$

15. $\sqrt{18} - \sqrt{200} + \sqrt{72}$

16. $\sqrt{75} + 2\sqrt{3} - \sqrt{48}$

17. $\dfrac{3}{4}\sqrt{7} - \dfrac{1}{4}\sqrt{28}$

18. $\sqrt{128x} - \sqrt{32x}$

19. $\dfrac{1}{4}\sqrt{24} + \dfrac{1}{3}\sqrt{96}$

20. $\sqrt{75y} - 2\sqrt{3y} + \sqrt{300y}$

21. $5x\sqrt{x^3} - 2x\sqrt{x}$

22. $\sqrt{16} + \dfrac{1}{\sqrt{4}}$

23. $\sqrt{8} + \dfrac{24}{\sqrt{8}}$

24. $\sqrt{\dfrac{45}{4}} + \dfrac{1}{3}\sqrt{125}$

25. $\sqrt{18} + \dfrac{4}{\sqrt{2}}$

26. $\dfrac{1}{\sqrt{12}} + \sqrt{27}$

27. $\dfrac{3}{\sqrt{32}} + \sqrt{8}$

28. $\sqrt{\dfrac{3}{4}} + \sqrt{\dfrac{4}{3}}$

29. $\dfrac{1}{\sqrt{9}} - \dfrac{1}{\sqrt{16}}$

30. $\dfrac{4\sqrt{5}}{5} - \sqrt{\dfrac{1}{5}}$

31. $\sqrt{2}(\sqrt{2} - \sqrt{8})$

32. $\sqrt{3}(\sqrt{15} + 2\sqrt{60})$

33. $\sqrt{8}(2\sqrt{3} - \sqrt{12})$

34. $\sqrt{5}(\sqrt{5} - \sqrt{20})$

35. $\sqrt[3]{4}(\sqrt[3]{2} - \sqrt[3]{16})$

36. $\dfrac{\sqrt{50} - \sqrt{8}}{\sqrt{4}}$

37. $\dfrac{\sqrt{21} - 2\sqrt{5}}{\sqrt{5}}$

38. $\dfrac{\sqrt{27} + 4\sqrt{3}}{\sqrt{12}}$

39. $\dfrac{3 - \sqrt{2}}{\sqrt{32}}$

40. $\dfrac{4\sqrt{30} - \sqrt{40}}{2\sqrt{3}}$

8.7   USING THE PYTHAGOREAN RELATIONSHIP

_____ KEY IDEAS _____

A **right triangle** is a triangle that contains a 90-degree (right) angle. Each of the sides that form the right angle is called a **leg** of the triangle. The side opposite the right angle is called the **hypotenuse**.

The lengths of the sides of a right triangle satisfy the following relationship, which is often referred to as the *Pythagorean theorem*:

$(\text{Leg 1})^2 + (\text{Leg 2})^2 = (\text{Hypotenuse})^2,$

$$a^2 \quad + \quad b^2 \quad = \quad c^2$$

APPLYING THE PYTHAGOREAN RELATIONSHIP. When the lengths of any two sides of a *right* triangle are known, the length of the third side may be found by the following procedure:

Step 1. Use a variable to represent the length of the unknown side.

Step 2. Substitute the given lengths into the Pythagorean relationship.

Step 3. Solve for the length of the unknown side.

Example ▰▰▰

1. For each triangle, find the value of *x*.

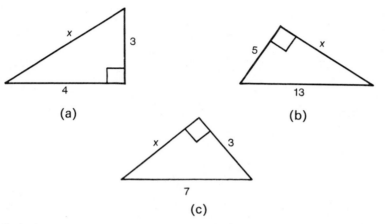

(a)

(b)

(c)

Solutions:

(a)
$$3^2 + 4^2 = x^2$$
$$9 + 16 = x^2$$
$$25 = x^2$$
$$\sqrt{x^2} = \pm\sqrt{25}$$
$$x = 5$$

(b)
$$x^2 + 5^2 = 13^2$$
$$x^2 + 25 = 169$$
$$x^2 = 169 - 25$$
$$\sqrt{x^2} = \pm\sqrt{144}$$
$$x = 12$$

(c)
$$x^2 + 3^2 = 7^2$$
$$x^2 + 9 = 49$$
$$x^2 = 49 - 9$$
$$\sqrt{x^2} = \pm\sqrt{40}$$
$$x = \sqrt{40} = \sqrt{4} \cdot \sqrt{10}$$
$$= 2\sqrt{10}$$

Note: In each of these examples the negative value of *x* is discarded since the length of a side of a triangle cannot be negative. ▰▰▰

The Pythagorean relationship is useful when solving a variety of geometric problems.

Example ▰▰▰

2. If the length of a diagonal of a square is 10, what is the length of a side of the square?

Solution: Let x = length of a side of the square.

A diagonal of a figure such as a square (or rectangle) is a line segment that connects any two nonconsecutive corners (called **vertices**) of the figure.

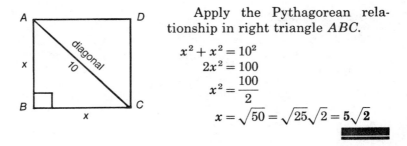

Apply the Pythagorean relationship in right triangle ABC.

$$x^2 + x^2 = 10^2$$
$$2x^2 = 100$$
$$x^2 = \frac{100}{2}$$
$$x = \sqrt{50} = \sqrt{25}\sqrt{2} = 5\sqrt{2}$$

PYTHAGOREAN TRIPLES. A **Pythagorean triple** is a set of positive integers $\{a, b, c\}$ that satisfy the equation $a^2 + b^2 = c^2$. There are many Pythagorean triples. The sets

$$\{3, 4, 5\} \qquad \text{and} \qquad \{5, 12, 13\} \qquad \text{and} \qquad \{8, 15, 17\}$$

are some commonly encountered Pythagorean triples. Observe that:

$3^2 + 4^2 = 5^2$	$5^2 + 12^2 = 13^2$	$8^2 + 15^2 = 17^2$
$9 + 16 \mid 25$	$25 + 144 \mid 169$	$64 + 255 \mid 289$
$25 = 25 \checkmark$	$169 = 169 \checkmark$	$289 = 289 \checkmark$

Whole-number multiples of any Pythagorean triple also comprise a Pythagorean triple. For example, if each member of the set $\{3, 4, 5\}$ is multipled by 2, the set $\{6, 8, 10\}$ that is obtained is also a Pythagorean triple since $6^2 + 8^2 = 10^2$ ($36 + 64 = 100$). If each member of the set $\{3, 4, 5\}$ is multipled by 3, the set $\{9, 12, 15\}$, which is also a Pythagorean triple since $9^2 + 12^2 = 15^2$ ($81 + 144 = 225$), is obtained.

Example ▬▬

3. Which of the following is *not* a Pythagorean triple?
(1) $\{9, 40, 41\}$ (3) $\{8, 12, 17\}$
(2) $\{15, 20, 25\}$ (4) $\{10, 24, 26\}$

Solution: Choice (1) represents a Pythagorean triple since

$9^2 + 40^2 = 41^2$
$81 + 1600 \mid 1681$
$1681 = 1681 \checkmark$

Choice (2) is a multiple of $\{3, 4, 5\}$ where each element is multipled by 5. Choice (4) is a multiple of $\{5, 12, 13\}$ where each element is multipled by 2. In choice (3) you can easily verify that $8^2 + 12^2 \neq 17^2$, so $\{8, 12, 17\}$ is *not* a Pythagorean triple. The correct answer is **choice (3)**. ▬▬

Some problems become easier to solve if we recognize that a set of numbers forms a Pythagorean triple.

Examples

4. A ladder 13 feet in length rests against a vertical building. The foot of the ladder is 5 feet from the building. How far up the building does the ladder reach?

Solution: The ladder forms the hypotenuse of a right triangle. Notice that the sides of the right triangle form a 5-12-13 Pythagorean triple. The ladder reaches **12 feet** up the building.

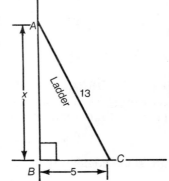

If you did not recognize that the lengths form a Pythagorean triple, you could have solved this problem by letting $x = AB$ and proceeding as follows:

$$x^2 + 5^2 = 13^2$$
$$x^2 + 25 = 169$$
$$x^2 = 169 - 25$$
$$x = \sqrt{144} = 12$$

5. The perimeter of a right triangle is 60. If the length of the hypotenuse is 26, find the length of the shorter leg of the triangle.

Solution: The sum of the lengths of the legs = $60 - 26 = 34$.

Let x = length of the shorter leg.
Then $34 - x$ = length of the remaining leg.
$$x^2 + (34 - x)^2 = 26^2$$
$$x^2 + x^2 - 68x + 1156 = 676$$
$$2x^2 - 68x + 1156 - 676 = 0$$
$$2x^2 - 68x + 480 = 0$$
$$\frac{2x^2}{2} - \frac{68x}{2} + \frac{480}{2} = \frac{0}{2}$$
$$x^2 - 34x + 240 = 0$$
$$(x - 10)(x - 24) = 0$$
$$(x - 10 = 0) \vee (x - 24 = 0)$$
$$x = 10 \vee \qquad x = 24$$

The length of the shorter leg of the right triangle is **10**.

CONVERSE OF THE PYTHAGOREAN RELATIONSHIP. If the lengths of a side of a triangle satisfy the Pythagorean relationship, then the triangle is a right triangle.

Example ▰▰▰▰

6. The lengths of the sides of a triangle are 2, $\sqrt{5}$, and 3. Determine whether the triangle is a right triangle.

    Solution: $\dfrac{2^2 + (\sqrt{5})^2 = 3^3}{4 + 5 \mid 9}$

                      $9 = 9.\checkmark$

Therefore the triangle is a right triangle. ▰▰▰▰

EXERCISE SET 8.7

1–10. In right triangle ABC, angle C is the right angle. The length of the side opposite vertex A is labeled a, the length of the side opposite vertex B is labeled b, and the side opposite vertex C is labeled c. Complete the accompanying table.

	a	b	c
1.	30	40	?
2.	7	24	?
3.	?	$3\sqrt{7}$	8
4.	5	13	?
5.	?	17	15
6.	1	2	?
7.	5	?	$\sqrt{34}$
8.	$\sqrt{11}$	$\sqrt{5}$	?
9.	4	4	?
10.	$2\sqrt{3}$	9	?

11. Find the length of the diagonal of a rectangle whose length is 15 and whose width is 20.

12. The length of a rectangle is twice its width. If the length of the diagonal of the rectangle is $\sqrt{15}$, find the width of the rectangle.

13. Find the length of a diagonal of a square if the length of a side is
    (a) 8   (b) 14   (c) 20   (d) 15   (e) $\sqrt{7}$

14. Find the length of a side of a square if the length of a diagonal is:
    (a) 12   (b) 9   (c) $16\sqrt{2}$ (d) $2\sqrt{6}$ (e) 1

15. A ladder 41 feet in length rests against a vertical building. The foot of the ladder is 9 feet from the building. How far up the building does the ladder reach?

16. The length and the width of a rectangle are in the ratio of 3:4. If the length of the diagonal of the rectangle is 100, what are the length and the width of the rectangle?

17–20. In the accompanying table, a and b represent the lengths of the legs of a right triangle, and c represents the length of the hypotenuse. In each case, find the value of x.

	a	b	c
17.	x	x	18
18.	$x-1$	x	$x+1$
19.	$x+1$	$3x$	$5x-7$
20.	$x-1$	$\dfrac{x}{2}$	$x+1$

21. The diagonal of a rectangle exceeds the length by 2, and exceeds twice the width by 1. Find the length and the width of the rectangle.

22. The hypotenuse of a right triangle exceeds the length of one leg by 1, and is 3 less than four times the length of the other leg. Find the length of the shorter leg of the right triangle.

23. Determine whether each of the following sets of numbers can represent the lengths of the sides of a right triangle:

(a) 15, 8, 17   (b) 2, 7, $\sqrt{53}$ (c) $\dfrac{1}{3}, \dfrac{1}{4}, \dfrac{1}{5}$ (d) $3\sqrt{5}, \sqrt{29}, 8$

24. The perimeter of a right triangle is 180. If the length of the hypotenuse is 82, find the length of the shorter leg of the triangle.

25. The perimeter of a right triangle is 132. If the length of the hypotenuse is 61, find the length of the shorter leg of the triangle.

CHAPTER 8 REVIEW EXERCISES

REGENTS REVIEW. *Problems included in this section are similar in form and difficulty to those found on the New York State Regents Examination for Course I of the Three-Year Sequence for High School Mathematics. Problems preceded by an asterisk have actually appeared on a previous Course I Regents Examination.*

*1. The legs of a right triangle have lengths of 2 and 7. Express, in radical form, the length of the hypotenuse.

*2. Find $\sqrt{23}$ to the nearest tenth.

*3. Simplify $\sqrt{50} + 3\sqrt{2}$.

4. Express the product $(-3\sqrt{6})(2\sqrt{10})$ in simplest form.

5. Express $0.4\overline{7}$ as the ratio of two integers.

6. Express as a monomial in simplest form: $\sqrt{24} - 6\sqrt{\dfrac{2}{3}}$.

*7. What is the length of the diagonal of a rectangle whose dimensions are 5 by 7?

    (1) 5   (2) 8   (3) $\sqrt{24}$ (4) $\sqrt{74}$

*8. The expression $(3\sqrt{75} - 2\sqrt{27})$ is equivalent to:

    (1) $57\sqrt{3}$ (2) 9   (3) $9\sqrt{3}$ (4) $\sqrt{48}$

*9. The expression $\sqrt{125} + 2\sqrt{5}$ is equivalent to:

    (1) 35   (2) $7\sqrt{5}$ (3) $3\sqrt{5}$ (4) $3\sqrt{130}$

*10. The value of π is:
    (1) rational and equal to 3.14
    (2) irrational and equal to 3.14
    (3) rational and between 3.14 and 3.15
    (4) irrational and between 3.14 and 3.15

*11. The sum of $6\sqrt{6}$ and $\sqrt{54}$ is:

    (1) $3\sqrt{6}$ (2) $6\sqrt{60}$ (3) $9\sqrt{6}$ (4) $15\sqrt{6}$

*12. Which is a rational number?

    (1) $\sqrt{6}$ (2) $\sqrt{2}$ (3) $\sqrt{3}$ (4) $\sqrt{4}$

*13. The longer leg of a right triangle is 7 more than the shorter leg. The hypotenuse is 8 more than the shorter leg. The perimeter of the triangle is 30. Find the length of each leg.

*14. Let p represent "Triangle ABC is a right triangle."
Let q represent "The square of the hypotenuse is equal to the sum of the squares of the legs."
    (a) Write in words: $p \to q$.
    (b) Write in words the contrapositive of $p \to q$.
    (c) If the hypotenuse is 19 and the legs are 13 and 14, respectively, is q a true statement?
    (d) If p is false, what is the truth value of $p \to q$?
    (e) Using your answer to part (d), determine the truth value of the contrapositive of $p \to q$.

CUMULATIVE REVIEW EXERCISES FOR CHAPTERS 1–8

REGENTS REVIEW. *Problems included in this section are similar in form and difficulty to those found on the New York State Regents Examination for Course I of the Three-Year Sequence for High School Mathematics. Problems preceded by an asterisk have actually appeared on a previous Course I Regents Examination.*

*1. Solve for x: $\dfrac{2}{3}x + 1 = 13$.

*2. Factor: $x^2 - x - 12$.

*3. If $xy^2 = 18$, find x when $y = -3$.

*4. Solve for x: $0.03x + 7.2 = 8.34$.

*5. Solve for y: $6(y + 3) = 2y - 2$.

*6. From $2x^2 - 3x - 5$ subtract $x^2 - x - 6$.

*7. Solve for x: $7x < 4x + 18$.

*8. Solve for a: $\dfrac{a+2}{12} = \dfrac{5}{3}$.

*9. The perimeter of a square is represented by $8x - 8$. Express the length of one side of the square in terms of x.

*10. Express the product $(2x - 7)(x + 3)$ as a trinomial.

*11. What percent of 25 is 10?

*12. Solve for p in terms of r, s, and t: $rp + s = t$.

*13. The inverse of a statement is $p \rightarrow {\sim}q$. What is the statement?

*14. Factor: $4x^2 - 9$.

*15. Thirty percent of what number is 12?

16. Find the greatest common factor of $3x^3 + 6x$.

17. Find a negative number in the solution set of $(x - 1)(x + 2) = 0$.

18. If $(x + 3)$ is one factor of $2x^2 + 11x + 15$, what is the other factor?

19. If 32 meters of wire weighs 8 kilograms, what is the weight, in kilograms, of 40 meters of the same wire?

20. Find the positive square root of 43 to the *nearest tenth*.

21. The denominator of a fraction is 7 more than its numerator. If the numerator is increased by 3 and the denominator is decreased by 2, the new fraction equals $\dfrac{4}{5}$. Find the original fraction.

*22. Find the positive root of the equation $x^2 - x - 6 = 0$.

23. Express $0.4\overline{39}$ as the ratio of two integers.

*24. Let x represent the smaller of two integers whose sum is greater than 40. The larger integer is 7 times the smaller. Find the *smallest* possible value of x.

*25. One positive number is 4 more than another. The sum of their squares is 40. Find the numbers.

*26. The area of a rectangle is represented by $x^2 + 2x - 3$. If the width of the rectangle is represented by $x - 1$, the length may be represented by:
(1) $x - 3$ (2) $x - 2$ (3) $x + 3$ (4) $x + 4$

*27. Which statement is false when p is false and q is false?
(1) $p \wedge q$ (2) $p \rightarrow q$ (3) $\sim p \rightarrow \sim q$ (4) $p \leftrightarrow q$

*28. The quotient of $\dfrac{-4a^6b^2}{2a^2b}$ is:
(1) $2a^3b^2$ (2) $-2a^4b^2$ (3) $-2a^4b$ (4) $-6a^3b$

*29. Which number is *not* a member of the solution set of $3x \leq 6$?
(1) 0   (2) -1 (3) 3   (4) $\dfrac{1}{2}$

*30. Which statement is the converse of "If it rains today, I'll stay home"?
(1) If I stay home, then it will rain today.
(2) If it rains today, then I'll stay home.
(3) If I don't stay home, then it won't rain today.
(4) If it doesn't rain today, then I won't stay home.

*31. Let p represent the statement "$x \geq 5$," and let q represent the statement "$2x = 4$." Which is true if $x = 6$?
(1) $p \wedge q$ (2) $p \vee q$ (3) $p \rightarrow q$ (4) $p \leftrightarrow q$

*32. The expression $\sqrt{48} + \sqrt{27}$ is equivalent to:
(1) $7\sqrt{3}$ (2) $\sqrt{75}$ (3) $6\sqrt{3}$ (4) $4\sqrt{6}$

*33. The solution set of the equation $x^2 - 5x - 6 = 0$ is:
(1) $\{6, -1\}$ (2) $\{3, -2\}$ (3) $\{3, 2\}$ (4) $\{-6, 1\}$

*34. Find three positive consecutive odd integers such that the largest decreased by twice the second is equal to 10 less than the smallest.

*35. Given the replacement set $\{5, 6, 7, 8\}$, which member of the replacement set will make the statement $(x < 6) \vee (x < 8)$ *false*?

*36. The length of a side of a square is 1 more than twice the length of a side of another square. The perimeters of the two squares differ by 24 centimeters. Find, in centimeters, the length of a side of the *smaller* square.

*37. Find two consecutive positive integers such that the square of the smaller is 1 more than four times the larger.

*38. Below are three statements symbolized by p, q, and r:
Let p represent: 7 is an even number.
Let q represent: 9 is a prime number.
Let r represent: 25 is a perfect square.
(a) Write in words and tell whether the statement is *true* or *false*:
   (1) $p \vee r$ (2) $r \to q$ (3) $\sim p \wedge \sim q$
(b) Write in symbolic form and give the truth values of the following statements:
   (1) 25 is a perfect square if and only if 7 is an even number.
   (2) 9 is not a prime number or 7 is not an even number

39. (a) Construct a truth table for the statement
$$(q \to \sim p) \leftrightarrow (\sim p \vee \sim q).$$
(b) Is $(q \to \sim p) \leftrightarrow (\sim p \vee \sim q)$ a tautology?
(c) Give a reason for your answer to part (b).

40–42. Perform the indicated operations and express the result in simplest form.

40. $\left(\dfrac{8a^2b^3}{3c}\right)\left(\dfrac{3c^2 + 6c}{4ab}\right)$

41. $\dfrac{y^2 + 5y}{2y^2 - 8} \div \dfrac{3y + 15}{y^2 + 4y - 12}$

42. $\dfrac{6x + 5}{10x} - \dfrac{x^2 + 10x}{15x^2}$

43–50. What integer value(s) of x, if any, will make the following statements true?

43. $(x^2 = 9) \wedge (x + 2) = 5$
44. $(x > -1) \wedge (x < 6)$
45. $(4x > 5x - 2) \wedge (x = 2)$
46. $(x^2 = 16) \vee (2x - 1 = 3)$
47. $(x^2 - 3x = 0) \wedge (x^2 - 2x - 3 = 0)$
48. $\left(\dfrac{2x}{3} - 1 = 7\right) \wedge (12x = x^2)$
49. $(x^2 + 4x = 5) \wedge (x^2 - 1 = 0)$
50. $(x^2 = 2x + 48) \vee (x^2 - 64 = 0)$

UNIT III: GEOMETRY

CHAPTER 9

Fundamental Ideas in Geometry

9.1 BUILDING A GEOMETRY VOCABULARY

KEY IDEAS

Cement and bricks are used to give a house a strong foundation. The building blocks of geometry take the form of *undefined terms, defined terms, postulates,* and *theorems.*

UNDEFINED TERMS.   Some basic terms in geometry can be described but cannot be defined by using simpler terms. *Point, line,* and *plane* are undefined terms.

A **point** indicates position and has no size or dimensions. A point is represented by a dot and named by a capital letter (Figure 9.1).

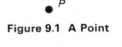

Figure 9.1 A Point

A **line** is a set of continuous points that form a straight path that extends without ending in two opposite directions. A line has no width or thickness. A line is identified by naming two points on the line or by writing a lower case letter next to the line (Figure 9.2). The notation $\overleftrightarrow{AB}$ is read as "line AB" and refers to the line that contains points A and B.

Figure 9.2 A Line

A **plane** is a flat surface that has no thickness and extends without ending in all directions. A plane is represented by a "window pane" and named by writing a capital letter in one of its corners (Figure 9.3).

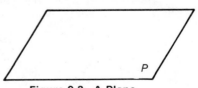

Figure 9.3 A Plane

DEFINED TERMS.   Defined terms are terms whose distinguishing characteristics can be explained by using either undefined or previously defined terms. Table 9.1 lists some basic geometric terms and their definitions.

TABLE 9.1

Term	Definition	Illustration
Line segment	A **line segment** is a part of a line consisting of two points, called endpoints, and the set of all points between them.	 Notation: $\overline{AB}$
Ray	A **ray** is a part of a line consisting of a given point, called the endpoint, and the set of all points on one side of the endpoint.	 Notation: $\overrightarrow{LM}$ A ray is always named by using two points, the first of which must be the endpoint. The arrow on top must always point to the right.
Opposite rays	**Opposite rays** are rays that have the same endpoint and that form a line.	 $\overrightarrow{KX}$ and $\overrightarrow{KB}$ are opposite rays.
Angle	An **angle** is the union of two rays having the same endpoint. The endpoint is called the vertex of the angle; the rays are called the sides of the angle.	 Vertex: K Sides: $\overrightarrow{KJ}$ and $\overrightarrow{KL}$
Collinear points	**Collinear points** are points that lie on the same line.	 Points A, B, and C are collinear. Points B, C, and D are *not* collinear.

NAMING ANGLES. An angle may be named in several different ways.

1. By using three letters, with the middle letter corresponding to the vertex of the angle and the other letters naming one point on each side of the angle. In Figure 9.4, the name of the angle may be $\angle RTB$ *or* $\angle BTR$.

2. By placing a number at the vertex and in the interior of the angle. The angle may then be referred to by the number. In Figure 9.4, the name of the angle may be $\angle 1$ *or* $\angle RTB$ (*or* $\angle BTR$).

3. By using a *single* capital letter that corresponds to the vertex, provided that this causes no confusion. In Figure 9.5, there is no question that $\angle A$ is another name for $\angle BAD$. On the other hand, $\angle D$ may not be used since it is not clear whether it names $\angle ADB$ *or* $\angle CDB$ *or* $\angle ADC$.

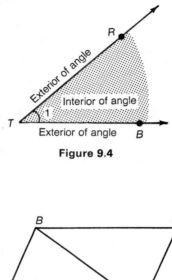

Figure 9.4

Figure 9.5

BEGINNING POSTULATES. A **postulate** is a statement that is assumed to be true. For example, we accept as postulates the following statements:

Postulate 1 Exactly one line may be drawn between two given points.

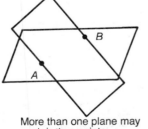

A second *line* cannot be drawn through points A and B. Thus two points determine a line.

Postulate 2 Exactly one plane contains three noncollinear points.

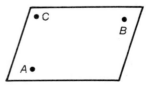

More than one plane may contain *two* points.

Exactly one plane contains *three* noncollinear points.

Postulate 3 If two lines intersect, they meet in exactly one point.

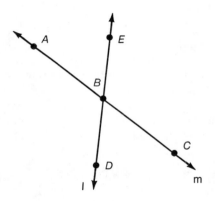

Intersecting lines cannot meet in more than one point.

THEOREMS. A **theorem** is a generalization that can be demonstrated to be true. The Pythagorean relationship ($a^2 + b^2 = c^2$) is a theorem since it can be proved to be true for *any* right triangle.

EXERCISE SET 9.1

1. In the accompanying diagram:
   (a) Name four rays having point B as an endpoint.
   (b) Name line l in three different ways.
   (c) Name line m in three different ways.
   (d) Name four angles that have the same vertex.
   (e) Name two pairs of opposite rays.

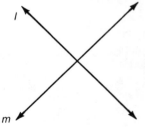

Use the following diagram for Exercises 2 and 3:

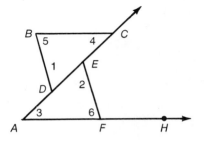

2. Name the vertex of each of the following angles:
   (a) 1 (b) 3 (c) 5

3. Use three letters to name each of the following angles:
   (a) 2 (b) 4 (c) 6

Use the following diagram for Exercises 4–11:

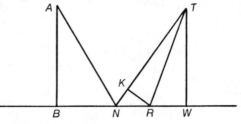

4. Name four collinear points.

5. If point N is the midpoint of $\overline{BW}$, name two segments that have the same length.

6. Name the different triangles that appear in the diagram.

7. Name each angle that has point R as its vertex.

8. Name an angle that is not an angle of a triangle.

9. Name two pairs of opposite rays.

10. Name a segment that is a side of two different triangles.

11. In order to conclude that R is the midpoint of $\overline{WN}$, which two segments must have the same length?

9.2 MEASURING SEGMENTS AND ANGLES

——— KEY IDEAS ———

The familiar *ruler* is used for measuring the length of a segment, and the *protractor* is used to measure an angle. Comparing the measures of segments and measures of angles leads to new terms and concepts.

MEASURING SEGMENTS. The length (or measure) of a line segment is the distance between its endpoints. If the distance between points A and B is 2 inches, the length of $\overline{AB}$ is 2 inches; this may be abbreviated by writing $AB = 2$. Notice that $\overline{AB}$ represents a line segment, while AB (without the top bar) represents the *length* of $\overline{AB}$.

MEASURING ANGLES. If you imagine the vertex as a pivot point, then the measure of an angle refers to the amount of rotation from the first side to the second side. The amount of rotation is measured by a protractor (Figure 9.6), on which the customary unit of measurement is the degree, represented by the symbol $°$. A ray that sweeps out one complete circle rotates 360 degrees. One degree is therefore defined to be $\frac{1}{360}$ of one complete rotation of a ray.

The measure of an angle corresponds to some number on the protractor, greater than 0 and less than *or* equal to 180. In Figure 9.6, the degree measure of angle *ABC* is 60 degrees. We abbreviate this by writing m∠*ABC*=60, read as "the measure of angle *ABC* is 60." It is customary to omit the degree symbol (°); we never write m∠*ABC*=60° or ∠*ABC*=60 (omitting the "m").

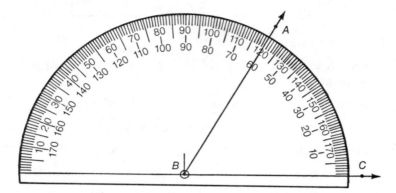

Figure 9.6   A Protractor

Example

1. In the accompanying figure, find the measures of these angles:
(a) ∠*APZ*   (b) ∠*FPZ*   (c) ∠*WPB*   (d) ∠*ZPB*   (e) ∠*SPZ*

Solutions:
(a) m∠*APZ*=**50** (read lower scale).
(b) m∠*FPZ*=**130** (read upper scale).
(c) m∠*WPB*=110−90=**20**.
(d) m∠*ZPB*=90−50=**40**.
(e) m∠*SPZ*=130−50=**80**.

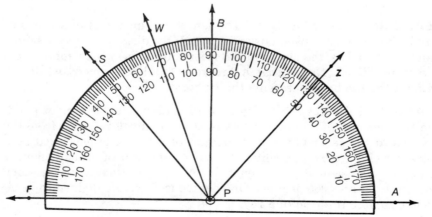

RIGHT ANGLES AND PERPENDICULARS.   An L-shaped angle is called a *right* angle. A **right angle** is an angle whose measure is 90. Lines or segments that intersect to form a right angle are said to be *perpendicular*.

Perpendicular lines are two lines that intersect to form a right angle. If line l is perpendicular to line m, we may write $l \perp m$, where the symbol $\perp$ is read as "is perpendicular to."

CLASSIFYING ANGLES.   An angle whose sides form a straight line is called a **straight** angle and has a measure of 180. Other angles having measures between 0 and 180 may be classified according to whether their measures are less than 90 or greater than 90. Figure 9.7 shows the four types of angles.

Acute Angle

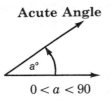

$0 < a < 90$

Right Angle

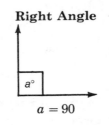

$a = 90$

Obtuse Angle

$90 < a < 180$

Straight Angle

$a = 180$

Figure 9.7   Types of Angles

Example

2.   The measure of angle R is represented by $x + 15$. If angle R is acute, what is the set of all possible values of x?

Solution: Since angle R is acute, its measure must be greater than 0 *and* less than 90.

$$(m \angle R > 0) \wedge (m \angle R < 90)$$
$$(x + 15 > 0) \wedge (x + 15 < 90)$$
$$(x > -15) \wedge (x < 75)$$

The set of all possible values of x is $\{x | x > -15 \text{ } and \text{ } x < 75\}$, which may also be written as $\{x | -15 < x < 75\}$.

CONGRUENT SEGMENTS AND ANGLES.   Objects that have the same size and shape are said to be **congruent**. Line segments are congruent if they have the same length. Angles are congruent if they have the same degree measure. Since all right angles have 90 as their measure, *all right angles are congruent.*

NOTATION. The symbol ≅ is translated as "is congruent to." If $AB = 2$ and $RS = 2$, then $\overline{AB} \cong \overline{RS}$; this is read as "line segment *AB is congruent to* line segment *RS.*" If $m\angle J = 60$ and $m\angle K = 60$, then $\angle J \cong \angle K$, read as "angle *J is congruent to* angle *K.*"

When comparing diagrams, it is sometimes helpful to indicate which pairs of segments or angles, if any, are congruent. Matching bars drawn through segments are used to indicate that pairs of line segments are congruent. In Figure 9.8, $\overline{AB} \cong \overline{CD}$ and $\overline{BC} \cong \overline{AD}$. As shown in the diagram, congruent angles may also be identified by drawing matching bars. Angles 1 and 2 are marked off as being congruent. According to the diagram, angles 3 and 4 are also congruent.

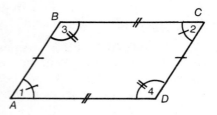

Figure 9.8   Congruent Angles and Line Segments

BISECTOR AND MIDPOINT. A **bisector** of a line segment is any line, line segment, or ray that divides the segment into two congruent segments. If line *l bisects* $\overline{AB}$, then the point at which line *l* intersects $\overline{AB}$ is the *midpoint* of $\overline{AB}$ (Figure 9.9). In general, a point *M* is the **midpoint** of $\overline{AB}$ if points *A*, *B*, and *M* are collinear and $AM = MB$. A line segment has exactly one midpoint, but an infinite number of bisectors.

An **angle bisector** is a ray that divides an angle into two congruent angles. In Figure 9.10, $\angle ABD \cong \angle CBD$ so that $\overrightarrow{BD}$ bisects $\angle ABC$. An angle has exactly one bisector.

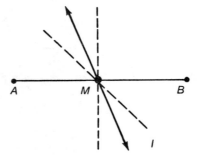

Figure 9.9   Bisection and Midpoint

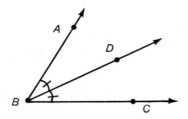

Figure 9.10   Angle Bisector

Examples ▬▬▬

3. In the accompanying figure, point M is the midpoint of $\overline{RS}$. If $RM = 18$ and the length of $\overline{SM}$ is represented by $3x - 6$, find the value of x.

Solution: Since M is the midpoint of $\overline{RS}$, SM = RM, so

$$3x - 6 = 18$$
$$3x = 18 + 6$$
$$\frac{3x}{3} = 24$$
$$x = 8$$

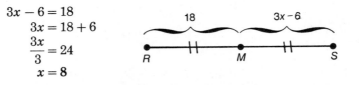

4. For the accompanying figure, draw a conclusion, given that:
   (a) $\overline{AL}$ bisects $\overline{BC}$.
   (b) $\overline{BK}$ bisects $\angle ABC$.
   (c) $\overline{BK}$ bisects $\overline{AL}$.
   (d) $\overline{AL}$ bisects $\angle CAB$.

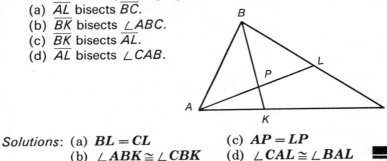

Solutions: (a) $BL = CL$ (c) $AP = LP$
             (b) $\angle ABK \cong \angle CBK$ (d) $\angle CAL \cong \angle BAL$ ▬▬

EXERCISE SET 9.2

1. In the acompanying diagram, classify each of the following angles as acute, right, obtuse, or straight:
   (a) $\angle TOM$
   (b) $\angle LOM$
   (c) $\angle SOM$
   (d) $\angle LOR$
   (e) $\angle ROT$
   (f) $\angle LOT$
   (g) $\angle ROS$
   (h) $\angle MOR$

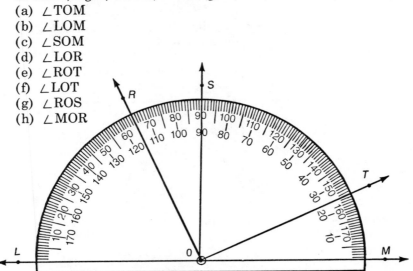

2. In the accompanying diagram, pairs of angles and segments are indicated as congruent. Using the letters in the diagram, write the appropriate congruence relationships.

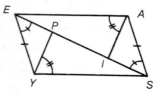

3. Line $\overleftrightarrow{HG}$ passes through point P in such a way that P lies between points H and G.
    (a) If $HP = 3$ and $PG = 5$, find HG.
    (b) If point X is the midpoint of $\overline{HG}$, find the length of $\overline{XP}$.

4. Points, P, I, and Z are collinear, and $IZ = 8$, $PI = 14$, and $PZ = 6$.
    (a) Which of the three points is between the other two?
    (b) If point M is the midpoint of $\overline{PI}$ and point N is the midpoint of $\overline{IZ}$, what is the length of $\overline{MN}$?

5. $\overrightarrow{PL}$ lies in the interior of $\angle RPH$. If $m\angle RPL = x - 5$, $m\angle LPH = 2x + 18$, and $m\angle HPR = 58$, what is the measure of the smallest angle formed that has ray PL as one side?

6. $\overleftrightarrow{XY}$ bisects $\overline{RS}$ at point M. If $RM = 6.5$, find the length of $\overline{RS}$.

7. $\overrightarrow{PQ}$ bisects $\angle HPJ$. If $m\angle HPJ = 83$, find $m\angle QPJ$.

8. $\overrightarrow{BP}$ bisects $\angle ABC$. If $m\angle ABP = 4x + 5$ and $m\angle CBP = 3x + 15$:
    (a) find the value of x
    (b) classify $\angle ABC$ as acute, right, or obtuse

9. If R is the midpoint $\overline{XY}$, and $XR = 3n + 1$, and $YR = 16 - 2n$:
    (a) find the value of n
    (b) find the length of $\overline{XY}$

10. If M is the midpoint of $\overline{AB}$, find the value of x and fill in each missing length in the following table:

	AB	**AM**	**MB**
(a)	x	3.6	?
(b)	?	$3x - 14$	x
(c)	$8x$	$3x + 24$	?
(d)	?	$2x + 13$	$5x - 14$
(e)	$x - 5$	?	$x + 9$

11. Find the set of all possible values of x if
    (a) angle A is acute and $m\angle A = 3x - 9$
    (b) angle A is right and $m\angle A = 2x + 6$
    (c) angle A is obtuse and $m\angle A = 5x - 15$

In Exercises 12 to 14, mark off each diagram with the given information, and draw an appropriate conclusion.

12. Given: $\overline{BF}$ bisects $\overline{AC}$.
Conclusion: ?

13. Given: $\overline{PT}$ bisects $\angle STO$.
Conclusion: ?

14. Given: $\overline{AC}$ bisects $\overline{BD}$.
$\overline{BD}$ bisects $\angle ADC$.
Conclusion: ?

9.3 CLASSIFYING POLYGONS AND TRIANGLES

────────── KEY IDEAS ──────────

Any figure that can be represented by stretching and/or twisting a rubber band is an example of a **closed figure.** If the rubber band does not cross over itself, then the figure is called a *simple* closed figure.

(1)   (2)   (3)   (4)

Figure (1) is *not* a simple closed curve since the curve crosses over itself. Figure (2) is *not* a simple closed curve since the "rubber band *snapped*" and the curve is "open." Figures (3) and (4) are examples of simple closed curves.

CLASSIFYING POLYGONS. A **polygon** is a simple closed curve that consists entirely of line segments. Each line segment is called a **side** of the polygon. Each corner of the polygon in which two sides intersect is called a **vertex** of the polygon. Polygons may be classified by the number of their sides. The names of some commonly referred to polygons are listed in Table 9.2.

TABLE 9.2 Names of Some Polygons

Number of Sides	Name
3	Triangle
4	Quadrilateral
5	Pentagon
6	Hexagon
8	Octagon
10	Decagon
12	Dodecagon

A polygon of any number of sides may also be referred to as an "*n*-gon," where *n* represents the number of its sides. For example, a polygon having 13 sides may be referred to as a 13-gon.

REGULAR POLYGONS.   If each side of a polygon has the same length, the polygon is **equilateral**. If each angle of a polygon has the same measure, the polygon is **equiangular**. If a polygon is both equilateral *and* equiangular, it is called a **regular polygon**. Figure 9.11 shows some different types of quadrilaterals.

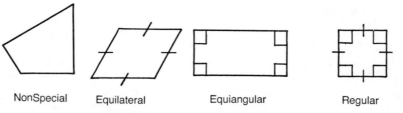

NonSpecial   Equilateral   Equiangular   Regular

Figure 9.11   Types of Quadrilaterals

Examples

1. Find the perimeter of an equilateral pentagon if the length of one of its sides is 4.6 inches.

Solution: The perimeter of a polygon is equal to the sum of the lengths of its sides. A pentagon has five sides, and, since it is regular, each side has the same length, so

$$\text{Perimeter} = 4.6 + 4.6 + 4.6 + 4.6 + 4.6$$
$$= 5(4.6)$$
$$= \textbf{23 inches}$$

2. Find the measure of each angle of a regular hexagon if the sum of the degree measures of its angles is 720.

Solution: Since a hexagon has six sides, it must have six interior angles. Each angle of a regular hexagon has the same degree measure.

Let x = measure of one interior angle.
$$6x = 720$$
$$x = \frac{720}{6} = 120$$

3. If the perimeter of an equilateral polygon having seven sides is represented by $14x - 35$, express the length of one of its sides in terms of x.

Solution: Let s = length of a side.
$$7s = 14x - 35$$
$$\frac{7s}{7} = \frac{14x - 35}{7}$$
$$s = \frac{7(2x - 5)}{7}$$
$$s = 2x - 5$$

CLASSIFYING TRIANGLES. A triangle may be classified according to the number of congruent sides that it contains (Figure. 9.12).

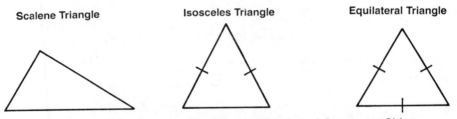

Scalene Triangle   Isosceles Triangle   Equilateral Triangle

Figure 9.12   Triangles Classified by Number of Congruent Sides

A triangle may also be classified by the measure of its greatest angle (Figure. 9.13).

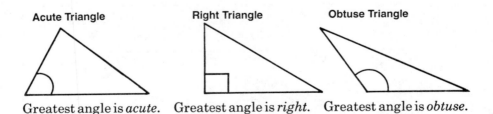

Acute Triangle   Right Triangle   Obtuse Triangle

Greatest angle is *acute*.   Greatest angle is *right*.   Greatest angle is *obtuse*.

Figure 9.13   Triangles Classified by Greatest Angle Measurement

EXERCISE SET 9.3

1. Find the perimeter of a regular octagon if the length of a side is 4.

2. Express in terms of x the perimeter of a regular hexagon if the length of a side is represented by $3x + 2$.

3. If the perimeter of a regular decagon is 78, find the length of a side.

4. If the sum of the measures of the angles of a regular 9-gon is 1260, find the measure of an angle of the 9-gon.

5. If the perimeter of a regular quadrilateral is represented by $24x^2 - 8x$, represent in terms of x the length of a side of the quadrilateral.

6. The perimeter of an equilateral triangle is equal to the perimeter of a certain equilateral quadrilateral. If the length of a side of the triangle exceeds the length of a side of the quadrilateral by 5, find the length of a side of the quadrilateral.

7. The perimeter of a regular pentagon is equal to the perimeter of a certain regular hexagon. If the length of a side of the pentagon exceeds the length of a side of the hexagon by 2, find the perimeter of each polygon.

8–10. Classify $\triangle ABC$ as scalene, isosceles, or equilateral.

8. Perimeter $= 45$; $AB = x + 7$, $BC = 2x - 1$, and $AC = 3x - 9$.

9. Perimeter $= 59$; $AB = 2x$, $BC = 3x - 10$, and $AC = x + 9$.

10. Perimeter $= 66$; $AB = x + 10$, $BC = 2x$, and $AC = 3x - 10$.

11. Fill in the following table, given that the indicated polygon is regular.

	Polygon	Length of Side	Measure of Angle	Perimeter	Sum of Angle Measures
(a)	Pentagon	7.4	?	?	540
(b)	7-gon	1.8	?	?	900
(c)	Octagon	?	135	28	?
(d)	Decagon	6.7	?	?	1440
(e)	Dodecagon	?	150	45.6	?

9.4 INVESTIGATING SPECIAL PAIRS OF ANGLES

_____ KEY IDEAS _____

Important geometric results often rely on whether a special relationship exists between two angles. *Supplementary, complementary,* and *vertical* angle pairs are of special importance.

ADJACENT ANGLES. Two angles are **adjacent** if they have the same vertex and share a common side, but do not have any interior points in common (they don't overlap). In Figure 9.14, angles 1 and 2 are adjacent angles. Point A is the vertex of each angle, and $\overrightarrow{AS}$ is the common side of the two angles.

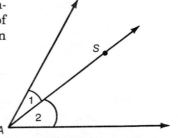

Figure 9.14   Adjacent Angles

SUPPLEMENTARY ANGLES. Two angles are **supplementary** (Figure 9.15) if the sum of their measures is 180. If $m\angle A = 60$ and $m\angle B = 120$, then $\angle A$ and $\angle B$ are supplementary, and either angle is called the *supplement* of the other angle. Observe that $m\angle A = 180 - m\angle B$, and $m\angle B = 180 - m\angle A$.

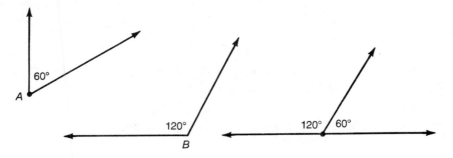

$\angle A$ is the supplement of $\angle B$, and $\angle B$ is the supplement of $\angle A$.

If two *adjacent* angles are supplementary, their noncommon (exterior) sides form a straight line.

Figure 9.15   Supplementary Angles

COMPLEMENTARY ANGLES. Two angles are **complementary** (Figure 9.16) if the sum of their measures is 90. If $m \angle A = 40$ and $m \angle B = 50$, then $\angle A$ and $\angle B$ are complementary, and either angle is called the *complement* of the other angle. Observe that $m \angle A = 90 - m \angle B$, and $m \angle B = 90 - m \angle A$.

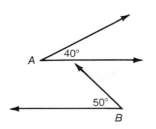

$\angle A$ is the complement of $\angle B$, and $\angle B$ is the complement of $\angle A$.

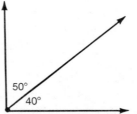

If two *adjacent* angles are complementary, their noncommon (exterior) sides are perpendicular.

Figure 9.16 Complementary Angles

Examples

1. In the accompanying diagram, find the value of *x*.

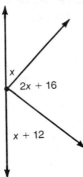

Solution: The sum of the measures of the adjacent angles having point P as their vertex is 180, so

$$x + (2x + 16) + (x + 12) = 180$$
$$4x + 28 = 180$$
$$4x = 180 - 28$$
$$4x = 152$$
$$x = \frac{152}{4} = \mathbf{38}$$

2. The measures of two complementary angles are in the ratio of $2 : 13$. Find the measure of the smaller angle.

Solution: Let $2x$ = measure of the smaller angle.
Then $13x$ = measure of the larger angle.
$$2x + 13x = 90$$
$$15x = 90$$
$$\frac{15x}{15} = \frac{90}{15}$$
$$x = 6$$
$$2x = 2(6) = 12.$$
The measure of the smaller angle is **12**.

3. If the measure of an angle exceeds twice its supplement by 30, find the measure of the angle.

Solution:　Let x　= measure of the angle.

Then $180 - x$ = measure of the angle's supplement.

$$x = 2(180 - x) + 30$$
$$x = 360 - 2x + 30$$
$$x + 2x = 390$$
$$\frac{3x}{3} = \frac{390}{3}$$
$$x = 130$$

VERTICAL ANGLES.　If two different lines intersect, four angles are formed having the point of intersection of the lines as their vertex. Non-adjacent (opposite) pairs of these angles are called **vertical angles.** In Figure 9.17, angles 1 and 3 are vertical angles. Also, angles 2 and 4 are vertical angles.

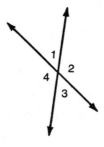

Suppose that $m\angle 1 = 50$. Then $m\angle 2 = 180 - m\angle 1 = 180 - 50 = 130$. Also, $m\angle 3 = 180 - m\angle 2 = 180 - 130 = 50$. And $m\angle 4 = 180 - m\angle 1 = 130$.

Therefore　$m\angle 1 = m\angle 3$,　and $m\angle 2 = m\angle 4$. This suggests the following theorem:

Figure 9.17　Vertical Angles

THEOREM:　*Vertical angles are equal in measure and are, therefore, congruent.*

Example

4.　In the accompanying diagram, find the value of y:

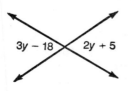

$3y - 18$　$2y + 5$

Solution:　Since vertical angles are equal in measure,

$$3y - 18 = 2y + 5$$
$$3y = 2y + 5 + 18$$
$$3y - 2y = 23$$
$$y = 23$$

SUMMARY OF ANGLE PAIR RELATIONSHIPS

Let $m\angle A = a$, and $m\angle B = b$.

If $\angle A$ and $\angle B$ are:	Then:
Supplementary	$a + b = 180$
Complementary	$a + b = 90$
Vertical	$a = b$

EXERCISE SET 9.4

1. For the accompanying diagram, list all pairs of adjacent,
   supplementary, and vertical
   angles.

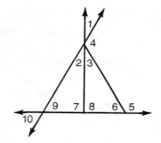

2. For each of the following, find the value of x:

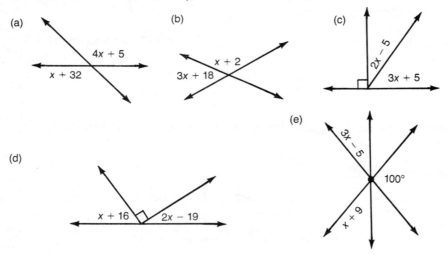

(a)

$4x + 5$
$x + 32$

(b)

$x + 2$
$3x + 18$

(c)

$2x - 5$
$3x + 5$

(d)

$x + 16$ $2x - 19$

(e)

$3x - 5$
$100°$
$x + 9$

3. If two angles are supplementary, find the measure of the smaller
   angle if the measures of the two angles are in the ratio of:
   (a) $1:8$ (b) $3:5$ (c) $3:1$ (d) $5:7$ (e) $7:11$

4. If two angles are complementary, find the measure of the smaller angle if the measures of the two angles are in the ratio of:
    (a) $2:3$ (b) $1:2$ (c) $4:5$ (d) $3:1$ (e) $1:5$

5. The measure of an angle exceeds three times its supplement by 4. Find the measure of the angle.

6. The measure of an angle exceeds four times the measure of its complement by 6. Find the measure of the angle.

7. The measure of an angle is 22 less than three times the measure of the complement of the angle. Find the measure of the angle.

8. The measure of the supplement of an angle is three times as great as the measure of the angle's complement. What is the measure of the angle?

9. Find the measure of an angle if it is 12 less than twice the measure of its complement.

10. The difference between the measures of an angle and its complement is 14. Find the measure of the smaller of the two angles.

11. The difference between the measures of an angle and its supplement is 22. Find the measure of the smaller of the two angles.

12. The measure of the supplement of an angle is three times as great as the measure of the complement of the same angle. What is the measure of the angle?

13. If the measure of angle A is represented by $3x - 18$, express each of the following in terms of x:
    (a) the measure of the supplement of angle A
    (b) the measure of the complement of angle A
    (c) the measure of the supplement of angle A diminished by the measure of the complement of angle A

14–16. Lines AB *and* CD *intersect at point* H. *Fill in the missing values in the accompanying table, solving for* x *where necessary*:

	$m\angle AHC$	$m\angle AHD$	$m\angle DHB$	$m\angle CHB$
14.	42	?	?	?
15.	?	$3x - 7$	?	$2x + 17$
16.	$5x - 2$	$2x + 21$	?	?

17. $\overleftrightarrow{XY}$ and $\overleftrightarrow{AB}$ intersect at point C. If $m\angle XCB = 4y - 9$ and $m\angle ACY = 3y + 29$, find $m\angle XCB$.

18. State whether each of the following statements is *true* or *false*. If a statement is false, provide an example that shows that your answer is correct.

   (a) If an angle is congruent to its supplement, then the angle is a right angle.

   (b) If two lines intersect to form congruent vertical angles, then the lines are perpendicular.

   (c) If a pair of angles are congruent, then they are vertical angles.

   (d) If two angles are supplementary, then they are adjacent.

   (e) If two lines intersect to form congruent adjacent angles, then the lines are perpendicular.

   (f) Vertical angles are never right angles.

   (g) If two angles are complementary, then their sides are perpendicular to each other.

   (h) A line that bisects one of two vertical angles also bisects the other vertical angle.

   (i) If two angles are each complementary to the same angle, then the original two angles are congruent.

9.5 WORKING WITH PARALLEL LINES

KEY IDEAS

Lines that lie in the same plane and never meet are called **parallel lines**. The symbol ‖ means "is parallel to," so that $l \parallel m$ is read as "line l is parallel to line m." To identify parallel lines, mark them with arrowheads that point in the same direction. In the accompanying diagram, the corresponding pairs of arrowheads indicate that $\overline{AD} \parallel \overline{BC}$ and $\overline{AB} \parallel \overline{CD}$.

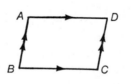

TRANSVERSALS AND SPECIAL ANGLE PAIRS. A line that intersects two or more lines in different points is called a **transversal**. In Figure 9.18, line t represents a transversal since it intersects lines l and m at two different points. Angles 1, 2, 5, and 6 lie *between* lines l and m and are called **interior angles**. Angles 3, 4, 7, and 8 lie *outside* lines l and m and are called **exterior angles**.

Table 9.3 further classifies special pairs of these angles.

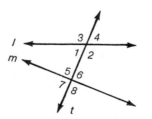

Figure 9.18 Transversal and Angle Pairs

TABLE 9.3 Special Angle Pairs

Type of Angle Pair	Distinguishing Features	Examples (Figure 9.18)
Alternate interior angles	● Angles are interior angles. ● Angles are on opposite sides of the transversal. ● Angles do not have the same vertex.	Angles 1 and 6; angles 2 and 5.
Corresponding angles	● One angle is an interior angle; the other angle is an exterior angle. ● Angles are on the same side of the transversal. ● Angles do not have the same vertex.	Angles 3 and 5; angles 4 and 6; angles 1 and 7; angles 2 and 8.

In analyzing diagrams, alternate interior angle pairs may be identified by their Z shape, while corresponding angles form an F shape (Figure 9.19). The Z and F shapes, however, may be rotated so that the letter may appear reversed or upside down.

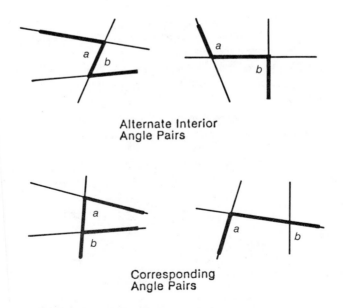

Alternate Interior
Angle Pairs

Corresponding
Angle Pairs

Figure 9.19 Z and F Shapes Formed by Angle Pairs

Example

1. For the accompanying diagram, name all pairs of:
    (a) alternate interior angles
    (b) corresponding angles

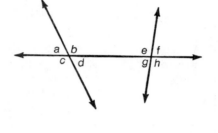

Solutions:
    (a) Alternate interior angle pairs: *b* and *g*; *d* and *e*.
    (b) Corresponding angle pairs: *a* and *e*; *b* and *f*; *c* and *g*; *d* and *h*.

ANGLES FORMED BY PARALLEL LINES. In Figure 9.20 line *t* intersects parallel lines *l* and *m*. If you took a protractor and compared the measures of ∠1 and ∠2, you would find that the measures of these alternate interior angles are equal. This experiment is consistent with the following postulate:

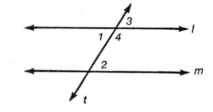

Figure 9.20 Angles Formed by Parallel Lines

Postulate 1: If two lines are parallel, then alternate interior angles have the same measure and are, therefore, congruent.

Referring to Figure 9.20, suppose that m ∠ 1 = *x*. Then m ∠ 2 = *x* since alternate interior angles of parallel lines have the same measure. Since angles 1 and 3 are vertical angles, $m \angle 3 = m \angle 1 = x$. The measures of angles 3 and 2 are each represented by *x*. Corresponding angles of parallel lines have the same measure and are, therefore, *congruent*. Since angles 1 and 4 are supplementary, m ∠ 4 = 180 − m ∠ 1 = 180 − *x*. Comparing the measures of angles 2 and 4, we see that *interior angles on the same side of the transversal* are *supplementary*. These results suggest the following theorems:

THEOREM 1: *If two lines are parallel, then corresponding angles have the same measure and are, therefore, congruent.*

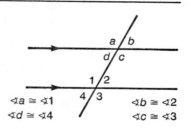

THEOREM 2: *If two lines are parallel, then interior angles on the same side of the transversal are supplementary.*

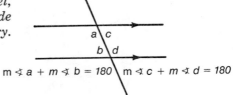

$$m \sphericalangle a + m \sphericalangle b = 180 \qquad m \sphericalangle c + m \sphericalangle d = 180$$

Examples

2. Given that the indicated lines in the accompanying diagrams are parallel, determine the value of *x*.

(a)

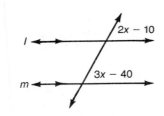

(b)

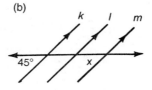

Solutions:

(a) From Theorem 1,
$$3x - 40 = 2x - 10$$
$$3x = 2x + 30$$
$$x = \mathbf{30}$$

(b) Using vertical angles and Postulate 1 gives

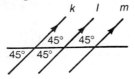

3. Two parallel lines are cut by a transversal so that the measures of a pair of interior angles on the same side of the transversal are in the ratio of $5 : 13$. Find the measure of the smaller of these angles.

Solution: Let $5x =$ measure of the smaller interior angle. Then $13x =$ measure of the other interior angle.

Since the lines are parallel, interior angles on the same side of the transversal are supplementary, so the sum of their measures is 180.

$$5x + 13x = 180$$
$$18x = 180$$
$$x = \frac{180}{18} = 10$$
$$5x = 5(10) = 50$$

The measure of the small interior angle is **50**.

4. If $l \parallel m$ and $r \parallel s$ in the accompanying diagram, find x and y.

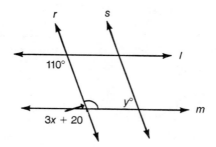

Solution: Since $l \parallel m$, alternate interior angles are equal.

$$3x + 20 = 110$$
$$3x = 110 - 20$$
$$x = \frac{90}{3} = 30$$

Since $r \parallel s$, interior angles on the same side of the transversal are supplementary.

$$y + (3x + 20) = 180$$
$$y + 110 = 180$$
$$y = 180 - 110 = 70$$

SUMMARY OF ANGLE PAIRS

When a transversal intersects a pair of parallel lines, the angles in any pair that is formed are either supplementary or have the same measure.

Type of Angle Pair	Relationship	Diagram
Alternate interior angles	$c = e; \ d = f$	
Corresponding angles	$a = e; \ c = g$ $b = f; \ d = h$	
Interior angles on the same side of the transversal	$d + e = 180$ $c + f = 180$	

DETERMINING WHEN LINES ARE PARALLEL. Although the converse of a true statement is not necessarily true, the converses of the preceding postulate and theorems are true. These converses provide a way of knowing when lines are parallel.

Converse of Postulate 1 of Section 9.5:
If a pair of alternate interior angles have the same measure, then the lines are parallel.

Converse of Theorems 1 and 2 of Section 9.5:
1. If a pair of corresponding angles have the same measure, then the lines are parallel.
2. If a pair of interior angles on the same side of the transversal are supplementary, then the lines are parallel.

Example ■■■

5. Which of the accompanying diagrams contains a pair of parallel lines?

(1)

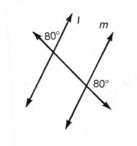

(3)

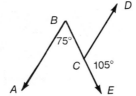

(2) (4)

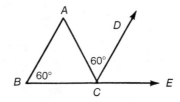

Solution: In choice (3), m∠$BCD = 180 - 105 = 75$. Since alternate interior angles are equal in measure, $\overline{BA} \| \overline{CD}$. The correct answer is **choice (3)**.

EXERCISE SET 9.5

1. In the accompanying diagram, $l \parallel m$. Find the value of x if:
   (a) $m \angle 1 = x$ and $m \angle 7 = 68$
   (b) $m \angle 2 = 53$ and $m \angle 7 = x$
   (c) $m \angle 3 = 64$ and $m \angle 8 = x$
   (d) $m \angle 3 = 76$ and $m \angle 5 = 3x - 5$
   (e) $m \angle 6 = 128$ and $m \angle 2 = 4x$
   (f) $m \angle 2 = 3x - 15$ and $m \angle 5 = x + 29$
   (g) $m \angle 8 = 2x - 11$ and $m \angle 5 = 3x - 47$
   (h) $m \angle 4 = 3x + 7$ and $m \angle 3 = x + 5$
   (i) $m \angle 1 = 3x$ and $m \angle 5 = 7x$
   (j) $m \angle 4 = x$ and $m \angle 8 = 5x$
   (k) $m \angle 3 = 4x - 35$ and $m \angle 8 = x + 7$

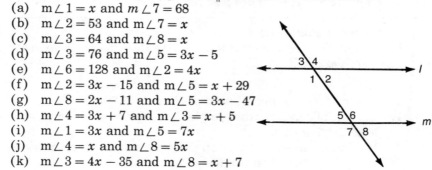

2–10. Given that $1 \parallel m$, *find the value of* x.

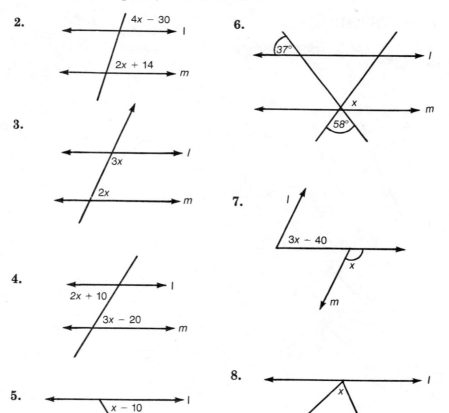

2. $4x - 30$ l
     $2x + 14$ m

3. $3x$
     $2x$ m l

6. $37°$ l
     x
     $58°$ m

7. l
     $3x - 40$
     x
     m

4. $2x + 10$ l
     $3x - 20$ m

8. l
     x
     $40°$ $100°$ m

5. l
     $x - 10$
     $x + 10$ m

9.

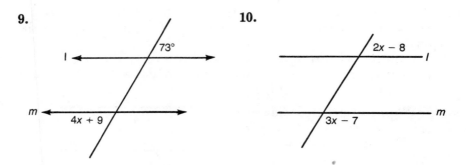

10.

11. In each of the following, find the values of x and y:

(a)

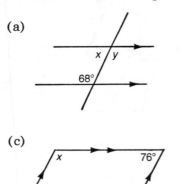

(b)

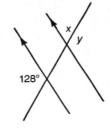

(c)

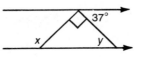

(d)

(e)

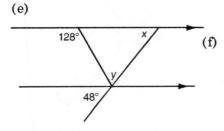

(f)

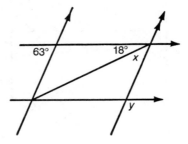

12. In the accompanying diagram, $\overleftrightarrow{AB} \parallel \overleftrightarrow{CD}$ and $\overline{EF}$ bisects angle AFG.
   (a) If $m \angle 1 = 100$, find the measure of each numbered angle.
   (b) If $m \angle 3 = 4x - 9$ and $m \angle 5 = x + 19$, find the measure of each numbered angle.

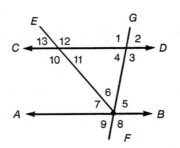

13. Two parallel lines are cut by a transversal. Find the measures of a pair of interior angles on the same side of the transversal if the angles:
  (a) are represented by $5x - 32$ and $x + 8$
  (b) have measures such that the measure of one angle is four times the measure of the other

14. In the accompanying diagram $\overleftrightarrow{AB} \parallel \overleftrightarrow{CD}$ and $\overrightarrow{FG}$ bisects $\angle EFD$. If $m\angle EFG = x$ and $m\angle FEG = 4x$, find x.

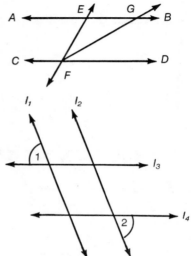

15. In the accompanying diagram, lines l_1 and l_2 are parallel and $m\angle 1 = 70$. What must $m\angle 2$ be so that lines l_3 and l_4 will be parallel?

16–20. In each of the following, determine whether $l \parallel m$:

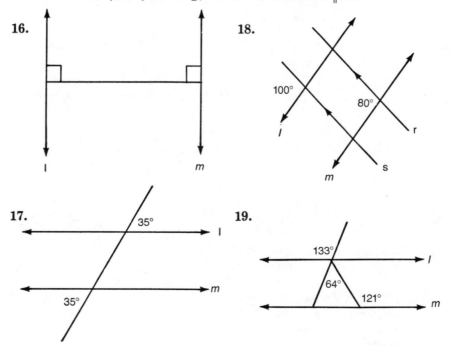

16.

18.
100°
80°

17.
35°
35°

19.
133°
64°
121°

20.

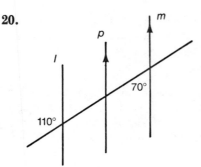

21. If in the accompanying dia-
gram, $L_1 \parallel L_2$ and $L_3 \parallel L_4$, then
angle x is *not* always congruent
to which angle?
(1) a (2) b (3) c (4) d

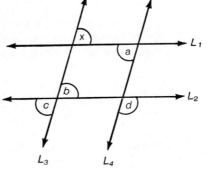

22. Two parallel lines are cut by a transversal, and the two interior
angles on the same side of the transversal are bisected. What kind of
angle is formed where the two angle bisectors meet?
(1) Right   (2) Obtuse   (3) Acute   (4) Straight

23. In the accompanying diagram,
$\overrightarrow{AD} \parallel \overrightarrow{BC}$ and $\overrightarrow{AC}$ bisects
$\angle BAD$. If $m\angle BAD = x$, ex-
press $m\angle 1$ in terms of x.

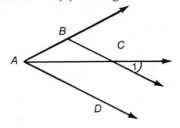

24. Given that lines p and q are parallel, determine whether line l is
parallel to line m.

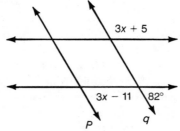

25. Two parallel lines are cut by a transversal in such a way that the measure of one interior angle is one-half the measure of the other interior angle that lies on the same side of the transversal. Find the measure of the smaller of these angles.

26. In the accompanying diagram, angles 1 and 3 are *alternate exterior* angles, and angles 1 and 2 are *exterior* angles on the same side of the transversal. By representing the measure of angle 1 by x and using previously learned angle relationships, informally prove that, if two lines are parallel, then:
   (a) alternate exterior angles are equal in measure.
   (b) exterior angles on the same side of the transversal are supplementary.

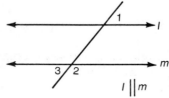

$l \parallel m$

9.6   MEASURING ANGLES OF A TRIANGLE

KEY IDEAS

The accompanying diagrams illustrate that, after "tearing off" angles 1 and 3, their sides can be aligned with one of the sides of angle 2 so that their exterior sides form a straight line.

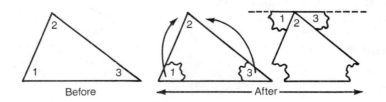

Since the measure of a straight angle is 180, this experiment suggests that the sum of the measures of angles 1, 2, and 3 is 180 and, therefore, the sum of the measures of the angles of *any* triangle is 180.

ANGLES OF A TRIANGLE.   In order to *prove* that the sum of the measures of the angles of a triangle is 180, a proof that does not depend on "tearing off" angles is needed. In Figure 9.21, a line has been drawn parallel to a side of the triangle and through one of its vertices. Since $l \parallel \overrightarrow{AC}$, alternate interior angles are equal in measure:

$$m\angle 1 = m\angle 4,$$

and

$$m\angle 3 = m\angle 5.$$

The sum of the measures of the angles formed at vertex B is 180:

$$m\angle 4 + m\angle 2 + m\angle 5 = 180.$$

We may therefore substitute in the above equation $m\angle 1$ for $m\angle 4$ and $m\angle 3$ for $m\angle 5$:

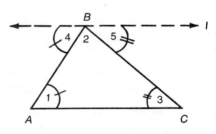

Figure 9.21 Angles of a Triangle

$$m\angle 1 + m\angle 2 + m\angle 3 = 180.$$

This analysis provides an "informal" proof of the following theorem.

THEOREM 1:
The sum of the measures of the angles of a triangle is 180.

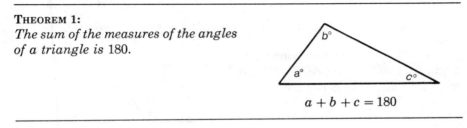

$$a + b + c = 180$$

Examples

1. The degree measures of the acute angles of a right triangle are represented by x and $2x - 30$. Find x.

Solution: A right triangle contains a right angle, which has a degree measure of 90. The remaining two angles of the right triangle are acute, and their measures must add up to 90, so that the sum of the three angles is 180.

$$x + (2x - 30) = 90$$
$$3x - 30 = 90$$
$$3x = 90 + 30$$
$$x = \frac{120}{3}$$
$$x = 40$$

2. If a triangle is equiangular, what is the measure of each of its angles?

Solution: An equiangular triangle is a triangle in which all of the angles have the same measure. If x represents the measure of each angle, then

$$x + x + x = 180$$
$$3x = 180$$
$$x = \frac{180}{3} = 60$$

Each angle of an equiangular triangle has a degree measure of **60**.

3. The measures of the angles of a triangle are in the ratio of $2 : 3 : 5$. What is the measure of the smallest angle of the triangle?

Solution: Let $2x$ = measure of the smallest angle of triangle. Then $3x$ and $5x$ = measures of the remaining angles.

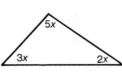

$$2x + 3x + 5x = 180$$
$$10x = 180$$
$$\frac{10x}{10} = \frac{180}{10}$$
$$x = 18$$
$$2x = 2(18) = 36$$

The measure of the smallest angle of the triangle is **36**.

4. In the accompanying diagram, $\overline{DE} \perp \overline{AEC}$. If $m\angle ADB = 80$ and $m\angle CDE = 60$, what is $m\angle DAE$?

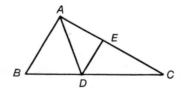

Solution: Since angles ADB, ADE, and CDE form a straight angle, the sum of their measures is 180. Hence

$$80 + m\angle ADE + 60 = 180$$
$$m\angle ADE = 180 - 140 = 40$$

In $\triangle ADE$,

$$m\angle DAE + m\angle ADE + m\angle AED = 180$$
$$m\angle DAE + \quad 40 \quad + \quad 90 \quad = 180$$
$$m\angle DAE + \quad 130 \quad = 180$$
$$m\angle DAE = 180 - 130 = \mathbf{50}$$

5. In the accompanying diagram, $\overline{AD} \parallel \overline{EC}$, $\overline{DF} \parallel \overline{CB}$, $m\angle DAE = 34$, and $m\angle DFE = 57$. Find $m\angle ECB$.

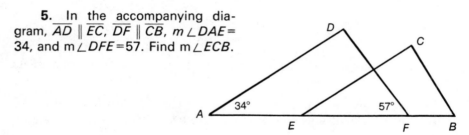

Solution: Since $\overline{AD} \parallel \overline{EC}$, transversal $\overline{AEFB}$ forms congruent corresponding angles, so that $m\angle CEB = m\angle DAE = 34$. Since $\overline{DF} \parallel \overline{CB}$, transversal $\overline{AEFB}$ forms congruent corresponding angles, so that $m\angle CBE = m\angle DFE = 57$. In $\triangle CEB$,

$$m\angle ECB + m\angle CEB + m\angle CBE = 180$$
$$m\angle ECB + \quad 34 \quad + \quad 57 \quad = 180$$
$$m\angle ECB + \qquad 91 \qquad = 180$$
$$m\angle ECB = 180 - 91$$
$$m\angle ECB = 89$$
■■■■■

EXTERIOR ANGLES OF A TRIANGLE.   At each vertex of a triangle an *exterior* angle of the triangle may be formed by extending one of the sides of the triangle (Figure 9.22). Notice that:

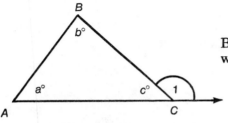

$$(a + b) + c = 180,$$
$$m\angle 1 + c = 180.$$

By comparing these two equations, we may conclude that:

$$m\angle 1 = a + b.$$

Figure 9.22   Exterior Angles of a Triangle

The angles whose measures are represented by a and b are the two interior angles of the triangle that are the most remote from $\angle 1$. With respect to $\angle 1$, these angles are nonadjacent. We may generalize as follows:

The measure of an exterior angle of a triangle is equal to the sum of the measures of the two remote (nonadjacent) interior angles of the triangle.

Example ■■■■■

6.   In the accompanying diagrams, find the value of *x*.

(a)   (b)

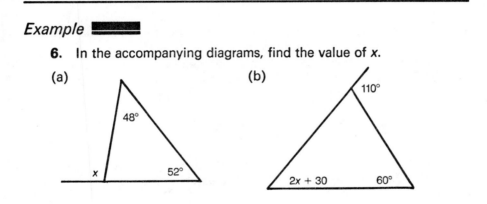

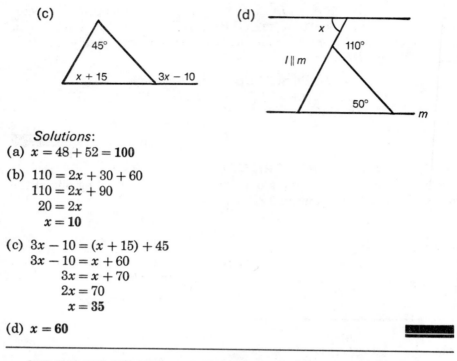

(c)

45°

x + 15   3x − 10

(d)

l ∥ m

x

110°

50°

m

Solutions:
(a) $x = 48 + 52 = 100$

(b) $110 = 2x + 30 + 60$
$110 = 2x + 90$
$20 = 2x$
$x = 10$

(c) $3x - 10 = (x + 15) + 45$
$3x - 10 = x + 60$
$3x = x + 70$
$2x = 70$
$x = 35$

(d) $x = 60$

SUMMARY OF ANGLE RELATIONSHIPS IN A TRIANGLE

b°

a°   *c°*   *d°*

$a + b + c = 180$
$c + d = 180$
$d = a + b$

EXERCISE SET 9.6

1. Determine whether each of the following statements is *true* or *false*. In either case, give a reason for your answer.
   (a) A triangle may not contain more than one obtuse angle.
   (b) The acute angles of a right triangle are supplementary.
   (c) A triangle may not contain more than one right angle.
   (d) If a triangle is regular, then each angle has measure 60.
   (e) The sum of the measures of the exterior angles of a triangle, one formed at each of the three vertices of the triangle, is 360.

2. Find the measure of the smallest angle of a triangle if the measures of the three angles of the triangle are in the ratio:
   (a) $1 : 2 : 6$ (b) $2 : 3 : 10$ (c) $1 : 1 : 2$ (d) $3 : 4 : 5$ (e) $2 : 7 : 9$

3. In right triangle ABC, the measure of acute angle A exceeds twice the measure of $\angle B$ by 27. Find the measure of the smallest angle of the triangle.

4. When a ray bisects an angle of an equiangular triangle, what type of angle does it always form with the opposite side of the triangle?
   (1) Acute   (2) Right   (3) Obtuse   (4) Straight

5. For each of the following, the measures of the angles of $\triangle ABC$ are represented in terms of x. Find the value of x, and classify the triangle as acute, right, or obtuse.
   (a) $m\angle A = 3x + 8$ (b) $m\angle A = x + 24$ (c) $m\angle A = 3x - 5$
       $m\angle B = x + 10$ $m\angle B = 4x + 17$ $m\angle B = x + 14$
       $m\angle C = 5x$ $m\angle C = 2x - 15$ $m\angle C = 2x - 9$

6. In $\triangle ABC$, $\overline{BD} \perp \overline{AC}$. If $m\angle A = 72$ and $m\angle ABC = 54$, find $m\angle CBD$.

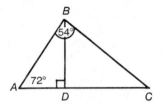

7. Given that $l \parallel m$, $m\angle 2 = 110$, and $m\angle 6 = 70$, find each remaining numbered angle.

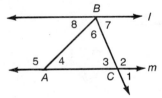

8–25. In each of the following, find the value of x:

8.

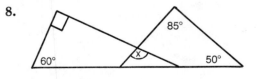

9.

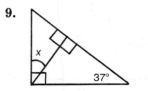

10.

$\overline{AB} \parallel \overline{DE}$

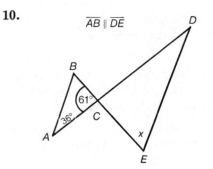

15.

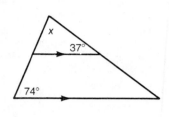

11.

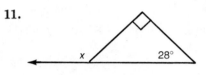

16.

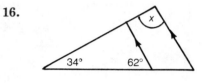

12.

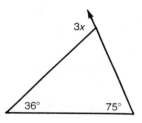

17.

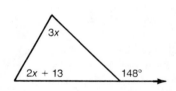

13.

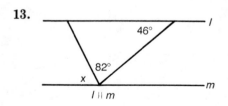

18.

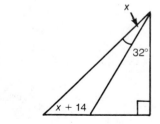

14.

19.

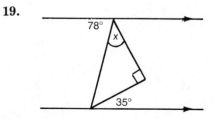

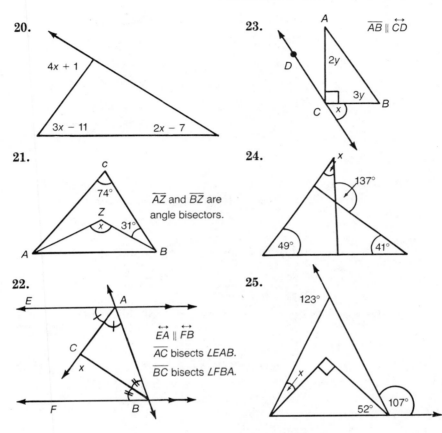

20.

4x + 1

3x − 11   2x − 7

21.

$\overline{AZ}$ and $\overline{BZ}$ are
angle bisectors.

c

74°

Z

x   31°

A   B

22.

E   A

C

x

F   B

$\overleftrightarrow{EA} \parallel \overleftrightarrow{FB}$

$\overline{AC}$ bisects $\angle EAB$.

$\overline{BC}$ bisects $\angle FBA$.

23.

A

$\overline{AB} \parallel \overleftrightarrow{CD}$

D

2y

3y

C   x   B

24.

x

137°

49°   41°

25.

123°

x

52°   107°

9.7   CLASSIFYING QUADRILATERALS AND THEIR ANGLE RELATIONSHIPS

KEY IDEAS

In quadrilaterals, as in triangles, special angle relationships exist.

ANGLES OF A QUADRILATERAL. divides quadrilateral *ABCD* into two triangles. The sum of the degree measures of the four angles of a quadrilateral can be found by combining the measures of the angles of the two triangles; this gives a sum of 360. This analysis leads to the following generalization:

In Figure 9.23, diagonal $\overline{BD}$

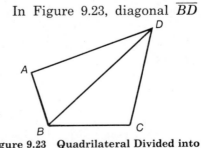

Figure 9.23   Quadrilateral Divided into Triangles

The sum of the degree measures of the angles of a quadrilateral is 360.

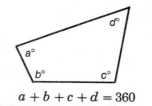

$$a + b + c + d = 360$$

Example ■■■■

1. The degree measures of three angles of a quadrilateral are 72, 119, and 67. What is the degree measure of the remaining angle of the quadrilateral?

Solution:

Let x = measure of the remaining angle of the quadrilateral.

$x + 72 + 119 + 67 = 360$

$x + 258 \qquad\quad = 360$

$\qquad x = 360 - 258 = 102$

The degree measure of the remaining angle of the quadrilateral is **102.** ■■■■

PARALLELOGRAMS. A **parallelogram** (Figure 9.24) is a quadrilateral having *two* pairs of parallel sides. The notation $\square ABCD$ is read as "parallelogram $ABCD$." The letters A, B, C, and D represent consecutive vertices of the parallelogram, and the symbol preceding these letters is a miniature parallelogram. Two angles that have a common side are called **consecutive angles**. Angles A and B are consecutive angles, as are B and C, C and D, and A and D. Two angles that do *not* share a common side are called **opposite angles**. Angles A and C are opposite angles, as are angles B and D.

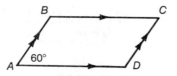

Figure 9.24 Parallelogram

Suppose that m$\angle A = 60$. Angles A and B are interior angles on the same side of transversal $\overline{AB}$. Since $\overline{BC} \parallel \overline{AD}$, $\angle A$ and $\angle B$ are supplementary, so that m$\angle B = 120$. For the same reason, $\angle D$ and $\angle A$ are supplementary, so that m$\angle D = 120$. Since the sum of the angles of a quadrilateral is 360,

$$\text{m}\angle C = 360 - (60 + 120 + 120) = 360 - 300 = 60.$$

Notice that consecutive angles of the parallelogram are supplementary, while opposite angles of the parallelogram have the same measure.

SUMMARY OF RELATIONSHIPS IN A PARALLELOGRAM

1. Opposite sides are parallel: $\overline{AB} \parallel \overline{CD}$ and $\overline{BC} \parallel \overline{AD}$.

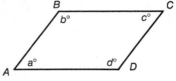

2. The sum of the degree measures of the four angles is 360:

$$a + b + c + d = 360.$$

3. Consecutive angles are supplementary:

$$a + b = 180, \quad c + b = 180,$$
$$a + d = 180, \quad c + d = 180.$$

4. Opposite angles have the same degree measure:

$$a = c \quad \text{and} \quad b = d.$$

Examples

2. In parallelogram *JKLM,* shown in the accompanying diagram, $m \angle K = 3x - 5$ and $m \angle M = 100$. Find the value of *x.*

Solution: Since the opposite angles of a parallelogram have the same degree measure,

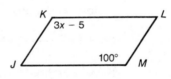

$$m \angle K = m \angle M$$
$$3x - 5 = 100$$
$$3x = 100 + 5$$
$$x = \frac{105}{3} = \mathbf{35.}$$

3. In parallelogram *ABCD,* shown in the accompanying diagram, the measures of $\angle A$ and $\angle B$ are in the ratio of 1 : 3. What is the measure of $\angle A$?

Solution: Let $x =$ measure of $\angle A$.
Then $3x =$ measure of $\angle B$.

Points *A* and *B* are consecutive vertices of the parallelogram, so the measures of $\angle A$ and $\angle B$ are supplementary.

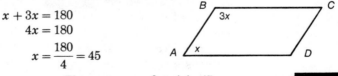

$$x + 3x = 180$$
$$4x = 180$$
$$x = \frac{180}{4} = 45$$

The measure of $\angle A$ is **45.**

SPECIAL TYPES OF QUADRILATERALS. Table 9.4 classifies some special types of quadrilaterals. A *trapezoid* is the only quadrilateral appearing in the table that is *not* a parallelogram. A rhombus, a rectangle, and a square all have the special properties of a parallelogram.

TABLE 9.5   Special Quadrilaterals

Name	Description	Figure
Rhombus	A parallelogram having four equal sides.	
Rectangle	A parallelogram having four right angles.	
Square	A rhombus with four right angles *or* a rectangle with four sides having the same length.	
Trapezoid	A quadrilateral having exactly *one* pair of parallel sides, which are called the *bases*. The nonparallel sides are called the *legs*. If the legs have the same length, then the trapezoid is isosceles.	Base Leg Leg Base

EXERCISE SET 9.7

1–4. In each of the following, find the value of x:

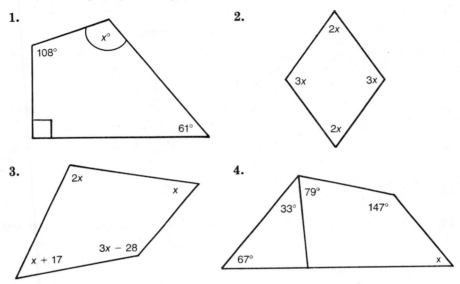

1. 108°   x°   61°

2. 2x   3x   3x   2x

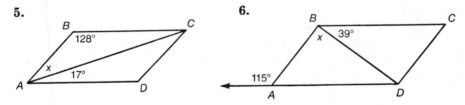

3. 2x   x   x + 17   3x − 28

4. 79°   33°   147°   67°   x

5–6. In parallelogram ABCD, *find the value of* x.

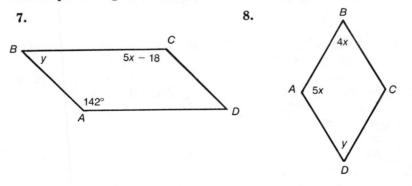

5. B   128°   C   x   17°   A   D

6. B   39°   x   115°   A   D   C

7–8. In parallelogram ABCD, *find the value of* x *and* y.

7. B   y   C   5x − 18   142°   A   D

8. B   4x   A   5x   C   y   D

9. In parallelogram $ABCD$, m$\angle A = 3x$ and m$\angle B = x + 40$. What is the value of x?

10. In parallelogram *MATH* the measure of $\angle T$ exceeds the measure of $\angle H$ by 30. Find the measure of each angle of the parallelogram.

11. In parallelogram *TRIG*, $m\angle R = 2a + 9$ and $m\angle G = 4a - 17$. Find the measure of each angle of the parallelogram.

12. In parallelogram *ABCD* the degree measure of $\angle A$ is 76. Diagonal *BD* is drawn in such a way that the degree measure of $\angle CBD$ is 34. What is the measure of $\angle ABD$?

13. In rhombus *ABCD*, $AB = 3x + 12$ and $BC = 5x$. What is the value of x?

14. In rhombus *STAR*, $ST = 4y - 9$ and $TA = 2y + 5$. What is the perimeter of rhombus *STAR*?

15. If the measures of two consecutive angles of a parallelogram differ by 20, find the degree measure of the smaller angle.

16. In parallelogram *ABCD* a line from *B* is drawn perpendicular to *AD*, intersecting *AD* at point *H*. If $m\angle D = 119$, what is the measure of $\angle ABH$?

17. Which of the following quadrilaterals is *not* a parallelogram?
(1) A rhombus   (3) A rectangle
(2) A square   (4) A trapezoid

18. In which of the following quadrilaterals are the sides in a pair of adjacent sides always congruent?
(1) A parallelogram   (3) A rectangle
(2) A rhombus   (4) A trapezoid

19. In quadrilateral *ABCD*, $m\angle B = 150$, and $m\angle D = 70$. Which of the following statements is true?
(1) *ABCD* is a parallelogram.   (3) *ABCD* is a rhombus.
(2) *ABCD* is a trapezoid.   (4) *ABCD* is a rectangle.

20–24. Classify quadrilateral ABCD as a parallelogram, rectangle, trapezoid, or nonspecial quadrilateral.

20. $m\angle A = 6x$, $m\angle B = 4x + 30$, $m\angle C = 9x - 45$, and $m\angle D = 90$.

21. $m\angle A = 90$, $m\angle B = 3x + 15$, $m\angle C = 4x$, and $m\angle D = 2x + 30$.

22. $m\angle A = 10x - 39$, $m\angle B = 2x + 9$, $m\angle C = x + 27$, and $m\angle D = 129$.

23. $m\angle A = 3x$, $m\angle B = 5x - 12$, $m\angle C = 2x + 21$, and $m\angle D = 4x + 15$.

24. $m\angle A = 4x + 15$, $m\angle B = 5x$, $m\angle C = 6x - 42$, and $m\angle D = 7x - 31$.

25. It was shown that a quadrilateral could be divided into two triangles by drawing a diagonal from one of its vertices.

    (a) Draw polygons having five, six, seven and eight sides. Choose a vertex of each one of the polygons, and draw as many different diagonals as possible. Find a relationship between the number of sides of a polygon and the number of different triangles into which the polygon can be separated.

    (b) Using the results of part (a), write a formula that tells how to find the sum of the measures of the angles of a polygon, given the number of sides, n. Use this formula to find the sum of the measures of the angles of a polygon having 12 sides.

26. Using the formula written in part (b) of Problem 25, find the sum of the measures of the angles of a polygon having:

    (a) 5 sides   (b) 6 sides   (c) 7 sides   (d) 8 sides   (e) 13 sides

CHAPTER 9 REVIEW EXERCISES

REGENTS REVIEW. *Problems included in this section are similar in form and difficulty to those found on the New York State Regents Examination for Course I of the Three-Year Sequence for High School Mathematics. Problems preceded by an asterisk have actually appeared on a previous Course I Regents Examination.*

*1. The measures of the angles of a triangle are represented by x, $2x$, and $(x + 20)$. Find the number of degrees in the measure of the *smallest* angle of the triangle.

*2. Two angles are supplementary and congruent. How many degrees are in the measure of each angle?

*3. In the accompanying diagram $\overleftrightarrow{AB} \parallel \overleftrightarrow{CD}$ and $\overleftrightarrow{EF}$ intersects $\overleftrightarrow{AB}$ at G and $\overleftrightarrow{CD}$ at H. If the degree measure of $\angle AGH$ is $(3x - 10)$ and the degree measure of $\angle GHD$ is 80, find the value of x.

*4. In the accompanying diagram, parallel lines $\overleftrightarrow{AB}$ and $\overleftrightarrow{CD}$ are intersected by transversal $\overleftrightarrow{GH}$ at E and F, respectively. The degree measure of $\angle AEG$ is $(6x + 10)$ and of $\angle CFE$ is 130. Find x.

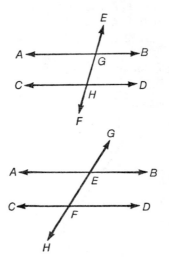

*5. As shown in the accompanying diagram, $\overleftrightarrow{AB}$ and $\overleftrightarrow{CD}$ intersect at point *E*. If the degree measures of vertical angles *AED* and *CEB* are represented by $(3x + 20)$ and $(8x - 5)$, find the value of *x*.

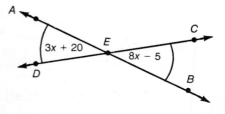

*6. The measures of two complementary angles are in the ratio of 2 : 3. Find the measure of the *larger* angle.

*7. In the accompanying diagram, $m \angle A = 70$ and $m \angle B = 30$. Find the measure of exterior angle *BCD*.

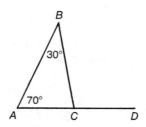

*8. Two angles of a right triangle are congruent. What is the number of degrees in the measure of each of these angles?

*9. The measures of two supplementary angles are in the ratio of 5 : 1. What is the measure of the *smaller* angle?

*10. In $\triangle ABC$, the ratio of the measure of $\angle A$ to the measure of $\angle B$ is 3 : 5. The measure of $\angle C$ is 20 more than the sum of the measures of $\angle A$ and $\angle B$. What is the measure of each angle in $\triangle ABC$?

*11. Given the true statement "If a triangle is equilateral, then it is isosceles," which statement must also be true?
(1) If a triangle is not equilateral, then it is not isosceles.
(2) If a triangle is not equilateral, then it is isosceles.
(3) If a triangle is not isosceles, then it is not equilateral.
(4) If a triangle is isosceles, then it is equilateral.

12–15. Lines $\overleftrightarrow{AB}$ *and* $\overleftrightarrow{CD}$ *are parallel. Find the value of* x.

12.

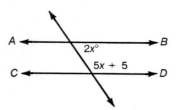

13.

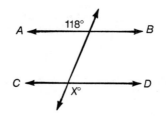

14.

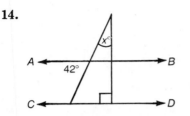

15.

16. In the accompanying diagram of $\triangle ABC$, $\overline{BD}$ bisects $\angle ABC$ and $\overline{CDE}$ bisects $\angle ACB$. If $m\angle BDE = 70$ and $m\angle BCE = 40$, find $m\angle A$.

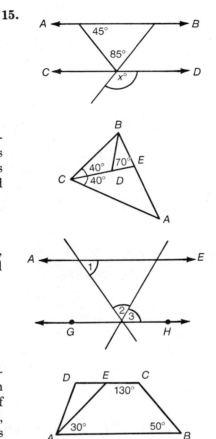

17. In the accompanying diagram, $\overleftrightarrow{AF} \parallel \overleftrightarrow{GH}$, $m\angle 1 = 45$, and $m\angle 2 = 80$. What is $m\angle 3$?
(1) 35   (3) 100
(2) 55   (4) 135

18. In the accompanying diagram, E is a point on $\overline{DC}$ such that $\overline{AE}$ bisects $\angle DAB$. If $m\angle EAB = 30$, $m\angle ABC = 50$, and $m\angle BCD = 130$, what is $m\angle ADC$?
(1) 30   (3) 120
(2) 60   (4) 150

19. In rhombus $PLUS$, $LU = 3n - 7$ and $US = 5n - 19$. What is the perimeter of rhombus $PLUS$?
(1) 6   (2) 24   (3) 34   (4) 44

*20. Let p represent "The polygon has exactly three sides," and let q represent "All angles of the polygon are right angles." What is true if the polygon is a rectangle?
(1) $p \wedge q$ (2) $p \vee q$ (3) p (4) $\sim q$

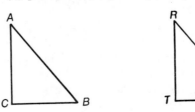

CHAPTER 10

COMPARING AND MEASURING GEOMETRIC FIGURES

10.1 PROVING TRIANGLES ARE CONGRUENT

_____ KEY IDEAS _____

The size and the shape of a triangle are determined by the measures of its six parts: the lengths of its three sides and the degree measures of its three angles. Triangles that have the same size and shape are *congruent*.

CONGRUENT TRIANGLES. In Figure 10.1, if it were possible to "slide" $\triangle ABC$ to the right, we could determine whether the two triangles can be made to coincide. If the triangles can be made to coincide, then $\triangle ABC$ is congruent to $\triangle RST$.

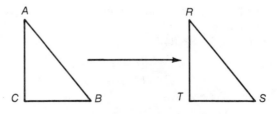

Figure 10.1 Testing Whether Triangles Coincide

Observe that, when "sliding" $\triangle ABC$, we would try to match vertex A with vertex R, vertex B with vertex S, and vertex C with vertex T. Vertices that are paired off in this way are called *corresponding* vertices. Corresponding vertices of the two triangles determine corresponding angles. Corresponding sides of the two triangles lie opposite corresponding angles.

Corresponding Angles	Corresponding Sides
$\angle A$ and $\angle R$	$\overline{BC}$ and $\overline{ST}$
$\angle B$ and $\angle S$	$\overline{AC}$ and $\overline{RT}$
$\angle C$ and $\angle T$	$\overline{AB}$ and $\overline{RS}$

Congruent triangles are triangles whose vertices can be paired off so that corresponding angles are congruent *and* corresponding sides are congruent. In naming pairs of congruent triangles, corresponding vertices must be written in the same order:

$$\triangle ABC \quad \cong \quad \triangle RST$$

Here are some other ways in which this correspondence may be written:

$$\triangle CAB \cong \triangle TRS \qquad \triangle BAC \cong \triangle SRT \qquad \triangle CBA \cong \triangle TSR.$$

INCLUDED ANGLES AND SIDES. In Figure 10.2, $\angle A$ is said to be *included* by sides $\overline{AB}$ and $\overline{AC}$ since $\angle A$ is formed by the intersection of these sides. Side $\overline{BC}$ is said to be included by $\angle B$ and $\angle C$ since it is a side of both angles.

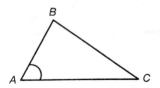

Figure 10.2   Included Angle and Side

PROVING THAT TRIANGLES ARE CONGRUENT. Two *polygons* are congruent if and only if their corresponding angles are congruent *and* their corresponding sides are congruent. If the polygons are triangles, then it is sufficient to show that only *three* pairs of parts are congruent, provided that they are a particular set of congruent parts.

You may conclude that two triangles are congruent if any one of the following conditions is true:

1. Three sides of one triangle are congruent to their corresponding sides in the other triangle. This is referred to as the **SSS** (side–side–side) method.

2. Two sides and the included angle of one triangle are congruent to the corresponding parts of the other triangle. This is referred to as the **SAS** (side–angle–side) method.

3. Two angles and the included side of one triangle are congruent to the corresponding parts of the other triangle. This is referred to as the **ASA** (angle–side–angle) method.

4. Two angles and the not-included side of one triangle are congruent to the corresponding parts of the other triangle. This is referred to as the **AAS** (angle–angle–side) method.

Example ▰▰▰▰

Using the parts marked off in the accompanying figures as being congruent, determine in each case whether △I is congruent to △II. Give a reason for your answer.

(a)

(b)   (c)

(d)   (e)

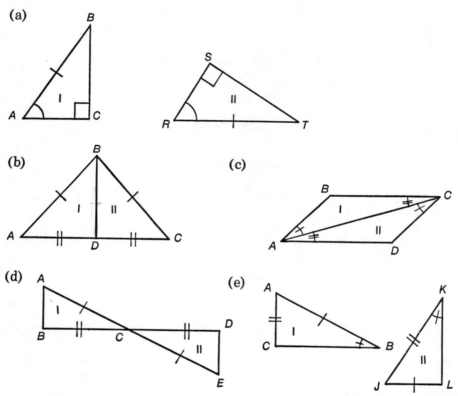

Solution: (a) △**ACB** ≅ △**RST** by applying the *AAS* method. Note that ∠*C* and ∠*S* are congruent since all right angles are congruent.

(b) △**ADB** ≅ △**CDB**. Since $\overline{BD}$ is congruent to itself, the *SSS* method may be applied.

(c) △**ABC** ≅ △**CDA**. Since $\overline{AC}$ is congruent to itself, the *ASA* method may be used.

(d) △**ABC** ≅ △**EDC**. Since vertical angles are congruent, ∠*ACB* and ∠*ECD* are congruent. These angles are included by congruent pairs of corresponding sides, so that the *SAS* method may be used.

(e) △**ABC** is **not congruent** to △**JKL**. The pairs of angles that are congruent are *not* included by the congruent pairs of corresponding sides.

▰▰▰▰

APPLYING CONGRUENT TRIANGLES TO PARALLELOGRAMS.

In Figure 10.3, diagonal $\overline{BD}$ divides parallelogram $\overline{ABCD}$ into two triangles. Comparing $\triangle BAD$ and $\triangle DCB$, we see that the following parts are congruent:

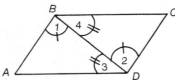

Angle: $\angle 1 \cong \angle 2$
Side: $\overline{BD} \cong \overline{BD}$
Angle: $\angle 3 \cong \angle 4$

Figure 10.3   Parallelogram Divided into Two Triangles

Angles 1 and 2 are congruent since they are alternate interior angles formed by parallel lines. Angles 3 and 4 are congruent for the same reason. Triangle *BAD* is congruent to $\triangle DCB$ as proved by the ASA method. Since corresponding parts of congruent triangles are congruent, $\overline{AD} \cong \overline{BC}$ and $\overline{AB} \cong \overline{CD}$. This establishes the following important result:

Opposite sides of a parallelogram are congruent, and have, therefore, the same length.

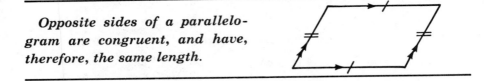

SUMMARY OF METHODS FOR PROVING THAT TRIANGLES ARE CONGRUENT

You may conclude that two triangles are congruent if it can be shown that:

1. Three sides of one triangle are congruent to the corresponding parts of the other triangle.

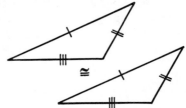

Method: SSS $\cong$ SSS

2. Two sides and the included angle of one triangle are congruent to the corresponding parts of the other triangle.

Method: SAS $\cong$ SAS

3. Two angles and the included side of one triangle are congruent to the corresponding parts of the other triangle.

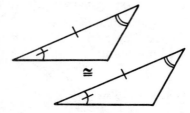

Method: ASA ≅ ASA

4. Two angles and the side opposite one of them are congruent to the corresponding parts of the other triangle.

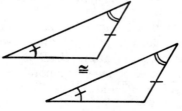

Method: AAS ≅ AAS

You may *not* conclude that two triangles are congruent when:

1. Two sides and an angle that is *not* included of one triangle are congruent to the corresponding parts of the other triangle.

SSA ≇ SSA

2. Three angles of one triangle are congruent to the corresponding parts of the other triangle.

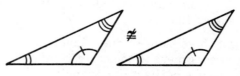

AAA ≇ AAA

EXERCISE SET 10.1

1. If $\triangle RST \cong \triangle HOP$, name three pairs of congruent angles and three pairs of congruent sides.

2. In parallelogram $ABCD$, $BC = 5x - 17$ and $AD = 63$. What is the value of x?

3. In parallelogram $ABCD$, $AB = 4x - 17$ and $CD = 2x + 13$. What are the lengths of $\overline{AB}$ and $\overline{CD}$?

4. Which of the following is *not* a valid method for proving triangles
   are congruent?
   (1) ASA ≅ ASA   (3) SSA ≅ SSA
   (2) SAS ≅ SAS   (4) AAS ≅ AAS

*5–12. Using the parts marked off as being congruent in the accompanying
figures, determine whether △I is congruent to △II. In each case, give a
reason for your answer.*

5.

9.

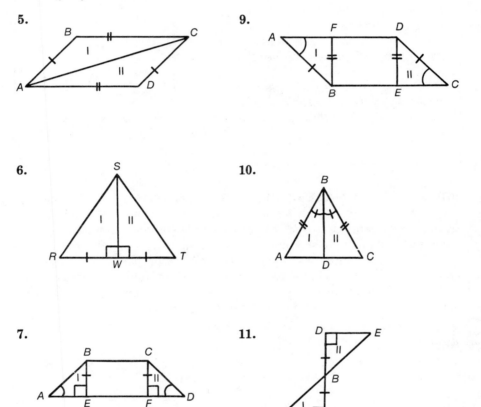

6.

10.

7.

11.

8.

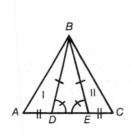

12.

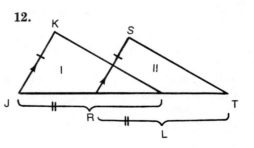

10.2   MEASURING ANGLES OF AN ISOSCELES TRIANGLE

KEY IDEAS

In an isosceles triangle, the congruent sides are called the **legs**. *The angles that are opposite the legs are called the* **base angles***, and the side that they include is called the* **base***. The angle opposite the base is called the* **vertex angle.**

In an isosceles triangle the base angles have the same degree measure and are, therefore, congruent.

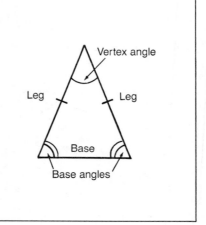

PROVING THAT BASE ANGLES ARE CONGRUENT.   If a special line segment such as the bisector of the vertex angle of an isosceles triangle is drawn, the isosceles triangle can be "folded" along this line in such a way that the base angles exactly coincide.

This relationship may be proved using the properties of congruent triangles. In Figure 10.4, the bisector of the vertex angle is drawn, so that $\angle ABC$ is divided into two congruent angles. Comparing $\triangle ABD$ and $\triangle CBD$, we see that the following parts are congruent:

Side: $\overline{AB} \cong \overline{BC}$
Angle: $\angle 1 \cong \angle 2$
Side: $\overline{BD} \cong \overline{BD}$

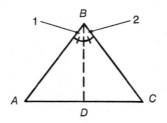

Figure 10.4   Proving Base Angles are Congruent

Triangles ABD and CBD are congruent as proved by the SAS method. Since the triangles are congruent, every pair of corresponding parts must be congruent. Therefore $\angle A \cong \angle C$. We have informally proved the following important relationship:

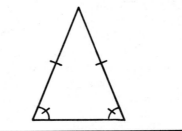

Base angles of an isosceles triangle are congruent and have, therefore, the same measure.

Examples

1. If the measure of the vertex angle of an isosceles triangle is 80, what is the degree measure of each base angle?

Solution: Let x = measure of each base angle.
$$x + x + 80 = 180$$
$$2x = 180 - 80$$
$$x = \frac{100}{2}$$
$$x = \mathbf{50}$$

2. If the measure of an exterior angle formed by extending the base of an isosceles triangle is 112, what is the degree measure of the vertex angle?

Solution: $m \angle A = 180 - 112 = 68$
Therefore $m \angle C$ must also equal 68
$$68 + 68 + m \angle C = 180$$
$$136 + m \angle C = 180$$
$$m \angle C = 180 - 136$$
$$m \angle C = \mathbf{44}$$

3. The degree measure of a base angle of an isosceles triangle exceeds twice the degree measure of the vertex angle by 15. Find the measure of the vertex angle.

Solution: Let x = measure of the vertex angle.
Then $2x + 15$ = measure of a base angle.
$$(2x + 15) + (2x + 15) + x = 180$$
$$5x + 30 = 180$$
$$5x = 180 - 30$$
$$x = \frac{150}{5}$$
$$x = \mathbf{30}$$

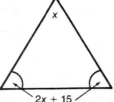

$2x + 15$

EQUILATERAL TRIANGLES.   Since an equilateral triangle (Figure 10.5) has three equal sides, it is also an isosceles triangle, in which any pair of angles may be considered the base angles. Each angle of the trian- gle must, therefore, have the same measure.

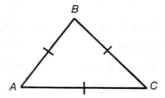

Figure 10.5   Equilateral Triangle

An   equilateral   triangle   is equiangular, so that each angle has a degree measure of 60.

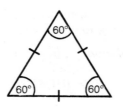

EXERCISE SET 10.2

1. Find the measure of the vertex angle of an isosceles triangle if the measure of a base angle is:
    (a) 30   (b) 59   (c) 74   (d) 60   (e) 8.5

2. Find the measure of each base angle of an isosceles triangle if the measure of the vertex angle is:
    (a) 50   (b) 90   (c) 43   (d) 100   (e) 19.5

3. Find the measure of each angle of an isosceles triangle if the ratio of the measure of a base angle to the measure of the vertex angle is:
    (a) 2:1   (b) 3:2   (c) 1:4   (d) 3:4   (e) 2:5

4. The degree measure of a base angle of an isosceles triangle exceeds three times the degree measure of the vertex angle by 13. Find the measure of the vertex angle.

5. The measure of an exterior angle at the base of an isosceles triangle is 108. What is the measure of the vertex angle of the triangle?

6. The measure of the vertex angle of an isosceles triangle is 96. What is the measure of an exterior angle at the base of the triangle?

7. The degree measure of the vertex angle of an isosceles triangle is 5 less than three times the degree measure of a base angle. What is the degree measure of each base angle?

8. In the accompanying figure, *ABCD* is a parallelogram. If *EB = AB* and m∠*CBE* = 57, what is the value of *x*?

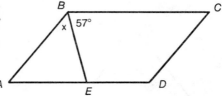

9. If the degree measure of an exterior angle formed at the vertex of an isosceles triangle is 118, what is the degree measure of each base angle?

10. The degree measure of an exterior angle of an isosceles triangle exceeds the measure of a base angle by 32. What is the degree measure of each base angle of the triangle?

11. In the accompanying diagram, *ABC* is an *isosceles right triangle* with *AC = BC*.
(a) What are m∠*A* and m∠*B*?
(b) If *AC* = 5, find *AB*. (*Hint:* Use the Pythagorean theorem.)
(c) If *AB* = 8, find *BC*.

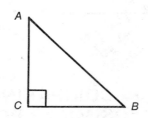

12. The length of a leg of an isosceles right triangle is 10. Find the length of the altitude drawn to the hypotenuse of the right triangle.

13–20. In each of the following, find the value of x:

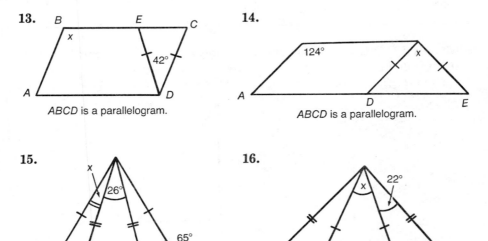

13. *ABCD* is a parallelogram.

14. *ABCD* is a parallelogram.

15.

16.

17.

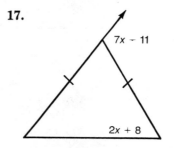

7x – 11

2x + 8

18.

38°

x

74°

19.

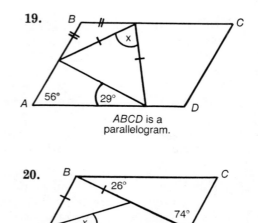

B

C

x

A 56° 29° D

ABCD is a
parallelogram.

20.

B 26° C

74°

A x D

ABCD is a
parallelogram.

10.3 COMPARING LENGTHS OF SIDES OF SIMILAR POLYGONS

KEY IDEAS

When a photograph is enlarged, the original and enlarged figures are *similar* since they have exactly the same shape. In making a blueprint, every object must be drawn to scale so that the figures in the blueprint are in proportion and are similar to their real-life counterparts.

SIMILAR POLYGONS. Congruent polygons have the same shape *and* the same size, while similar figures have the same shape, but may differ in size. The triangles in Figure 10.6 are similar.

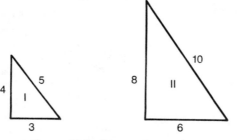

5

4

I

3

10

8

II

6

Figure 10.6 Similar Triangles

Notice that the lengths of corresponding sides of triangles I and II have the same ratio and are, therefore, in proportion:

$$\frac{\text{Side in } \triangle I}{\text{Side in } \triangle II} = \frac{3}{6} = \frac{4}{8} = \frac{5}{10} = \frac{1}{2} \text{ or } 1:2.$$

Two triangles (or any other two polygons having the same number of sides) are **similar** if both of the following conditions are met:

1. Corresponding angles have the same degree measure.

2. The lengths of corresponding sides are in proportion.
The symbol for similarity is $\sim$. The notation $\triangle ABC \sim \triangle RST$ is read as "triangle *ABC* is *similar to* triangle *RST*."

Also observe that the perimeters of two similar triangles have the same ratio as the lengths of a pair of corresponding sides:

$$\frac{\text{Perimeter of } \triangle I}{\text{Perimeter } \triangle II} = \frac{3+4+5}{6+8+10} = \frac{12}{24} = \frac{1}{2} \text{ or } 1:2.$$

The perimeters of two similar triangles have the same ratio as the lengths of any pair of corresponding sides.

Examples ▬▬▬

1. Quadrilateral *ABCD* is similar to quadrilateral *RSTW*. The lengths of the sides of quadrilateral *ABCD* are 6, 9, 12, and 18. If the length of the longest side of quadrilateral *RSTW* is 24, what is the length of its shortest side?

Solution: Let $x =$ length of the shortest side of quadrilateral *RSTW*. Since the lengths of corresponding sides of similar polygons must have the same ratio, the following proportion is true:

$$\frac{\text{Shortest side of quad } ABCD}{\text{Shortest side of quad } RSTW} = \frac{\text{Longest side of quad } ABCD}{\text{Longest side of quad } RSTW}.$$

$$\frac{6}{x} = \frac{18}{24}$$

Write $\frac{18}{24}$ in lowest terms: $\quad \dfrac{6}{x} = \dfrac{3}{4}$

Cross-multiply: $\quad 3x = 24$

$$x = \frac{24}{3} = 8$$

The length of the shortest side of quadrilateral *RSTW* is **8**.

2.   The longest side of a polygon exceeds twice the length of the longest side of a similar polygon by 3. If the ratio of the perimeters of the two polygons is 4 : 9, find the length of the longest side of each polygon.

Solution: Let x = length of longest side in smaller polygon.
   Then $2x + 3$ = length of longest side in larger polygon.

$$\frac{\text{Perimeter of smaller polygon}}{\text{Perimeter of larger polygon}} = \frac{\text{Longest side of smaller polygon}}{\text{Longest side of larger polygon}}$$

$$\frac{4}{9} = \frac{x}{2x + 3}$$

Cross-multiply: $9x = 4(2x + 3)$
$$9x = 8x + 12$$
$$9x - 8x = 12$$
$$x = 12$$
$$2x + 3 = 2(12) + 3 = 24 + 3 = 27$$

The length of the longest side in the smaller polygon is **12**, and the length of the longest side in the larger polygon is **27**.   ▬▬▬

PROVING THAT TRIANGLES ARE SIMILAR.   To prove that two *polygons* are similar, it is necessary to demonstrate that *all* pairs of corresponding angles have the same degree measure *and* the lengths of all pairs of corresponding sides have the same ratio. If two *triangles* are drawn having two pairs of congruent angles, then:

1.   The remaining pair of angles is also congruent since the measures of the three angles of a triangle must always add up to 180.

2.   The ratios of the lengths of the corresponding sides of the triangles are determined so that they are in proportion. Thus the two triangles are similar.

This suggests the following shortcut method for proving that two triangles are similar:

To prove that two triangles are similar, it is sufficient to show that two pairs of angles are congruent.

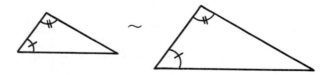

Examples

3. In the accompanying figure, $\overline{DE} \parallel \overline{AB}$.

(a) Is $\triangle DEC \sim \triangle ABC$? Give a reason for your answer.

(b) If $CD = 6$, $CA = 18$, and $DE = 4$, what is the length of AB?

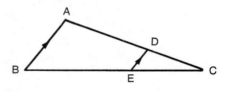

Solutions: (a) $\overline{DE} \parallel \overline{AB}$, so transversal $\overline{AC}$ forms congruent corresponding angles, making $m \angle A = m \angle CDE$. Also, transversal $\overline{BC}$ forms congruent corresponding angles, making $m \angle B = m \angle CED$. **Triangle DEC** $\sim \triangle ABC$ since two angles of $\triangle DEC$ are equal in degree measure to two angles of $\triangle ABC$.

(b) Let x = length of $\overline{AB}$.

Since the lengths of corresponding sides of similar triangles are in proportion,

$$\frac{CD}{CA} = \frac{DE}{AB}$$

$$\frac{6}{18} = \frac{4}{x}$$

$$\frac{1}{3} = \frac{4}{x}$$

$$x = 3 \cdot 4 = 12$$

The length of $\overline{AB}$ is **12**.

4. A pole 10 feet high casts a 15-foot-long shadow on level ground. At the same time a man casts a shadow that is 9 feet in length. How tall is the man?

Solution: By assuming that the shadows are perpendicular to the pole and the man, we may use right triangles to represent these situations, where x represents the height of the man.

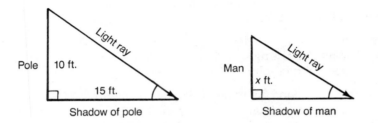

We also assume that in each triangle the light rays make angles with the ground that have the same degree measure. Since all right angles have the same degree measure, the two right triangles are similar and the lengths of their sides are in proportion.

$$\frac{\text{Height of pole}}{\text{Height of man}} = \frac{\text{Shadow of pole}}{\text{Shadow of man}}$$

$$\frac{10}{x} = \frac{15}{9}$$

$$\frac{10}{x} = \frac{5}{3}$$

$$5x = 3 \cdot 10$$

$$x = \frac{30}{5} = 6$$

The man is **6 feet** tall.

EXERCISE SET 10.3

1. The lengths of the corresponding sides of two similar polygons are 3 and 4, respectively. If the perimeter of the smaller polygon is 18, find the perimeter of the larger polygon.

2. Triangle ABC is similar to $\triangle XYZ$, $AB:XY = 5:3$, and $BC = 20$. What is the length of $\overline{YZ}$?

3. A person 6 feet tall casts a shadow 4 feet long. At the same time, a nearby tower casts a shadow 32 feet long. How many feet are in the height of the tower?

4. Given that $\triangle ABC \sim \triangle RST$, fill in the missing lengths in the following table:

	AB	BC	AC	RS	ST	RT
(a)	7	24	?	14	?	50
(b)	12	?	12	?	9	8
(c)	10	?	25	?	18	15

5. The ratio of the perimeters of two similar triangles is $1:3$. If the length of the smallest side of the smaller triangle is 3, what is the length of the smallest side of the larger triangle?

6. The lengths of three sides of a triangle are 6, 8, and 10. If the perimeter of a similar triangle is 72, what is the length of the *shortest* side of the second triangle?

7. A vertical antenna 75 meters tall casts a shadow 35 meters long. At the same time, a flagpole nearby casts a shadow 14 meters long. What is the number of meters in the height of the flagpole?

8. The lengths of the sides of a triangle are 5, 6, and 9. If the length of the *shortest* side of a similar triangle is 15, find the perimeter of the larger triangle.

9. In two similar triangles the ratio of the lengths of a pair of corresponding sides is 5:8. If the perimeter of the larger triangle exceeds the perimeter of the smaller triangle by 12, find the perimeter of the larger triangle.

10. In the accompanying diagram, $\overline{DE} \parallel \overline{AB}$.
    (a) Explain why $\triangle DCE \sim \triangle BCA$.
    (b) If $DE = 6$, $AB = 10$, and $BC = 15$, find DC.
    (c) If $CE = 8$, $EA = 6$, and $BC = 21$, find BD.

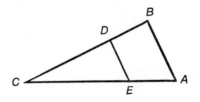

11. In the accompanying diagram, $\overline{AB} \perp \overline{BC}$ and $\overline{DC} \perp \overline{BC}$.
    (a) Explain why $\triangle ABE \sim \triangle DCE$.
    (b) If $CD = 9$, $AB = 6$, and $DE = 12$, find AE. $AB = 4$.
    (c) If $BC = 20$ and $CD = 12$, find BE.

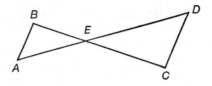

12. Given that $\triangle ABC \sim \triangle RST$, $\overline{BH} \perp \overline{AC}$, and $\overline{SK} \perp \overline{RT}$.
    (a) Explain why $\triangle ABH \sim \triangle RSK$.
    (b) If $AB:RS = 4:9$ and $SK = 18$, find BH.

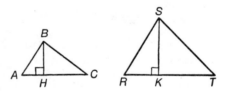

10.4 FINDING AREAS OF A RECTANGLE, SQUARE, AND PARALLELOGRAM

_____ KEY IDEAS _____

In the accompanying figure, a rectangle encloses a total of 36 square boxes, so that its area is 36 square units. When we speak of the *area* of a figure, we simply mean the total number of square boxes that the figure can enclose. If a side of each little square box measures 1 centimeter (cm), then the area of the rectangle is 36 cm², where cm² is read as "square centimeters."

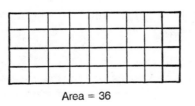

Area = 36

AREA OF A RECTANGLE AND SQUARE.   The formulas for the areas of a rectangle and a square should be familiar to you.

The area of a rectangle is equal to the product of the length and the width.	w $\boxed{A = lw}$ l

The area of a square is equal to the product of two sides.	s $\boxed{A = s^2}$ s

Sometimes one side of a rectangle is referred to as the **base**, and an adjacent side (which is perpendicular to the base) is called the **altitude** or **height**. The formula for the area of a rectangle may be expressed alternatively as

$$A = bh,$$

where b represents the length of the base and h represents the length of the height or altitude. The terms *base* and *altitude* are also used in connection with the area formulas for other types of geometric figures.

Examples ▰

1. Find the area of a rectangle whose base has a length of 8 and whose diagonal has a length of 10.

Solution: Drawing diagonal $\overline{AC}$ of rectangle $ABCD$ forms right triangle ABC, in which the diagonal is the hypotenuse. The lengths of the sides of this right triangle form a 6-8-10 Pythagorean triple, where height $AB = 6$.

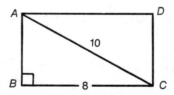

Area of rectangle $= bh = 8 \times 6 = \mathbf{48}$.

2. If the length of a side of a square is doubled, what change occurs in each of the following?

(a) The perimeter of the square   (b) The area of the square

Solutions: In the formulas for perimeter and area, replace s by $2s$.

(a) Perimeter of original square $= 4s$

Perimeter of new square $= 4(2s)$ or $2(4s)$

The perimeter of the square is **doubled**.

(b) Area of original square $= s^2$

Area of new square $= (2s)^2 = 4(s^2)$

The area of the square is multiplied by **4**.

3. Find the length of a side of a square that has the same area as a rectangle whose base is 27 and whose height is 3.

Solution: Area of rectangle $= bh = (27)(3) = 81$
Area of square $= s^2 = 81$.
Therefore the length of each side of the square is **9**.

4. A certain rectangle and square have the same area. The base of the rectangle exceeds three times its altitude by 4. If the length of a side of the square is 8, find the dimensions of the rectangle.

Solution: Let $x =$ length of altitude of rectangle.
Then $3x + 4 =$ length of base of rectangle.
Area of rectangle = Area of square
Base × Altitude = (Side)²
$$(3x + 4)x = 8^2$$
$$3x^2 + 4x = 64$$
$$3x^2 + 4x - 64 = 0$$
$$(3x + 16)(x - 4) = 0$$
$(3x + 16) = 0 \quad \lor \quad (x - 4) = 0$
$3x = -16 \qquad\qquad x = 4$
$x = \dfrac{-16}{3} \qquad$ Altitude $= x = 4$
Reject $\qquad\qquad$ Base $= 3(4) + 4 = $ **16**

Check: The area of the square is 64 since $8^2 = 64$. The rectangle has the same area since $4 \times 16 = 64$. ▬▬▬

AREA OF A PARALLELOGRAM. Any side of a parallelogram may be considered the base. The height or altitude of the parallelogram is the length of a segment ($\overline{BH}$ in Figure 10.7) drawn perpendicular to the base from any point on the opposite side. The altitude is usually dropped from a vertex of the parallelogram. In future courses you will prove that

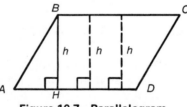

Figure 10.7 **Parallelogram**

a parallelogram and a rectangle that have equal bases and altitudes have equal areas.

The area of a parallelogram is equal to the product of the length of the base and the length of the altitude drawn to that base.

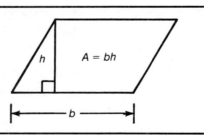

Examples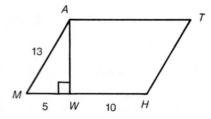

5. In the accompanying diagram, quadrilateral *MATH* is a parallelogram. If $MA = 13$, $MW = 5$, and $HW = 10$, what is the area of parallelogram *MATH*?

Solution: $\triangle MAW$ is a right triangle whose sides form a 5-12-13 Pythagorean triple, where $AW = 12$. Base $MH = MW + HW = 5 + 10 = 15$.

$$\begin{aligned}
\text{Area of } \square MATH &= \text{Base} \times \text{Altitude} \\
&= MH \times AW \\
&= 15 \times 12 \\
&= \textbf{180 square units}
\end{aligned}$$

6. The area of parallelogram *ABCD* is 40. $\overline{BH}$ is the altitude drawn to base $\overline{AD}$. If $BH = 5$, what is the length of $\overline{BC}$?

Solution:
$$\begin{aligned}
\text{Area of } \square ABCD &= \text{Base} \times \text{Height} \\
40 &= AD \times BH \\
40 &= AD \times 5 \\
\frac{40}{5} &= AD \\
8 &= AD
\end{aligned}$$

Since opposite sides of a parallelogram have the same length, $BC = AD = 8$.

EXERCISE SET 10.4

1. If the area of a rectangle is 108, find its dimensions if:
   (a) the length is three times the width.
   (b) the width and the length have a ratio of $1:12$.
   (c) the length exceeds six times the width by 3.
   (d) the sum of the length and the width is 21.

2. If the area of a parallelogram is 52 and the length of a side is 13, find the length of the altitude drawn to that side.

3. Find the area of a square whose perimeter is:
   (a) 40   (b) 18   (c) $32x$ (d) $20x - 4$

4. Find the perimeter of a square whose area is: (a) 100   (b) $49x^2$

5. Fill in the following table, where A represents the area of a rectangle, b is the length of its base, h is the height, and d is the length of a diagonal:

	b	h	d	A
(a)	?	5	13	?
(b)	40	?	41	?
(c)	7	?	25	
(d)	15	?	?	120

6. The base of a parallelogram is represented by $x + 5$, and the altitude drawn to that base is represented by $x - 5$. Express the area of the parallelogram as a binomial in terms of x.

7. If the length and the width of a rectangle are each doubled, what change occurs in each of the following?
   (a) The perimeter of the rectangle   (b) The area of the rectangle

8. If the perimeter of a square is tripled by increasing the length of each side by the same amount, what change occurs in the area of the square?

9. The length of a rectangle is 4 less than three times its width. If its area is 119, what are the dimensions of the rectangle?

10. If the length of a side of a square is doubled and the length of an adjacent side is diminished by 3, a rectangle is formed whose area is 80. Find the original dimensions of the square.

11. In parallelogram $ABCD$, the base and the altitude drawn to that base are in the ratio of $5:3$. If the area of the parallelogram is 60, find the lengths of the base and the altitude.

12. The length of a rectangle is three times its width. If the length of the rectangle is decreased by 7 and the width increased by 3, a square is formed whose area is 64 square units. Find the dimensions of the original rectangle.

13. An altitude is drawn from vertex B of rhombus $ABCD$, intersecting $\overline{AD}$ at point H. If $AB = 10$ and $AH = 6$, what is the area of rhombus $ABCD$?

14. The base of a parallelogram exceeds the length of the altitude drawn to that base by 5. If the area of the parallelogram is 84, find the length of the altitude.

15. The base of a rectangle exceeds three times its height by 1. If the height of the rectangle is represented by x, and the area is represented by $2x^2 + 12$, find the dimensions of the rectangle.

16. The length of a rectangle exceeds its width by 7. If the rectangle has the same area as a square whose perimeter is 48, find the dimensions of the rectangle.

17. The lengths of two adjacent sides of a parallelogram are 10 and 15. If the length of the altitude drawn to the shorter side of the parallelogram is 9, find the length of the altitude drawn to the longer side of the parallelogram.

18. Find the area of a square whose diagonal has a length of:
    (a) 10   (b) 18   (c) 15   (d) $6\sqrt{2}$

    (*Hint*: First find the length of a side of the square by using the Pythagorean theorem.)

10.5 FINDING AREAS OF A TRIANGLE AND TRAPEZOID

KEY IDEAS

The formula for the area of a triangle is also expressed in terms of the length of a base and the length of the altitude drawn to that base. Any side of a triangle may be the base. The altitude is the perpendicular dropped to the base from the opposite vertex of the triangle.

A trapezoid has *two* bases, which are the parallel sides of the trapezoid. The altitude is a segment drawn from any point on one base and perpendicular to the opposite side. The nonparallel sides are called *legs*.

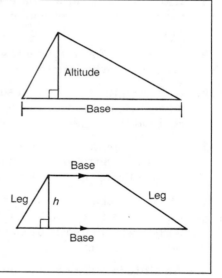

AREA OF A TRIANGLE.   A diagonal of a parallelogram divides the parallelogram into two congruent triangles (Figure 10.8). The area of each triangle is the same and is equal, therefore, to one-half the area of the entire parallelogram.

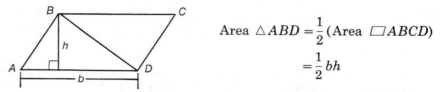

$$\text{Area } \triangle ABD = \frac{1}{2}(\text{Area } \square ABCD)$$

$$= \frac{1}{2}bh$$

Figure 10.8   Parallelogram Divided into Two Congruent Triangles

> **The area of a triangle is equal to one-half the product of the lengths of the base and the altitude drawn to that base.**

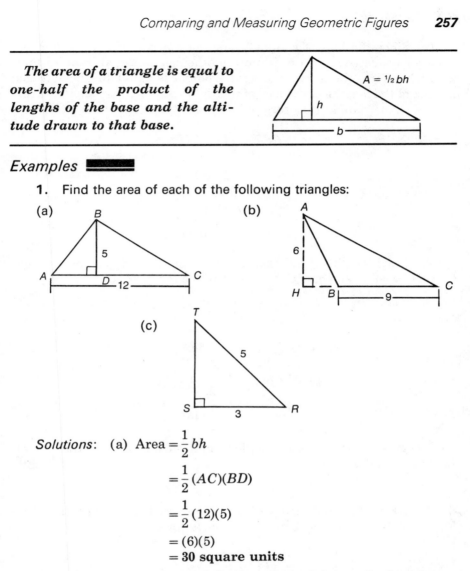

$A = \frac{1}{2}bh$

Examples

1. Find the area of each of the following triangles:

(a)

(b)

(c)

Solutions: (a) Area $= \frac{1}{2}bh$

$$= \frac{1}{2}(AC)(BD)$$

$$= \frac{1}{2}(12)(5)$$

$$= (6)(5)$$

$$= \textbf{30 square units}$$

(b) This example illustrates the fact that, whenever the base is one of the sides that include an obtuse angle of a triangle, the altitude falls *outside* the triangle and the base must be extended.

$$\text{Area} = \frac{1}{2}bh$$

$$= \frac{1}{2}(AH)(BC)$$

$$= \frac{1}{2}(6)(9)$$

$$= (3)(9)$$

$$= \textbf{27 square units}$$

(c) Since the legs of a right triangle are perpendicular, either leg may be considered the base, while the other leg is the altitude to that base. Therefore, the area of a *right* triangle is equal to one-half the product of the lengths of the legs of the right triangle. The lengths of the sides of right triangle RST form a 3-4-5 right triangle in which $ST = 4$.

$$\text{Area } \triangle RST = \frac{1}{2}(RS)(ST)$$

$$= \frac{1}{2}(3)(4)$$

$$= \frac{1}{2}(12)$$

$$= \textbf{6 square units}$$

2.   If the lengths of the base and the altitude of a triangle are each doubled, what is the change in the area of the triangle?

Solution: In the formula for the area of a triangle, replace b by $2b$ and h by $2h$.

$$\text{Area of original } \triangle = \frac{1}{2}bh$$

$$\text{Area of new } \triangle = \frac{1}{2}(2b)(2h)$$

$$= \frac{1}{2}(4bh) \text{ or } 4\left(\frac{1}{2}bh\right)$$

The area of the original triangle is multiplied by **4** to get the area of the new triangle.

AREAS OF SIMILAR TRIANGLES.   For any two triangles I and II (Figure 10.9) the ratio of their areas is as follows:

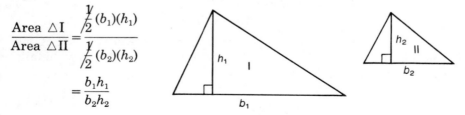

$$\frac{\text{Area } \triangle \text{I}}{\text{Area } \triangle \text{II}} = \frac{\frac{1}{2}(b_1)(h_1)}{\frac{1}{2}(b_2)(h_2)}$$

$$= \frac{b_1 h_1}{b_2 h_2}$$

Figure 10.9   Areas of Similar Triangles

If $\triangle$I is similar to $\triangle$II, then the altitudes drawn to corresponding sides of these triangles are in proportion to the lengths of these sides. Hence we can replace the ratio of the altitudes, $\dfrac{h_1}{h_2}$, with the ratio of the bases.

$$\frac{\text{Area } \triangle \text{I}}{\text{Area } \triangle \text{II}} = \frac{b_1}{b_2} \cdot \frac{h_1}{h_2} = \frac{b_1}{b_2} \cdot \frac{b_1}{b_2} = \left(\frac{b_1}{b_2}\right)^2.$$

Since the ratio of the lengths of the bases must be the same as the ratio of the lengths of any other pair of corresponding sides of the similar triangles, we draw the following conclusion:

The ratio of the areas of two similar triangles is equal to the square of the ratio of the lengths of any pair of corresponding sides.

$$\frac{\text{Area } \triangle_{\text{I}}}{\text{Area } \triangle_{\text{II}}} = \left(\frac{\text{Side I}}{\text{Side II}}\right)^2$$

provided that $\triangle \text{I} \sim \triangle \text{II}$.

Examples

3. If the length of the longest side of a triangle is 10 and the length of the longest side of a similar triangle is 20, how many times greater is the area of the larger triangle than the area of the smaller triangle?

Solution: The ratio of the area of the larger triangle to the area of the smaller triangle is equal to the square of the ratio of 20 to 10.

$$\frac{\text{Area of larger } \triangle}{\text{Area of smaller } \triangle} = \left(\frac{20}{10}\right)^2 = \left(\frac{2}{1}\right)^2 = \frac{4}{1}$$

The area of the larger triangle is **four** times as great as the area of the smaller triangle.

4. The areas of two similar triangles are in the ratio of 4:9. If the length of the shortest side of a similar triangle is 6, find the length of the shortest side of the larger triangle.

Solution: Let $x =$ length of the shortest side of the larger triangle.

$$\frac{\text{Area of smaller } \triangle}{\text{Area of larger } \triangle} = \left(\frac{\text{Side of smaller}}{\text{Corresponding side of larger}}\right)^2$$

$$\frac{4}{9} = \left(\frac{6}{x}\right)^2 = \frac{36}{x^2}$$

Cross-multiply: $4x^2 = 9.36$

$$4x^2 = 324$$

$$x^2 = \frac{324}{4} = 81$$

$$x = \sqrt{81} = 9$$

The length of the shortest side of the larger triangle is **9**.

AREA OF A TRAPEZOID.   To find a formula for the area of a trapezoid, add the areas of the two triangles that are formed when a diagonal of the trapezoid is drawn. In Figure 10.10, the altitude drawn from B to lower base AD (b_1) is labeled with the letter h. The altitude drawn from D to upper base BC extended (b_2) is labeled with the same letter, h. The two altitudes have the same length since they are drawn between two parallel lines and parallel lines always remain the same distance apart. We obtain the following formula:

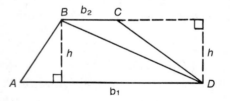

Figure 10.10   Trapezoid

$$\text{Area trap } ABCD = \text{Area } \triangle ABD + \text{Area } \triangle BCD$$

$$= \frac{1}{2} b_1 h + \frac{1}{2} b_2 h.$$

Since $\frac{1}{2}$ and h are factors of each monomial term, they can be factored out:

$$\text{Area trap } ABCD = \frac{1}{2} h(b_1 + b_2).$$

The formula states the following:

The area of a trapezoid is equal to the product of one-half the length of the altitude and the sum of the lengths of the bases $A = \frac{1}{2} h \, (b_1 + b_2)$.

Examples

5.   Find the area of trapezoid *ABCD*.

(a)   (b)

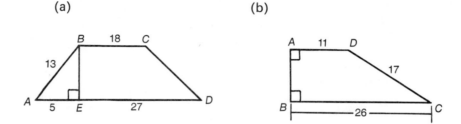

Solutions: (a) The lengths of the sides of right triangle AEB form a 5-12-13 Pythagorean triple, where altitude $BE = 12$. The length of lower base $AD = AE + ED = 5 + 27 = 32$.

Area trap $ABCD = \dfrac{1}{2}h(b_1 + b_2)$

$\qquad\qquad\quad = \dfrac{1}{2}(BE)(AD + BC)$

$\qquad\qquad\quad = \dfrac{1}{2}(12)(32 + 18)$

$\qquad\qquad\quad = 6(50)$

$\qquad\qquad\quad = \textbf{300 square units}$

(b) Drawing altitude $\overline{DE}$ forms rectangle $ABED$. Since opposite sides of a rectangle have the same length, $EB = 11$; therefore $EC = 26 - 11$ or 15. The lengths of the sides of right triangle DEC form a 8-15-17 Pythagorean triple in which the length of altitude $DE = 8$.

Area trap $ABCD = \dfrac{1}{2}h(\text{b}_1 + \text{b}_2)$

$\qquad\qquad\quad = \dfrac{1}{2}(DE)(BC + AD)$

$\qquad\qquad\quad = \dfrac{1}{2}(8)(26 + 11)$

$\qquad\qquad\quad = 4(37)$

$\qquad\qquad\quad = \textbf{148 square units}$

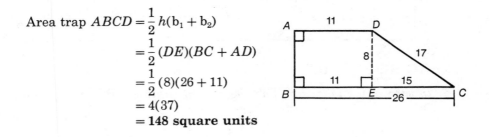

6. In trapezoid $RTSW$ the length of base $\overline{RW}$ is twice the length of base $\overline{ST}$. If the area of the trapezoid is 42 square inches and the length of the altitude is 4, find the length of the shorter base.

Solution: Let $x =$ length of base $\overline{ST}$.
$\qquad\qquad$ Then $2x =$ length of base $\overline{RW}$.

Area of trap $RTSW = \dfrac{1}{2}h(x + 2x)$

$\qquad\qquad 42 = \dfrac{1}{2}(4)(3x)$

$\qquad\qquad 42 = 6x$

$\qquad\qquad \dfrac{42}{6} = \dfrac{6x}{6}$

$\qquad\qquad\;\; 7 = x$

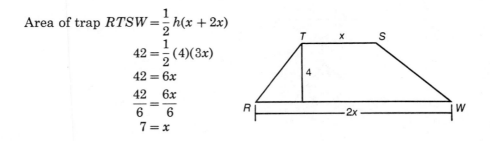

The length of the shorter base is **7 inches.**

SUMMARY OF AREA FORMULAS	
Figure	**Area Formula**
Rectangle	$A = \textbf{\textit{l}}\text{ength} \times \textbf{\textit{w}}\text{idth}$ *or* $= \textbf{\textit{b}}\text{ase} \times \textbf{\textit{h}}\text{eight}$
Square	$A = (\textbf{\textit{s}}\text{ide})^2$
Parallelogram	$A = \textbf{\textit{b}}\text{ase} \times \textbf{\textit{h}}\text{eight}$
Triangle	$A = \dfrac{1}{2} \times \textbf{\textit{b}}\text{ase} \times \textbf{\textit{h}}\text{eight}$
Trapezoid	$A = \dfrac{1}{2} \times \textbf{\textit{h}}\text{eight} \times (\textbf{\textit{b}}\text{ase}_1 + \textbf{\textit{b}}\text{ase}_2)$

EXERCISE SET 10.5

1–7. In each of the following, find the area of either $\triangle ABC$ *or trapezoid* ABCD:

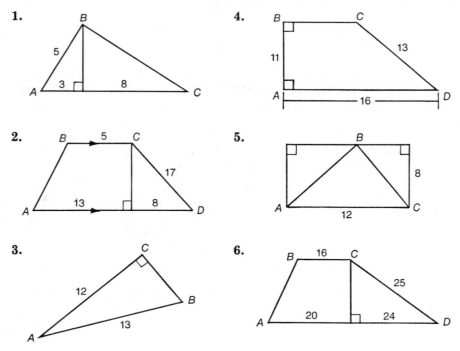

1.

2.

3.

4.

5.

6.

7.

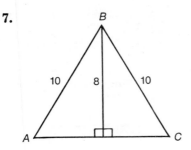

8. The area of a triangle is 28. Find the length of the base if the length of the altitude drawn to that base is 7.

9. The base and the altitude of a triangle are in the ratio of 1 : 2. If the area of the triangle is 36, find the length of the base.

10. Find the length of an altitude of a trapezoid if:
(a) its area is 72, and the sum of the lengths of its bases is 36.
(b) the ratio of the lengths of the altitude, the lower base, and the upper base is 1 : 2 : 3, and the area of the trapezoid is 147.
(c) the sum of the lengths of the bases is numerically equal to one third of the area of the trapezoid.

11. The lengths of the bases of a trapezoid are in the ratio of 1 : 3. If the area of the trapezoid is 140 and the length of an altitude is 5, what is the length of the shorter base?

12. The length of the base of a triangle is 1 less than twice the length of an altitude drawn to it. If the area of the triangle is 33, what are the lengths of the base and the altitude?

13. Triangle $JKL \sim \triangle RST$. If $JL = 20$ and $RT = 15$, find the ratio of the areas of the two triangles.

14. The area of two similar triangles are 25 and 81. What is the ratio of the lengths of a pair of corresponding sides?

15. The area of a trapezoid is 50, and the length of an altitude is 4. If the length of one of the bases is 7, find the length of the other base.

16. The area of two similar triangles are 81 and 121. If the perimeter of the smaller triangle is 45, find the perimeter of the larger triangle.

17. The lengths of a pair of corresponding sides of a pair of similar triangles are in the ratio of 5 : 8. If the area of the smaller triangle is 75, find the area of the larger triangle.

18. The length of the longer base of a trapezoid exceeds twice the length of the shorter base by 3. If the length of an altitude is 9 and the area of the trapezoid is 81, find the length of the shorter base.

19. In a certain trapezoid the lengths of the shorter base and the altitude are the same. The length of the longer base is 11, and the area of the trapezoid is 63. What are the lengths of the shorter base and the altitude?

20. The sum of the lengths of the legs of a right triangle is 31. If the area of the triangle is 84, find the lengths of the legs and the hypotenuse of the triangle.

21. As shown in the accompanying diagram, *ABCD* is a rectangle and a line segment drawn from *B* intersects $\overline{CD}$ at *E*.

    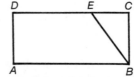

    (a) If the measure of $\overline{AB}$ is 9 and the area of the rectangle is 36, find *AD*.
    (b) Point *E* separates $\overline{DC}$ into two segments such that $DE : EC = 2 : 1$. Find *DE* and *EC*.
    (c) Find *BE*.
    (d) Find the area of trapezoid *ABED*.

10.6 FINDING CIRCUMFERENCE AND AREA OF A CIRCLE

KEY IDEAS

> If you were able to locate and connect all points that were a distance of 5 inches from a given point, a *circle* having a *radius* of 5 inches would be formed. The distance around the circle is called the *circumference* of the circle. The region enclosed by the circle represents the *area* of the circle.
>
> The size of a circle depends on the length of its radius. The longer the radius, the greater the circumference and the area of the circle.

SOME PARTS OF A CIRCLE.   A **circle** (Figure 10.11) is the set of all points at a given distance from a fixed point. The fixed point is called the **center** of the circle. The center of a circle is named by a single capital letter. If the center of a circle is named by the letter *O*, then the circle is referred to as *circle O*. Any segment drawn from the center of the circle to a point on the circle is called a **radius** (plural: *radii*) of the circle. All radii of the same circle have the same length. A **diameter** is a line segment that passes through the center of a circle and whose endpoints are points on the circle. The length of a diameter is twice the length of a radius.

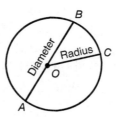

Figure 10.11   Circle

Any curved section of the circle is called an **arc** of the circle. A diameter divides a circle into two congruent arcs, each of which is called a **semicircle**. In Figure 10.11, $\overarc{AB}$ (read as "arc AB") is a semicircle. Also, $\overarc{ACB}$ (read as "arc ACB") is a semicircle.

CIRCUMFERENCE OF A CIRCLE. When a circle's **circumference** (that is, the distance around the circle), is divided by its diameter, the number obtained is always the same regardless of the size of the circle. This constant value is represented by the Greek letter π and is read as "pi."

$$\frac{\text{Circumference}}{\text{Diameter}} = \frac{C}{D} = 3.1415926\ldots = \pi \text{ (pi)}$$

Since the length of a diameter D is twice the length of the radius r, the circumference C may also be expressed in the following equivalent ways:

$$C = \pi D \quad \text{and} \quad C = 2\pi r.$$

The number π is an irrational number that takes the form of an infinite, nonrepeating decimal number. When an estimate of the value of the circumference is needed, π may be replaced by a rational approximation, such as 3.14 or $\frac{22}{7}$. An exact value of the circumference is represented whenever the circumference is written in terms of π.

Examples ▬▬▬

1. For a circle having a diameter of 5, find each of the following:
(a) an approximation for the circumference of the circle (Use $\pi = 3.14$.)
(b) the exact value of the circumference of the circle

Solutions: (a) $C = \pi D = 3.14 \times 5 = \mathbf{15.7}$
(b) $C = \pi D = \pi(5) = \mathbf{5\pi}$

2. Find an approximation for the length of a semicircle having 14 as its radius. (Use $\pi = \frac{22}{7}$.)

Solution: First find the circumference of the *entire* circle. The length of the semicircle will be one half of this amount.

$$C = 2\pi r = 2\pi(14) = 28\pi = 28 \times \frac{22}{7} = 88$$

$$\text{Circumference of semicircle} = \frac{1}{2}(88) = \mathbf{44} \quad \text{▬▬▬}$$

AREA OF A CIRCLE. To find the area, A, of a circle, multiply π by the square of the radius, r:

$$A = \pi r^2.$$

Examples ▬▬

3. Find the exact area of a circle whose radius is 6.

Solution: $A = \pi r^2 = \pi(6)^2 = 36\pi$

4. Express in terms of π the circumference of a circle whose area is 49π.

Solution:
$$A = \pi r^2$$
$$49\pi = \pi r^2$$
$$\frac{49\pi}{\pi} = \frac{\pi r^2}{\pi}$$
$$49 = r^2$$
$$r = \sqrt{49} = 7.$$
$$C = 2\pi r = 2\pi(7) = 14\pi$$

COMPARING CIRCLES.   If the radius of a circle is represented by r_1 and the radius of a second circle is represented by r_2, then

$$\frac{C_1}{C_2} = \frac{2\pi r_1}{2\pi r_2} = \frac{r_1}{r_2} \quad and \quad \frac{A_1}{A_2} = \frac{\pi(r_1)^2}{\pi(r_2)^2} = \frac{(r_1)^2}{(r_2)^2} = \left(\frac{r_1}{r_2}\right)^2.$$

In words, the circumferences of two circles have the same ratio as their radii, and the areas of two circles have the same ratio as the *square* of their radii. To illustrate, if the length of the radius of one circle is twice the length of the radius of another circle, then we may draw two conclusions:

1. The *circumference* of the larger circle is twice the circumference of the other circle since

$$\frac{\text{Circumference of larger circle}}{\text{Circumference of smaller circle}} = \frac{\text{Radius of larger}}{\text{Radius of smaller}} = \frac{2}{1}.$$

2. The *area* of the larger circle is *four* times the area of the other circle since

$$\frac{\text{Area of larger circle}}{\text{Area of smaller circle}} = \left(\frac{\text{Radius of larger}}{\text{Radius of smaller}}\right)^2 = \left(\frac{2}{1}\right)^2 = \frac{4}{1}.$$

Example ▬▬

5. The ratio of the areas of two circles is $9 : 16$. If the radius of the larger circle is 20 units, what is the length of the radius of the smaller circle?

Solution: Let $x = $ radius of the smaller circle.

$$\frac{9}{16} = \left(\frac{x}{20}\right)^2$$

Since $\frac{9}{16}$ is a perfect square, solve the proportion by taking the square root of each side of the equation:

$$\sqrt{\frac{9}{16}} = \sqrt{\left(\frac{x}{20}\right)^2}$$

$$\frac{3}{4} = \frac{x}{20}$$

Cross-multiply: $4x = 60$

$$x = \frac{60}{4} = 15$$

The radius of the smaller circle is **15 units**.

INSCRIBED AND CIRCUMSCRIBED POLYGONS. In Figure 10.12 square $ABCD$ is *circumscribed* about circle O. A polygon is **circumscribed** about a circle if each of its sides intersects the circle in exactly one point. Drawing diameter $\overline{EF}$ forms rectangle $ABEF$. Since opposite sides of a rectangle have the same length, side AB = diameter EF. In general, a side of a square circumscribed about a circle has the same length as a diameter of the circle.

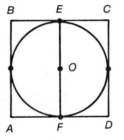

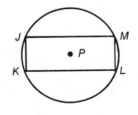

Figure 10.12 A Circumscribed Polygon   Figure 10.13 An Inscribed Polygon

In Figure 10.13 rectangle $JKLM$ is *inscribed* in circle P. A polygon is **inscribed** in a circle if each of its vertices lies on the circle. The circle is *circumscribed* about rectangle $JKLM$. In subsequent courses you will be able to show that the diagonals of the rectangle are also diameters of the circle.

As illustrated in Figure 10.14, it is also true that, if one of the sides of an inscribed triangle is a diameter of the circle, then the triangle is a *right* triangle and the diameter is the hypotenuse.

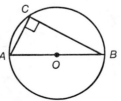

Figure 10.14 Inscribed Right Triangle

Examples ▰▰▰▰▰

6. A square having a perimeter of 32 is circumscribed about circle *P*. Find, in terms of π, the area of circle *P*.

Solution: Since the perimeter of the square is 32, the length of each side is 8 (32 ÷ 4 = 8). The diameter of the circle is, therefore, also 8. The radius of the circle is 4, so

$$A = \pi r^2$$
$$= \pi(4^2) = \mathbf{16\pi}$$

7. In the accompanying figure, $\overset{\frown}{AB}$ is a semicircle of circle *O*. Find the area of the semicircle.

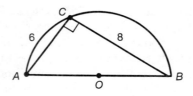

Solution: Since a side of $\triangle ABC$ is a diameter of the circle, the triangle is a right triangle, in which $\overline{AB}$ is the hypotenuse. The lengths of the sides of right triangle *ABC* form a 6-8-10 Pythagorean triple, in which $AB = 10$.

The radius of circle *O* is 5 (10 ÷ 2 = 5). To find the area, *A*, of circle *O* use the formula

$$A = \pi r^2 = \pi(5^2) = 25\pi$$

Since the area of the *entire* circle is 25π, the area of the semicircle must be one half of 25π. The area of semicircle *O* is $\dfrac{25}{2}\pi$ or **12.5π**. ▰▰▰▰▰

EXERCISE SET 10.6

1. Fill in the following table:

	Radius	Diameter	Circumference	Area
(a)	5	?	?	
(b)	?	9	?	?
(c)	?	?	?	49π
(d)	?	?	18π	?
(e)	?	?	?	$\dfrac{64}{25}\pi$

2. The ratio of the areas of two circles is 1 : 9. If the radius of the smaller circle is 5, find the length of the radius of the larger circle.

3. The ratio of the lengths of the radii of two circles is 4 : 25. If the area of the smaller circle is 8 cm², find the area of the larger circle.

4. Find the circumference and the area of the semicircle whose diameter is 16.

5. Find the area of a square that is inscribed in a circle having a radius of:
   (a) 3   (b) 4.5   (c) $2x$ (d) π

6. Find the area of a circle that is inscribed in a square having a perimeter of:

   (a) 12   (b) 28   (c) $40x$ (d) $\dfrac{4}{\pi}$

7. If the length of the radius of a circle is doubled, what is the change in each of the following?
   (a) The circumference of the circle   (b) The area of the circle

8. In the accompanying figure, find the area of $\triangle ABC$.

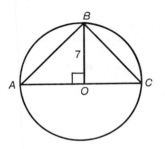

9. In the accompanying figure, find the area of semicircle $\overset{\frown}{ACB}$

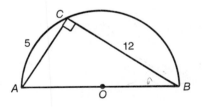

10.7 FINDING AREAS OF MORE COMPLICATED REGIONS

────────────── KEY IDEAS ──────────────

To find the area of a region whose boundaries are formed by intersecting geometric shapes, it may be necessary to apply more than one area formula.

FINDING AREAS USING ADDITION. In Figure 10.15, arcs AB, BC, and CD are semicircles with diameters $\overline{AB}$, $\overline{BC}$, and $\overline{CD}$, respectively. $ABCD$ is a rectangle, $BC = 20$, and $AB = 12$. To find the area of the entire region, we must calculate the areas of the rectangle and the three semicircles. The sum of these areas equals the area of the entire region. When finding the area of a semicircle, remember to multiply the area of the circle by $\frac{1}{2}$.

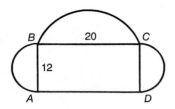

Figure 10.15 Semicircles

Area of rectangle $ABCD$:
$$\text{Area} = (BC)(AB) = (20)(12) = 240$$

Area of semicircle BC:

$$\text{Radius} \qquad r = \frac{1}{2}(20) = 10$$

$$\text{Area of semicircle } BC = \frac{1}{2}(\pi r^2)$$

$$= \frac{1}{2}(\pi)(10^2)$$

$$= \frac{1}{2}(100\pi) = 50\pi$$

Area of semicircle AB:

$$\text{Radius } r = \frac{1}{2}(12) \qquad = 6$$

$$\text{Area of semicircle } AB = \frac{1}{2}(\pi r^2)$$

$$= \frac{1}{2}(\pi)(6^2)$$

$$= \frac{1}{2}(36\pi) = 18\pi$$

Area of semicircle CD: Since opposite sides of a rectangle have the same length, the diameter and, therefore, the radii of semicircles AB and CD are equal. As a result, they must also have equal areas.

Area of semicircle CD = Area of semicircle AB = 18π

Area of entire region $= 240 + 50\pi + 18\pi + 18\pi$
$= \mathbf{240 + 86\pi}$

FINDING AREAS USING SUBTRACTION. When one geometric figure lies within another, the difference in their area represents the area of the region that they do not have in common. For example, in Figure 10.16, the radius of the inner circle is 5 and the radius of the outer circle is 8. The two circles are **concentric circles** since they have the same center, but have radii of different lengths. The shaded region represents the area which the concentric circles do *not* have in common. This area may be found by *subtracting* the area of the inner circle from the area of the outer circle.

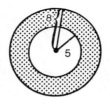

Figure 10.16   Concentric Circles

$$\begin{array}{l} \text{Area of outer circle} = \pi(8^2) = 64\pi \\ \underline{-\text{Area of inner circle} = \pi(5^2) = 25\pi} \\ \text{Area of shaded region} \qquad = \mathbf{39\pi} \end{array}$$

Examples

1. In the accompanying diagram, *ABCD* is a square. Find the area of the shaded region.

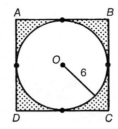

Solution: The diameter of the inscribed circle is 12, so the length of a side of the circumscribed square is also 12.

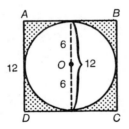

Area of shaded region = Area of square − Area of circle

$$= s^2 \qquad\qquad -\pi r^2$$
$$= (12)^2 \qquad\qquad -\pi(6)^2$$
$$= 144 \qquad\qquad -36\pi$$

2. In the accompanying diagram, $\triangle BCE$ is inscribed in square $ABCD$. If the length of side $\overline{BC}$ is 4 centimeters, what is the area, in square centimeters, of the shaded portion of the diagram?

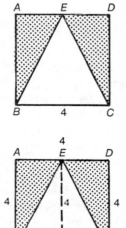

Solution: Draw an altitude of $\triangle BCE$ from E to $\overline{BC}$. Since parallel lines ($\overline{AD}$ and $\overline{BC}$) are always the same distance apart, $EH = AB = 4$.

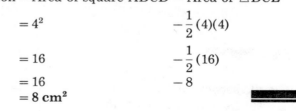

Area of shaded region = Area of square $ABCD$ − Area of $\triangle BCE$

$$= 4^2 \qquad\qquad -\frac{1}{2}(4)(4)$$
$$= 16 \qquad\qquad -\frac{1}{2}(16)$$
$$= 16 \qquad\qquad -8$$
$$= 8 \text{ cm}^2$$

EXERCISE SET 10.7

1. In the accompanying diagram, find the area of the region bounded by square $ABCD$ and semicircle BC.

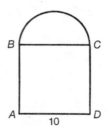

2. In the accompanying diagram, find the area of the region bounded by isosceles right triangle *ABC* and semicircle *BC*.

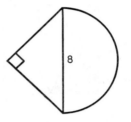

3. In the accompanying diagram, find the area of the region that is inside the circle *O* and outside circle *O'*.

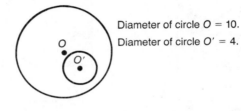

Diameter of circle *O* = 10.
Diameter of circle *O'* = 4.

4. In the accompanying diagram find the area between the two concentric circles.

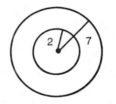

5. The area of square *ABCD* as shown in the accompanying diagram is 121. $\overline{EKF}$ is drawn parallel to $\overline{AD}$, and $\overline{GKH}$ is drawn parallel to $\overline{AB}$, so as to form the smaller squares *AGKE* and *FCHK*. If the area of *AGKE* is 36, find the area of *FCHK*.

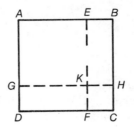

6–8. In the accompanying diagrams ABCD is a square. Find the area of the shaded regions.

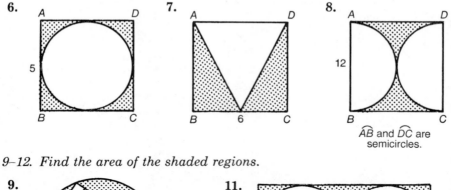

6.

5

7.

6

8.

12

$\overset{\frown}{AB}$ and $\overset{\frown}{DC}$ are semicircles.

9–12. Find the area of the shaded regions.

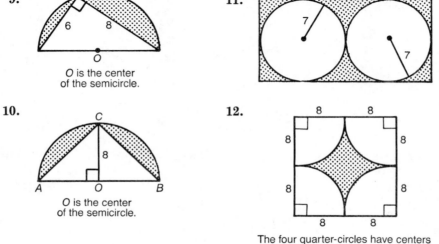

9.

6   8

O

O is the center
of the semicircle.

11.

7

7

10.

C

8

A   *O*   *B*

O is the center
of the semicircle.

12.

8   8

8   8

8   8

8   8

The four quarter-circles have centers
at the vertices of the square.

13. In the accompanying diagram, $\triangle RST$ is inscribed in circle *O* with diameter $\overline{RT}$. Radius $\overline{OS}$ is an altitude of $\triangle RST$, and $OS = 4$.

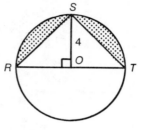

S

4

R   *O*   *T*

(a) Find *RT*.
(b) Express, in terms of π, the area of circle *O*.
(c) Find the area of $\triangle RST$.
(d) Express, in terms of π, the area of the shaded region.
(e) Find *RS*. (Answer may be left in radical form.)

14. In the accompanying diagram, $\overline{AD}$ is a diameter of circle O, $\overline{BC}$ is a diameter of circle P, $ABCD$ is a square, and side $AB = 12$. (Answers may be left in terms of π.)

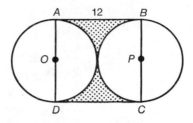

(a) Find the circumference of circle O.
(b) Find the area of circle O.
(c) Find the area of a semicircle of circle P.
(d) Find the area of square $ABCD$.
(e) Find the area of the shaded portion.

10.8 MEASURING VOLUMES OF PRISMS AND PYRAMIDS

KEY IDEAS

The amount of space that a solid encloses is represented by its volume. The volume of a solid, expressed in cubic units, is the number of cubes having an edge length of 1 unit that the solid can enclose.

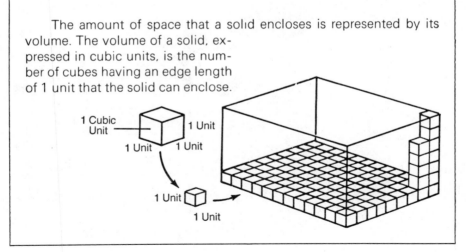

SPECIAL PRISMS. A polygon is "flat" since all its sides lie in the same plane. The figure that is the counterpart of a polygon in space is called a **polyhedron.**

A **prism** (Figure 10.17) is a special type of polyhedron. The sides of a prism are called **faces.** All prisms have these two properties:

1. Two of the faces, called **bases,** are congruent polygons lying in parallel planes.

2. The faces that are not bases, called **lateral faces,** are parallelograms.

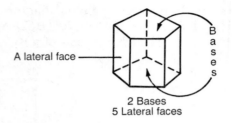

Figure 10.17 A Prism

A **rectangular solid** (Figure 10.18) is a prism whose two bases and four lateral faces are rectangles. If the bases and lateral faces are squares, then the rectangular solid is called a **cube.**

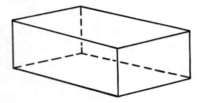

Figure 10.18 A Rectangular Solid

VOLUME OF RECTANGULAR SOLIDS. The volume, V, of *any* prism is equal to the product of the area of its base, B, and its height, h:

Volume of a prism: $V = Bh$.

By using this relationship, special formulas can be derived for determining the volumes of a cube and a rectangular solid:

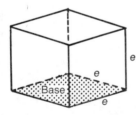

A Cube

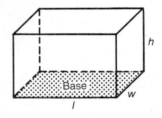

A Rectangular Solid

Volume of a cube:

$V = Bh = (e^2)e$
$V \text{ cube} = e^3$

Volume of a rectangular solid:

$V = Bh = (l \times w)h$
$V \text{ rect solid} = lwh$

Examples

1. What is the volume of a rectangular solid having a length, width, and height of 5 cm, 4 cm, and 3 cm, respectively?

Solution: $V = lwh = (5)(4)(3) = \textbf{60 cm}^3$

2. A rectangular solid has the same volume as a cube whose edge length is 6. What is the height of the rectangular solid if its length is 8 and its width is 3?

Solution: Volume of rectangular solid = Volume of cube

$$lwh = e^3$$
$$(8)(3)h = 6^3$$
$$24h = 216$$
$$h = \frac{216}{24} = 9$$

The height of the rectangular solid is **9**.

3. What is the change in volume of a cube whose edge length is doubled?

Solution: In the formula $V = e^3$, replace e with $2e$, so that the new volume is $V = (2e)^3 = 8e^3$.

The new volume is 8 times as great as the original volume. ■

VOLUME OF A PYRAMID.   A **pyramid** (Figure 10.19) is a solid figure formed by connecting each vertex of a polygon base to a given point that lies in a different plane. A prism has two bases, whereas a pyramid has *one* base. The vertex of the pyramid is the point at which the triangular faces intersect. The *altitude* of the pyramid is the perpendicular segment dropped from the vertex to the plane that contains the base. The length of this segment is the *height* of the pyramid. The volume, V, of a pyramid is *one-third* the volume of a prism having the same base area (B) and height (h):

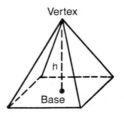

Figure 10.19   Pyramid

$$\text{Volume of a pyramid: } V \text{ pyramid} = \frac{1}{3}Bh.$$

Examples ▆▆▆

4. A pyramid 12 cm high has a square base that has a perimeter of 20 cm. What is the volume of the pyramid?

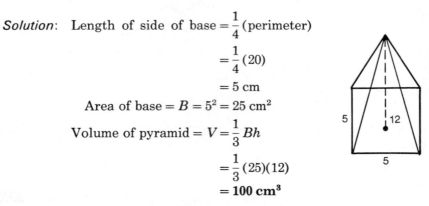

Solution: Length of side of base $= \dfrac{1}{4}$ (perimeter)

$$= \frac{1}{4}(20)$$

$$= 5 \text{ cm}$$

Area of base $= B = 5^2 = 25 \text{ cm}^2$

Volume of pyramid $= V = \dfrac{1}{3} Bh$

$$= \frac{1}{3}(25)(12)$$

$$= \mathbf{100 \text{ cm}^3}$$

5. The volume of a pyramid having an isosceles right triangle as its base is 48 cm³. If the length of a leg of the right triangle is 6 cm, what is the height of the pyramid?

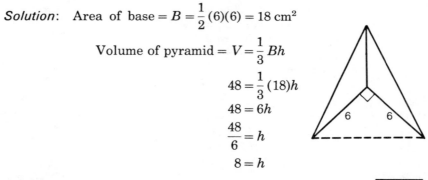

Solution: Area of base $= B = \dfrac{1}{2}(6)(6) = 18 \text{ cm}^2$

Volume of pyramid $= V = \dfrac{1}{3} Bh$

$$48 = \frac{1}{3}(18)h$$

$$48 = 6h$$

$$\frac{48}{6} = h$$

$$8 = h$$

The height of the pyramid is **8 cm**. ▆▆▆

COMPARING VOLUMES OF SIMILAR SOLIDS.   If two solids are similar, then their volumes have the same ratio as the cube of the ratio of any pair of corresponding dimensions. For example, the volumes V_1 and V_2 of two rectangular solids have the same ratio as the cube of the ratio of their lengths, widths, or heights:

$$\frac{V_1}{V_2} = \left(\frac{l_1}{l_2}\right)^3 = \left(\frac{w_1}{w_2}\right)^3 = \left(\frac{h_1}{h_2}\right)^3.$$

Example ▆▆▆

6. The volumes of two rectangular solids are 8 cm³ and 27 cm³. If the height of the smaller solid is 2 cm, find the height of the larger solid.

Solution: $\dfrac{V_1}{V_2} = \left(\dfrac{h_1}{h_2}\right)^3$

$$\frac{8}{27} = \left(\frac{2}{h}\right)^3 = \frac{8}{h^3}$$

Cross-multiply: $8h^3 = (8)(27)$

$$h^3 = \frac{(8)(27)}{8} = 27$$

$$h = \sqrt[3]{27} = 3 \text{ cm}$$

EXERCISE SET 10.8

1. Find the volume of a cube whose edge length is:

   (a) 4   (b) 10   (c) $\dfrac{2}{3}$ (d) 1.5   (e) $5x$ (f) $3y^2$

2. Find the volume of a rectangular solid if its dimensions are:

   (a) $l = 2$, $w = 5$, and $h = 7$
   (b) $l = 3$, $w = 4$, $h = 7.6$
   (c) $l = \dfrac{1}{2}$, $w = \dfrac{3}{4}$, $h = \dfrac{8}{9}$
   (d) $l = 1\dfrac{1}{2}$, $w = \dfrac{4}{9}$, $h = 0.75$
   (e) $l = x^2$, $w = 3x$, $h = 4$
   (f) $l = 5x^3$, $w = 2$, $h = 6x^2$

3. Find the height of a rectangular solid if its other dimensions and its volume are:

   (a) $l = 10$, $w = 2.5$, $V = 75$
   (b) $l = 8$, $w = 3.2$, $V = 128$
   (c) $l = 6.2$, $w = 4$, $V = 37.2$
   (d) $l = 4$, $w = 2.6$, $V = 18.2$

4. A rectangular solid has the same volume as a cube whose edge length is 4. What is the height of the rectangular solid if its length is 2 and its width is 8?

5. A cube has the same volume as a pyramid whose base has an area of 25 and whose height is 15. What is the edge length of the cube?

6. If the edge length of a cube is tripled, by what number is the volume multiplied?

7. If the length and the height of a rectangular solid are each doubled, by what number is the volume multiplied?

8. A certain prism has the same length and the same volume as a pyramid. If the area of the base of the pyramid is 42, what is the area of the base of the prism?

9. A pyramid has a height of 6 cm and a right triangle as a base. If the length of the hypotenuse of the right triangle is 10 cm and the length of one of the legs is 8 cm, what is the volume of the pyramid?

10. The height of a rectangular solid is 3, and its length exceeds twice its width by 1. If the volume of the solid is 30, find the length and the width.

11. A pyramid having a square base has a volume of 98 cm³. If a side of the square is 7 cm, what is the height of the pyramid?

12. The volumes of two cubes are 27 and 216. If the length of an edge of the smaller cube is 4.5, what is the length of an edge of the larger cube?

13. If V_1 and V_2 represent the volumes of two rectangular solids, and w_1 and w_2 represent their widths, fill in the missing dimensions in the following table:

	V_1	V_2	W_1	W_2
(a)	80	270	9	?
(b)	?	125	24	30
(c)	54	?	6	8
(d)	200	?	5	2

14. The smaller of two boxes of breakfast cereal has a volume of 12, while the larger box has a volume of 96. If the height of the smaller box is 8, what is the height of the larger box?

15. A pyramid having a rectangular base has a volume of 182 cm³ and a height of 6 cm. If the length of the base is 1 less than twice the width, find the dimensions of the base of the pyramid.

10.9 MEASURING VOLUMES OF CIRCULAR SOLIDS

_____ KEY IDEAS _____

When the term *cylinder* is used, we will always mean a right circular cylinder, which can be visualized as a tin can. Similarly, when discussing a *cone*, we will be referring to a right circular cone, whose shape may be thought of as being the same as that of an ice cream cone.

VOLUME OF A CYLINDER.   A cylinder (Figure 10.20) has *two* bases that are congruent circles lying in parallel planes. Like a prism, the volume of a cylinder is also given by the formula $V = Bh$. The area of a cylinder's circular base is πr^2, so

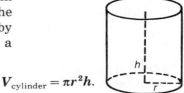

$$V_{\text{cylinder}} = \pi r^2 h.$$

Figure 10.20   Cylinder

VOLUME OF A CONE.   A **cone** (Figure 10.21), like a pyramid, has one base and a volume given by the formula $V = \frac{1}{3} Bh$. Here B represents the area of its circular base, so

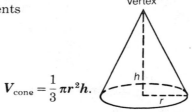

Vertex

$$V_{\text{cone}} = \frac{1}{3} \pi r^2 h.$$

Figure 10.21   Cone

Examples

1.   The radius of a base of a cylinder is 5 and its height is 6. What is its volume?

Solution: $V = \pi r^2 h$
$\qquad = \pi (5^2) 6 = \pi (25)(6) = 150\pi$

2.   The *slant height, l,* of a cone is a segment that connects the vertex to a point on the circular base. What is the volume of a cone having a radius of 6 and a slant height of 10?

Solution: The slant height is the hypotenuse of a right triangle whose legs are a radius and the altitude of the cone. The lengths of this right triangle form a 6-8-10 right triangle, where 8 represents the height of the cone. Therefore

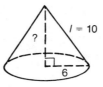

$l = 10$
?
6

$$V = \frac{1}{3} \pi r^2 h$$

$$= \frac{1}{3} \pi (6)^2 \cdot 8$$

$$\overset{12}{=\frac{1}{\cancel{3}}\pi(\cancel{36})\cdot 8}$$
$$\underset{1}{}$$
$$= 96\pi$$

3. The circumference of the base of a cone is 8π cm. If the volume of the cone is 16π cm³, what is the height?

Solution: Since $C = \pi D = 8\pi$, the diameter is 8 cm; this means that the radius of the base is 4 cm.

$$V = \frac{1}{3}\pi r^2 h$$
$$16\pi = \frac{1}{3}\pi(4^2)h$$
$$48\pi = 16\pi h$$
$$\frac{48\pi}{16\pi} = h$$
$$3 = h$$

The height of the cone is **3 cm**.

VOLUME OF A SPHERE. A sphere (Figure 10.22) is a solid that represents the set of all points in space that are at a given distance from a fixed point. Its volume, V, can be determined using the formula

$$V_{\text{sphere}} = \frac{4}{3}\pi r^3.$$

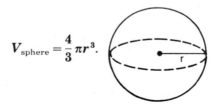

Figure 10.22 Sphere

Examples

4. Find the volume of a sphere whose diameter is 6 cm.

Solution: Radius $= \frac{1}{2}(6) = 3$

$$V = \frac{4}{3}\pi(3)^3$$
$$= \frac{4}{3}\pi(27)$$
$$= 4\pi(9)$$
$$= \mathbf{36\pi \ cm^3}$$

5. The radius of a sphere is twice as long as the radius of a smaller sphere. How many times greater is the volume of the larger sphere than the volume of the smaller sphere?

Solution: If the radii of the two spheres are represented by r_1 and r_2, then their volumes, V_1 and V_2, have the ratio

$$\frac{V_1}{V_2} = \frac{\frac{4}{3}\pi(r_1)^3}{\frac{4}{3}\pi(r_2)^3} = \frac{r_1^3}{r_2^3} = \left(\frac{r_1}{r_2}\right)^3.$$

Since the radii are in the ratio of $2:1$,

$$\frac{V_1}{V_2} = \left(\frac{2}{1}\right)^3 = \frac{8}{1}.$$

The volume of the larger sphere is 8 times the volume of the smaller sphere.

SUMMARY OF VOLUME FORMULAS

Figure	Volume Formula
Rectangular Solid	$V = $ length $\times$ width $\times$ height $= lwh$
Cube	$V = $ edge $\times$ edge $\times$ edge $= ($edge$)^3$
Pyramid	$V = \dfrac{1}{3} \times$ area of base $\times$ height
Cylinder	$V = \pi \times ($radius$)^2 \times$ height $= \pi r^2 h$
Cone	$V = \dfrac{1}{3} \times \pi \times ($radius$)^2 \times$ height $= \dfrac{1}{3}\pi r^2 h$
Sphere	$V = \dfrac{4}{3} \times \pi \times ($radius$)^3$ $= \dfrac{4}{3}\pi r^3$

EXERCISE SET 10.9

1. Find the volume of each cone.

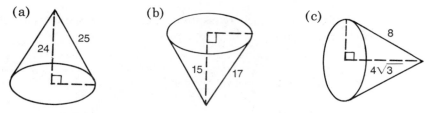

2. Find the volume of a sphere if the length of its radius is:

   (a) 6   (b) $\dfrac{3}{2}$ (c) π (d) $3x$

3. Fill in the missing volumes in the following table:

	r	h	V_{cylinder}	V_{cone}
(a)	7	3	?	?
(b)	4.5	10	?	?
(c)	6	?	36π	?
(d)	?	5	45π	?
(e)	4	?	?	96π

4. Fill in the missing values in the following table, where l represents the slant height of a cone:

	r	h	l	V_{cone}
(a)	3	4	?	?
(b)	5	?	13	?
(c)	?	9	41	?
(d)	$\sqrt{15}$	?	?	35π

5. If the radius of the base of a cone is multiplied by 3 while its height remains the same, by what number is its volume multiplied?

6. If the radius of a sphere is tripled, by what number is its volume multiplied?

7. The circumference of a cylinder is 10π cm, and its height is 3.5 cm. What is the volume of the cylinder?

8. A cylinder and a cone have congruent bases and equal heights. How many times greater is the volume of the cylinder than the volume of the cone?

9. The radius of a sphere is 6, and the radius of a cylinder is 4. If these solids have the same volume, what is the height of the cylinder?

10. The radii of two spheres are 30 and 50. If the volume of the smaller sphere is 270π, what is the volume of the larger sphere?

11. The volumes of two spheres are 343π and 729π. If the radius of the larger sphere is 18, what is the radius of the smaller sphere?

12. A right triangle whose legs are 8 cm and 15 cm is revolved in space about the shorter leg. What is the volume of the resulting solid of revolution?

13. A container having the shape of a cylinder with a radius of 2 cm and a height of 9 cm is filled with sand. What is the radius of a container having the shape of a sphere that can hold the same amount of sand?

14. A sphere is inscribed in a cube having an edge length of 8. What is the volume of the sphere?

15. A sphere having a volume $32/3$ π cm^3 is inscribed in a cube. What is the volume of the cube?

CHAPTER 10 REVIEW EXERCISES

REGENTS REVIEW. *Problems included in this section are similar in form and difficulty to those found on the New York Regents Examination for Course I of the Three-Year Sequence for High School Mathematics. Problems preceded by an asterisk have actually appeared on a previous Course I Regents Examination.*

*1. If the base of a triangle is represented by $2x$ and the altitude drawn to that base is equal to 10, express the area of the triangle in terms of x.

*2. A building casts a shadow 15 feet long at the same time that a woman 6 feet tall casts a shadow 5 feet long. Find the number of feet in the height of the building.

*3. If the diameter of a circle is 14, find the area of the circle.

*4. The sides of a triangle are, in centimeters, 24, 20, and 8. The longest side of a similar triangle is 12 centimeters. Find the number of centimeters in the *shortest* side of this triangle.

*5. Find the radius of a circle if its circumference is 48π.

*6.   The area of a triangle is 48. If the base of this triangle is 12, what is the length of the altitude to this base?

*7.   In the accompanying figure, $\triangle ABC$ is congruent to $\triangle RST$, $\overline{AB} \cong \overline{RS}$, $\overline{BC} \cong \overline{ST}$, and $\overline{AC} \cong \overline{RT}$. What angle in $\triangle RST$ is congruent to $\angle BAC$?

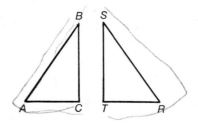

*8.   In the accompanying diagram, $\triangle ABC$ is similar to $\triangle XYZ$, with $\angle A \cong \angle X$, $\angle B \cong \angle Y$, and $\angle C \cong \angle Z$. If $AB = 35$, $XY = 7$, $BC = 10$, and $YZ = 2$, how many times larger is side $\overline{AC}$ than side $\overline{XZ}$?

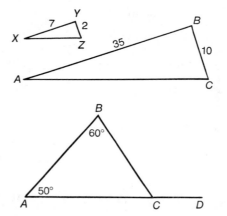

*9.   In the accompanying figure, $\angle BCD$ is an exterior angle to $\triangle ABC$ at vertex C. If $m\angle A = 50$ and $m\angle B = 60$, find the number of degrees in the measure of $\angle BCD$.

*10.   The area of square $ABCD$ is 36 square centimeters. What is the number of centimeters in the perimeter of the square?

*11.   If the edge of a cube is $3x$, the volume of the cube is:
    (1) $27x^3$ (2) $9x^3$ (3) $3x^3$ (4) $9x^2$

*12.   If the radius of a circle is tripled, then the area of the circle is multiplied by:
    (1) 27   (2) 9   (3) 3   (4) 6

*13.   The volume of a cylinder is found by using the formula $V = \pi r^2 h$. If h is doubled, then the volume is:
    (1) doubled
    (2) increased by 2
    (3) increased by 4
    (4) multiplied by 4

*14.   In the accompanying figure, quadrilateral $ABCD$ is a trapezoid with $\overleftrightarrow{AB} \parallel \overleftrightarrow{DC}$, $\overleftrightarrow{AD} \perp \overleftrightarrow{AB}$, and $\overleftrightarrow{DB} \perp \overleftrightarrow{BC}$; $AB = AD = 4$, and $DC = 8$.

(a) Find DB in radical form.
(b) Find the area of $\triangle ABD$.
(c) Find the area of trapezoid $ABCD$.
(d) Find the area of $\triangle DBC$.

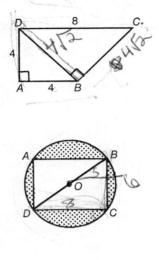

*15. In the accompanying figure, rectangle $ABCD$ is inscribed in circle O and $\overline{DB}$ is a diameter. The radius of the circle is 5. (Answers may be left in terms of π.)

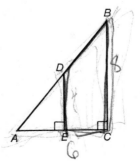

(a) Find the area of the circle.
(b) If $CD = 8$, find BC.
(c) Find the area of $\triangle BCD$.
(d) Find the area of rectangle $ABCD$.
(e) Find the area of the shaded portion of the figure.

*16. In the accompanying figure, $\triangle ABC$ is an isosceles triangle, $AB = CB$, the measure of $\angle BCA$ is $2x$, and the measure of the exterior angle DAB is $3x$.

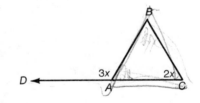

(a) Express the measure of $\angle BAC$ in terms of x.
(b) What is the value of x?
(c) How many degrees are in the measure of $\angle BAC$?
(d) How many degrees are in the measure of $\angle BAD$?
(e) How many degrees are in the measure of $\angle ABC$?

*17. In the diagram below, $\triangle ABC$ is a right triangle with the right angle at C. Segment $\overline{DE}$ is perpendicular to $\overline{AC}$ at E, $BC = 8$, $AC = 6$, and $DF : BC = 1 : 2$.
(a) Find DE.
(b) Find AB.
(c) Find AE.
(d) Find the area of $\triangle ABC$.
(e) Find the area of trapezoid $ECBD$.

*18. In the diagram of parallelogram *ABCD*, $\overline{DE}$ is perpendicular to $\overline{AB}$, *AD* = 15, and
AE = 9.
(a) Find *DE*.
(b) If *BE* is 2 less than twice
AE, find *BE*.
(c) Find *AB*.
(d) Find the area of $\triangle AED$.
(e) Find the area of *ABCD*.
(f) Find the area of trapezoid
EBCD.

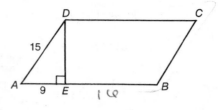

*19. In the accompanying diagram, *ABCD* is a rectangle and *AGE* is an
isosceles triangle with *AG* = *EG*, $\overline{GF} \perp \overline{AD}$, *E* is the midpoint of
$\overline{AD}$, *AF* = *FE*, *AB* = 8, and *AD* = 24.

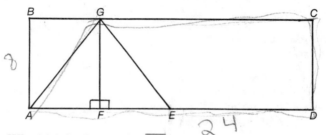

(a) What is the length of $\overline{AE}$?
(b) What is the length of $\overline{AF}$?
(c) What is the length of $\overline{AG}$?
(d) What is the area of $\triangle AGE$?
(e) What is the area of trapezoid *ADCG*?

*20. In the accompanying diagram, *ABCD* is a rectangle, *E* is a point on
$\overline{AB}$, *DE* = 10, *AE* = 6, and *DC* = 15. Circle *O* has a radius of 3.

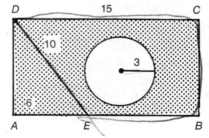

(a) Find *AD*.
(b) Find the area of $\triangle ADE$.
(c) Find the area of circle *O*.
(d) Find the area of trapezoid *EBCD*.
(e) Find the area of the shaded portion.

UNIT IV: ELEMENTS OF CORDINATE GEOMETRY AND TRANSFORMATIONS

CHAPTER 11

Equations of Lines; Introduction to Transformations

11.1 GRAPHING POINTS IN THE COORDINATE PLANE

KEY IDEAS

A **coordinate plane** may be created by drawing a horizontal number line called the **x-axis** and a vertical number line called the **y-axis**. The x-axis and the y-axis are sometimes referred to as the **coordinate axes**, and their point of intersection is called the **origin**. The process of locating a point or a series of points in the coordinate plane is called **graphing**.

GRAPHING ORDERED PAIRS. Each point in the coordinate plane is located (see Figure 11.1) using an ordered pair of numbers of the form (x, y), in which the first number of the pair is the x-coordinate, and the second number is the y-coordinate. The x-coordinate, sometimes called the **abscissa**, tells the number of units the point is located to the right $(x > 0)$ or to the left $(x < 0)$ of the origin. The y-coordinate, sometimes called the **ordinate**, gives the number of units the point is located above $(y > 0)$ or below $(y < 0)$ the

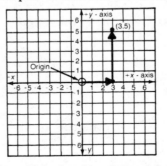

Figure 11.1 Graphing Ordered Pairs

289

origin. For example, to graph the point (3, 5), start at the origin, move 3 units to the right, and then 5 units up.

THE FOUR QUADRANTS.   The coordinate axes divide the plane into four regions called **quadrants**. As shown in Figure 11.2, the quadrants are numbered in counterclockwise order, beginning at the upper right and using Roman numerals. Notice that the points $A(2, 3)$, $B(-4, 5)$, $C(-3, -6)$, and $D(3, -3)$ lie in different quadrants. The signs of the x- and y-coordinates of a point determine the quadrant in which a point lies.

Coordinates	Location of Point
$(+, +)$	Quadrant I
$(-, +)$	Quadrant II
$(-, -)$	Quadrant III
$(+, -)$	Quadrant IV

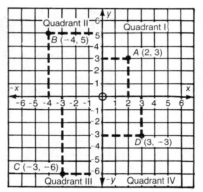

Figure 11.2   The Four Quadrants

LENGTHS OF HORIZONTAL AND VERTICAL SEGMENTS.   In Figure 11.3, the line segment joining $L(2, 5)$ and $M(6, 5)$ is parallel to the x-axis. The length of $\overline{LM}$ may be obtained in one of two ways:

1.   By counting the number of boxes between points L and M. There are four square boxes between points L and M, so the length of $\overline{LM}$ is 4 units.

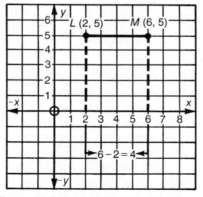

Figure 11.3   Lengths of Line Segments

2.   By subtracting to find the difference between the corresponding coordinates of the two points that are different. Since the y-coordinates of points L and M are the same, subtract the x-coordinates of these points: $LM = 6 - 2 = 4$. Keep in mind that, since length must be a positive number, you must always subtract the smaller coordinate from the larger coordinate.

Examples

1. Find the length of the line segment joining points $A(3, -2)$ and $B(3, 5)$.

Solution: $\overline{AB}$ is parallel to the y-axis, and its length is equal to the difference in the y-coordinates: $5 - (-2) = 5 + 2 = \mathbf{7\ units}$.

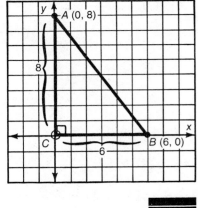

2. Find the area of the triangle whose vertices are $A(0, 8)$, $B(6, 0)$, and $C(0, 0)$.

Solution: The vertices determine a right triangle, whose right angle is at C. First find the lengths of the legs of the right triangle.

$$AC = 6 - 0 = 6$$
$$BC = 8 - 0 = 8$$

$$\text{Area } \triangle ABC = \frac{1}{2} bh$$
$$= \frac{1}{2}(6)(8)$$
$$= 3(8)$$
$$= \mathbf{24\ square\ units}$$

FINDING THE AREAS OF SOME POLYGONS USING COORDINATES.

The area of a triangle and the areas of certain special quadrilaterals can be easily found if at least one of their sides is parallel to a coordinate axis. The altitude drawn to that base will be parallel to the other coordinate axis, so that the lengths of the base and the altitude can then be determined by counting boxes or by subtracting coordinates. Substituting these lengths into the appropriate area formula gives the area of the figure.

Examples

3. Graph a parallelogram whose vertices are $A(2, 2)$, $B(5, 6)$, $C(13, 6)$, and $D(10, 2)$, and then find its area.

Solution: In the accompanying graph, altitude $\overline{BH}$ has been drawn to base $\overline{AD}$. Count boxes to find the lengths of these segments.

Area of $\square ABCD = bh$

$$= (AD)(BH)$$
$$= (8)(4)$$
$$= 32 \text{ square units}$$

4. Graph a trapezoid whose vertices are $A(-4, 0)$, $B(-4, 3)$, $C(0, 6)$ and $D(0, 0)$, and then find its area.

Solution: In the accompanying graph, $\overline{AB}$ and $\overline{CD}$ are the bases of trapezoid $ABCD$. $\overline{AD}$ may be considered an altitude since it is perpendicular to both bases.

Area of trap $ABCD = \dfrac{1}{2} h(b_1 + b_2)$

$$= \frac{1}{2}(AD)(AB + CD)$$

$$= \frac{1}{2}(4)(3 + 6)$$

$$= 2(9)$$

$$= 18 \text{ square units}$$

EXERCISE SET 11.1

1. Starting at the origin, move up 3 units and move to the right 2 units. Then move to the left 5 units and down 1 unit. Label this point A. What are the coordinates of point A?

2. Graph points $(-3, -3)$, $(0, 0)$, and $(2, 2)$, and then draw a line through them.
   (a) Using a protractor, determine the angle that the line makes with the positive x-axis.
   (b) Give the coordinates of three other points on the line.

3. In what quadrant is point $P(x, y)$ located if $xy < 0$ and $y > x$?

4. Graph the line segment determined by each of the following pairs of points, and then determine its length:
   (a) $(3, 8)$ and $(7, 8)$ (d) $(-2, 5)$ and $(-6, 5)$
   (b) $(9, 4)$ and $(1, 4)$ (e) $(-3, -8)$ and $(-3, 2)$
   (c) $(0, -1)$ and $(0, 5)$ (f) $(7, -1)$ and $(-7, -1)$

5. Find the area of the triangle whose vertices are:
(a) $A(0, 5)$, $B(6, 0)$, $C(0, 0)$ (c) $A(2, 2)$, $B(2, 7)$, $C(5, 2)$
(b) $A(-4, 0)$, $B(0, 0)$, $C(0, -9)$ (d) $A(-3, 0)$, $B(0, 8)$, $C(3, 0)$

6. Sketch the triangle determined by vertices $A(1, 4)$, $B(1, 1)$, and $C(5, 1)$, and find the length of $\overline{AC}$.

7. The rectangle whose vertices are $A(0, 0)$, $B(0, 5)$, $C(h, k)$, and $D(8, 0)$ lies in the first quadrant.
(a) What are the values of h and k?
(b) What is the area of rectangle $ABCD$?

8. Find the area of the parallelogram whose vertices are:
(a) $A(2, 3)$, $B(5, 9)$, $C(13, 9)$, $D(10, 3)$
(b) $A(-4, -2)$, $B(-2, 6)$, $C(10, 6)$, $D(8, -2)$

9. Find the area of the trapezoid whose vertices are:
(a) $A(0, 0)$, $B(0, 5)$, $C(7, 11)$, $D(7, 0)$
(b) $A(-3, 0)$, $B(-3, 2)$, $C(5, 6)$, $D(5, 0)$
(c) $A(0, 0)$, $B(-2, -6)$, $C(9, -6)$, $D(7, 0)$
(d) $A(-4, -4)$, $B(-1, 5)$, $C(6, 5)$, $D(9, -4)$

10. Find the area of the hexagon whose vertices are $A(4, 5)$, $B(7, 0)$, $C(4, -5)$, $D(-4, -5)$, $E(-7, 0)$, and $F(-4, 5)$.

11.2   FINDING THE SLOPE OF A LINE

--------- KEY IDEAS ---------

If you imagine that a line represents a hill, you realize that some lines will be more difficult to "walk up" than other lines. In the accompanying figure, line *l* will be more difficult to climb than line *k* since line *l* is *steeper* than line *k*. Another name for steepness is *slope*. If, as you move along a line from left to right, you are "walking *uphill*," then the line has a *positive* slope; if you are "walking *downhill*," then the line has a *negative* slope.

DEFINING SLOPE.   The **slope** of a line is a measure of its steepness and may be expressed as a number. To do this, select any two different points on the line. In traveling from one point to the other, find the ratio of the change in the vertical distance (difference in the y-coordinates) to the change in the horizontal distance (difference in the x-coordinates). Sometimes the notation Δy (read as "delta y") is used to represent the change in the vertical distance, and Δx (read as "delta x") to represent the change in the horizontal distance.

In general, the slope, m, of a nonvertical line that passes through points $A(x_1, y_1)$ and $B(x_2, y_2)$ (Figure 11.4) is given by the ratio of the change in the values of their y-coordinates to the change in the value of their x-coordinates:

$$\text{Slope} = m = \frac{\Delta y}{\Delta x} = \frac{y_2 - y_1}{x_2 - x_1}$$

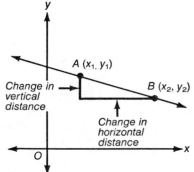

Figure 11.4   Slope of a Line

Example

1. Determine the slope of the line that contains each of the following pairs of points:

(a) $A(4, 2)$ and $B(6, 5)$ (c) $J(4, 3)$ and $K(8, 3)$

(b) $P(0, 3)$ and $Q(5, -1)$ (d) $W(2, 1)$ and $C(2, 7)$

Solutions: (a) See Figure (a).

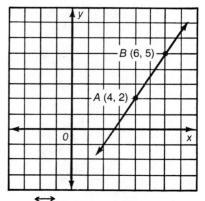

To find the slope of $\overleftrightarrow{AB}$, observe that:

$$\Delta y = 5 - 2 = 3$$

$$A(4, 2) \qquad\qquad\qquad B(6, 5)$$

$$\Delta x = 6 - 4 = 2$$

$$m = \frac{\Delta y}{\Delta x} = \frac{y_2 - y_1}{x_2 - x_1} = \frac{5 - 2}{6 - 4} = \frac{3}{2}$$

The slope of $\overleftrightarrow{AB}$ is $\frac{3}{2}$. The slope of $\overleftrightarrow{AB}$ was calculated assuming that point B was the second point. When using the slope formula, either of the two points may be considered the second point. For example, let's repeat the slope calculation considering point A to be the second point (that is, $x_2 = 4$ and $y_2 = 2$):

$$m = \frac{\Delta y}{\Delta x} = \frac{y_2 - y_1}{x_2 - x_1} = \frac{2-5}{4-6} = \frac{-3}{-2} = \frac{3}{2}$$

The same value, 3/2, is obtained for the slope of $\overleftrightarrow{AB}$, regardless of whether A is taken as the first or the second point.

(b) See Figure (b).

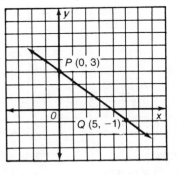

$$m = \frac{\Delta y}{\Delta x} = \frac{y_2 - y_1}{x_2 - x_1} = \frac{-1-3}{5-0} = \frac{-4}{5}$$

The slope of $\overleftrightarrow{PQ}$ is $-4/5$. The slope of $\overleftrightarrow{AB}$ in part (a) was *positive* in value, and the slope of $\overleftrightarrow{PQ}$ has a *negative* value. Compare the directions of these lines. Notice that, if a line has a positive slope, it climbs up *and* to the right; if a line has a negative slope, it falls down *and* to the right.

These observations may be restated as follows: As you move along a line from left to right, (that is, as the values of the x-coordinates increase), if the values of the y-coordinates also increase, then the line has a positive slope; if, as the values of the x-coordinates increase, the values of the y-coordinates decrease, then the line has a negative slope.

(c) See Figure (c).

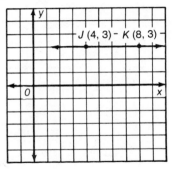

Since the line $\overleftrightarrow{JK}$ is horizontal, there is no change in y, so that $\Delta y = 0$.

$$m = \frac{\Delta y}{\Delta x} = \frac{0}{\Delta x} = 0$$

The slope of $\overleftrightarrow{JK}$ is **0**.

(d) See Figure (d).

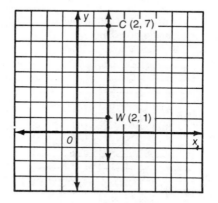

Since the line is vertical, there is no change in x, so that $\Delta x = 0$. The slope of $\overleftrightarrow{WC}$ *is* **undefined** since division by 0 is undefined.

THREE GENERALIZATIONS CONCERNING SLOPE

1.   An **oblique** line is a line that is *not* parallel to a coordinate axis. The slope of an oblique line may be either positive or negative.

If, as x increases, the line *rises*, then the slope m of the line is *positive*.

If, as x increases, the line *falls*, then the slope m of the line is *negative*.

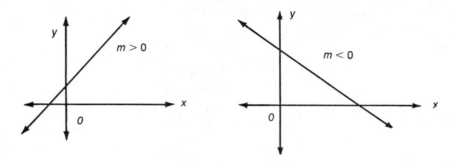

2. The slope m of a horizontal line is 0.

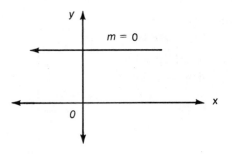

3. The slope m of a vertical line is not defined.

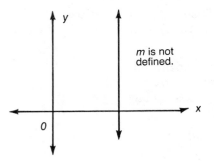

SLOPES OF PARALLEL LINES. In Figure 11.5, the slope of the line containing $A(1, 3)$ and $B(6, 8)$ is the same as the slope of the line containing $C(3, 0)$ and $D(7, 4)$. The graphs of the two lines determined by these points show that the lines are parallel.

Slope of $\overleftrightarrow{AB} = \dfrac{8-3}{6-1}$

$\qquad = \dfrac{5}{5} = 1$

Slope of $\overleftrightarrow{CD} = \dfrac{4-0}{7-3}$

$\qquad = \dfrac{4}{4} = 1$

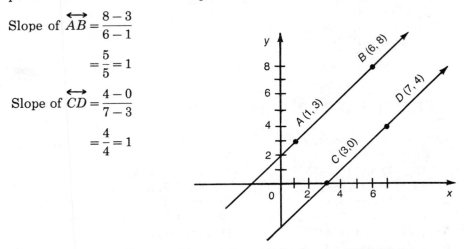

Figure 11.5 Slopes of Parallel Lines

Here are two generalizations about parallel lines and slope (Figure 11.6):

● If two nonvertical lines are parallel, then their slopes are equal.

● If two nonvertical lines have the same slope, then they are parallel.

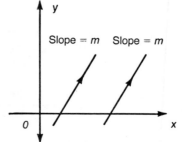

Figure 11.6 Parallel Lines and Slope

Example ▬▬▬

2. The coordinates of the vertices of quadrilateral *MATH* are $M(-3, 2)$, $A(4, 8)$, $T(15, 5)$, and $H(8, y)$. If *MATH* is a parallelogram, find the value of y.

Solution: The opposite sides of a parallelogram are parallel and have, therefore, the same slope.

Slope $\overline{MA}$ = Slope $\overline{HT}$

$$\frac{8-2}{4-(-3)} = \frac{y-5}{8-15}$$

$$\frac{6}{7} = \frac{y-5}{-7}$$

$$7(y-5) = 6(-7)$$
$$7y - 35 = -42$$
$$7y = -42 + 35$$
$$7y = -7$$
$$y = -\frac{7}{7} = -1$$

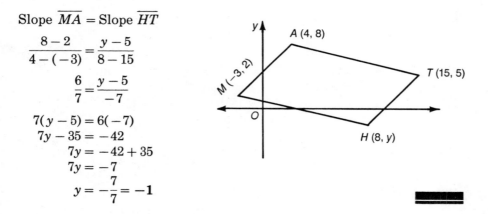

▬▬▬

EXERCISE SET 11.2

1–12. Find the slope of the line that passes through each of the following pairs of points:

1. $(2, -7)$ and $(5, -7)$
2. $(4, 3)$ and $(4, -1)$
3. $(-3, 5)$ and $(4, 7)$
4. $(5, 4)$ and $(-7, 8)$
5. $(-2, 3)$ and $(-4, 5)$
6. $(-1, 4)$ and $(5, 9)$
7. $(-3, -4)$ and $(3, 8)$
8. $(5, -6)$ and $(0, -6)$
9. $(0, -7)$ and $(-2, -3)$
10. $(-4, 9)$ and $(-4, -9)$
11. $(5, -1)$ and $(-11, 7)$
12. $(-1, -3)$ and $(2, 3)$

13. In each of the following cases, determine whether $\overleftrightarrow{AB}$ is parallel to $\overleftrightarrow{CD}$:
    (a) $A(1, 5)$, $B(-1, 9)$; $C(2, 6)$, $D(1, 8)$
    (b) $A(-2, 7)$, $B(1, 4)$; $C(-8, 3)$, $D(-7, 4)$
    (c) $A(1, -5)$, $B(-4, 5)$; $C(0, -7)$, $D(4, 9)$
    (d) $A(-3, 6)$, $B(1, 1)$; $C(-7, 3)$, $D(1, -7)$

14. The slope of $\overleftrightarrow{AB}$ is $\dfrac{3}{5}$, and the slope of $\overleftrightarrow{CD}$ is $\dfrac{9}{k}$. If $\overleftrightarrow{AB}$ is parallel to $\overleftrightarrow{CD}$, what is the value of k?

15. Points $A(2, k)$ and $B(6, 10)$ determine a line whose slope is $\dfrac{1}{2}$. Find k.

16. Which is true of the line segment joining $(-5, 2)$ and $(-5, -7)$?
    (1) Its slope is -2
    (2) Its slope is $\dfrac{7}{2}$.
    (3) Its slope is undefined.
    (4) Its slope is zero.

17. The coordinates of the vertices of parallelogram $ABCD$ are $A(0, 0)$, $B(5, 0)$, $C(8, 1)$, and $D(x, 1)$. The value of x is:
    (1) 1   (2) 2   (3) 3   (4) 4

18. The coordinates of the vertices of parallelogram $ABCD$ are $A(1, y)$, $B(4, 10)$, $C(12, 10)$, and $D(9, 4)$. Find the value of y.

19. The line joining $A(-2, 0)$ and $B(10, 3)$ is parallel to the line joining $C(5, 7)$ and $D(1, k)$. Find the value of k.

20. In quadrilateral $ABCD$, the coordinates of the vertices are $A(3, 10)$, $B(11, 10)$, $C(3, -2)$, and $D(-5, -2)$.
    (a) Using graph paper, draw quadrilateral $ABCD$.
    (b) Using slopes, show that $ABCD$ is a parallelogram.
    (c) Find the area of $ABCD$.

21. The coordinates of the vertices of quadrilateral $ABCD$ are $A(2, 0)$, $B(10, 2)$, $C(6, 7)$, and $D(2, 6)$.
    (a) Using slopes, show that $\overline{AB}$ is parallel to $\overline{CD}$, and state a reason for your conclusion.
    (b) Using slopes, show that quadrilateral $ABCD$ is *not* a parallelogram, and state a reason for your conclusion.

22. The coordinates of the vertices of trapezoid $ABCD$ are $A(1, 5)$, $B(7, k)$, $C(2, -4)$, and $D(-7, -1)$. If $\overline{AB}$ and $\overline{DC}$ are the bases of the trapezoid, find the value of k.

23. In trapezoid $ABCD$ with bases $\overline{AD}$ and $\overline{BC}$, the coordinates of the vertices are $A(3, 1)$, $B(1, 7)$, $C(4, 9)$, and $D(k, 5)$.
    (a) What is the slope of $\overline{BC}$?
    (b) Using your answer in part (a), find k.

24. The vertices of parallelogram $STWU$ are $S(1, 1)$, $T(-2, 3)$, $W(0, b)$, and $U(3, -5)$.
    (a) Find the slope of $\overline{ST}$.   (b) Find the value of b.

25. Parallelogram $ABCD$ has vertices $A(2, -1)$, $B(8, 1)$, and $D(4, k)$. The slope of $\overline{AD}$ is equal to 2.
    (a) Find k.   (b) Find the coordinates of C.

26. The vertices of a triangle are $P(1, 2)$, $Q(-3, 6)$, and $R(4, 8)$.
    (a) Find the slope of $\overline{PR}$.
    (b) A line through point Q is parallel to $\overleftrightarrow{PR}$ If this line contains point $(x, 14)$, find the value of x.

27. Three points lie on the same line if the slope of the line determined by the first two points is the same as the slope of the line determined by the first and the last point. Determine whether the points in each of the following sets are collinear:
    (a) $(-4, -5)$, $(0, -2)$, and $(8, 4)$ (c) $(1, 2)$, $(5, 8)$, and $(-3, -4)$
    (b) $(-3, 2)$, $(4, 2)$, and $(-5, 2)$ (d) $(2, 1)$, $(10, 7)$, and $(-4, -6)$

28. If $D(7, k)$ is a point on the line joining $A(1, 1)$ and $B(10, 4)$, what is the value of k?

29. If $E(5, h)$ is a point on the line joining $A(0, 1)$ and $B(-2, -1)$, what is the value of h?

30. The coordinates of the vertices of trapezoid $ABCD$ are $A(3, 0)$, $B(7, 0)$, $C(7, 11)$, and $D(3, 8)$.
    (a) Using graph paper, draw the trapezoid.
    (b) Find the slope of diagonal $\overline{BD}$.
    (c) Find the area of the trapezoid.
    (d) Find the perimeter of the trapezoid.

31. In the accompanying diagram, find:
    (a) the slope of $\overleftrightarrow{AB}$
    (b) the slope of $\overleftrightarrow{CD}$

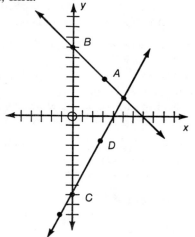

11.3 USING THE SLOPE-INTERCEPT FORM OF A LINEAR EQUATION

KEY IDEAS

In a *linear equation* the highest power of any variable is 1. The equation $x + y = 5$ is an example of a linear equation. A linear equation may also have a single variable. The equations $x = 2$ and $y = -1$ are also examples of linear equations.

In general, a **linear equation** is any equation that can be written in the form

$$Ax + By + C = 0,$$

where A, B, and C are constants and A and B are not both equal to 0. The graph of a linear equation is a straight line.

EQUATIONS OF LINES.   The solution set of the equation $x + 2 = 5$ has exactly *one* member, which is 3. The solution set of the equation $x + y = 5$ contains *all* ordered pairs of numbers such that the sum of the x- and y-coordinates is 5. Thus, there are an *infinite* number of ordered pairs in the solution set. Some of these are:

$$(1, 4) \text{ since } 1 + 4 = 5, \quad (-3, 8) \text{ since } -3 + 8 = 5,$$
$$(2, 3) \text{ since } 2 + 3 = 5, \quad (2.5, 2.5) \text{ since } 2.5 + 2.5 = 5.$$

The graph of each of these ordered pairs of numbers (Figure 11.7) is a different point on the same line. The line represents the set of *all* ordered pairs of numbers that satisfy the equation $x + y = 5$.

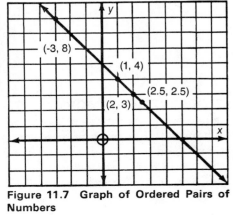

Figure 11.7   Graph of Ordered Pairs of Numbers

Examples

1. The graph of $3x - y = 6$ contains which of the following points?
(1) $(0, 2)$ (2) $(5, 9)$ (3) $(4, -6)$ (4) $(1, 9)$

Solution: Through trial and error determine the point that satisfies the equation. Substituting the values in choice (2) gives

$$\begin{array}{r} 3x - y = 6 \\ \hline 3(5) - (9) \hspace{0.3em}\Big| \\ 15 - 9 \hspace{0.6em}\Big| \\ 6 = 6\checkmark \end{array}$$

The correct answer is choice **(2)**.

2.   The line whose equation is $y = 3x - 1$ contains point $A(2, k)$. What is the value of k?

Solution: Since the point lies on the line, its coordinates must satisfy the equation of the line. To find k, replace x by 2 and y by k in the original equation.

$$\begin{aligned} k &= 3x - 1 \\ &= 3(2) - 1 \\ &= 6 - 1 = \mathbf{5} \end{aligned}$$

3.   The line whose equation is $Ax + 3y = 13$ passes through point $(8, -1)$. What is the value of A?

Solution: Since the line passes through the point, the coordinates of the point must satisfy the equation. To find the value of A, replace x by 8 and y by -1.

$$\begin{aligned} Ax + 3y \hspace{1.5em} &= 13 \\ 8A + 3(-1) &= 13 \\ 8A - 3 \hspace{1.5em} &= 13 \\ 8A &= 13 + 3 \\ \frac{8A}{8} &= \frac{16}{8} \\ A &= \mathbf{2} \end{aligned}$$

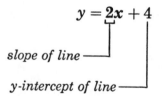

SLOPE-INTERCEPT FORM.   The y-coordinate of the point at which a nonvertical line intersects the y-axis is called the **y-intercept** of the line. Whenever a linear equation is written in the form $y = mx + b$, the equation is said to be in *slope-intercept* form since the graph of this equation (Figure 11.8) is a nonvertical line that has a slope of m and intersects the y-axis at (o,b). For example,

$$y = \underset{\text{slope of line}}{\underline{2x}} + 4$$

slope of line ⏤⏤⏤

y-intercept of line ⏤⏤⏤

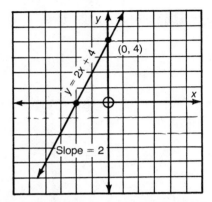

Figure 11.8 Graph of an Equation in Slope-Intercept Form

FINDING THE SLOPE AND THE Y-INTERCEPT OF A LINEAR EQUATION. To determine the slope and the y-intercept of a line from its equation, write the equation in the form $y = mx + b$. In order to do this, it may be necessary to solve the equation for y in terms of x.

Examples ▬▬▬

4. Find the slope and the y-intercept of a line whose equation is:

(a) $y = x + 2$ (c) $y - 5x = 0$

(b) $y = \dfrac{2x}{5} - 3$ (d) $y + 2x - 7 = 0$

Solutions: (a) $y = x + 2 = 1 \cdot x + 2$. The slope is **1**, and the y-intercept is **2**.

(b) The slope is $\dfrac{2}{5}$, and the y-intercept is **−3**.

(c) $y - 5x = 0$ may be rewritten as $y = 5x + 0$. The slope is **5**, and the y-intercept is **0**. Note that, if the y-intercept of a line is 0, then the line passes through the origin.

(d) Solve for y in terms of x:

$$y + 2x - 7 = 0$$

Subtract $2x$ from each side: $y - 7 = -2x$

Add 7 to each side: $y = -2x + 7$

The slope of the line is **−2**, and the y-intercept is **7**.

5. Find the slope of a line that is parallel to the line whose equation is $2x + 3y = 12$.

Solution: First determine the slope of the line whose equation is obtained by solving for y in terms of x:

$$2x + 3y = 12$$

Subtract $2x$ from each side: $3y = -2x + 12$

Divide each side by 3:
$$\frac{\overset{1}{\cancel{3}}y}{\cancel{3}} = \frac{-2x}{3} + \frac{\overset{4}{\cancel{12}}}{\cancel{3}}$$

$$y = \frac{\overset{1}{-2x}}{3} + 4$$

The slope of the given line is $\frac{-2}{3}$. Since parallel lines have the same slope, the slope of the line parallel to the line whose equation is $2x + 3y = 12$ is also $\frac{-2}{3}$.

6. Determine whether the line whose equation is $2y - 4x = 9$ is parallel to the line whose equation is $y + 4 = 2x$.

Solution: Compare the slopes of the two lines after expressing each equation in the form $y = mx + b$:

$$
\begin{array}{l|l}
2y - 4x = 9 & y + 4 = 2x \\
\quad 2y = 4x + 9 & \quad y = 2x - 4 \\
\dfrac{2y}{2} = \dfrac{4x}{2} + \dfrac{9}{2} & \\
\quad y = 2x + \dfrac{9}{2} &
\end{array}
$$

Since the slope of each line is 2, **the lines are parallel.**

WRITING AN EQUATION OF A LINE.   Knowing certain information about a line allows us to determine the values of m and b in the equation $y = mx + b$.

Examples

7. Write an equation of a line whose slope is -2 and which passes through point (1 4).

Solution   Step 1. Find the value of b.

$$y = mx + b$$

Replace m by -2: $y = (-2)x + b$

Replace x by 1 and y by 4: $4 = (-2)(1) + b$

Simplify: $4 = -2 + b$

Solve for b: $4 + 2 = b$

$$6 = b$$

Step 2. Replace m and b with their numerical values.

Since $m = -2$ and $b = 6$, the equation of the line is $y = -2x + 6$.

8. Write an equation of the line that contains points $A(6, 0)$ and $B(2, -6)$.

Solution: *Step 1.* Find the slope of the line.

$$m = \text{slope of } \overleftrightarrow{AB} = \frac{-6-0}{2-6}$$

$$= \frac{-6}{-4} = \frac{3}{2}$$

Step 2. Using the x and the y value of either point, find the value of b.

$$y = mx + b$$

Replace m by $\dfrac{3}{2}$: $\qquad y = \dfrac{3}{2}x + b$

Replace x by 6 and y by 0: $\qquad 0 = \dfrac{3}{2}(6) + b$

Simplify: $\qquad\qquad\qquad\quad 0 = 9 + b$

Solve for b: $\qquad\qquad\quad -9 = b$

Step 3. Replace m and b with their numerical values.

Since $m = \dfrac{3}{2}$ and $b = -9$ an equation of the line is $y = \dfrac{3}{2}x - 9$.

9. Write an equation of the horizontal line whose y-intercept is -7.

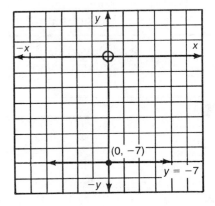

Solution: The slope of a horizontal line is 0, so $y = mx + b$ becomes $y = 0x - 7 = -7$.

10. Write an equation of the line that is parallel to the *y*-axis and 4 units to the right of the origin.

Solution: The desired line is a vertical line, so the *x*-coordinate of each point is always equal to the same number. Since the line is 4 units to the right of the origin, *x* is always equal to 4.

An equation of the line is **x = 4.**

The preceding examples suggest the following generalizations:

General Form of Equation	Description
$x = a$	● Vertical line (parallel to *y*-axis). ● Each point on the line has *a* as its *x*-coordinate.
$y = b$	● Horizontal line (parallel to *x*-axis). ● Each point on the line has *b* as its *y*-coordinate.
$y = mx + b$	● Nonvertical line whose slope is equal to *m* and whose *y*-intercept is *b*.

EXERCISE SET 11.3

1. Which point lies on the graph of $2x + y = 10$?
   (1) (0, 8)   (2) (10, 0)   (3) (3, 4)   (4) (4, 3)

2. Which point does *not* lie on the graph of $3y - x = 7$?
   (1) (2, −1)   (2) (3, 2)   (3) (−1, 4)   (4) (1, −4)

3. Which of the following pairs of points determines a line that is parallel to the x-axis?
   (1) (3, 5) and (5, 3) (3) (3, 5) and (3, −2)
   (2) (3, 5) and (−3, −5) (4) (3, 5) and (−2, 5)

4. Which of the following pairs of points determines a line that is parallel to the y-axis?
   (1) (4, 7) and (7, 4) (3) (4, 7) and (−4, 7)
   (2) (4, 7) and (4, −7) (4) (4, 7) and (−4, −7)

5. Which of the following is an equation of a line that is parallel to the y-axis and 2 units to the right of it?
   (1) $x = 2$ (2) $x = -2$ (3) $y = 2$ (4) $y = -2$

6. Which of the following is an equation of a line that is parallel to the x-axis and 3 units below it?
   (1) $x = 3$ (2) $x = -3$ (3) $y = 3$ (4) $y = -3$

7. The line whose equation is $3x + Ay = 17$ passes through point (3, 2). What is the value of A?

8. The line whose equation is $2y + x = 9$ contains point $P(-1, k)$. What is the value of k?

9–20. Find the slope and the y-intercept of the graphs of each of the following equations:

9. $y - 3x = 1$
10. $y + 4x - 2 = 0$
11. $y + 1 = \dfrac{2}{5}x$
12. $3y + x = 6$
13. $2y - x = 10$
14. $4y - 3x = 12$
15. $2x + y = 7$

16. $5y + 10 = 4x$
17. $\dfrac{1}{2}y + x = -3$
18. $2y - \dfrac{1}{3}x + 8 = 0$
19. $\dfrac{1}{4}y - \dfrac{1}{4}x = 2$
20. $\dfrac{1}{3}y + \dfrac{1}{2}x = 1$

21–24. If m represents the slope of a line and b its y-intercept, write an equation of the line when:

21. $m = -2$ and $b = 3$
22. $m = 4$ and $b = \dfrac{2}{5}$
23. $m = \dfrac{1}{3}$ and $b = -1$
24. $m = 0$ and $b = -2$

25. In the following table, determine the value of p:

	Equation of Line	Point on Line	Value of p
(a)	$x - 3y = p$	$(2, -5)$	?
(b)	$y = px$	$(3, -6)$	?
(c)	$3y + 2x = 7$	$(-1, p)$	?
(d)	$py - x = 11$	$(1, -3)$	?
(e)	$2y + 3x - 9 = 0$	$(p, 6)$	?
(f)	$2y - px = p$	$(-5, 5)$	?

26. Write an equation of a line that is parallel to the x-axis and passes through the given point.
(a) $(2, 5)$ (b) $(-3, 7)$ (c) $(-4, -2)$ (d) $(8, 0)$

27. Write an equation of a line that is parallel to the y-axis and passes through the given point.
(a) $(5, 4)$ (b) $(9, -6)$ (d) $(-3, -1)$ (e) $(0, 3)$

28–33. Find an equation of the line that has slope m *and contains the given point.*

28. $m = 1; (2, 2)$
29. $m = 3; (-1, 4)$
30. $m = -2; (5, -3)$
31. $m = \dfrac{1}{2}; (-4, -5)$
32. $m = 0; (3, 1)$
33. m is undefined; $(-2, 7)$
34. Write an equation of a horizontal line that:
(a) is 4 units above the y-axis
(b) has a y-intercept of -1
(c) contains point $(-2, 3)$
(d) has the same y-intercept as the line whose equation is $6y - 4x = 3$

35. Write an equation of a vertical line that:
(a) is 5 units to the right of the y-axis
(b) has an x-intercept of -3
(c) contains point $(-8, -7)$
(d) has the same x-intercept as the line whose equation is $2x - 3y = 5$

36. (a) Find the slope of the line parallel to the line whose equation is $2y = x + 3$.
(b) Write an equation of the line that contains point $(4, -1)$ and is parallel to the line whose equation is $2y = x + 3$.

37. (a) Find the area of the triangle whose vertices are $A(0, 6)$, $B(0, 0)$, and $C(-8, 0)$.

  (b) Write an equation of the line that passes through B and is parallel to $\overline{AC}$.

38. Determine whether the lines whose equations are given are parallel.

  (a) $2y - x = 9$
  $y = \dfrac{1}{2}x + 5$

  (b) $3x - y = 6$
  $2y + 6x = 12$

  (c) $2x - 4y = 8$
  $2y - x = 9$

  (d) $3y - 2x = 10$
  $6x - 4 = 9y$

39–48. Write an equation of the line that is determined by each pair of points.

39. $(1, 5), (2, 1)$
40. $(-1, 2), (0, 0)$
41. $(-2, 9), (1, -6)$
42. $(2, -4), (-3, -4)$
43. $(5, 7), (3, 6)$
44. $(-8, -3), (-1, 4)$
45. $(-3, 8), (-3, -1)$
46. $(9, -2), (6, 2)$
47. $\left(\dfrac{1}{2}, 5\right), \left(\dfrac{3}{2}, 2\right)$
48. $\left(4, \dfrac{9}{5}\right), \left(2, 1\right)$

49. Write an equation of one of the lines that are parallel to the line whose equation is $3y - 12x = 6$ and which intersects the line whose equation is $y + 2x = 10$.

50. (a) For the accompanying graph, determine and then write an equation of line l in slope-intercept form.

  (b) Determine and then write an equation of line m in slope-intercept form.

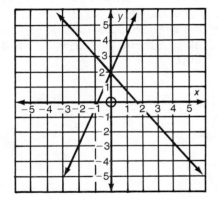

11.4 GRAPHING LINEAR EQUATIONS

KEY IDEAS

Here are some general guidelines for graphing linear equations:

● Draw the coordinate axes on graph paper, using a straightedge.

● Label the horizontal axis *x*, and the vertical axis *y*.

● Label the origin, and number the boxes along each axis sequentially.

● Choose one of the methods illustrated in this section.

● Graph the line, and label it with its equation.

THREE-POINT METHOD. To draw the graph of a linear equation, we must obtain the coordinates of at least two points that satisfy the equation. Graphing a third point and verifying that this point also lies on the line serves as a check. To graph the line whose equation is $y - 2x = 3$, using the three-point method, follow these steps:

Step	Example
1. Solve the original equation for *y* in terms of *x*.	$y - 2x = 3$ $y = 2x + 3$

2. Choose any three convenient values for *x*, and then calculate the corresponding values of *y*. The numbers -1, 0, and 1 are often good choices for *x*. It is helpful to organize your work in a table.

x	$y = 2x + 3$	(x, y)
-1	$y = 2(-1) + 3$ $= -2 + 3 = 1$	$(-1, 1)$
0	$y = 2(0) + 3$ $= 0 + 3 = 3$	$(0, 3)$
1	$y = 2(1) + 3$ $= 2 + 3 = 5$	$(1, 5)$

Step	Example
3. Graph the three points obtained in step 2. Use a straight-edge to draw the line. Label the line with its equation, $y - 2x = 3$. If the three points do *not* lie on the same line, check your work since at least one of the points has been graphed incorrectly. Make certain that you have correctly numbered the axes and that each of the points has been accurately graphed. If the graphing of the points is correct, then return to step 2 and verify that the coordinates you are using are correct.	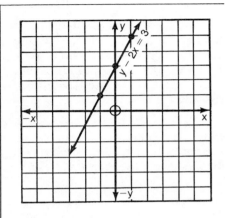

INTERCEPT METHOD.   An oblique line that does not pass through the origin intersects the x-axis at a value of x called the *x-intercept* and the y-axis at a value of y called the *y-intercept*. To graph the equation $2x - 3y = 12$, using the intercept method, follow these steps:

Step	Example
1. Find the x-intercept by setting $y = 0$ in the original equation and then solving for x. Note that $y = 0$ all along the x-axis.	$$2x - 3y = 12$$ $$2x - 3(0) = 12$$ $$2x = 12$$ $$x = \frac{12}{2} = 6$$ The x-intercept is 6.
2. Find the y-intercept by setting $x = 0$ in the original equation and then solving for y. Note that $x = 0$ all along the y-axis.	$$2x - 3y = 12$$ $$2(0) - 3y = 12$$ $$-3y = 12$$ $$y = \frac{12}{-3} = -4$$ The y-intercept is -4.

Step	Example

3. Use the intercepts to graph the points where the line crosses the axes, and then draw a line through these points. Label the line with its equation, $2x - 3y = 12$.

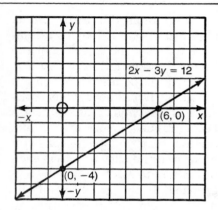

Note 1: As a check, choose any convenient point that lies on the line and verify algebraically that its coordinates satisfy the equation.

Note 2: Lines that have equations of the form $y = mx$ pass through the origin and, therefore, intersect the x- and y-axes at the same point, so this method cannot be used for such equations.

SLOPE-INTERCEPT METHOD.   To graph a linear equation such as $y = \frac{2}{5}x + 1$, using the slope-intercept method, follow these steps:

Step	Example

1. Use the y-intercept to graph the point where the line crosses the y-axis. The coordinate of the y-intercept of $y = \frac{2}{5}x + 1$ is 1, so the line crosses the y-axis at $A(0, 1)$.

2. Find another point of the given line, using the slope. The slope of $y = \frac{2}{5}x + 1$ is $\frac{2}{5}$. Start at $A(0, 1)$, and move up 2 units. Then move 5 units to the right. Label this point B. Note that the coordinates of B are $(5, 3)$.

3. Find another point that will serve as a check point by moving up 2 units from point B, and then moving 5 units to the right. Label this point C. The coordinates of C are $(10, 5)$.

4. Draw $\overline{AB}$ and label the line with its equation, $y = \frac{2}{5}x + 1$.

Example ▆▆▆

Use the slope-intercept method to graph the line whose equation is $y + 3x = 5$.

Solution: Put the equation in slope-intercept form.

$$y + 3x = 5$$
$$y = -3x + 5$$

Obtain two points on the line by following these steps:

Step 1. Use the y-intercept, 5. The coordinates of the intersection of $y = -3x + 5$ with the y-axis are $A(0, 5)$.

Step 2. Graph another point of the given line, using the slope. The slope of $y = -3x + 5$ is -3 or $-3/1$. Since the numerator is *negative*, start at $A(0, 5)$ and move 3 units *down*. Then move 1 unit to the right. Label this point B. Note that the coordinates of B are $(1, 2)$.

Step 3. Starting at B, find another point that will serve as a check by moving 3 units down from point B, and then moving 1 unit to the right. Label this point C. The coordinates of C are $(2, -1)$.

Step 4. Draw $\overline{AB}$, which represents the graph of $y = -3x + 5$ (or $y + 3x = 5$).

▆▆▆

DIRECT VARIATION AND LINEAR EQUATIONS.   In general, if the ratio of two variables always remains the same, then the variables vary directly with one another. If variables x and y vary directly with one another, then:

1.   The direct variation is expressed as $y/x = k$, where k is *the constant of variation.*

2.   The graph that describes the direct variation between x and y is a line that, when extended, passes through the origin, and whose slope is the constant of variation. This follows from the fact that $y/x = k$ can also be written as $y = kx$, or $y = kx + 0$.

3. If the value of one variable is multiplied by a number, then the corresponding value of the other variable must also be multiplied by the same number, so that the ratio of the variables remains constant. For example, the length of a side s of a square varies directly with the perimeter P of the square ($P/s = 4$ or $P = 4s$), so that, if the length of a side of a square is doubled, then its perimeter is also doubled.

EXERCISE SET 11.4

1–12. Using graph paper, draw the graph of each equation using the three-point method.

1. $y = 3x$
2. $y = -3x$
3. $y = x + 2$
4. $y = -2x + 1$
5. $y + 3 = x$
6. $y - 3x + 5 = 0$
7. $y = \dfrac{1}{2}x$
8. $y = \dfrac{3x}{5} - 2$
9. $2y - 4x = 10$
10. $3y + 6x = 12$
11. $x - 2y = 8$
12. $2x - 5y = 15$

13–18. Using graph paper, draw the graph of each equation using the x- and y-intercepts method.

13. $x + y = 7$
14. $2y - x = 8$
15. $y + 3x - 7 = 0$
16. $3y - 2x = 6$
17. $6y + 18 = 4x$
18. $3x - 5y = 20$

19–30. Using graph paper, draw the graph of each equation using the slope-intercept method.

19. $y = 3x - 1$
20. $y = -2x + 4$
21. $y = \dfrac{3}{4}x + 8$
22. $2y - x = 10$
23. $x = 2y + 5$
24. $4x - 6y = 12$
25. $2x - 5y = 15$
26. $x - 2y = 3$
27. $\dfrac{y}{2} - x = 4$
28. $\dfrac{y}{3} - \dfrac{x}{2} = 1$
29. $\dfrac{y}{5} + \dfrac{x}{2} = 0$
30. $\dfrac{y - 1}{2} = 2x$

31–39. Using graph paper, draw the graph of each equation using any method.

31. $y = -2x$
32. $5x = 3y$
33. $3y - 2x = 18$
34. $x + 3y = 6$
35. $y - 2x + 9 = 0$
36. $y = \dfrac{1}{2}x + 4$
37. $3y - 2x = 12$
38. $5x - y = 10$
39. $8 - 2y = x$

40. Write several ordered pairs of numbers in which the x-coordinate represents the length of a side of a square and the y-coordinate represents the perimeter of that square. Graph the relationship between the length of a side of a square and the perimeter of the square.

11.5 MOVING SETS OF POINTS IN THE PLANE

KEY IDEAS

The process of moving each point of a figure according to some given rule is called a **transformation**. Each point of the new figure corresponds to exactly one point of the original figure and is called the **image** of that point. *Reflections, translations, rotations, and dilations* are special types of transformations; each uses a different rule for locating the images of points of the figure that are undergoing the transformation.

REFLECTIONS. A **reflection** may be thought of as the "mirror image" of a point or set of points. In Figure 11.9, the letter E is reflected "in line l." Line l serves as a "mirror" and is referred to as the *line of symmetry*. In general, when a figure is reflected in line l, each point P of the figure is moved according to the following rules:

Line of symmetry

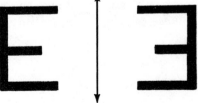

Figure 11.9 Reflection

1. If point P does *not* lie on line l, then the reflection of P is the endpoint P' of $\overline{PP'}$ drawn so that line l is the perpendicular bisector of $\overline{PP'}$. P' is the *image* of point P.

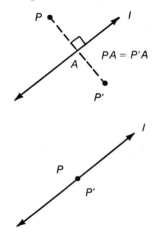

$PA = P'A$

2. If point P lies on line l, then the reflection of point P is the point P', which coincides with P.

Examples

1. Given $P(3, -2)$, find the coordinates of the image of point P when P is reflected in (across): (a) the x-axis (b) the y-axis

Solutions:

(a)   (b)

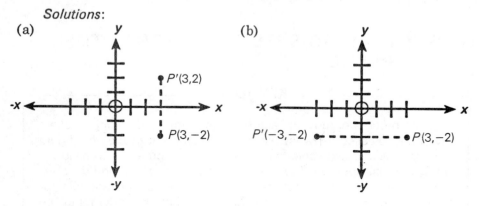

$P'(3, 2)$ is the image of $P(3, -2)$ $P'(-3, -2)$ is the image of
across the x-axis. $P(3, -2)$ across the y-axis.

Note: In general, the reflection of point $P(x, y)$ across the x-axis is the point whose coordinates are $(x, -y)$. The reflection of point $P(x, y)$ across the y-axis is the point whose coordinates are $(-x, y)$.

2. For the accompanying diagram, sketch the reflection of $\triangle ABC$ in line *l*.

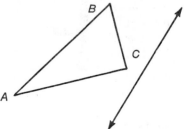

Solution: Sketch the reflection of points A, B, and C in line *l*. Then draw line segments $\overline{A'B'}$, $\overline{B'C'}$, and $\overline{A'C'}$.

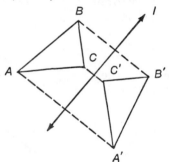

Note: $\overline{AB} \cong \overline{A'B'}$, $\overline{BC} \cong \overline{B'C'}$, and $\overline{AC} \cong \overline{A'C'}$, so $\triangle ABC \cong \triangle A'B'C'$ by the SSS method. In general, the image of a figure that is reflected is congruent to the original figure. ▅▅▅▅

TRANSLATIONS. A **translation** may be thought of as a "slide" of a figure in a plane. Each point of a figure that is translated is moved the same distance in the same direction.

Example ▅▅▅▅

3. The coordinates of the vertices of $\triangle ABC$ are $A(1, 1)$, $B(1, 4)$, and $C(5, 1)$. Sketch the image of $\triangle ABC$ obtained by translating the triangle 3 units to the right and 2 units up.

Solution: Translate each vertex of the original triangle by adding 3 units to its x-coordinate and 2 units to its y-coordinate.

$\triangle ABC$		$\triangle A'B'C'$
$A(1, 1)$	$\longrightarrow$	$A'(1+3, 1+2) = A'(4, 3)$
$B(1, 4)$	$\longrightarrow$	$B'(1+3, 4+2) = B'(4, 6)$
$C(5, 1)$	$\longrightarrow$	$C'(5+3, 1+2) = C'(8, 3)$

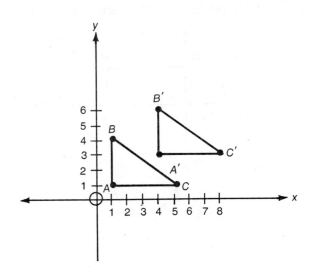

Note: The translation preserves the lengths of the sides of the triangle so that $\triangle ABC \cong \triangle A'B'C'$ by the SSS method. In general, the image of a figure that is translated is congruent to the original figure. ▅▅▅▅

ROTATIONS.   In Figure 11.10, *A'* is the image of point *A* under **a** rotation of 45° clockwise about point *P*. The image of *P* is the same as point *P*. Notice that rays *PA* and *PA'* form an angle having a degree measure of 45. Point *A* has been rotated, using point *P* as a point of reference, 45° in the clockwise direction. A **rotation** is a transformation that may be thought of as a turn of a figure a given number of degrees about some fixed point in the plane. The point about which the figure is turned is called the *center of rotation* and is its own image. A rotation may change the orientation of a figure with respect to the center of rotation, but it does not change the size or shape of the figure.

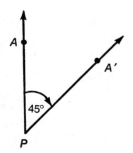

Figure 11.10   Rotation

Example

4. In the accompanying diagram, sketch the counterclockwise rotation of rectangle *ABCD* (a) 90°, (b) 180°, and (c) 270° about point *A*.

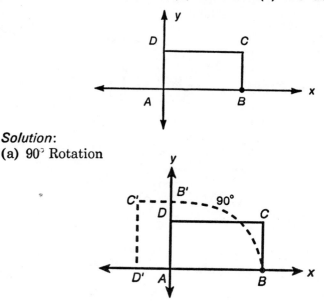

Solution:
(a) 90° Rotation

(b) 180° Rotation

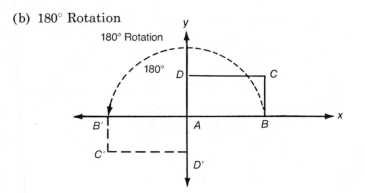

(c) 270° Rotation

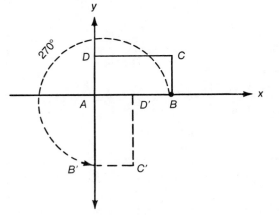

DILATIONS.   Reflections, translations, and rotations produce figures that are *congruent* to the original figures since under these transformations the lengths of the sides and the measures of the angles of the figures remain the same. A *dilation* is an example of a type of transformation that produces a figure that is *similar* to the original figure. A **dilation** shrinks or magnifies the size of the original figure by a fixed amount with respect to a given point of reference called the *center of dilation*.

Example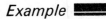

5.   For the accompanying diagram, dilate △*ABC* with respect to any point *P* so that the length of each side of the new triangle is twice the length of the corresponding side of the original triangle.

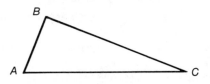

Solution: Step 1. Choose any point as the center of dilation, and label it *P*. Then draw rays $\overrightarrow{PA}$, $\overrightarrow{PB}$, and $\overrightarrow{PC}$.

Step 2. Using a ruler, align the zero marking at point *P*.

Step 3. Locate point *A'* on ray $\overrightarrow{PA}$ by measuring off a segment $\overline{PA'}$ such that *PA'* equals twice *PA*.

Step 4. Similarly, locate point *B'* on ray $\overrightarrow{PB}$ and point *C'* on ray $\overrightarrow{PC}$.

Step 5. Draw the sides of the triangle determined by points *A'*, *B'*, and *C'*.

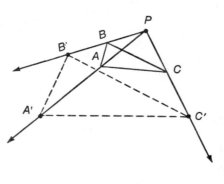

EXERCISE SET 11.5

1. Which of the following types of transformations produces a figure similar to the original figure?
   (1) Reflection   (2) Dilation   (3) Translation   (4) Rotation

2. Find the coordinates of the reflection of the given point in the *y*-axis.
   (a) $(2, 5)$ (b) $(-3, 7)$ (c) $(4, -1)$ (d) $(-2, -6)$ (e) (a, b)

3. Find the coordinates of the reflection of the given point in the *x*-axis.
   (a) $(1, 4)$ (b) $(2, -9)$ (c) $(-3, 0)$ (d) $(-4, -5)$ (e) (a, b)

4. Find the coordinates of the image of each of the following points after a counterclockwise rotation of 90° about the origin:
   (a) $(3, 0)$ (b) $(0, -5)$ (c) $(0, 4)$ (d) $(-2, 0)$

5. Find the coordinates of the image of each of the following points after a closkwise rotation of 180° about the origin:
   (a) $(1, 0)$ (b) $(0, 2)$ (c) $(-3, 0)$ (d) $(0, -6)$

6. If the line segment joining $A(2, 3)$ and $B(9, 3)$ is rotated 90° about point *A*, then the coordinates of the image of point *B* are:
   (1) $(2, -4)$ (2) $(2, 10)$ (3) $(-9, 3)$ (4) $9, -3)$

7. Which property is *not* preserved under a line reflection?
   (1) Collinearity   (3) Congruence of angles
   (2) Congruence of line segments   (4) Orientation

8. The coordinates of the vertices of $\triangle ABC$ are $A(1, 1)$, $B(3, 6)$ and $C(-2, 7)$. Sketch the image of $\triangle ABC$ obtained by translating the triangle:
    (a) 2 units to the right and 1 unit up
    (b) 4 units to the left and 3 units up
    (c) 1 unit to the right and 5 units down
    (d) 3 units to the left and 2 units down

9. Under a transformation the image of $P(2, 3)$ is $P'(1, 5)$. Under the same transformation, what are the possible coordinates of the image of $A(-1, 4)$?

10. Under a transformation the image of $P(x, y)$ is $P'(x + 3, y - 2)$. Find the coordinates of Q if its image under the same transformation is $Q'(6, 2)$.

11. In the accompanying diagram, sketch the clockwise rotation of right triangle ABC:
    (a) 90° about point A
    (b) 180° about point A
    (c) 270° about point A
    (d) 360° about point A

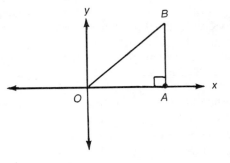

12. Draw square $ABCD$. Dilate square $ABCD$ with respect to any convenient point P so that the length of a side of its image is three times as long as a side of the original square.

13. Sketch the counterclockwise rotation of the figure in the accompanying diagram 180° about point P.

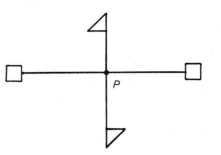

14. Sketch the counterclockwise rotation of rectangle *ABCD* about point *E*.
    (a) 90°   (b) 180°   (c) 270°   (d) 360°

B   C

• E

A   D

15. Draw equilateral triangle *ABC* and rotate it 120° clockwise about point *A*.

11.6   OBSERVING SYMMETRY

─────────── KEY IDEAS ───────────

There are many examples of symmetry in nature. People's faces, leaves, and butterflies have real or imaginary "lines of symmetry" which divide the figures into two parts that are mirror images. If a geometric shape has line symmetry, then it can be "folded" along the line of symmetry so that the two parts coincide.

LINE SYMMETRY.   A figure has line symmetry if a line can be drawn which divides the figure into two parts that are mirror images. The line of symmetry may be a horizontal line, a vertical line, or neither.

The shapes in Figure 11.11 have horizontal line symmetry.

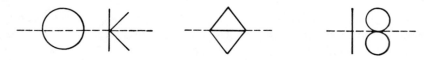

Figure 11.11   Horizontal Line Symmetry

The examples in Figure 11.12 have vertical line symmetry.

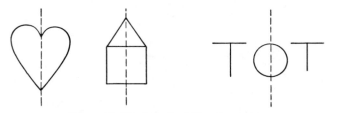

Figure 11.12   Vertical Line Symmetry

Figure 11.13 has a line of symmetry that is neither horizontal nor vertical.

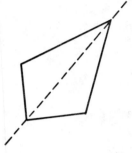

Figure 11.13 Neither Horizontal nor Vertical Line Symmetry

Figure 11.14 illustrates that a figure may have both a horizontal and a vertical line of symmetry.

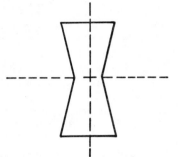

Figure 11.14 Both Horizontal and Vertical Line Symmetry

As shown in Figure 11.15, a figure may have more than one line of symmetry or may have no lines of symmetry.

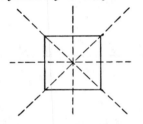
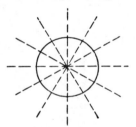
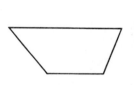

Four lines of symmetry   An infinite number of   No lines of symmetry
                           lines of symmetry

Figure 11.15 Figures with More Than One or No Lines of Symmetry

Examples

1. Which letter has both a vertical and a horizontal line of symmetry?
(1) A   (2) M   (3) T   (4) X

Solution: The correct choice is X since:

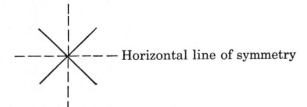

Horizontal line of symmetry

Vertical line of symmetry

The correct answer is **choice (4)**.

2. Which of the following triangles has line symmetry?
(1) Right   (2) Isosceles   (3) Obtuse   (4) Scalene

Solution· A line (angle bisector or altitude) through the vertex
angle of an isosceles triangle divides
the triangle into two mirror-image
(that is, congruent) triangles.
The correct answer is **choice (2)**.

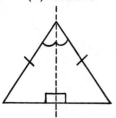

3. Which word has a horizontal line of symmetry?
(1) MOM   (2) EVE   (3) DAD   (4) BOB

Solution: The correct choice is BOB since ~~BOB~~.
The correct answer is **choice (4)**.

POINT SYMMETRY.   A figure has **point symmetry** if, after undergoing a rotation of 180° in either direction about a fixed point *P*, the
figure coincides with itself. The figure in Figure 11.16 has point symmetry.

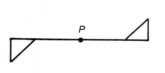

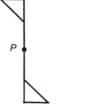

Original Figure   Clockwise
(or Counterclockwise)
Rotation of 90°
about Point *P*

Clockwise
(or Counterclockwise)
Rotation of 180°
about Point *P*

Figure 11.16   Point Symmetry

A right triangle (Figure 11.17) is an example of a figure that does *not* have
point symmetry.

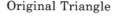

Original Triangle   Triangle after a 180° Clockwise
Rotation with Respect to Point *B*

Figure 11.17   Lack of Point Symmetry

REFLECTIONS IN THE ORIGIN. Rotating a point P 180° about the origin reflects the point in the origin. Picture this reflection as a 180° rotation about the origin of the line segment $\overline{PP''}$ determined by P and the origin O, where $OP = OP''$. In Figure 11.18, the reflection of $P(x, y)$ in the origin is located in the quadrant diagonally opposite to P and has the coordinates $P''(-x, -y)$. The reflection of a point in the origin is equivalent, therefore, to consecutive reflections in the x-axis and y-axis:

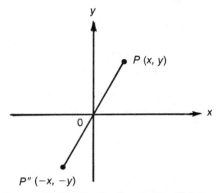

Figure 11.18 Reflection in the Origin

$$P(x, y) \xrightarrow[\text{in } x\text{-axis}]{\text{reflection}} P'(x, -y) \xrightarrow[\text{in } y\text{-axis}]{\text{reflection}} P''(-x, -y).$$

EXERCISE SET 11.6

1. For each of the following groups of letters of the alphabet, state whether each capital letter in the group has line symmetry, horizontal line symmetry, both vertical and horizontal line symmetry, a line of symmetry other than a horizontal or vertical line, or no symmetry:
   (a) letters A through I
   (b) letters J through Q
   (c) letters R through Z

2. Which letter has point symmetry?
   (1) A   (2) B   (3) N   (4) T

3. Which symbol has an image that coincides with itself after a rotation of 90°?
   (1) X   (2) H   (3) S   (4) 8

4. What kind of symmetry does a rectangle have?
   (1) Line symmetry only   (3) Both line and point symmetry
   (2) Point symmetry only   (4) Neither line nor point symmetry

5. Determine the number of lines of symmetry, if any, for each of the following figures or words:
   (a) a parallelogram   (g) a right triangle
   (b) a trapezoid   (h) OX
   (c) HOE   (i) a regular pentagon
   (d) an equilateral triangle   (j) BIB
   (e) WOW   (k) ECHO
   (f) SIX   (l) a regular hexagon

6. Determine the kind of line symmetry, if any, for each numerical symbol.
   (a) 11   (b) 38   (c) 22   (d) 101   (e) 818   (f) 100

7. Find the coordinates of the reflections of each of the following points in (1) the x-axis, (2) the y-axis, and (3) the origin:
   (a) $(-8, 0)$ (b) $(2, -1)$ (c) $(-7, 9)$ (d) $(-6, -5)$ (e) (p, q)

8. Determine which of the following figures have point symmetry with respect to point P:

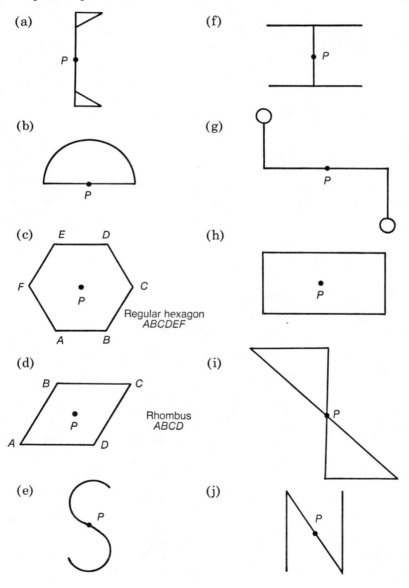

(a)

(f)

(b)

(g)

(c) Regular hexagon ABCDEF

(h)

(d) Rhombus ABCD

(i)

(e)

(j)

9. Make up a figure that has line symmetry but does not have point symmetry.

10. Make up a figure that has point symmetry but does not have line symmetry.

11. Make up a figure that has both line and point symmetry.

12. Determine whether square $ABCD$ has point symmetry with respect to point C.

CHAPTER 11 REVIEW EXERCISES

REGENTS REVIEW. *Problems included in this section are similar in form and difficulty to those found on the New York State Regents Examination for Course I of the Three-Year Sequence for High School Mathematics. Problems preceded by an asterisk have actually appeared on a previous Course I Regents Examination.*

*1. The graph of which equation has a slope of 3 and a y-intercept of -2?
   (1) $y = 3x - 2$ (2) $y = 3x + 2$ (3) $y = 2x - 3$ (4) $y = 2x + 3$

*2. If $(r, 3)$ is in the solution set of $2x + y = 7$, then the value of r must be:
   (1) 1   (2) 2   (3) 3   (4) 4

*3. A point on the graph of $x + 3y = 13$ is:
   (1) $(4, 4)$ (2) $(-2, 3)$ (3) $(-5, 6)$ (4) $(4, -3)$

*4. The graph of $y = 3x - 4$ is parallel to the graph of:
   (1) $y = 4x - 3$ (2) $y = 3x + 4$ (3) $y = -3x + 4$ (4) $y = 3$

*5. What is the slope of the line whose equation is $2y = 3x - 7$?
   (1) $\dfrac{2}{3}$ (2) -2 (3) 3   (4) $\dfrac{3}{2}$

*6. The coordinates of the vertices of a triangle are $(1, 1)$, $(3, 1)$, and $(3, 5)$. The triangle formed is:
   (1) a right triangle   (3) an isosceles triangle
   (2) an obtuse triangle   (4) an equilateral triangle

*7. The graph of $3x - y = 3$ intersects the x-axis at point:
   (1) $(1, 0)$ (2) $(0, 1)$ (3) $(0, 3)$ (4) $(3, 0)$

*8. Which point does not lie on the graph of $x - 2y = 10$?
   (1) $(0, -5)$ (2) $(2, -4)$ (3) $(5, 0)$ (4) $(6, -2)$

9. Which letter has horizontal but *not* vertical line symmetry?
   (1) X   (2) O   (3) V   (4) E

10. If point $P(4, -3)$ is reflected in the y-axis, what are the coordinates of its image?

    (1) $(-4, 3)$ (2) $(-4. -3)$ (3) $(-3, 4)$ (4) $(4, 3)$

11. If point $A(-6, 1)$ is reflected in the x-axis, what are the coordinates of its image?

    (1) $(-6, -1)$ (2) $(6, -1)$ (3) $(6, -1)$ (4) $(1, -6)$

*12. Find the area of a triangle whose vertices are $(0, 0)$, $(0, 4)$, and $(5, 0)$.

*13. If point $(2, 3)$ lies on the graph of the equation $2x + ky = -2$, find the value of k.

*14. What is the point of intersection of the graphs of $x = 1$ and $y = 4$?

15. The triangle whose vertices are $A(0, 7)$, $B(8, 0)$, and $C(0, 0)$ is rotated 90° about point C in the clockwise direction. What are the coordinates of the images of A, B, and C?

*16. After each, write the number that makes the statement correct for each graph that is shown.

(a) The equation of the graph
    shown is:
    (1) $y = x$
    (2) $y = -x$
    (3) $y = 2x$
    (4) $y = -2x$

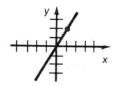

(b) The equation of the graph
    shown is:
    (1) $x = 3$
    (2) $x = -3$
    (3) $y = 3$
    (4) $y = -3$

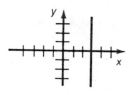

(c) The graph shown has a
    slope of:
    (1) 1
    (2) -1
    (3) -4
    (4) 4

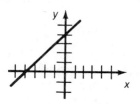

(d) The slope of the graph
    shown is:
    (1) 1
    (2) 2
    (3) 0
    (4) undefined

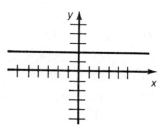

17. Which figure has both line and point symmetry?
    (1) A circle
    (2) A parallelogram
    (3) A trapezoid
    (4) An equilateral triangle

18. Which kind of symmetry does the word TOOT have?
    (1) Vertical line symmetry only
    (2) Horizontal line symmetry only
    (3) Both vertical and horizontal line symmetry
    (4) Neither horizontal nor vertical line symmetry

19. Which kind of symmetry does a rhombus have?
    (1) Line symmetry only
    (2) Point symmetry only
    (3) Both line and point symmetry
    (4) Neither line nor point symmetry

20. Which transformation can product an image triangle with an area that is *not* equal to the area of the original triangle?
    (1) Translation
    (2) Line reflection
    (3) Dilation
    (4) Rotation

CHAPTER 12

Solving Systems of Equations and Inequalities

12.1   GRAPHING SYSTEMS OF EQUATIONS

─────────────── KEY IDEAS ───────────────

Solving a group or *system* of linear equations means finding the set of all ordered pairs of numbers that make each of the equations true at the same time. One approach is to graph each equation on the same set of axes and then determine the coordinates of their points of intersection, if any.

SOLVING A SYSTEM OF LINEAR EQUATIONS GRAPHICALLY.
The graph of each equation of the system

$$y = 2x$$
$$x + y = \ \ 6$$

is shown in Figure 12.1. The lines intersect at point (2, 4), so the solution set of this system of linear equations is {(2, 4)}, that is

$$(y = 2x) \wedge (x + y = 6) = (2, 4).$$

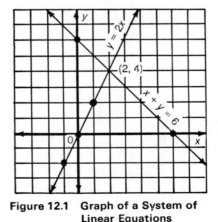

Figure 12.1   Graph of a System of Linear Equations

Examples

1. Solve the following system of equations graphically, and check by substitution:

$$2x + y = 5$$
$$y - x = -4$$

Solution: Graph each equation on the same set of axes. Using the slope-intercept method, you must first write each equation in the form $y = mx + b$:

$$2x + y = 5 \qquad y - x = -4$$
$$y = -2x + 5 \quad y = x - 4$$

The solution is **(3, −1)**.

Check: Replace x by 3 and y by −1 in each of the *original* equations:

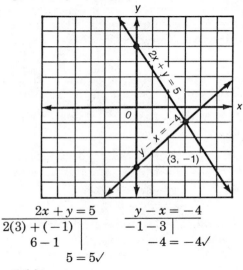

$$\begin{array}{c|c}
2x + y = 5 & y - x = -4 \\
\hline
2(3) + (-1) & -1 - 3 \\
6 - 1 & -4 = -4\checkmark \\
5 = 5\checkmark &
\end{array}$$

2. Solve by graphing:

$$6y - 3x = 18$$
$$2y = x + 1$$

Solution: Express each equation in the $y = mx + b$ form:

$$6y - 3x = 18$$
$$6y = 3x + 18$$
$$y = \frac{3x}{6} + \frac{18}{6}$$
$$= \frac{x}{2} + 3$$
$$2y = x + 1$$
$$y = \frac{x}{2} + \frac{1}{2}$$

The value of m for each line is $\frac{1}{2}$. Since the lines have the same slope but *different* y-intercepts, they are parallel and, therefore, do *not* intersect. There is *no* ordered pair of numbers that satisfies both equations simultaneously, so that the solution set is the empty set, which may be written as $\{\ \ \}$ or $\varnothing$.

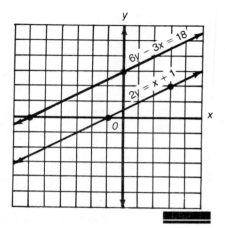

As Example 2 illustrates, systems of linear equations do not necessarily have one ordered pair in their solution sets. When the graphs of a pair of linear equations are drawn on the same set of axes, one of the following must be true:

1. The lines intersect in exactly one point, so that the system of equations has one ordered pair in its solution set.

2. The lines are parallel so that the system of equations has no ordered pairs in its solution set.

3. The lines coincide, meaning that the equations graphed are equivalent. For example, consider the system of equations

$$y = 2x - 3$$
$$4x = 2y + 6.$$

Points $(-1, -5)$, $(0, -3)$ and $(1, -1)$ can be used to graph the first equation. These points also satisfy the second equation, so that the graphs of these equaitons are two lines that coincide. The solution set is the infinite set of ordered pairs that lie on the single line defined by these equations.

In this course we will restrict our attention to solving systems of equations consisting of lines that intersect at one point.

EXERCISE SET 12.1

1–15. Solve graphically, and check by substitution.

1. $2x + y = 8$
$y = x + 2$

2. $x + 2y = 7$
$y = 2x + 1$

3. $y = 3x + 1$
$x = y - 3$

4. $2x - y = 10$
$x + 2y = 10$

5. $y = 2x - 4$
$x + 2y = -7$

6. $x + 2y = 6$
$4x + y = -4$

7. $x + y = 8$
$2x - y = 7$

8. $2x + y = 6$
$x - 2y = 8$

9. $2y = -5x$
$y - x = 7$

10. $x - 2y = 4$
$x = y + 2$

11. $2y = x + 6$
$y = 3x - 2$

12. $y - 2x = 5$
$x + 2y = 0$

13. $x - 3y = 9$
$2x + y = 4$

14. $3x - 2y = 4$
$3x + 2y = 8$

15. $y - x = -1$
$2y + x = 4$

16. (a) On the same set of coordinate axes, graph the three lines whose equations are (1) $y = 2x + 1$, (2) $y = 1$, and (3) $x = 2$.

(b) Write the coordinates of the three vertices of the triangle formed by the lines graphed in part (a).

17–20. Graph the triangle formed by the lines in each of the following systems of equations, and then determine its area:

17. $y = 2x$; $x = 5$; positive x-axis.
18. $y = x$; $y = -x$; $y = 8$
19. $y = -2x + 17$; $2y - 3x = 6$; $y = 3$
20. $x + y = 5$; $6y - 5x + 25 = 0$; $y = 5$

12.2 GRAPHING LINEAR INEQUALITIES
KEY IDEAS

In the accompanying graph, the line $y = 3$ serves as a *boundary* line dividing the coordinate plane into two *half-planes*. The region *above* the line $y = 3$ represents the solution set of the inequality $y > 3$ since every point in this region has a y-coordinate *greater than* 3. The region below the line $y = 3$ represents the solution set of the inequality $y < 3$ since the y-coordinate of every point in this region is *less than* 3. A half-plane that does *not* include the boundary line, such as $y < 3$ or $y > 3$, is referred to as an *open half-plane*. A *closed half-plane*, such as $y \le 3$ or $y \ge 3$, includes the boundary line.

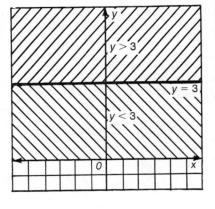

GRAPHING A LINEAR INEQUALITY. To graph a linear inequality, proceed as follows:

1. Mentally replace the inequality with an equals symbol and graph the resulting equation.

2. If the inequality relation is $<$ or $>$, draw the graph of the related equation as a broken or dashed line to indicate that points on the boundary line are *not* included in the solution set. If the inequality relation is $\le$ or $\ge$, draw the boundary line as a continuous line which indicates that points on the line are included in the solution set.

3. Decide which half-plane represents the solution set. This can be done by choosing a test point on either side of the boundary line and determining which point makes the inequality a true statement.

Examples ▬▬

1. Graph $y > 3x + 1$.

Solution: *Step 1.* Draw the graph of $y = 3x + 1$, using the slope-intercept method.

Step 2. Since the inequality is $>$, draw the boundary line as broken.

Step 3. Choose test points. Whenever the line does not contain the origin, it is usually convenient to use $(0, 0)$ as one of the test points.

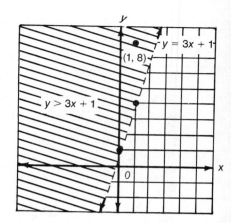

Test $(0, 0)$	Test $(2, 8)$
$y > 3x + 1$	$y > 3x + 1$
$0 > 3(0) + 1$	$8 > 3(2) + 1$
$0 > 1$ *False*	$8 > 6 + 1$ *True*

Step 4. Shade in the half-plane that contains $(2, 8)$, which is the region *above* the boundary line.

2. Which ordered pair is in the solution set of $x + 2y > 7$?

(1) $(5, 1)$ (2) $(2, 6)$ (3) $(3, 1)$ (4) $(7, 0)$

Solution: The ordered pair $(2, 6)$ is correct since, if x is replaced by 2 and v is replaced by 6, then

$$x + 2y = 2 + 2(6) = 2 + 12 = 14,$$

which is greater than 7. Note that for choices (1) and (4) the value of $x + 2y = 7$, making the inequality $x + 2y > 7$ false.

The correct answer is **choice (2)**.   ▬▬▬

GRAPHING SYSTEMS OF INEQUALITIES.   A system of inequalities can be solved graphically by graphing each of the inequalities on the same set of axes and then determining the region in which the solution set of the individual inequalities overlap.

Examples ▬▬

3. Graph each of the following systems of inequalities, and identify the solution set:

(a) $y > x$ (b) $y > 2$
     $x \le 5$ $y < -3$

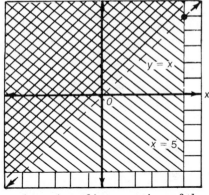

Solution: (a) *Step 1.* Graph $y > x$. The open half-plane above the line $y = x$ represents the solution set of $y > x$.

Step 2. Graph $x \leq 5$ on the same set of axes. The closed half-plane to the left of $x = 5$ represents the solution set of $x \leq 5$.

The cross-hatched shading indicates the region where the solution sets of the two inequalities overlap.

Notice that an open circle appears at the point of intersection of the two boundary lines. Since this point is *not* a member of the solution set of $y > x$, it is not a member of the solution set of the *system* of inequalities.

(b) As the accompanying graph illustrates, the solution sets of the two inequalities do *not* overlap, so the solution of this system of inequalities is $\emptyset$

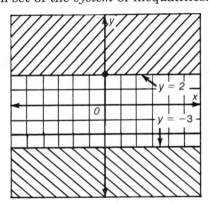

4. Graph the following systems of inequalities, and label the solution set S:

$$y + 3x > 6$$
$$y \leq 2x - 4$$

Solution: *Step 1.* Rewrite the first inequality as $y > -3x + 6$. Use the slope-intercept method to graph the line $y = -3x + 6$. Since the inequality relation is $<$, the graph of the related equation is drawn as a broken line

Step 2. Determine the open-half plane that represents the solution set to $y + 3x > 6$. Shade in the region *above* and to the right of the boundary line.

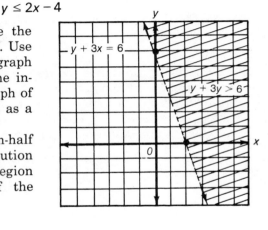

Step 3. On the same set of axes graph the line $y = 2x - 4$, using the slope-intercept method. Since the inequality relation is $\geq$, the graph of the related equation is drawn as a continuous line.

Step 4. Determine the closed half-plane that represents the solution set to $y \leq 2x - 4$. Shade in the region *below* and to the right of the boundary line.

Step 5. Label the region in which the shaded regions overlap as *S.* This cross-hatched area represents the solution set of the system of inequalities.

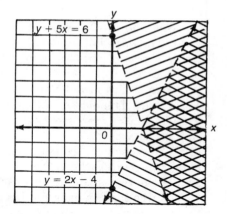

Keep in mind that any point in the region labeled as *S* is a member of the solution set of the conjunction $(y + 3x > 6) \wedge (y \leq 2x - 4)$.

EXERCISE SET 12.2

1–8. Graph each of the following inequalities:

1. $x < -1$

2. $y \geq 6$

3. $y + x \leq 0$

4. $y \geq 5x$

5. $y + 2x \geq 3$

6. $y - 3x < 1$

7. $2y - 3x > 6$

8. $x - 3y \leq 9$

9. Which ordered pair is in the solution set of $x < 6 - y$?

    (1) $(0, 6)$ (2) $(6, 0)$ (3) $(0, 5)$ (4) $(7, 0)$

10. Which is *not* a member of the solution set of $2x - 3y \geq 12$?

    (1) $(0, -4)$ (2) $(-3, -6)$ (3) $(10, 3)$ (4) $(6, 0)$

11–25. (a) On the same set of coordinate axes, graph the system of inequalities and label the solution set S.

    (b) Write the coordinates of a point in the solution set S.

    (c) Check algebraically that the coordinates of the point found in part (b) satisfy both inequalities.

11. $y > 3x$
     $x \leq 2$

12. $y > 2x + 5$
     $y < 1$

13. $2x + y < 6$
$y \geq 2$
14. $x > -1$
$y > x + 2$
15. $y < x - 5$
$y + 2x \geq 4$
16. $y > 3x + 6$
$y \leq 2x - 4$
17. $2y \geq x - 4$
$y < 3x$
18. $2x - y \leq 3$
$3x + y < 7$
19. $x + y > 6$
$y + 5 \leq 2x$

20. $2y \geq x - 6$
$x + y < 2$
21. $y + 3x > 6$
$y \leq 2x - 4$
22. $x + y < 8$
$y > x - 4$
23. $3y < 2x + 12$
$4x + y < -1$
24. $x > y + 2$
$2x \geq 1 - y$
25. $y + 2x > 7$
$y + 3 \leq 3x$

26. (a) On the same set of coordinate axes, graph the following system of inequalities:

$$y > x + 4$$
$$x + y \leq 2$$

(b) Which of the following points is in the solution set of the graph drawn in answer to part (a)?
    (1) $(2, 3)$ (2) $(-5, 2)$ (3) $(0, 6)$ (4) $(-1, 0)$

27. (a) On the same set of coordinate axes, graph the following system of inequalities:

$$y \leq 3x + 4$$
$$y + x > 2$$

(b) Write the coordinates of one point that is *not* in the solution set of both inequalities.

28. (a) On the same set of coordinate axes, graph the following system of inequalities:

$$y + 2 < x$$
$$y + 2x \geq 4$$

(b) Write the coordinates of a point that is *not* in the solution set of both inequalities.

12.3   SOLVING SYSTEMS OF EQUATIONS ALGEBRAICALLY: SUBSTITUTION METHOD

———— KEY IDEAS ————

The accompanying system of linear equations may be solved algebraically as well as graphically. Algebraic solutions of systems of linear equations are based on reducing the original system of equations to a single equation that contains one variable.

$$y = 2x\}$$

$$3x + y = 10$$

One way of solving the given system is to rewrite the second equation, replacing y with its equivalent, $2x$. The resulting equation has one variable, so it can be solved.

$$3x + 2x = 10$$
$$5x = 10$$
$$x = \frac{10}{5} = \mathbf{2}$$
$$y = 2x = 2(2) = \mathbf{4}$$

USING THE SUBSTITUTION METHOD.   In some systems of linear equations one of the given equations expresses one variable in terms of the other variable. In this situation, the *substitution method* provides a convenient way of obtaining one equation with one variable so that the solution set can be easily found.

Example

1. Solve the following system of equations algebraically, and check:

$$x + 2y = 7$$
$$y = 2x + 1$$

Solution: Eliminate variable y in the first equation by subtituting $2x + 1$ for y.

$$x + 2y = 7$$
$$x + 2(2x + 1) = 7$$
$$x + 4x + 2 = 7$$
$$5x + 2 = 7$$
$$5x = 7 - 2$$
$$5x = 5$$
$$x = \frac{5}{5} = 1$$

Find the corresponding value of y by substituting 1 for x in the second equation.

$$y = 2x + 1$$
$$= 2(1) + 1$$
$$= 2 + 1 = 3$$

The solution set is $\{(1, 3)\}$.

Check. Subtitute 1 for x and 3 for y in each of the original equations.

$$\frac{x + 2y = 7}{1 + 2(3)}$$
$$1 + 6$$
$$7 = 7 \checkmark$$

$$\frac{y = 2x + 1}{3 \;\vert\; 2(1) + 1}$$
$$3 \;\vert\; 2 + 1$$
$$3 = 3 \checkmark$$

In some systems of linear equations one equation can easily be transformed into an equivalent equation in which one variable is expressed in terms of the other variable. After this has been accomplished, the substitution method can be used to find the solution set.

Examples

2. Solve the following system of equations algebraically, and check:

$$3x - 2y = 42$$
$$2x - y = 26$$

Solution: Solve the second equation for y in terms of x.

Subtract $2x$ from each side: $\qquad -y = -2x + 26$

Divide each member of
  both sides of the equation by -1: $\qquad y = 2x - 26$

Substitute $2x - 26$ for y in the first equation.

$$3x - 2y = 42$$
$$3x - 2(2x - 26) = 42$$
$$3x - 4x + 52 = 42$$
$$-x + 52 = 42$$
$$-x = 42 - 52$$
$$= -10$$
$$x = 10$$

Find the corresponding value for y by substituting 10 for x in the equation $y = 2x - 6$.

$$y = 2x - 26$$
$$= 2(10) - 26$$
$$= 20 - 26 = -6$$

The solution set is $\{(10, -6)\}$. The check is left for you.

3. Solve the following system of equations algebraically, and check:

$$\frac{x}{2} = y + 5$$
$$4y - x = 6$$

Solution: Solve the first equation for x by multiplying each member of both sides of the equation by 2.

$$2\left(\frac{x}{2}\right) = 2(y + 5)$$
$$x = 2y + 10$$

In the second equation, replace x by $2y + 10$.

$$4y - x = 6$$
$$4y - (2y + 10) = 6$$
$$4y - 2y - 10 = 6$$
$$2y - 10 = 6$$
$$2y = 6 + 10$$
$$2y = 16$$
$$y = \frac{16}{2} = 8$$

Find the corresponding value for x by substituting 8 for y in the equation $x = 2y + 10$:

$$x = 2y + 10$$
$$= 2(8) + 10$$
$$= 16 + 10 = 26$$

The solution set is $\{(26, 8)\}$. The check is left for you.

4. Two angles are supplementary. If five times the measure of the smaller angle is subtracted from twice the measure of the larger angle, the result is 10. What is the measure of each angle?

Solution: Let x = measure of the smaller angle,
and y = measure of the larger angle.

Since the angles are supplementary, the sum of their measures is 180.

$$x + y = 180 \qquad \text{Equation (1)}$$

The second condition of the problem may be translated as follows:

$$2y - 5x = 10 \qquad \text{Equation (2).}$$

From equation (1), $y = 180 - x$, so y may be eliminated in equation (2).

$$2(180 - x) - 5x = 10$$
$$360 - 2x - 5x = 10$$
$$360 - 7x = 10$$
$$-7x = 10 - 360$$
$$x = \frac{-350}{-7} = 50$$
$$y = 180 - x = 180 - 50 = 130$$

The measures of the two angles are **50** and **130**. Check that these numbers satisfy the conditions in the original statement of the problem.

Condition 1: Are the two angles supplementary? Yes, since $50 + 130 = 180$.

Condition 2: Is five times the measure of the smaller angle subtracted from twice the measure of the larger angle equal to 10? Yes, since $2(130) - 5(50) = 260 - 250 = 10$.

5. The denominator of a fraction is 7 more than its numerator. If the numerator is increased by 3 and the denominator is decreased by 2, the new fraction equals $\frac{4}{5}$. Find the original fraction.

Solution: Let x = numerator of the fraction,
and y = denominator of the fraction.
$$y = x + 7 \qquad \text{Equation (1)}$$
$$\frac{x + 3}{y - 2} = \frac{4}{5} \qquad \text{Equation (2)}$$

Cross-multiply:
$$5(x + 3) = 4(y - 2)$$
$$5x + 15 = 4y - 8$$
$$5x = 4y - 8 - 15$$
$$5x = 4y - 23$$
$$5x - 4y = -23$$

From equation (1), replace y with $x + 7$:

$$5x - 4(x + 7) = -23$$
$$5x - 4x - 28 = -23$$
$$x - 28 = -23$$
$$x = 28 - 23 = 5$$
$$y = x + 7 = 5 + 7 = 12$$

The original fraction is $\frac{5}{12}$. The check is left for you.

EXERCISE SET 12.3

1–20. Solve each of the following systems algebraically, and check:

1. $y = 2x$
    $2x - 3y = 16$

2. $x = 3y$
    $5x - 9y = 18$

3. $y + 5x = 0$
    $3x - 2y = 26$

4. $\dfrac{y}{4} = x$
    $2y - 3x = 7$

5. $5c - n = 0$
    $3n + 4c = -19$

6. $a + b = 0$
    $5a - 2b = 14$

7. $y - 1 = x$
    $-3x + 7y = -1$

8. $y = 3x + 1$
    $x = y - 3$

9. $\dfrac{x}{3} - y = 0$
    $y - 2x = 10$

10. $y - 5 = x$
    $2y - 8 = 3x$

11. $x + 1 = 3y$
    $4x + 3y = 11$

12. $y - x = 1$
    $7y - 11x = -5$

13. $y + 2x = 3$
    $4x - 3y = 21$

14. $3y - 3x = 9$
    $7y - 6x = 58$

15. $x + y = 28$
    $x - 3y = 0$

16. $\dfrac{x}{4} - \dfrac{y}{2} = 1$
    $5x + 4y = 11$

17. $0.3y - 0.2x = 1.5$
    $0.75y = 2.25x$

18. $3(y + 1) = x$
    $2x + y = -8$

19. $\dfrac{a}{2} - \dfrac{b}{5} = 1$
    $b - 2a = 3$

20. $\dfrac{x - 2}{3} = y$
    $2x + 3y = -5$

21. Two angles are complementary. The difference between four times the measure of the smaller and the measure of the larger angle is 10. Find the degree measure of each angle.

22. The length of a side of one equilateral triangle exceeds twice the length of a side of another equilateral triangle by 1. If the difference in the perimeters of the triangles is 15, find the length of a side of each triangle.

23. The denominator of a fraction is 8 more than the numerator. If 5 is added to both the numerator and the denominator, the resulting fraction is equal to $\dfrac{1}{2}$. Find the original fraction.

24. The denominator of a fraction is three times the numerator. If 8 is added to the numerator and 6 is subtracted from the denominator, the value of the resulting fraction is $\dfrac{8}{9}$. Find the original fraction.

25. Mary is 1 year less than three times as old as Sue. In 10 years the ratio of Sue's age to Mary's age will be 1 : 2. What are the present ages of Mary and Sue?

12.4 SOLVING SYSTEMS OF EQUATIONS ALGEBRAICALLY: ADDITION METHOD

KEY IDEAS

The accompanying system of linear equations is difficult to solve using the substitution method, but can be easily solved by adding corresponding sides of each equation.

The resulting equation does not contain variable y since the coefficients of y in the original equations are additive inverses (opposites), so their sum is 0.

$$2x - 9y = 17$$
$$5x + 9y = 11$$
$$\overline{7x + 0 = 28}$$
$$x = \frac{28}{7} = \mathbf{4}$$

USING THE ADDITION METHOD. To use the *addition method* to solve a system of linear equations, write each equation in the form $Ax + By = C$ and then compare the coefficients of like variables. If the numerical coefficients of either the x terms or the y terms are additive inverses (opposites), then this variable can be eliminated by adding corresponding sides of both equations.

Examples ▰▰▰

1. Solve the following system of equations algebraically, and check:

$$3y = 2x - 1$$
$$5y + 2x = 25$$

Solution: Write the first equation in the form $Ax + By = C$, and then compare the numerical coefficients of the like variables.

$$3y - 2x = -1$$
$$5y + 2x = 25$$

The coefficients of variable x are opposites, so this variable can be eliminated if the equations are added:

$$3y - 2x = -1$$
$$\underline{5y + 2x = 25}$$
$$8y \quad\ = 24$$
$$y = \frac{24}{8} = 3$$

Find the corresponding value of x by replacing y by 3 in one of the equations:

$$3y = 2x - 1$$
$$3(3) = 2x - 1$$
$$9 = 2x - 1$$
$$1 + 9 = 2x$$
$$10 = 2x$$
$$x = \frac{10}{2} = 5$$

The solution set is $\{(5, 3)\}$.

Check. Replace x by 5 and y by 3 in each of the original equations.

$3y = 2x - 1$		$5y + 2x = 25$	
$3(3)$	$2(5) - 1$	$5(3) + 2(5)$	
9	$10 - 1$	$15 + 10$	
$9 = 9\checkmark$		$25 = 25\checkmark$	

2. The sum of two positive numbers is 27, and their difference is 13. What are the numbers?

Solution: Let $x =$ larger of the two numbers,
and $y =$ the other number.

The sum of the numbers is 27:

The difference of the numbers is 13:

Add the equations:

$$x + y = 27$$
$$x - y = 13$$
$$2x = 40$$
$$x = \frac{40}{2} = 20$$

To find y, replace x by 20 in one of the equations:

$$x + y = 27$$
$$20 + y = 27$$
$$y = 27 - 20 = 7$$

The two numbers are **20** and **7**.

Check. Do these numbers satisfy the conditions in the original statement of the problem?

Condition 1: Is the sum of 20 and 7 equal to 27? Yes, since $20 + 7 = 27$.

Condition 2: Is the difference of 20 and 7 equal to 13? Yes, since $20 - 7 = 13$.

3. Solve the following system of equations algebraically, and check:

$$x - \frac{1}{2}y = 4$$
$$x + y = 7$$

Solution: Begin by clearing the first equation of fractions by multiplying each member by 2.

$$2(x) - 2\left(\frac{1}{2}y\right) = 2(4) \rightarrow 2x - y = 8$$

Rewrite the second equation: $x + y = 7$
Add the equations: $\dfrac{3x \qquad = 15}{}$

$$x = \frac{15}{3} = 5$$

To find y, replace x by 5 in one of the equations.

$$x + y = 7$$
$$5 + y = 7$$
$$y = 7 - 5 = 2$$

The solution set is $\{(5, 2)\}$. The check is left for you. ▅▅▅▅▅

SOLVING SYSTEMS OF EQUATIONS USING MULTIPLIERS.

Sometimes one or both of the equations in a system of linear equations must be multiplied by an appropriate number in order to obtain a pair of like variables that have opposite numerical coefficients.

Examples ▬▬▬

4. Solve the following system of equations algebraically, and check:

$$3x + 2y = 4$$
$$9x + 2y = 16$$

Solution: The coefficients of y have the same value. Therefore multiply each member of one of the equations by -1 so that the coefficient of y in the resulting equation will be -2.

Multiply the first equation by -1: $-3x - 2y = -4$
Rewrite the second equation: $\dfrac{9x + 2y = 16}{}$
Add the equations: $6x \qquad = 12$

$$x = \frac{12}{6} = 2$$

Find the corresponding value for y by replacing x by 2 in one of the equations:

$$3x + 2y = 4$$
$$3(2) + 2y = 4$$
$$6 + 2y = 4$$
$$2y = 4 - 6$$
$$2y = -2$$
$$y = -\frac{2}{2} = -1$$

The solution set is $\{(2, -1)\}$. The check is left for you.

5. Solve the following system of equations algebraically, and check:

$$3x - 4y = -1$$
$$5x + 12y = 73$$

Solution: Compare the coefficients of like variables of the two equations. The coefficient of y in the second equation is an integer multiple of the coefficient of y in the first equation. Therefore variable y is the more likely choice for elimination. Multiply each member of the first equation by 3, since this will change the coefficient of y to -12, which is the opposite of the coefficient of y in the second equation.

Multiply the first equation by 3:	$(3)3x - (3)4y = (3)(-1)$
Simplify:	$9x - 12y = -3$
Rewrite the second equation:	$5x + 12y = 73$
Add the equations:	$14x = 70$
	$x = \dfrac{70}{14} = 5$

Find the corresponding value of y by substituting 5 for x in one of the original equations:

$$3x - 4y = -1$$
$$3(5) - 4y = -1$$
$$15 - 4y = -1$$
$$-4y = -1 - 15$$
$$-4y = -16$$
$$y = \frac{-16}{-4} = 4$$

The solution set is $\{(\mathbf{5, 4})\}$. The check is left for you.

6. Solve the following system of equations algebraically, and check:

$$3x + 4y = 9$$
$$5x + 6y = 13$$

Solution: There is no clear advantage in choosing x or in choosing y as the variable to eliminate. To eliminate x, determine the lowest common multiple of the coefficients of x, which is 15. To obtain *opposite* numerical coefficients for x, multiply the first equation by 5 and the second equation by -3. This will produce equivalent equations having coefficients of x of 15 and -15. An equally acceptable approach is to multiply the first equation by -5 and the second equation by 3.

$$(5)3x + (5)4y = (5)9 \quad \rightarrow \quad 15x + 20y = 45$$

$$(-3)5x + (-3)6y = (-3)13 \rightarrow \underline{-15x - 18y = -39}$$

Add the equations:
$$2y = 6$$
$$y = \frac{6}{2} = 3$$

Find the corresponding value of x by substituting 3 for y in one of the equations:

$$3x + 4y = 9$$
$$3x + 4(3) = 9$$
$$3x + 12 = 9$$
$$3x = 9 - 12$$
$$3x = -3$$
$$x = \frac{-3}{3} = -1$$

The solution set is $\{(-1, 3)\}$. The check is left for you.

Note: Another way of solving this system of equations is to eliminate y by multiplying the first equation by 3 and the second equation by -2. This produces equivalent equations having coefficients of y of 12 in the first equation and -12 in the second equation. ▬▬▬▬

EXERCISE SET 12.4

1–6. Solve for x.

1. $x + y = 4$
  $x - y = 2$

2. $2x - y = 12$
  $x + y = 3$

3. $2x + y = 5$
  $3x = y + 8$

4. $3x + y = 13$
  $x + y = 5$

5. $y - x = 6$
  $x + y = 4$

6. $3x + 4y = -4$
  $2x - y = -10$

7–12. Solve for y.

7. $3x + 2y = 7$
  $-3x + y = 8$

8. $2y + x = 8$
  $y + x = 5$

9. $3x - 2y = 12$
  $x + y = 4$

10. $4x - 3x = 15$
  $2x + 3y = 9$

11. $3x + 7y = 10$
  $3x - 2y = -8$

12. $7x - 3 = 3y$
  $7x - y = -1$

13. Which ordered pair is the solution of the following system of equations?

$$3x + y = 10$$
$$2x - y = 5$$

(1) $(1, 3)$ (2) $(5, -5)$ (3) $(3, 1)$ (4) $(-5, 5)$

14. Which ordered pair is the solution of the following system of equations?

$$6x + 2y = 14$$
$$3x + 2y = 8$$

(1) $(1, 2)$ (2) $(2, 1)$ (3) $(1, 4)$ (4) $(4, -2)$

15. The ordered pair $(2, -1)$ is the solution to which of the following systems of equations?

   (1) $x = 2y$
      $3x + 4y = -10$
   (2) $2x + 5y = -1$
      $x - y = 3$
   (3) $5x + 4y = 6$
      $x + 2y = 0$
   (4) $3x - 6y = 12$
      $5x - 10y = 4$

16. Solve algebraically for c and d, and check.

   (a) $3c - d = 7$
      $c + 2d = 7$
   (b) $\dfrac{c}{2} + d = 5$
      $c - 2d = 8$
   (c) $0.4c + 1.5d = -1$
      $1.2c - d = 8$
   (d) $0.6c - 1.8d = 7.2$
      $0.4c - 0.9d = -3.9$

17–30. Use the addition method to solve the system of equations for x *and* y, *and check.*

17. $3x - 2y = 42$
    $2x - y = 26$
18. $x + 2y + 1 = 0$
    $x - 2y + 3 = 0$
19. $7x - 2y = 8$
    $2y = 3x$
20. $2x + y = 6$
    $x - 3y = 10$
21. $3x - 2y = -1$
    $2x + 3y = 8$
22. $5x + 3y = 7$
    $6x + 5y = 17$
23. $\dfrac{x}{2} - 3y = -11$
    $2x + 3y = 1$

24. $4x + 3y - 1 = 0$
    $2x + 5y + 3 = 0$
25. $5x + 2y = 9$
    $2x + 5y = 12$
26. $3x = 7y - 48$
    $5x + 4y = 14$
27. $-3y + 7x = -15$
    $4x + 4y = -20$
28. $5 = 11x + 8y$
    $17 = 3x + 10y$
29. $3x - 3y = -15$
    $2x + 2y = 18$
30. $5x + 3y = 3$
    $\dfrac{x}{3} + \dfrac{y}{2} = 2$

31–33. Solve algebraically for a *and* b, *and check.*

31. $\dfrac{3b}{2} = 5a$
    $8a - 5b = -13$

32. $3a - 2b = 6$
    $\dfrac{b-1}{a} = \dfrac{1}{2}$

33. $\dfrac{a}{b+1} = \dfrac{2}{3}$
    $a + b = 9$

34–42. Solve each of the following problems algebraically, using a system of equations:

34. The sum of two numbers is 21. The smaller number is one half of the larger number. Find the two numbers.

35. The difference between two positive numbers is 9. If four times the larger number is ten times the smaller, what are the two numbers?

36. The sum of two numbers is 13. If twice the larger number is increased by 2, the result is equal to five times the smaller number. Find the numbers.

37. Bob has 21 coins in dimes and quarters in his pocket. If the total value of these coins is $3.30, how many dimes and how many quarters does Bob have in his pocket?

38. Two angles are supplementary. The difference between the measure of the larger angle and twice the measure of the smaller angle is 15. Find the degree measure of each angle.

39. The difference between the length and the width of a rectangle is 4. If the perimeter of the rectangle is 20, find the length and the width of the rectangle.

40. In a certain isosceles triangle three times the length of the base is equal to twice the length of a leg. If the perimeter of the triangle is 32, find the length of a leg and the length of the base.

41. The sum of the perimeters of two squares is 52. If the difference in the lengths of their sides is 5, find the area of each square.

42. Three shirts and two neckties cost $69. At the same prices, two shirts and three neckties cost $61. What is the cost of one shirt and one necktie?

12.5 USING SYSTEMS OF EQUATIONS TO SOLVE PROBLEMS

KEY IDEAS

Some word problems can be solved only by using two variables. Others can be solved by using either one or two variables. Using two variables often makes the process of translating the conditions of a word problem into mathematical terms easier than if one variable is used. An algebraic solution using two variables, however, is generally more difficult than if the same problem is solved using a single variable.

BUSINESS AND INVESTMENT PROBLEMS. Business problems involve this relationship:

$$\text{Price} \times \text{Quantity} = \text{Cost}.$$

Investment problems use the following principle:

Interest rate × Amount of money invested = Income from investment.

These types of problems usually can be solved either by using two variables or by using one variable.

Examples ▆▆▆▆

1. Total attendance of ticket holders at a school play was 850. The tickets for senior citizens were $1.50 each, and the regular tickets were $2.00 each. If the total receipts were $1650, how many tickets of each kind were sold?

Solution:

Method 1: Two Variables   ▆▆▆▆▆▆▆

Two kinds of tickets were sold, so that the number sold of each kind of ticket may be represented by a different variable. The receipts for each type of ticket sold are found by multiplying the number of tickets sold by the price of that type of ticket.

Let x = number of tickets sold to senior citizens,
and y = number of regular tickets sold.

Total attendance was 850: $\qquad x + y = 850$
Total receipts were 1650: $\qquad 1.5x + 2y = 1650$

The system can be solve by using either the addition or the substitution method. To use the substitution method, solve for y in the first equation, obtaining $y = 850 - x$. Replace y with $850 - x$ in the second equation:

$$1.5x + 2y = 1650$$
$$1.5x + 2(850 - x) = 1650$$
$$1.5x + 1700 - 2x = 1650$$
$$-0.5x = 1650 - 1700$$
$$-0.5x = -50$$

Multiply each side by 10: $\qquad -5x = -500$

$$x = \frac{-500}{-5} = 100$$
$$y = 850 - x = 850 - 100 = 750$$

100 senior citizen and **750** regular tickets were sold.

Check: 100 senior citizen tickets × $1.50 = \$ \ 150$
$\qquad\qquad$ 750 regular tickets × $2.00 = \$1500$
$\qquad\qquad\qquad$ Total receipts $= \overline{\$1650}$

Method 2: One Variable

Let x = number of tickets sold to senior citizens,
Then $850 - x$ = number of regular tickets sold.

$$1.5x + 2(850 - x) = 1650$$
$$1.5x + 1700 - 2x = 1650$$
$$-0.5x = 1650 - 1700$$
$$x = \frac{-50}{-0.5} = \mathbf{100}$$
$$850 - x = 850 - 100 = \mathbf{750}$$

2. Part of $5000 is invested in stocks at 12% interest, and the remainder in bonds at 9% interest. The total annual income from both investments is $555. Find the number of dollars invested at each rate.

Solution: Let $x =$ amount of dollars invested in stocks,
and $y =$ amount of dollars invested in bonds.

A total of $5000 is invested, so

$$x + y = 5000. \qquad \text{Equation (1)}$$

Multiply the interest rate for one investment, expressed as a decimal, by the amount invested (x or y) in order to obtain the income from that investment. Then do the same for the other investment. The sum of these products equals the total annual income:

$$0.12x + 0.09y = 555. \qquad \text{Equation (2)}$$

Clear equation (2) of decimal coefficients by multiplying each member of the equation by 100:

$$12x + 9y = 55,500.$$

From equation (1), $y = 5000 - x$, which can be used to eliminate y from the preceding equation:

$$12x + 9(5000 - x) = 55,500$$
$$12x + 45,000 - 9x = 55,500$$
$$3x = 55,500 - 45,000$$
$$3x = 10,500$$
$$x = \frac{10,500}{3} = 3500$$
$$y = 5000 - x = 5000 - 3500 = 1500$$

$3500 was invested at 12%, and **$1500** was invested at 9%. The check is left for you.

This problem can also be solved using one equation:

Let $x =$ amount invested at 12%.
Then $5000 - x =$ amount invested at 9%.

$$0.12x + 0.09(5000 - x) = 555$$

PROBLEMS REQUIRING TWO VARIABLES. Some problems *must* be solved using two variables.

Example ▬▬▬

3. Six computer disks and two computer printer ribbons cost $19.00. Eight of the same disks and three of the same ribbons cost $27.00. What is the cost of one computer disk and the cost of one computer printer ribbon?

Solution: Let x = cost of one computer disk,
and y = cost of one computer printer ribbon.

$$6x + 2y = 19 \qquad \text{Equation (1)}$$
$$8x + 3y = 27 \qquad \text{Equation (2)}$$

Use the addition method. There is no clear advantage in choosing x or y as the variable to eliminate. To eliminate y, multiply equation (1) by 3 and equation (2) by -2. This will produce equivalent equations in which the coefficients of variable y are opposite numbers.

$$6x(3) + 2y(3) = 19(3) \qquad \longrightarrow \qquad 18x + 6y = 57$$
$$8x(-2) + 3y(-2) = 27(-2) \qquad \longrightarrow \qquad -16x - 6y = -54$$

Add the equations:
$$2x = 3$$
$$x = \frac{3}{2} = 1.5$$

Find the value of y by replacing x with 1.5 in either of the equations.

$$6x + 2y = 19 \qquad \text{Equation (1)}$$
$$6(1.5) + 2y = 19$$
$$9 + 2y = 19$$
$$2y = 19 - 9$$
$$y = \frac{10}{2} = 5$$

The cost of one computer disk is **$1.50**, and the cost of one computer printer ribbon is **$5.00**. The check is left for you.   ▬▬▬

DIGIT PROBLEMS.   This type of problem also requires two variables. Numbers such as 13, 48, and 69 are examples of two-digit numbers. The *tens* digit of 69 is 6, and the *units* digit of 69 is 9. An equivalent expression for 69 is $6 \cdot 10 + 9$. If the digits of the number 69 are interchanged, the resulting number is 96.

In general, if t represents the tens digit of a two-digit number and u represents the units digit, then the number may be represented by $10t + u$. The sum of the digits of a two-digit number may be represented by $t + u$. The number with its digits interchanged may be represented by $10u + t$.

Example ▬▬▬

4. The units digit of a two-digit number exceeds the tens digit by 1. The original number is 2 less than five times the sum of the digits. Find the number.

Solution: Let t = tens digit of the two-digit number, and u = units digit.
Then $10t + u$ = original number.

Condition 1:   Units digit exceeds the tens digit by 1.
Equation (1): $u = t + 1$

Condition 2:   Number is 2 less than five times sum of the digits.
Equation (2): $10t + u = 5(t + u) - 2$

Simplify the second equation:

$$10t + u = 5t + 5u - 2$$
$$10t - 5t + u - 5u = -2$$
$$5t - 4u = -2$$

Equation (1) allows us to replace u by $t + 1$ in the preceding equation:

$$5t - 4(t + 1) = -2$$
$$5t - 4t - 4 = -2$$
$$t - 4 = -2$$
$$t = -2 + 4 = 2$$
$$u = t + 1 = 2 + 1 = 3$$

The number is $10t + u = 10(2) + 3 = $ **23**. The check is left for you. ▬▬

EXERCISE SET 12.5

1–15. Solve each of the following problems algebraically, using two variables:

1. The difference of two numbers is 1. The sum of three times the larger and twice the smaller is 13. Find the numbers.

2. Tickets for a high school dance cost $1.50 each if purchased in advance of the dance, but were $2.25 each if bought at the door. For the dance, 100 tickets were sold and $180 was collected. How many tickets were sold at the door?

3. A two-digit number is eight times the sum of the digits. Four times the units digit is 1 more than the tens digit. Find the number.

4. A bank teller is holding 18 bills having a value of $195. If the bank teller is holding only $5 and $20 bills, how many of each type of bill are there?

5. The total receipts from the sale of 240 regular-size high school graduation rings and 75 large-size graduation rings were $18,450. If the price of the large-size ring was $15 more than the price of the regular-size ring, what was the selling price of rings of each size?

6. The tens digit of a two-digit number exceeds twice the units digit by 1. If 7 is added to the number, the result is equal to eight times the sum of the digits. Find the number.

7. A soda machine contains 20 coins; some of the coins are nickels and the rest are quarters. If the value of the coins is $4.40, find the number of coins of *each* kind.

8. Pat invests part of $10,000 at 8% interest and the remainder at 6% interest. If the total annual income from both investments is $720, find the number of dollars invested at *each* rate.

9. At a fast-food restaurant, a family bought four hamburgers and three bags of french fries for $4.20. At the same time, another family traveling with them bought five hamburgers and two bags of french fries for $4.55. What was the cost of one hamburger, and what was the cost of one bag of french fries?

10. Ms. Marino invested $3200 for 1 year, part at 7% and the remainder at 9%. If the total annual income from her investments was $254, find the number of dollars invested at *each* rate.

11. Two heads of lettuce and three pounds of tomatoes cost $2.85. Three heads of lettuce and two pounds of tomatoes cost $2.90. Find the cost of one head of lettuce and the cost of one pound of tomatoes.

12. The sum of the digits of a two-digit number is 11. The number obtained by interchanging the digits is 7 more than twice the original number. Find the original number.

13. The sum of the digits of a two-digit number is 7. If the digits are interchanged, the new number is 2 more than twice the original number. Find the original number.

14. Mr. Lerner invested $1000 more than did his wife. The annual income from both their investments at 9% was $450. How much did each invest?

15. The perimeter of a rectangle is 44 cm. If the length is doubled and the width is tripled, the perimeter is 106 cm. Find the number of centimeters in the length and in the width of the original rectangle.

CHAPTER 12 REVIEW EXERCISES

REGENTS REVIEW.   *Problems included in this section are similar in form and difficulty to those found on the New York State Regents Examination for Course I of the Three-Year Sequence for High School Mathematics. Problems preceded by an asterisk have actually appeared on a previous Course I Regents Examination.*

*1. Solve the following system of equations for x:

$$3x + y = 5$$
$$2x - y = 0$$

*2. Solve the following system of equations for y:

$$3x + 2y = 7$$
$$-3x + y = 8$$

*3. Solve the following system of equations for x:

$$3x + y = 5$$
$$y = 5x - 3$$

*4. Which ordered pair satisfies both of the following equations?

$$x + y = 5$$
$$y = 2$$

(1) $(3, 2)$ (2) $(2, 3)$ (3) $(5, 0)$ (4) $(0, 5)$

5. Which ordered pair satisfies the following system of inequalities?

$$y > x + 4$$
$$x + y \le 2$$

(1) $(2, 3)$ (2) $(-5, 2)$ (3) $(0, 6)$ (4) $(-1, 0)$

*6. When drawn on the same set of axes, the graphs of the equations

$$y = x - 1 \quad \text{and} \quad x + y = 5$$

intersect at the point whose coordinates are
(1) $(-5, 6)$ (2) $(2, 1)$ (3) $(3, 2)$ (4) $(4, 1)$

*7–10. *Solve algebraically, and check.*

7. $2c - d = -1$
    $c + 3d = 17$
8. $4x + 3y = 27$
    $y = 2x - 1$

9. $2x - 3y = 10$
    $5x + 2y = 6$
10. $x - 4y = 16$
    $y = 1 - x$

*11. Solve the following system of equations graphically, and check:

$$x + y = -3$$
$$2x - y = 6$$

*12. (a) On the same set of coordinate axes, graph the following system of inequalities:

$$y < -3x + 5$$
$$x - y \ge 2$$

(b) Write the coordinates of a point in the solution set of the graph drawn in answer to part (a).

*13. **(a)** On the same set of coordinate axes, graph the following system of inequalities: $y < 2x + 4$
$$x + y \leq 7$$

(b) On the basis of your answer to part (a), write the coordinates of a point that is *not* in the solution set of the system of inequalities.

*14. **(a)** On a set of coordinate axes, graph the following system of equations: $y = 2x - 1$
$$y - x = 1$$

(b) Solve algebraically the system of equations in part (a).

15. The sum of the digits of a two-digit number is 17. If 9 is subtracted from the number, the result is the original number with the digits interchanged. Find the original number.

16. A postal clerk sold 50 postage stamps for $7.00. Some were 2-cent stamps, and the rest were 22-cent stamps. Find the number of *each* kind of stamp that was sold.

*17. The accompanying diagram shows the graph of which inequality?

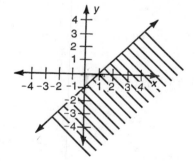

(1) $y > x - 1$ (2) $y \geq x - 1$ (3) $y < x - 1$ (4) $y \leq x - 1$

*18. *a* Solve the following system of equations algebraically and check:
$$y = 2x - 3$$
$$x - 3y = 24$$

b If the system of equations in part *a* were shown graphically, in which quadrant would the solution lie?

19. Write the letters (a) through (d). Next to *each* letter, write the *number* of the equality or inequality that is shown by the graph.

(a)   (c)

(b)   (d)

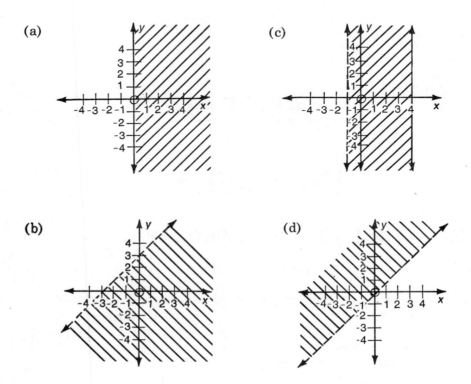

*20. *a* On the same set of coordinate axes, graph the following system of inequalities.

$$y \le \frac{1}{2}x - 3$$
$$y > -2x + 4$$

b Based on the graphs drawn in part *a*, in which solution set(s) does the point whose coordinates are (0,4) lie?

(1) $y \le \frac{1}{2}x - 3$, only

(2) $y > -2x + 4$, only

(3) both $y \le \frac{1}{2}x - 3$ and $y > -2x + 4$

(4) neither $y \le \frac{1}{2}x - 3$ nor $y > -2x + 4$

UNIT V: PROBABILITY AND STATISTICS

CHAPTER 13

Probability

13.1 FINDING SIMPLE PROBABILITIES

───────── KEY IDEAS ─────────

In probability an activity is sometimes referred to as an **experiment**, and a result of that experiment is called an **outcome**. An experiment may have more than one possible outcome. For example, flipping a coin has two possible outcomes: a head or a tail.

An **event** is a *specific* outcome of an experiment, such as getting a head when a coin is tossed. An event may occur in more than one way. For example, the event of getting an ace when a card is chosen from a standard deck of 52 playing cards may occur in four different ways (called *successes* or *favorable outcomes*) since a deck of cards includes four aces.

NOTATION AND SIMPLE PROBABILITY. Consider the experiment of placing seven slips of paper, each labeled with a different number from 1 to 7, in a hat, and then selecting one of the slips. What would be the probability of selecting a slip of paper having an odd number written on it? The set of all possible outcomes of the experiment, called the **sample space**, is the set {1, 2, 3, 4, 5, 6, 7}. Four members of the sample space (1, 3, 5, and 7) represent successful outcomes of the activity, that is, odd numbers. The number of successful ("favorable") outcomes is the number of different ways in which the desired event can occur.

The probability that a particular event will occur is found by dividing the number of ways the event can happen (number of "successes") by the number of total possible outcomes of the experiment. If the letter E represents the event of selecting an odd number, then the notation $P(E)$ is read as "the probability of selecting an odd number," and may be found by forming the following fraction:

$$P(E) = \frac{\text{Number of successes}}{\text{Number of total outcomes}} = \frac{4}{7}.$$

Examples ▬▬

1. A box contains two black marbles, four yellow marbles, and three red marbles. One marble is selected *at random* (without looking). What is the probability that the marble picked is yellow?

Solution: $P(\text{yellow}) = \dfrac{\text{Number of yellow marbles}}{\text{Total number of marbles}} = \dfrac{4}{9}$

2. A die is a cube whose faces are numbered 1 through 6. What is the probability of rolling a single die and obtaining each of the following?
  (a) A 5   (b) An even number   (c) A number greater than 4

Solutions: The sample space is $\{1, 2, 3, 4, 5, 6\}$, so the total number of possible outcomes is 6.
Let X = number on the die that shows up after the die is rolled.
(a) The sample space includes exactly *one* 5.

$$P(X = 5) = \frac{\text{Number of successes}}{\text{Number of total outcomes}} = \frac{1}{6}$$

(b) The sample space includes *three* even numbers (2, 4, and 6).

$$P(X = \text{even number}) = \frac{\text{Number of successes}}{\text{Number of total outcomes}} = \frac{3}{6} = \frac{1}{2}$$

(c) The sample space includes *two* numbers that are greater than 4 (5 and 6).

$$P(X > 4) = \frac{\text{Number of successes}}{\text{Number of total outcomes}} = \frac{2}{6} = \frac{1}{3} \qquad ▬▬$$

PROBLEMS WITH PLAYING CARDS.   A standard deck of playing cards includes 52 cards divided into four suits: hearts (red), diamonds (red), clubs (black), and spades (black). Each suit contains 13 cards: ace, 2, 3, 4, 5, 6, 7, 8, 9, 10, jack, queen, king. Jacks, queens, and kings are called *picture cards*. When a card is drawn from a playing deck, we always assume that it is drawn at a random, so that each card has an equally likely chance of being selected.

Example ▬▬▬

3. A single playing card is drawn from a standard deck of playing cards. Find the probability that the card is:
(a) an ace   (b) a club   (c) a red king

Solutions: In each case the sample space contains 52 possible outcomes since there are 52 different playing cards.

(a) A deck contains *four* aces, so

$$P(\text{ace}) = \frac{\text{Number of successes}}{\text{Number of total outcomes}} = \frac{4}{52} = \frac{1}{13}$$

'b' A deck contains *13* clubs, so

$$P(\text{club}) = \frac{\text{Number of successes}}{\text{Number of total outcomes}} = \frac{13}{52} = \frac{1}{4}$$

'c' There are four kings and *two* of these are red, so

$$P(\text{red king}) = \frac{\text{Number of successes}}{\text{Number of total outcomes}} = \frac{2}{52} = \frac{1}{26}$$ ▬▬▬

SOME PROBABILITY FACTS.   Since the probability of an event is defined as a fraction, certain conclusions can be drawn regarding the possible range of values of the probability of an event.

● **$P(E) = 0$ if event E is an impossibility.**   An event E is impossible if there are no ways in which E can happen. For example, the number of successes for the event of drawing a card with the number 19 from a standard playing deck is 0, so the probability of picking 19 is $\frac{0}{52}$ or 0. Since the number of successes can never be less than 0, the probability of an event can never be less than 0.

● **$P(E) = 1$ if event E is a certainty.**   An event E is a certainty whenever the number of successes equals the number of total possible outcomes. When finding $P(E)$, the same number appears in the numerator and the denominator of the probability fraction, so that the value of $P(E)$ is 1. For example, the probability of rolling a single die and getting a number less than 7 is $\frac{6}{6}$ or 1. Since the number of successes (numerator) can never be greater than the total number of outcomes (denominator), the probability fraction can never have a value greater than 1.

● **$0 \leq P(E) \leq 1$.**   The probability of an event must range between 0 and 1, possibly being equal to 0 or 1.

● **$P(\text{not } E) = 1 - P(E)$.**   Subtracting the probability that an event will occur from 1 gives the probability that the event will *not* occur. For example, suppose there is a 30% chance that it will rain tomorrow. The probability that it will *not* rain is 70% or 0.7 since

$$P(\text{not } R) = 1 - P(R)$$
$$= 1 - 30\%$$
$$= 1 - 0.3 = \mathbf{0.7} \text{ } or \text{ } \mathbf{70\%}.$$

EXERCISE SET 13.1

1. A letter from the word POLYGON is selected at random. What is the probability that the letter is an O?

2. A bag contains three green marbles and five white marbles. One marble is drawn at random. Find the probability of drawing:
   (a) a white marble   (b) *not* a white marble   (c) a blue marble

3. Find the probability of rolling a single die and obtaining:
   (a) a 3   (d) a prime number
   (b) an odd number   (e) an even number that is > 4
   (c) a number greater than 2   (f) a number less than 1

4. A letter is selected at random from the alphabet. What is the probability that it is *not* a vowel?

5. One of the angles of a right triangle is selected at random. What is the probability of each of the following?
   (a) The angle is obtuse.   (b) The angle is acute.

6. If all the letters of the word GEOMETRY are placed in a hat, what is the probability of drawing at random a letter that is a vowel?

7. If all the digits of the number 1987 are placed in a hat, what is the probability of drawing at random a number that is prime?

8. There are 13 boys and 17 girls in a class. If a teacher calls on a student at random, what is the probability that the student is a girl?

9. The numbers from 1 to 20, inclusive, are written on individual slips of paper and placed in a hat. What is the probability of selecting each of the following?
   (a) An even number   (d) A number divisible by 5 and by 10
   (b) A number divisible by 5   (e) A number that is at least 16
   (c) A number divisible by 10   (f) A prime number

10. A single playing card is drawn from a standard deck of cards. Find the probability that the card is:
    (a) a diamond   (d) the 2 of hearts
    (b) a 5   (e) a picture card
    (c) a queen   (f) a black ace

11. The probability that the Cougars will win when playing the Bengals at basketball is 60%. What is the probability that the Bengals will win when they play the Cougars on Saturday?

12. What is the probability of tossing a coin and *not* obtaining a head?

13. Given four geometric figures: an equiangular triangle, a square, a trapezoid, and a rhombus. If one of the figures is selected at random, what is the probability that the figure will be equilateral?

14. On a test the probability of getting the correct answer to a certain question is represented by $\frac{x}{10}$. Which *cannot* be a value of x?

    (1) -1 (2) 0   (3) 1   (4) 10

15. What is the probability that the average of two consecutive even integers is also an even integer?

    (1) 0   (2) $\frac{1}{2}$ (3) 1   (4) Impossible to determine

16. Express, in terms of x, the probability that an event will *not* happen if the probability that the event will happen is represented by:

    (a) x (b) $\frac{x}{4}$ (c) $x + 4$ (d) $4x - 1$

17. A jar contains x red marbles, $2x - 1$ blue marbles, and $2x + 1$ white marbles. One marble is drawn at random.
    (a) Express in terms of x the total number of marbles in the jar.
    (b) Express in terms of x the probability of drawing a blue marble.
    (c) If the probability of drawing a blue marble is $\frac{1}{3}$, find the value of x.
    (d) What is the probability of *not* drawing a red marble?

13.2   COUNTING OUTCOMES

KEY IDEAS

> Recall that a sample space is the set of all possible outcomes of an experiment. For more complicated experiments, the task of determining the outcomes in a sample space needs to be approached in a systematic fashion. There are several different ways in which this can be done.

LISTING OUTCOMES.   Suppose that a fair coin is tossed, and then a die is rolled. A *fair* coin is a coin that when tossed has equally likely chances of coming up heads (H) and tails (T). The sample space of this experiment may be described as a set of 12 pairs of outcomes:

$$\{(H, 1), (H, 2), (H, 3), (H, 4), (H, 5), (H, 6),$$
$$(T, 1), (T, 2), (T, 3), (T, 4), (T, 5), (T, 6)\}.$$

The first member of each pair represents the results of the coin toss, and the second member of the pair is a possible outcome of rolling the die.

Example: What is the probability of getting a head and rolling a 4? Since there are 12 possible outcomes in the sample space and only one of these outcomes is (H, 4), $P(\text{H and } 4) = \frac{1}{12}$.

Example: What is the probability of getting a tail and rolling an odd number? The outcomes (T, 1), (T, 3) and (T, 5) satisfy the conditions of the problem, so the probability of getting a tail and rolling an odd number is $\frac{3}{12}$ or $\frac{1}{4}$.

Example: What is the probability of getting a head *or* rolling a 6? The successful outcomes are (H, 1), (H, 2), (H, 3), (H, 4), (H, 5), (H, 6), and (T, 6), so $P(\text{H or } 6) = \frac{7}{12}$.

TREE DIAGRAMS. The sample space for the experiment described above can also be represented by using the tree diagram shown in Figure 13.1. The two primary branches correspond to the two possible outcomes of flipping a coin. Each primary branch has six secondary branches, which reflect the six different possible outcomes of rolling a die. Each of the 12 primary–secondary branches represents a possible outcome of the two events.

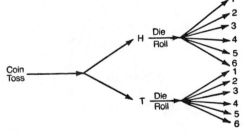

Example

1. A bag contains one red marble, one blue marble, and one green marble. Henry selects a marble at random from the bag, notes its color, and then places it back in the bag. Henry then selects another marble and notes its color.

(a) List the sample space as a set of ordered pairs that show all possible outcomes.

(b) Draw a tree diagram that shows all possible outcomes.

(c) What is the probability that Henry selected the red marble both times?

(d) What is the probability that two red marbles were not selected?

(e) What is the probability that Henry picked the blue marble *at least* once?

(f) What is the probability that Henry selected a marble of the same color both times?

Solutions: Let R = red marble, B = blue marble, and G = green marble.

(a) The first member of the ordered pair represents the color of the first marble selected, and the second member represents the color of the second marble selected.

(R, R), (R, B), (R, G)
(B, R), (B, B), (B, G)
(G, R), (G, B), (G, G)

(b)

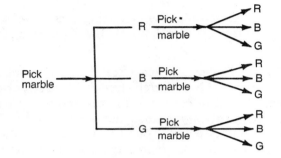

(c) The outcome (R, R) appears exactly once in a total of nine possible outcomes, so $P(\text{both red}) = \dfrac{1}{9}$.

(d) $P(\text{neither red}) = 1 - P(2 \text{ red})$

$$= 1 - \frac{1}{9}$$

$$= \frac{8}{9}$$

(e) There are five different outcomes in which the blue marble appears: (R, B), (B, R), (B, B), (B, G), and (G, B). Therefore the probability that Henry selected at least one blue marble is $\dfrac{5}{9}$.

(f) There are three different outcomes in which the color of the marble is the same: (R, R), (B, B) and (G, G). Therefore the probability that Henry selected a marble of the same color both times is equal to $\dfrac{3}{9}$ or $\dfrac{1}{3}$.

THE COUNTING PRINCIPLE. Notice that in the coin and die experiment the first activity has two possible outcomes, the second activity has six possible outcomes, and the total number of different ways in which both activities can occur is 2×6 or 12 ways. The generalization of this result, called the *counting principle*, may be stated as follows:

COUNTING PRINCIPLE
If one activity can be performed in p *ways and another activity in* q *ways, then there are* p × q *possible ways in which both activities may be performed.*

The counting principle may also be extended for more than two events; see part (b) of Example 2.

Examples ▬▬

2. A man has five different shirts and four different neckties.
(a) In how many ways can he choose a shirt and a necktie?
(b) If the man has three different sport jackets, how many different outfits consisting of a sport jacket, shirt, and a tie are possible?

Solutions: (a) Use the counting principle: 5 × 4 = 20. There are **20** different ways in which he can choose a shirt and a necktie.
(b) Use the counting principle for three activities: 5 × 4 × 3 = 60. There are **60** different outfits.

3. Find the probability that when two dice are rolled the sum of the numbers showing is:
(a) 7   (c) less than 13   (e) at least 10
(b) 1   (d) not greater than 5   (f) at most 3

Solution: The counting principle tells us that there is a total of 6 × 6 or 36 possible outcomes. These outcomes may be described as a set of ordered pairs in which the first member represents the number showing on one die and the second member represents the number showing on the other die.

$$(1, 1), (1, 2), (1, 3), (1, 4), (1, 5), (1, 6)$$
$$(2, 1), (2, 2), (2, 3), (2, 4), (2, 5), (2, 6)$$
$$(3, 1), (3, 2), (3, 3), (3, 4), (3, 5), (3, 6)$$
$$(4, 1), (4, 2), (4, 3), (4, 4), (4, 5), (4, 6)$$
$$(5, 1), (5, 2), (5, 3), (5, 4), (5, 5), (5, 6)$$
$$(6, 1), (6, 2), (6, 3), (6, 4), (6, 5), (6, 7)$$

(a) There are six successes: (1, 6), (2, 5), (3, 4), (4, 3), (5, 2), and (6, 1).

$$P(\text{sum} = 7) = \frac{6}{36} = \frac{1}{6}$$

(b) There are no outcomes in which the sum of the numbers is 1.

$$P(\text{sum} = 1) = \frac{0}{36} = 0$$

(c) The outcome (6, 6) has the largest sum, 12. Therefore each of the 36 outcomes has a sum that is less than 13.

$$P(\text{sum} < 13) = \frac{36}{36} = 1$$

(d) Finding outcomes whose sum is not greater than 5 is equivalent to finding outcomes whose sum is less than or equal to 5. There are ten such outcomes: (1, 1), (1, 2), (1, 3), (1, 4), (2, 1), (2, 2), (2, 3), (3, 1), (3, 2), and (4, 1).

$$P(\text{sum not} > 5) = P(\text{sum} \leq 5) = \frac{10}{36} = \frac{5}{18}$$

(e) Finding outcomes whose sum is at least 10 is equivalent to finding outcomes whose sum is greater than or equal to 10. There are six such outcomes: (4, 6), (5, 5), (5, 6), (6, 4), (6, 5), and (6, 6).

$$P(\text{sum at least} 10) = P(\text{sum} \geq 10) = \frac{6}{36} = \frac{1}{6}$$

(f) Finding outcomes whose sum is at most 3 is equivalent to finding outcomes whose sum is less than or equal to 3. There are three such outcomes: (1, 1), (1, 2), and (2, 1).

$$P(\text{sum is at most} 3) = P(\text{sum} \leq 3) = \frac{3}{36} = \frac{1}{12}$$

EXERCISE SET 13.2

1. A large parking lot has five entrances and seven exits. In how many different ways can a driver enter the parking lot and exit from it?

2. An ice cream parlor makes a sundae using one of six different flavors of ice cream, one of three different flavors of syrup, and one of four different toppings. What is the total number of different sundaes that this ice cream parlor sells?

3. Marcy has five skirts, six blouses, and three scarves. How many outfits can Marcy create consisting of one skirt, one blouse, and one scarf?

4. An experiment consists of tossing a fair coin, and then picking a card at random from a standard deck of playing cards. How many outcomes are contained in the sample space?

5. Two dice are rolled. Find the probability that:
    (a) their sum is 8.
    (b) the dice show the same number.
    (c) the dice show different numbers.
    (d) their sum is at least 9.
    (e) their sum is at most 6.
    (f) their sum is a prime number.

6. A fair coin and a fair die are tossed simultaneously.
   (a) Draw a tree diagram, or list the sample space showing all possible outcomes.
   (b) What is the probability of getting a head and an even number?
   (c) What is the probability of getting a 7 and a head?
   (d) What is the probability of getting a 5 or a tail?

7. A penny, a nickel, and a dime are in a box. Bob randomly selects a coin, notes its value, and returns it to the box. He then randomly selects another coin from the box.
   (a) Draw a tree diagram showing all possible outcomes.
   (b) List the possible outcomes as a set of ordered pairs.
   (c) What is the probability that the same coin was drawn both times?
   (d) What is the probability that a nickel was drawn *at least* once?
   (e) What is the probability that the total value of both coins which were selected would exceed 11¢?

8. A contest offers a first prize of $12,000 or a car. The second prize is $500 or a television set or a set of encyclopedias. In each case, the second place winner has the option of choosing between the two prizes offered.
   (a) Make a tree diagram, *or* list the sample space of all possible pairs of first and second prizes.
   (b) If each prize is equally likely to be chosen, find the probability that:
       (1) both prizes chosen are money.
       (2) neither prize chosen is money.
       (3) one prize chosen is money, but the other is not.

9. The letters A, E, N, T are written on four individual cards and placed in a container. Each has an equal likelihood of being drawn. One card is drawn from the container, the letter noted, and the card returned to the container. Then a second card is drawn and the letter noted.
   (a) Draw a tree diagram or list the sample space showing all possible outcomes after both drawings.
   (b) Find the probability that:
       (1) the two letters drawn are the same.
       (2) the first letter drawn is A and the second letter is T.
       (3) for both drawings the letter N does not appear.

10. The assembly committee of the River High School student council consists of four students whose ages are 14, 15, 16, and 17, respectively. One student will be chosen at random to be chairperson, and then, from the remaining three, one will be chosen at random to be the recording secretary.
    (a) Draw a tree diagram or list the sample space showing all possible outcomes after both drawings.
    (b) Find the probability that:
        (1) the chairperson is older than the recording secretary.
        (2) both students chosen are under the age of 16.
        (3) both students chosen are the same age.

11. A silver dollar, a half-dollar, a quarter, a dime, and a nickel are in a box. One coin is drawn at random. Without replacing the first coin, a second coin is drawn.
    (a) Draw a tree diagram or list the sample space showing all possible outcomes for this experiment.
    (b) Find the probability that:
        (1) the value of the first coin drawn is greater than the value of the second coin drawn.
        (2) the sum of the values of the two coins drawn is greater than $1.00.
        (3) the sum of the values of the two coins drawn is exactly $1.00.

12. A certain game requires spinning a marker and then tossing a single die. The marker must stop over one of three equally likely colors (red, green, blue), and the die is a standard fair six-sided type.

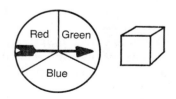

    (a) Draw a tree diagram or list the sample space of all possible pairs of outcomes for spinning the marker and tossing the die.
    (b) What is the probability of obtaining the result (red, 4)?
    (c) What is the probability of obtaining the result (green, 8)?
    (d) What is the probability of obtaining the result (blue, even number)?

13. A student has the following five books in his locker: math, history, Latin, science, and English. Without looking at the books, he pulls out one book and then, without replacing the first book, pulls out a second book.
    (a) Using the letters M, H, L, S, and E, draw a tree diagram, or write the sample space for pulling two books from the locker.
    (b) What is the probability that the student first pulled out the math book and then the English book?
    (c) What is the probability that he pulled out two different books?

14. The first step of an experiment is to pick one number from the set {1, 2, 3}. The second step of the experiment is to pick one number from the set {1, 4, 9}.
    (a) Draw a tree diagram or list the sample space of all possible pairs of outcomes.
    (b) Determine the probability that:
        (1) both numbers are the same.
        (2) the second number is the square of the first.
        (3) both numbers are odd.

13.3   FINDING PROBABILITIES INVOLVING *AND* and *OR*

─────────────────── KEY IDEAS ───────────────────

Some probability problems involve combining conditions or events using the connectives AND *and* OR. These problems can sometimes be made easier to understand by using the language and notation of sets. The notation $n(S)$ will be understood to mean the *n*umber of outcomes of event S or the *n*umber of elements in set S. If you are not familiar with the meaning of *intersection* ($\cap$) and *union* ($\cup$) of sets, review pages **2-3** of this book.

PROBABILITY INVOLVING *AND*.   An event E may involve more than one condition. For example, what is the probability of drawing a card from a standard playing deck that is both red *and* a king? Notice that there are two conditions: (1) the card is red, and (2) the card is a king. The set of successful outcomes is the *intersection* of the set of red cards and the set of kings, which is the set consisting of tne king of hearts and the king of diamonds. Since there are two successful outcomes,

$$P(E) = \frac{\text{Number of successes}}{\text{Total number of outcomes}} = \frac{2}{52} = \frac{1}{26}.$$

Example ▬▬▬

1. One number is selected from the set of integers from 1 to 12, inclusive. What is the probability that the number is an odd number and is prime?

Solution: The set of odd numbers in the original set is {1, 3, 5, 7, 9, 11}. The set of prime numbers in the original set is {2, 3, 5, 7, 11}.

$$\{1, 3, 5, 7, 9, 11\} \cap \{2, 3, 5, 7, 11\} = \{3, 5, 7, 11\}$$

Since there are four successful outcomes and 12 outcomes in the sample space, $P(E) = \dfrac{4}{12} = \dfrac{1}{3}$.

PROBABILITY INVOLVING *OR*.   Suppose that one number is selected from the set of integers from 11 to 20, inclusive. What is the probability that the number is an even number *or* is a prime number?

Let S = sample space = {11, 12, 13, 14, 15, 16, 17, 18, 19, 20},
  A = event of picking an even number,
  B = event of picking a prime number.

There are 5 numbers in the sample space that are even and 4 different numbers that are prime, so there is a total of 9 successes for the event. Hence

$$P(A \text{ or } B) = \frac{n(A \text{ or } B)}{n(S)} = \frac{9}{10}.$$

In probability problems involving OR, the same outcomes may be successes for both events. When this happens, be careful that you do not count these common outcomes twice. For example, in the preceding example what is the probability that the number picked is odd *or* is greater than 14?

Let A = event of picking an odd number,
  B = event of picking a number greater than 14.

In the sample space, {11, 12, 13, 14, 15, 16, 17, 18, 19, 20}, there are 5 odd numbers and 6 numbers that are greater than 14. However, $n(A \text{ or } B)$ cannot be equal to 11 $(5 + 6)$. If it were, then $P(A \text{ or } B)$ would equal $\dfrac{11}{10}$, which is greater than 1, and that is not possible. What is wrong? In finding $P(A \text{ or } B)$, the numbers 15, 17, and 19 were counted twice since they are both odd and greater than 14.

To avoid counting the same outcomes twice, subtract the number of outcomes that are successes for both events from the sum of successes for each event:

$$\begin{aligned} n(A \text{ or } B) &= n(A) + n(B) - n(A \text{ and } B) \\ &= 5 + 6 - 3 \\ &= 8. \end{aligned}$$

Therefore

$$P(A \text{ or } B) = \frac{n(A \text{ or } B)}{n(S)} = \frac{8}{10} = \frac{4}{5}.$$

We may express $P(A \text{ or } B)$ in terms of $P(A)$ and $P(B)$ by noting that $P(A) = \frac{5}{10}$, $P(B) = \frac{6}{10}$, $P(A \text{ and } B) = \frac{3}{10}$ (since three outcomes are common to both events), and

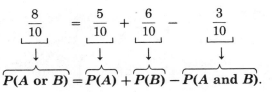

$$\underbrace{\frac{8}{10}}_{\downarrow} = \underbrace{\frac{5}{10}}_{\downarrow} + \underbrace{\frac{6}{10}}_{\downarrow} - \underbrace{\frac{3}{10}}_{\downarrow}$$

so that $\overbrace{P(A \text{ or } B)} = \overbrace{P(A)} + \overbrace{P(B)} - \overbrace{P(A \text{ and } B)}.$

Example ▬▬

2. Find the probability of drawing from a standard playing deck a card that is:

(a) a black 5   (b) a black card or a 5

Solution: (a) The set of successful outcomes is the *intersection* of the set of black cards and the set of 5's, which is the set consisting of the 5 of clubs and the 5 of spades. Since there are two successful outcomes,

$$P(E) = \frac{\text{Number of successes}}{\text{Total number of outcomes}} = \frac{2}{52} = \frac{1}{26}.$$

(b) There are 26 black cards (13 clubs and 13 spades), and four 5's. However, included in the 26 black cards are the 5 of clubs and the 5 of spades. Hence the number of successes is 28 since

$$26 + 4 - 2 = 28$$

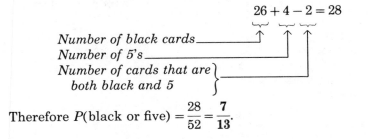

Number of black cards ———————↑ ↑ ↑
Number of 5's —————————————┘ │ │
Number of cards that are ⎫ ——————————┘ │
  both black and 5 ⎭ —————————————————┘

Therefore $P(\text{black or five}) = \frac{28}{52} = \frac{7}{13}.$ ▬▬

RELATING THE *OR* IN PROBABILITY TO SETS AND LOGIC.   The beginning of section 13.3 illustrated how the *AND* in probability is related to the concept of *intersection* of sets. The *OR* in probability can be related to the concept of *union* (symbol: $\cup$) of sets, and to disjunction (symbol: $\vee$) in logic. Let A and B represent events.

Case 1: $n(A \text{ and } B) = 0$ Equivalent Probability Expressions

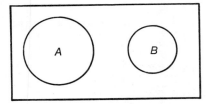

$$P(A \text{ or } B) = P(A) + P(B)$$
$$P(A \cup B) = P(A) \cup P(B)$$
$$P(A \vee B) = P(A) + P(B)$$

Case 2: $n(A \text{ and } B) \neq 0$ Equivalent Probability Expressions

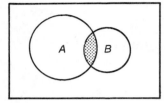

$P(A \text{ or } B) = P(A) + P(B) - P(A \text{ and } B)$
$P(A \cup B) = P(A) \cup P(B) - P(A \cap B)$
$P(A \lor B) = P(A) + P(B) - P(A \land B)$

EXERCISE SET 13.3

1. A letter is selected at random from the word TRAPEZOID. Find the probability that the letter is:
    (a) a vowel or a D
    (b) the first or the last letter of the alphabet
    (c) a vowel or the letter E
    (d) a vowel and the letter A

2. If $P(A) = 0.7$, $P(B) = 0.5$, and $P(A \text{ and } B) = 0.35$, then what is $P(A \text{ or } B)$?

3. Find the probability that, when a single die is rolled, the number rolled is:
    (a) odd and greater than 3
    (b) odd or greater than 3
    (c) prime and greater than 3
    (d) prime or greater than 3
    (e) prime and less than 3
    (f) prime or even

4. One number is selected from the set of integers from 1 to 10, inclusive. Find the probability that the number selected is:
    (a) even and prime
    (b) even or prime
    (c) prime and greater than 5
    (d) divisible by 3 or by 5
    (e) divisible by 3 and by 5
    (f) even or greater than 5
    (g) divisible by 2 and by 3
    (h) divisible by 2 or by 3

5. A card is selected at random from a standard playing deck. Find the probability that the card selected is:
    (a) red and an ace
    (b) red or an ace
    (c) a club or a diamond
    (d) a 7 of hearts or a 9 of clubs

(e) a 7 or a 9
(f) a picture card or a black card
(g) a picture card and a black card
(h) not a club and not a jack

13.4 FINDING PROBABILITIES OF EVENTS OCCURRING JOINTLY

KEY IDEAS

Two events are said to occur *jointly* when they both happen. The probability that two events, *A* and *B*, will occur jointly is the product of the probability that event *A* will occur and the probability that event *B* will occur.

JOINT PROBABILITIES.　As the counting principle suggests, to find the probability of two or more events occurring jointly, we multiply the probabilities of the individual events:

If the probability of one event occurring is p *and the probability of another event is* q, *then the probability of these events occurring together is* p × q.

Examples ▬▬▬

1.　A coin and a single die are tossed. What is the probability of getting a head *and* a number less than 3?

Solution:　$P(\text{H}) = \dfrac{1}{2}$. There are two numbers less than 3 (1 and 2), so $P(N < 3) = \dfrac{2}{6} = \dfrac{1}{3}$.

$$P(\text{H and } N > 3) = P(\text{H}) \times P(N < 3)$$
$$= \frac{1}{2} \times \frac{1}{3}$$
$$= \frac{1}{6}$$

2.　A card is drawn at random from a standard deck of playing cards, looked at, and then replaced. Another card is drawn and looked at. What is the probability that two aces were drawn?

Solution: There are four aces in a deck of 52 playing card, so

$$P(2 \text{ aces}) = P(1 \text{ ace}) \times P(1 \text{ ace})$$
$$= \frac{4}{52} \times \frac{4}{52}$$
$$= \frac{1}{13} \times \frac{1}{13}$$
$$= \frac{1}{169}.$$

3. The probability that the National League team will win the Allstar game from the American League team is $\frac{5}{7}$. What is the probability that the American League team will win the next two Allstar games?

Solution: The probability that the American League team will win the Allstar game is $1 - \frac{5}{7}$ or $\frac{2}{7}$.

$$P(\text{American League will win both games}) = \frac{2}{7} \times \frac{2}{7} = \frac{4}{9}.$$

4. What is the probability of flipping a coin three times and getting three heads?

Solution: To find the probability of three events occurring jointly, multiply the probabilities of the three events. The probability of getting a head on each toss of a coin is $\frac{1}{2}$, so

$$P(3 \text{ heads}) = P(H) \times P(H) \times P(H)$$
$$= \frac{1}{2} \times \frac{1}{2} \times \frac{1}{2}$$
$$= \frac{1}{8}.$$

PROBLEMS WITH AND WITHOUT REPLACEMENT.   An urn is a vase whose contents are not readily visible. If an object is taken out of an urn, examined, and then put back, we classify this as a problem "with replacement." The sample space for each withdrawal of an object with replacement remains the same.

In probability problems "without replacement," the object is *not* replaced after being drawn, so that the sample space changes for each succeeding withdrawal of an object.

Examples

5. An urn contains three red marbles, two white marbles, and four blue marbles. A marble is chosen at random from the urn and then replaced. Another marble is chosen.

(a) Find the probability that both marbles are white.

(b) If the first marble is not replaced, find the probability that both marbles are the same color.

Solutions: (a) There are nine marbles in the urn, so that the sample space for each selection with replacement is 9. On each selection from the urn, two white marbles are available to be picked. The probability that a white marble is selected on the first try is 2/9, and with replacement the probability that a white marble is picked on the second try is also 2/9. The probability that these events occur jointly is, therefore,

$$P(\text{both white}) = P(\text{first white}) \times P(\text{second white})$$

$$= \frac{2}{9} \times \frac{2}{9}$$

$$= \frac{4}{81}.$$

(b) $P(\text{same color}) = P(\text{both red}) + P(\text{both white}) + P(\text{both blue})$. Since there is no replacement, there are nine outcomes in the sample space for the first pick, and eight possible outcomes for the second pick. The outcome that is removed is assumed to be the color that the second pick is trying to match.

$$P(\text{both red}) = \frac{3}{9} \times \frac{2}{8} = \frac{6}{72}$$

$$P(\text{both white}) = \frac{2}{9} \times \frac{1}{8} = \frac{2}{72}$$

$$P(\text{both blue}) = \frac{4}{9} \times \frac{3}{8} = \frac{12}{72}$$

$$P(\text{same color}) = \qquad \frac{20}{72} = \frac{5}{18}.$$

6. From a standard deck of playing cards, two cards are drawn at random. Find the probability that both cards are jacks.

Solution: Drawing two cards from the deck implies that the second card is drawn without the first card being replaced. Since there are four jacks and a total of 52 playing cards, $P(\text{first jack}) = \frac{4}{52}$. If it is assumed that the first card picked is a jack and is not replaced, $P(\text{second jack}) = \frac{3}{51}$. To find the probability that these events occur jointly, multiply their individual probabilities:

$$P(\text{both jacks}) = P(\text{first jack}) \times P(\text{second jack})$$

$$= \frac{4}{52} \times \frac{3}{51}$$

$$= \frac{1}{13} \times \frac{1}{17}$$

$$= \frac{1}{221}.$$

EXERCISE SET 13.4

1. An urn contains three yellow marbles, five white marbles, and two black marbles. Two marbles are randomly selected, and their colors are noted. Find the probability of selecting without replacement:
   (a) one white and one black marble
   (b) two white marbles
   (c) two marbles having the same color
   (d) two marbles having different colors

2. Answer each part of Problem 1 assuming replacement.

3. The integers from 1 to 10, inclusive, are written on slips of paper and placed in an urn. Two slips of paper are drawn without replacement. Find the probability that:
   (a) both numbers are even
   (b) one number is even and one number is odd
   (c) both numbers are prime
   (d) both numbers are divisible by 3
   (e) both numbers are at least 5

4. Answer each part of Problem 3 assuming replacement.

5. The letters of the word PARALLELOGRAM are written on individual slips of paper and placed in an urn. Find the probability of drawing two letters at random and obtaining:
   (a) an L on both selections, assuming replacement after the first pick
   (b) an L on both selections without replacement
   (c) two letters that are *not* vowels, assuming replacement after the first pick
   (d) two letters that are *not* vowels without replacement
   (e) two letters that are the same, assuming replacement after the first pick
   (f) two letters that are the same without replacement

6. Two cards are drawn at random without replacement from a standard deck of playing cards. Find the probability that the two cards:
   (a) are both spades   (c) are picture cards
   (b) are in different suits   (d) have the same face value

7. Answer each part of Problem 6 assuming replacement.

8. A softball team plays two games each weekend, one on Saturday and the other on Sunday. The probability of winning on Saturday is $\frac{3}{5}$, and the probability of winning on Sunday is $\frac{4}{7}$. Find the probability of:
   (a) losing a Saturday game and winning a Sunday game
   (b) winning a Sunday game after already winning a Saturday game
   (c) winning both games
   (d) losing both games

9. John has 10 navy blue socks and 14 black socks in a drawer. If John selects two socks at random, what is the probability they will be the same color?

10. Mary chose at random one of the four numbers 1, 2, 3, and 6. She then chose at random one of the two numbers 1 and 5.
    (a) Draw a tree diagram or list the sample space of all possible pairs of numbers that Mary could choose.
    (b) Find the probability that Mary chose:
        (1) an even number first, followed by an odd number
        (2) *at least* one even number
        (3) the same two numbers
        (4) two even numbers

11. A coach has to purchase uniforms for a team. A uniform consists of one pair of pants and one shirt. The colors available for the pants are black and white. The colors available for the shirt are green, orange, and yellow.
    (a) Draw a tree diagram or list the sample space showing all possible color combinations for one pair of pants and one shirt.
    (b) Find the probability that in the uniform the coach chooses:
        (1) the pants are black and the shirt is orange
        (2) the shirt is green
        (3) the pants and the shirt are of different colors

12. Three coins are tossed simultaneously.
    (a) In how many different, equally likely ways can these coins fall? Draw a tree diagram or list the sample space showing all possible outcomes.
    (b) What is the probability that all three coins will come up the same?
    (c) In how many ways can a tail and two heads appear?
    (d) What is the probability of two tails and one head?

13.5 COUNTING ARRANGEMENTS OF OBJECTS: PERMUTATIONS

KEY IDEAS

A **permutation** is an arrangement of objects in which order matters. A special notation is useful when discussing permutations. The product of the integers from n to 1, inclusive, is called **n factorial** and is written as $n!$ For example,

$$5! = 5 \cdot 4 \cdot 3 \cdot 2 \cdot 1 = 120.$$

Note that n is defined only if n is a positive integer. 0! is defined to be equal to 1. Alternatively, $n!$ may be written as $_nP_n$. For example,

$$_4P_4 = 4! = 4 \cdot 3 \cdot 2 \cdot 1 = 24.$$

ARRANGING *N* OBJECTS IN *N* AVAILABLE POSITIONS. Consider the number of different ways in which the letters A, H, and W can be arranged in a row. There are *three* available letters that can be placed in position (1).

$$\frac{3}{(1)} \quad \frac{}{(2)} \quad \frac{}{(3)}$$

Once the first position is filled, then either of the *two* letters remaining can be inserted in position (2).

$$\frac{3}{(1)} \quad \frac{2}{(2)} \quad \frac{}{(3)}$$

There is *one* letter left, so it must be placed in position (3).

$$\frac{3}{(1)} \quad \frac{2}{(2)} \quad \frac{1}{(3)}$$

The counting principle may be applied in this instance, giving $3 \cdot 2 \cdot 1$ or **6** ways in which the three letters can be arranged. Also note that $3! = 3 \cdot 2 \cdot 1 = 6$. In general, we may state that:

---

n! *represents the number of different ways* **n** *objects can be arranged in* **n** *available positions.*

Since the number of available positions is equal to the number of objects being permuted, each object is used in every arrangement. This process is symbolized by the notation $_nP_n$, which is read as "the permutation of n objects taken n at a time." The notations $_nP_n$ and $n!$ are mathematically equivalent.

Examples ▬▬▬

1. In how many different ways can the letters of the word SQUARE be arranged?

Solution: There are six letters to be arranged.

$$_6P_6 = 6! = 6 \cdot 5 \cdot 4 \cdot 3 \cdot 2 \cdot 1 = 720.$$

The letters of the word SQUARE can be arranged in **720** different ways.

2. In how many ways can six students be arranged in a line if one particular student must be placed first?

Solution: There is only one choice for the first position. Each of the remaining five positions may be filled by any of the remaining five students. Therefore the students can be arranged in

$$1 \cdot {_5P_5} = 1 \cdot 5 \cdot 4 \cdot 3 \cdot 2 \cdot 1 = \textbf{120 ways.}$$

3. In how many different ways can the digits 1, 3, 5, and 7 be arranged to form a four-digit number if repetition of digits

(a) is allowed   (b) is *not* allowed

Solution: (a) There are $4 \cdot 4 \cdot 4 \cdot 4 = \textbf{256}$ ways in which the digits may be arranged, allowing for repetition of digits.

(b) Since each digit can be used only once, there are $_4P_4$ or $4 \cdot 3 \cdot 2 \cdot 1 = \textbf{24}$ ways in which the digits may be arranged without repeating a digit.

4. How many even four-digit numbers can be formed using the digits 1, 2, 3, and 9 if repetition is not allowed?

Solution: An integer is even if it ends in an even number. Therefore the last digit of the number must be 2. The first three positions of the number may be filled in $_3P_3$ ways, so the number of different even numbers that can be formed using these digits is $_3P_3 \cdot 1 = 3 \cdot 2 \cdot 1 \cdot 1 = \textbf{6.}$ ▬▬▬

ARRANGING *N* OBJECTS IN FEWER THAN *N* POSITIONS. Sometimes the number of objects to be arranged is greater than the number of positions that are allocated, so that not all of the objects are used in each possible arrangement. For example, in how many different ways can five students be seated in three chairs arranged in a row? Here the number of students ("objects" that are being permuted) exceeds the number of available positions. The first seat may be filled by any one of the five students. Once this seat is filled, there are four students who can be assigned the second seat, and then any one of the three remaining students can take the third seat:

$$\underset{\text{Seat 1}}{5} \times \underset{\text{Seat 2}}{4} \times \underset{\text{Seat 3}}{3} = \textbf{60 ways.}$$

Therefore, five "objects" can be arranged in three positions by using the three greatest factors of 5! This is indicated by using the notation $_5P_3$:

$$_5P_3 = 5 \cdot 4 \cdot 3 = 60.$$

In general, $_nP_r$ is read as "the permutation of n objects taken r at a time" and is equal to the r greatest factors of $n!$:

$$_nP_r = n(n-1)(n-2)(n-3) \ldots (n-r+1).$$

Example ▬▬▬

5. How many three-digit numbers greater than 500 can be formed from the digits 1, 2, 3, 4, 5, and 6:

(a) without repetition of digits?

(b) with repetition of digits allowed?

Solution: (a) Since the number being formed must be greater than 500, the first digit may be either a 5 or a 6. Any one of the remaining five digits can then be used for the second position, leaving four available digits for the last position:

$$\underset{\text{first digit}}{2} \times \underset{\text{second digit}}{5} \times \underset{\text{third digit}}{4} = 40 \text{ different numbers.}$$

(b) Again, the first digit may be either a 5 or a 6. Since repetition of digits is allowed, six digits are available for the second and the third position:

$$\underset{\text{first digit}}{2} \times \underset{\text{second digit}}{6} \times \underset{\text{third digit}}{6} = 72 \text{ different numbers.}$$

▬▬▬▬

EXERCISE SET 13.5

1. Evaluate each of the following:

(a) 6!   (c) $\dfrac{9!}{4!}$ (e) $\dfrac{7!}{6!}$ (g) $_5P_2$ (i) $_5P_4$

(b) $(9-1)!$ (d) $_4P_4$ (f) $\dfrac{(4+1)!}{(5-2)!}$ (h) $_7P_3$ (j) $2(_3P_3)$

2. Show that $_8P_3$ and $\dfrac{8!}{(8-3)!}$ are equivalent.

3–10. Find the number of ways in which each of the following activities can be performed:

3. Arranging a chemistry book, a calculus book, a history book, and a poetry book on a shelf.

4. Forming a three-digit number using the digits 1, 3, and 5.

5. Seating seven students in a row of seven chairs.

6. Forming six-letter arrangements using letters of the word SQUARE.

7. Forming four-letter arrangements using letters of the word SQUARE without using the same letter twice.

8. Forming a three-digit number using the digits 2, 4, 6, 8 in which repetition of digits is not allowed.

9. Forming a three-digit number using the digits 2, 4, 6, 8 in which repetition of digits is allowed.

10. Arranging the letters of the word TRIANGLE so that a vowel comes first.

11. How many three-digit numbers less than 400 can be formed from the digits 1, 2, 3, 4, and 5:
(a) without repetition of digits?
(b) with repetition of digits allowed?

12. How many four-digit numbers greater than 1000 can be formed from the digits 0, 1, 2, 3, 4, and 5:
(a) without repetition of digits?
(b) with repetition of digits allowed?

13. In how many ways can an odd number be formed from the digits 2, 4, 5, 6, and 8 if:
(a) all the digits are used without repetition.
(b) all the digits are used with repetition.
(c) three of the digits are used without repetition.
(d) three of the digits are used with repetition.

14. What is the probability that, when Allan, Barbara, John, Steve, and George line up, Barbara is first?

15. What is the probability that, when one red, one white, one blue, one green, and one orange marble are placed in a line, the red marble is first and the blue marble is last?

CHAPTER 13 REVIEW EXERCISES

REGENTS REVIEW. *Problems included in this section are similar in form and difficulty to those found on the New York State Regents Examination for Course I of the Three-Year Sequence for High School Mathematics. Problems preceded by an asterisk have actually appeared on a previous Course I Regents Examination.*

*1. In the accompanying figure, the spinner has five equal sections numbered 1 through 5. If the arrow is equally likely to land on any of the sections, what is the probability that it will land on an even number on the next spin?

*2. If the probability that Jones will win the election is 0.6, what is the probability that Jones will not win the election?

*3. A purse contains three pennies, two nickels, four dimes, and five quarters. If one coin is drawn at random from the purse, what is the probability of drawing a dime?

*4. The probability that an event will *not* occur is 7/12. What is the probability that the event will occur?

*5. How many different arrangements of four digits can be formed from the digits 2, 5, 6, and 7 if each digit is used only once in each arrangement?

*6. There are three ways of going from town A to town B and six ways of going from town B to town C. Find the total number of ways in which a person can go from town A to town B to town C.

*7. A fair coin and a fair die are tossed simultaneously. What is the total number of possible outcomes in the sample space?

*8. If one card is drawn from a standard deck of 52 playing cards, what is the probability that the card is a red 7?

*9. What integer does $\dfrac{4!}{3!}$ equal?

*10. From a standard deck of 52 cards, one card is drawn at random. What is the probability that the card is *not* a heart?

*11. A six-sided fair die is rolled. What is the probability of rolling a 3 or a 6?

*12. In how many different ways can the subjects math, English, social studies, and science be scheduled during the first four periods of the school day?

*13. An urn contains three red marbles and two green marbles. One marble is randomly selected, its color is noted, and it is *not* replaced. A second marble is then selected and its color is noted.
(a) Draw a tree diagram or list the sample space showing all possible outcomes.
(b) Find the probability that:
(1) both marbles selected are green.
(2) neither marble selected is green.
(3) at least one marble selected is green.

*14. A quarter, a dime, a nickel, and a penny are in a box. Ann draws one coin, replaces it, and draws a coin once again.
(a) Draw a tree diagram or list the sample of all possible pairs of outcomes for this experiment.
(b) What is the probability that the dime will be drawn at least once?
(c) What is the probability that the total value of the coins drawn will be exactly 30¢?

*15. In a certain class, there are four students in the first row: three girls, Ann, Barbara, and Cathy, and one boy, David. The teacher called one of these students to the board to solve a problem. When the problem was done, the teacher called one of the remaining students in the first row to do a second problem at the board.
(a) Draw a tree diagram or list the sample space of all possible pairs of names for calling two students to the board.
(b) Find the probability that the teacher called Ann first and Barbara second.
(c) Find the probability that the teacher called two girls to the board.
(d) Find the probability that David was one of the two students called.

*16. For a class picnic, the school cafeteria prepared a box lunch for each student, consisting of a sandwich and a cookie. The sandwiches were tuna, ham, or peanut butter, and the cookies were oatmeal or chocolate chip.

    (a) Draw a tree diagram or list a sample space showing all possible combinations of one sandwich and one cookie that could be in the boxes.

    (b) If each combination was equally likely to be in any one of the boxes, what is the probability that a box chosen at random contained:

        (1) a peanut butter sandwich and an oatmeal cookie

        (2) a ham sandwich

        (3) a sandwich that was *not* tuna

*17. The diagram below represents an arrow attached to a cardboard disk. The arrow is free to spin, but cannot land on a line. The disk is divided into three regions of equal area, one of which is red and the other is blue.

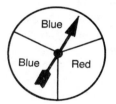

    (a) For any one spin, what is the probability of the arrow:

        (1) landing on red   (2) landing on blue

    (b) The arrow is spun twice and each outcome is recorded. What is the probability of the arrow:

        (1) landing on red on the first spin and blue on the second spin

        (2) landing on blue on both spins

        (3) *not* landing on blue on either spin

        (4) landing on the same color on both spins

CHAPTER 14

Statistics

14.1 FINDING THE MEAN, MEDIAN, AND MODE

_____ KEY IDEAS _____

Statistics is the branch of mathematics that is involved with methods of collecting, organizing, displaying, and interpreting *data*. **Data** are simply facts and figures. Numerical data may be referred to as *data values, scores,* or *numbers.* The *mean, mode,* and *median* are single numbers that help describe how the individual scores in a set are distributed in value.

THE MEAN. The **arithmetic mean** is another name for the average of a set of scores. The mean of a set of scores is found by dividing the sum of the scores by the number of scores. For example, the mean of 76, 82, and 85 is 81 since

$$\text{Mean} = \frac{76 + 82 + 85}{3} = \frac{243}{3} = \mathbf{81}.$$

Notice that, since the individual scores are fairly close in value, the mean of 81 represents a central value about which the scores in the original data set are clustered. The mean is an example of a **measure of central tendency.**

If a set of scores includes a number that differs by a large amount from the other numbers in the group, then the mean is *not* a good measure of central tendency. For example, the mean of the set of numbers 1, 2, 5, and 200 is 52 since

$$\text{Mean} = \frac{1 + 2 + 5 + 200}{4} = \frac{208}{4} = \mathbf{52}.$$

In this case, the mean does not provide useful information on how the individual data values in the set are distributed.

THE MODE.   The **mode** of a set of data values is the number in the set that appears most frequently. For example, in the set of numbers

$$19, 23, 19, 18, 27, 19, 15, 23, 16$$

the number 19 occurs three times, 23 occurs two times, and each of the remaining numbers appears only once. The mode of this set of numbers is 19.

A set of numbers may have *more than one* mode. The set 15, 9, 8, 9, 11, 15 has two modes, 15 and 9.

If every number in a set appears the same number of times, then the set of numbers has *no* mode. The set of numbers 2, 4, 6, 8, 10 has no mode

THE MEDIAN.   The mean, mode, and median are measures of central tendency. The **median** of a set of data values is the "middle" value after the data values are arranged in size order. To find the median of the set of numbers 18, 11, 50, 23, 37, arrange the numbers in increasing (or decreasing) order:

$$11, 18, \mathbf{23}, 37, 50$$

Median is the middle score.

The "middle" value is 23, so 23 is the median of this group of numbers. Notice that two numbers in the set are below the median and two numbers in the set are above the median. The median always divides a set of numbers into two groups that have the same number of values.

The following set of numbers contains an even number of values:

$$6, 17, 18, 22, 23, 31$$

Median is the average of the two middle values.

The median of this set is the *average* of the two middle values:

$$\text{Median} = \frac{18 + 22}{2} = \frac{40}{2} = \mathbf{20}$$

Examples

1. The average of a set of four numbers is 78. If three of the numbers in the set are 71, 74, and 83, what is the fourth number?

Solution: Let $x =$ fourth number of the set.

$$\frac{71 + 74 + 83 + x}{4} = 78$$

$$71 + 74 + 83 + x = 4(78)$$

$$228 + x = 312$$

$$x = 312 - 228 = \mathbf{84}$$

2. If a group of data consists of the numbers 2, 2, 5, 6, 15, which of the following is true?

    (1) Median > mean   (3) Mode < median

    (2) Mean = mode   (4) Median = mode

Solution: $\text{Mean} = \dfrac{2 + 2 + 5 + 6 + 15}{5} = \dfrac{30}{5} = 6$

                 $\text{Mode} = 2$

                 $\text{Median} = 5$

The mode is less than the median. The correct answer is **choice (3)**.

QUARTILES.   **Quartiles** are numbers that separate a set of scores arranged in size order into *four* equal groups, so that each group contains $\frac{1}{4}$ or 25% of the original number of scores. The median of the original set of data values divides the set into two equal subgroups. The first (lower) and third (upper) quartiles are the medians of these two subgroups. The median of the original set of scores is the second (middle) quartile.

Examples

3. Find the lower, second, and upper quartiles for the following set of scores: 33, 18, 65, 25, 21, 78, 84, 65, 52, 45, 60, and 72.

Solution: After arranging the scores in increasing order, find the median for the whole set. Then find the median of each subgroup.

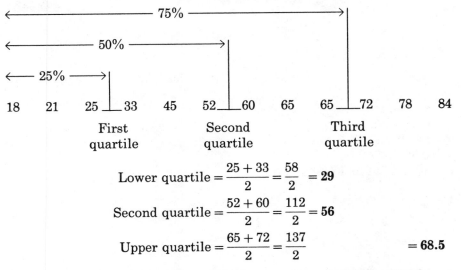

$$\text{Lower quartile} = \frac{25 + 33}{2} = \frac{58}{2} = \textbf{29}$$

$$\text{Second quartile} = \frac{52 + 60}{2} = \frac{112}{2} = \textbf{56}$$

$$\text{Upper quartile} = \frac{65 + 72}{2} = \frac{137}{2} = \textbf{68.5}$$

Keep in mind that 25% of the original scores are at or below the lower quartile mark of 29; 50% of the original scores are at or below the second quartile (median) mark of 56; 75% of the original scores are at or below the upper quartile mark of 68.5.

4. If a number is randomly selected from the set 8, 5, 13, 5, 7, and 10, find the probability that the number will be:
   (a) greater than the mean
   (b) greater than or equal to the mode
   (c) exactly equal to the median

Solutions: (a) Mean $= \dfrac{8 + 5 + 13 + 5 + 7 + 10}{6} = 8$

$$P(X > 8) = \frac{\text{Number of scores greater than 8}}{\text{Total number of scores}} = \frac{2}{6} = \frac{1}{3}$$

(b) The mode is 5. Every number in this set is greater than or equal to 5.

$$P(x > 5) = \frac{\text{Number of scores} \geq 5}{\text{Total number of scores}} = \frac{6}{6} = 1$$

(c) To find the median, first arrange the numbers in size order.

$$5, 5, 7, 8, 10, 13$$

The median is the middle score. Since there is an even number of scores,

$$\text{Median} = \frac{7 + 8}{2} = 7.5$$

$$P(X = \text{median} = 7.5) = \frac{0}{6} = 0$$

EXERCISE SET 14.1

1–8. Find the mean, the median, and the mode (if any) of each set of numbers.

1. 6, 9, 4, 2, 9

2. 60, 70, 80, 90

3. 34, 45, 68, 72, 51, 49

4. 0.84, 0.42, 0.16

5. 13, 14, 15, 16, 87, 86, 85, 84

6. $\dfrac{1}{3}, \dfrac{1}{2}, \dfrac{1}{4}, \dfrac{1}{3}, \dfrac{1}{5}, \dfrac{1}{3}, 1$

7. 123, 319, 214, 546, 189, 214, 123

8. $\dfrac{1}{2}, 0.6, \dfrac{3}{4}, 0.2, \dfrac{1}{5}, 0.3$

9. Express, in terms of x, the mean of
   (a) $(2x - 1)$ and $(6x + 1)$ (b) x, $(7x - 1)$, and $(4x + 7)$

10. The average of five numbers is 84. If four of the numbers are 71, 81, 94, and 77, what is the fifth number?

11. The average of a set of four numbers is 79. If the sum of three of the numbers is 231, what is the other number of the set?

12. Susan received 78, 89, and 82 on her first three exams in mathematics. What is the lowest score she can receive on her next mathematics exam and have an exam average of at least 85?

13. What is the mean number of sides in a group of polygons that consists of two triangles, one parallelogram, and one hexagon?

14. If a group of data consists of the numbers 8, 13, 8, 7, 4, which is true?
    (1) Median > mean   (3) Mode < median
    (2) Mean = mode   (4) Median = mode

15. For the group of data 3, 3, 5, 8, 18, which is true?
    (1) Median > mean   (3) Mean > mode
    (2) Mode > mean   (4) Median = mode

16. A number is selected at random from the set 2, 2, 2, 2, 3, 3, 3, 7. Find the probability that the number selected is:
    (a) the mode   (c) the median
    (b) the mean   (d) the upper quartile

17. Eight of Mr. Smith's students weigh 79, 60, 80, 50, 55, 100, 80, and 72 pounds. If one of the students is picked at random, find the probability that the student's weight will be:
    (a) greater than the mean
    (b) exactly equal to the median
    (c) less than the mode

18–21. For each of the following sets of numbers, find the lower, second, and upper quartiles:
18. 15, 18, 25, 31, 35, 35, 43, 50
19. 1, 3, 3, 4, 4, 4, 4, 5, 5, 5, 6, 6
20. 90, 56, 40, 65, 40, 36, 27, 82, 74, 89, 48, 69
21. 70, 51, 75, 89, 93, 35, 29, 64, 80, 56, 65, 65, 48, 79, 34, 60

14.2   CONSTRUCTING FREQUENCY TABLES AND HISTOGRAMS

───────────── KEY IDEAS ─────────────

The number of times a particular data value occurs in a data list is called the **frequency** of the data value. Large numbers of data may be more efficiently handled if the data are organized into a *frequency table* that lists each data value and its frequency. A *histogram* is a type of bar graph that provides a more visually appealing representation of the data contained in the frequency table.

MAKING FREQUENCY TABLES.   Data can be grouped by frequency for further analysis by inspecting the original list of data and *tallying* each occurrence of a data value. For example, suppose that a class of 25 students received the following scores on a mathematics exam: 58, 70, 60, 65, 68, 70, 90, 70, 72, 74, 70, 70, 75, 78, 80, 96, 75, 80, 83, 80, 83, 88, 90, 65, 75. Here is a more convenient way of representing the same set of data:

Exam Score	Tally	Frequency
58	/	1
60	/	1
65	//	2
68	/	1
70	##/	5
72	/	1
74	/	1
75	///	3
78	/	1
80	///	3
83	//	2
88	/	1
90	//	2
96	/	1

Sum = 25

The mode is 70 since it has a frequency of 5, which is the largest number in the frequency column. There are 25 scores; the median is the thirteenth score since 12 scores are below this score and 12 scores are above it. By adding the entries in the frequency column, you see that the twelfth score is 74. Since the next three scores are each 75, the *thirteenth* score is 75. The median, therefore, is **75**.

MAKING FREQUENCY TABLES USING INTERVALS.   Sometimes data are more easily managed if they are first divided into intervals having a convenient width. The data in the preceding example may be grouped by frequency within intervals having a uniform width of 10 points. The intervals must be selected so that they accommodate both the lowest and the highest score. Since the lowest score is 58, the first interval is 50–59. The highest score is 96, so the last interval is 90–99.

Interval	Tally	Frequency
50–59	/	-
60–69	////	4
70–79	₩₩ ₩₩ /	11
80–89	₩₩ /	6
90–99	///	3

Sum = 25

A quick glance at the table gives a good idea of how the test grades are distributed, with most of the scores falling between 70 and 79.

INTERPRETING FREQUENCY HISTOGRAMS.   Figure 14.1 is a histogram that shows the distribution of scores on a math test. Notice that the bars have the same width and are drawn next to one another. The heights of the bars represent the frequency (read from the vertical axis) for each interval of test scores. For example, two students had test scores between 71 and 75. No student received a score between 66 and 70. The total number of students who took the math test is 15 since

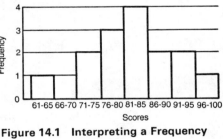

Figure 14.1   Interpreting a Frequency Histogram

$$1 + 2 + 3 + 4 + 2 + 2 + 1 = 15.$$

DRAWING FREQUENCY HISTOGRAMS.   Here is how to draw a frequency histogram based on the accompanying frequency table.

Interval	Frequency
50–59	1
60–69	4
70–79	11
80–89	6
90–99	3

Step 1. Using graph paper, draw the coordinate axes in the first quadrant. Call the vertical axis "Frequency," and the horizontal axis "Test scores."

Step 2. Label the vertical axis in units of 1.

Step 3. Label the horizontal axis so that each interval has the *same* width. The width may be of any convenient size.

Step 4. For each interval, draw vertical bars next to one another. The frequency of each interval determines the bar height.

Figure 14.2 shows the completed frequency histogram.

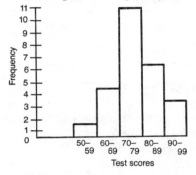

Figure 14.2 Drawing a Frequency Histogram

Examples

1. For the accompanying frequency table, answer the following questions:

(a) Which interval contains the median?

(b) Which interval contains the lower quartile?

(c) Which interval contains the upper quartile?

Interval	Frequency
1–15	1
16–30	2
31–45	6
46–60	4
61–75	2
76–90	5

Solutions: (a) There is a total of 20 scores. The median is the middle value, so it lies between the 10th and 11th scores. By accumulating frequencies, we know that the fourth interval contains the 10th, 11th, 12th, and 13th scores. Therefore, the interval **46–60** contains the median.

(b) The lower quartile is the number at or below which 25% of the scores fall. Since there is a total of 20 scores,

$$25\% \text{ of } 20 = \frac{1}{4} \times 20 = 5.$$

Adding frequencies shows that the 5th score is found in the third interval, so the lower quartile is contained in the interval **31–45**.

(c) The upper quartile is the number at or below which 75% of the scores fall. Since there is a total of 20 scores,

$$75\% \text{ of } 20 = \frac{3}{4} \times 20 = 15.$$

Adding frequencies reveals that the 15th score is found in the fifth interval, so the upper quartile is contained in the interval **61–75**.

2. A newspaper reporter stopped 20 people in the street and asked them how many times they had changed jobs. The results of this survey are summarized in the accompanying table.

Number of Job Changes	Frequency
0	4
1	5
2	4
3	2
4	4
5	1

(a) Draw a frequency histogram for these data.
(b) What is the mode?
(c) What is the mean number of job changes?
(d) If one of the people interviewed is selected at random, what is the probability that he or she never changed jobs?

Solutions: (a)

(b) The mode is **one** job change since its frequency, 5, is greater than any other frequency in the table.

(c) Find the sum of the number of job changes by multiplying each number of job changes by its frequency [see column (3) of the accompanying table] and adding these products. Then divide this sum by the total number of people [the sum of the frequencies in column (2)].

(1)	(2)	(3)
Number of Job Changes	**Frequency**	**Number × Frequency**
0	4	0
1	5	5
2	4	8
3	2	6
4	4	16
5	1	5

$$\text{Sum} = 20 \qquad\qquad \text{Total} = 40 \text{ job changes}$$

$$\text{Mean} = \frac{\text{Sum of column (3)}}{\text{Sum of column (2)}}$$

$$= \frac{40}{20} = 2$$

The mean is 2, so the group of people interviewed have an average of **2 job changes**

(d) $P(\text{job changes} = 0) = \dfrac{\text{Frequency of 0 job changes}}{\text{Sum of frequencies}}$

$$= \frac{4}{20} = \frac{1}{5}$$

EXERCISE SET 14.2

1. The distribution of grades in a college mathematics class is given in the accompanying table.

Grade	Frequency
A	2
B	6
C	8
D	3
F	1

(a) Using graph paper, draw a frequency histogram.
(b) How many students are in the class?
(c) Which grade is the mode?
(d) Which grade represents the lower quartile?

(e) What percent of students received a grade of B or higher?

(f) If a student from the class is selected at random, what is the probability that the student received a grade of at least C?

(g) If a student from the class is selected at random, what is the probability that the student did *not* receive a grade of F?

2. The test scores of 15 students are 86, 57, 69, 82, 91, 87, 75, 84, 68, 65, 91, 88, 81, 62, 72.

   (a) Copy and complete the table.

Interval	Frequency
90–99	
80–89	
70–79	
60–69	
50–59	

   (b) On graph paper, draw a frequency histogram based on the data.

   (c) In which interval does the median lie?

   (d) What is the probability that a student, selected at random, scored above 89 on this test?

3. The points scored by Rosa in 20 basketball games are 35, 33, 27, 35, 29, 37, 32, 35, 35, 32, 23, 37, 32, 29, 26, 30, 28, 31, 29, 35.

   (a) Find the mode.

   (b) Copy and complete the table below.

Interval	Tally	Frequency
35–37		
32–34		
29–31		
26–28		
23–25		

   (c) Construct a frequency histogram based on the table completed in part (b).

   (d) In what interval does the median lie?

4. The following data represent the heights of 14 students in a certain class: 65, 63, 68, 59, 74, 59, 68, 61, 64, 60, 69, 72, 55, 64.
    (a) Copy and complete the table below.

Interval	Number (frequency)
55–58	
59–62	
63–66	
67–70	
71–71	

   (b) On graph paper, construct a frequency histogram based on the data.
   (c) The median is contained in which interval?

5. A class record showed the following number of misspelled words in each of 25 essays.

Misspelled Words	Frequency (Number of Essays)
0	1
1	0
2	3
3	5
4	4
5	9
6	3

   (a) On graph paper, construct a frequency histogram based on the data.
   (b) Find the mean number of misspelled words.
   (c) Find the median number of misspelled words.
   (d) Find the mode number of misspelled words.

6. The following table represents the ages of the teachers at a school.

Interval	Number (f)
53–57	4
48–52	8
43–47	6
38–42	4
33–37	2
28–32	4
23–27	2

(a) In what interval is the median?
(b) A teacher is chosen at random from this school. What is the probability that the teacher's age is in the interval 33–37?
(c) What is the probability that the age of a teacher from this school is less than 38?
(d) What is the probability that a teacher from this school is older than 57?
(e) What percent of the teachers are in the interval 43–47?

7. Each of 20 students was asked to select *one* number from the following choices: 6, 7, 8, 9, 10. The table below gives the distribution of these selections.

Number	Frequency
6	3
7	10
8	1
9	4
10	2

(a) Draw a frequency histogram for the given data.
(b) Find the mode.
(c) What is the probability that a student selected the number 7?
(d) What is the probability that a student selected a number less than 6?

8. The table below gives the distribution of test scores for a class of 20 students.

Test Score Interval	Number of Students (frequency)
91–100	1
81–90	3
71–80	3
61–70	7
51–60	6

(a) Draw a frequency histogram for the given data.
(b) Which interval contains the median?
(c) Which interval contains the lower quartile?
(d) What is the probability that a student selected at random scored above 90?

14.3 CONSTRUCTING CUMULATIVE FREQUENCY HISTOGRAMS

_____ KEY IDEAS _____

Cumulative frequency tables and histograms display, for each given interval, the sum of the number of scores in all preceding intervals up to and including those contained in the interval being studied.

CONSTRUCTING CUMULATIVE FREQUENCY TABLES.　In order to answer questions based on the accompanying frequency table, such as "How many students received 79 or less on the exam?" or "In what interval does the median lie?" it is helpful to add a *cumulative frequency* column to the table. The first entry in this column is the frequency for the first interval. The entry in the cumulative frequency column for the next interval is obtained by adding the number in the frequency column for the current interval to the entry in the cumulative frequency column for the preceding interval. This process is repeated for each of the other intervals.

Interval	Frequency
50–59	1
60–69	4
70–79	11
80–89	6
90–99	3

Interval	Frequency	Cumulative	
		Frequency	Interval
50–59	1	1	50–59
60–69	4	5 $(4+1=5)$	50–69
70–79	11	16 $(11+5=16)$	50–79
80–89	6	22 $(6+16=22)$	50–89
90–99	3	25 $(3+22=25)$	50–99

Here are some observations that you can make from the cumulative frequency table:

● Sixteen students received grades of 79 or less on the exam.

● The lower quartile is contained in the third interval. Since there are 25 scores and

$$25\% \text{ of } 25 = \frac{1}{4} \times 25 = 6.25,$$

the lower quartile is located in the interval that includes the 6th and 7th scores, which is the interval 70–79.

● Eighty-eight percent ($\frac{22}{25} = 0.88 = 88\%$) of the class received grades of 89 or less.

DRAWING CUMULATIVE FREQUENCY HISTOGRAMS.
Cumulative frequency histograms are drawn using the same procedure as for frequency histograms.

Examples ▬▬▬

1. The accompanying table is a cumulative frequency table of student test scores.

Interval	Cumulative	
	Frequency	Interval
50–59	3	50–59
60–69	4	50–69
70–79	10	50–79
80–89	14	50–89
90–99	16	50–99

(a) Draw a cumulative frequency histogram.
(b) Which interval contains the lower quartile?
(c) Which interval contains the median?

Solutions: (a)

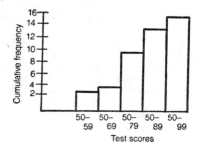

Figure 14.3   Cumulative Frequency Histogram

(b)   The lower quartile is the number at or below which 25% of the total number of scores falls. The total number of scores is 16, and

$$25\% \text{ of } 16 = \frac{1}{4} \times 16 = 4$$

The 4th score up from the lowest score falls in the **second interval, 60–69**.

(c) The median is the middle score. Since there are 16 scores, the median is between the 8th and 9th scores, which places it in the **third interval, 70–79**.   ▰▰▰▰

2.   On the basis of the cumulative frequency table in Example 1, construct a frequency histogram.

Solution: The frequency of an interval after the first can be obtained by finding the difference between its cumulative frequency and the cumulative frequency of the interval preceding it. Here are the frequency histogram and the completed frequency table on which it is based.

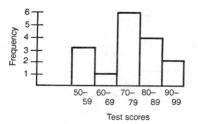

Frequency Histogram

Interval	Cumulative Frequency	Frequency	Interval
50–59	3	3	50–59
50–69	4	1 (=4 − 3)	60–69
50–79	10	6 (=10 − 4)	70–79
50–89	14	4 (=14 − 10)	80–89
50–99	16	2 (=16 − 14)	90–99

3. The accompanying cumulative frequency histogram shows the number of home runs hit by members of a high school baseball team.

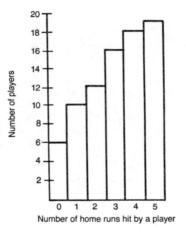

Cumulative Frequency Histogram

(a) How many students are on the baseball team?
(b) How many players each hit more than two home runs?
(c) What is the median number of home runs?
(d) Draw a frequency histogram.

Solution: (a) For each number of home runs in this cumulative frequency histogram, the height of the bar was obtained by adding the number of players who hit that number of home runs to the height of the preceding (lower) bar. The height of the last (tallest) bar can be interpreted as "19 *or fewer* players hit five home runs," so the total number of players is **19**.

(b) According to the height of the third bar, 12 players hit two *or fewer* home runs. Since there is a total of 19 players on the team, 19 − 12 or **7** players each hit more than two home runs.

(c) If the 19 players are arranged in order according to the number of home runs hit, then the median number of home runs is the number of home runs hit by the middle player. In a group of 19, the 10th player is in the middle. According to the graph, the first six players hit zero home runs, and the 7th, 8th, 9th, and 10th players each hit one home run. The median number of home runs is **one**.

(d) Make a table having the column headings "Home runs" and "Cumulative Frequency." Record in the "Cumulative Frequency" column the heights of the bars for 0, 1, 2, 3, 4, and 5 home runs. Extend the table to include the frequencies for each number of home runs. Each frequency after the first is obtained by subtracting each cumulative frequency from the cumulative frequency that comes before it. The frequency table and the frequency histogram are shown below.

Home runs	Cumulative Frequency	Home runs	Frequency
0	6	0	6
1 or less	10	1	4 (= 10 − 6)
2 or less	12	2	2 (= 12 − 10)
3 or less	16	3	4 (= 16 − 12)
4 or less	18	4	2 (= 18 − 16)
5 or less	19	5	1 (= 19 − 18)

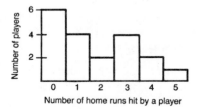

Number of home runs hit by a player

PERCENTILES AND CUMULATIVE FREQUENCY POLYGONS.   A vertical percent scale has been added to the cumulative frequency histogram in Figure 14.3. The height of the rightmost (tallest) bar represents the accumulated frequency of the test scores (16), so it is labeled as 100%. The point of intersection of the axes is labeled as 0% since there are clearly no scores at this level. The vertical segment determined by the 0% and 100% markings is then divided into four segments having the same length, with the division points labeled as 25%, 50%, and 75%. The vertical axis now represents the cumulative *relative* frequency.

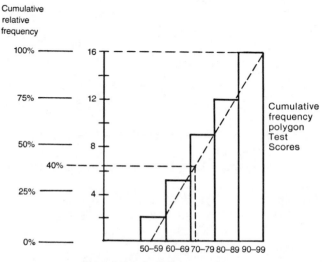

Cumulative Frequency Histogram

If the upper right vertices of the rectangular bars of a cumulative frequency histogram are joined with a line segment, the graph that is formed is called a cumulative frequency *polygon*.

Notice that the 40th *percentile* has been marked and is the point at which 40% of the total number of scores lie or fall below. *Percentile* is a more general term than *quartile*. Quartiles divide the scores into four equal groups, while percentiles divide the scores into 100 equal groups. A *percentile* is a number that represents the percent of the total number of scores that fall at or below that number. According to Figure 14.3, the 40th percentile falls in the interval 70–79 and is approximately equal to a score of 74. Since the 40th percentile is approximately 74, 40% of the total number of scores are less than or equal to 74.

EXERCISE SET 14.3

1. The table below shows the distribution of scores of 30 students on a test.

Scores	Frequency	Cumulative Frequency
91–100	3	
81–90	11	
71–80	8	
61–70	6	
51–60	1	
41–50	1	

(a) Using the data in the "Frequency" column of the table, draw a frequency histogram.
(b) Copy the table and fill in the column headed "Cumulative Frequency."
(c) Using the data in the "Cumulative Frequency" column of the table, draw a cumulative frequency histogram

2. The following table represents the ages of students hired for various summer jobs at a state park in New York:

Age Interval	Cumulative Frequency
11–12	2
13–14	6
15–16	9
17–18	15
19–21	20

(a) Draw a cumulative frequency histogram.
(b) What was the total number of students hired?
(c) In which interval does the median lie?
(d) How many students aged 13 or 14 were hired?

3. On a test, 15 students received the following grades: 17, 14, 16, 18, 17, 19, 15, 15, 16, 13, 17, 12, 18, 16, 17.

(a) Copy and complete the table below.

Grade	Frequency	Cumulative Frequency
12		
13		
14		
15		
16		
17		
18		
19		

(b) Find the median.
(c) Find the mode.
(d) Find the 75th percentile.

4. The following diagram is a cumulative frequency histogram of raw scores on a mathematics examination:

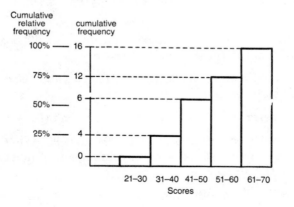

(a) How many students took the examination?
(b) How many students had scores less than or equal to 60?
(c) What percent of the students had scores less than or equal to 60?
(d) Which interval contains the median?
(e) Which interval contains the lower quartile?

5. The cumulative frequency histogram below shows the number of weeks of annual vacation for workers at a company.

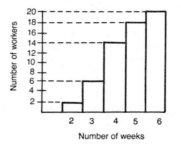

(a) How many workers are employed by the company?
(b) How many workers receive more than 4 weeks of vacation?
(c) Find the median number of weeks of vacation.
(d) Using the data from parts (a), (b), and (c), draw a frequency histogram.

CHAPTER 14 REVIEW EXERCISES

REGENTS REVIEW.   *Problems included in this section are similar in form and difficulty to those found on the New York State Regents Examination for Course I of the Three-Year Sequence for High School Mathematics. Problems preceded by an asterisk have actually appeared on a previous Course I Regents Examination.*

*1. The test results from a certain examination were 60, 65, 65, 70, 75, 90, and 95. What is the median test score?

*2. If student heights are 176 cm, 172 cm, 160 cm, and 160 cm, what is the mean height of these students?

*3. Express, in terms of x, the mean of $(2x - 8)$ and $(6x + 4)$.

*4. A student received test scores of 82, 94, and 96. What must she receive as a fourth test score so that the mean of her four scores will be exactly 90?

*5. Find the mode of the following data: 10, 12, 14, 20, 14, 15, 12, 17, 12.

*6. Express the mean of $(2x + 1)$, $(x + 1)$, and $(3x - 8)$ in terms of x

*7. On a math test, a score of 60 was the lower quartile (25th percentile). If 20 students took the test, how many students received scores of 60 or below?

*8. Which set of data has more than one mode?
(1) 2, 2, 4, 6, 7, 9　(3) 2, 2, 2, 6, 7, 9
(2) 2, 2, 4, 6, 9, 9　(4) 2, 3, 4, 6, 9, 9

*9. Five girls in a club reported the number of boxes of cookies that they sold: 20, 20, 40, 50, and 70. Which is true?
(1) The median is 20.　(3) The median is equal to the mean.
(2) The mean is 20.　(4) The median is equal to the mode.

*10. For which set of data do the mean, median, and mode all have the same value?
(1) 1, 3, 3, 3, 5　(3) 1, 1, 1, 2, 5
(2) 1, 1, 2, 5, 6　(4) 1, 1, 3, 5, 10

*11. For the data 2, 2, 4, 5, 12, which statement is true?
(1) mean = median　(3) mean < mode
(2) mean > mode　(4) mode = median

12. Let p represent the statement "The median is equal to the mode," and q represent the statement "The mean is equal to the median." For which set of numbers is $p \wedge q$ true?
(1) 2, 2, 5　(3) 2, 3, 3, 4
(2) 2, 5, 5　(4) 2, 2, 5, 5

13. A number is selected at random from the set 2, 2, 3, 3, 3, 4, 4, 4, 4. Find the probability that the number is:
(a) the mode　(b) the median　(c) the mean

*14. The accompanying histogram shows the distribution of student ages in a ninth grade class. Which age is the mode?

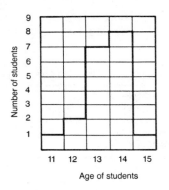

*15. The following data represent the heights of 15 students in a certain class: 63, 59, 64, 61, 62, 60, 58, 60, 62, 60, 67, 65, 68, 61, 60.
(a) Copy and complete the table below.

Height	Number (frequency)
58	
59	
60	
61	
62	
63	
64	
65	
66	
67	
68	

(b) Find the mean.
(c) Find the median.
(d) Find the mode.

*16. The following data are test scores for a class of 16 students: 96, 83, 91, 77, 58, 88, 80, 62, 89, 100, 87, 93, 64, 98, 88, 86.
(a) Copy and complete the following table.

Interval	Number (frequency)
91–100	
81–90	
71–80	
61–70	
51–60	

(b) On graph paper, construct a frequency histogram based on the data.
(c) Which interval contains the median?
(d) Which interval contains the lower quartile?

*17. The frequency histogram below shows the distribution of scores on a math test.

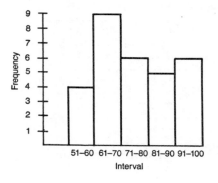

(a) Copy and complete the table.

Scores	Frequency	Cumulative Frequency
51–60		
61–70		
71–80		
81–90		
91–100		

(b) How many students took the math test?
(c) Which interval contains the upper quartile?
(d) How many students scored above 80?
(e) Using the table completed in part (a), draw a cumulative frequency histogram.

*18. The following table shows the distribution of test grades of students on a math test:

Interval	Cumulative Frequency
40–49	1
50–59	4
60–69	6
70–79	11
80–89	17
90–99	20

    (a) On graph paper, construct a cumulative frequency histogram based on the data.
    (b) Which interval contains the median?
    (c) Which interval contains the greatest number of scores?
    (d) Which interval contains the lower quartile?

*19. A math test was given to Ms. Jones' class. The table below shows the time the students took to complete the test.

Time (in minutes)	Frequency
38	7
36	3
34	1
32	6
30	10

Using the data in the table, determine the
    (a) mode   (b) median
    (c) mean, to the *nearest tenth*
    (d) probability that a student chosen at random completed the test in a time that was less than the mean

Answers to Chapter Review Exercises

CHAPTER 1

1. -4	14. 3	27. 4
2. -4	15. -13	28. 17/4
3. -4	16. $-1/4$	29. 36
4. 4	17. 8	30. 12
5. -70	18. -6	31. 128
6. $-1/32$	19. $-2/5$	32. -1
7. -14	20. 5/14	33. -17
8. -5	21. $-1/8$	34. v^{13}
9. -11	22. 1/6	35. e^{-1} or $1/e$
10. 3	23. $-2/9$	36. q^8
11. -2	24. 5/7	37. r^8
12. $-7/8$	25. 4	38. x^{10}
13. 9	26. 1	

39. (a) 48 (c) 144 (e) 1/81 (g) 0
    (b) -36 (d) 144 (f) -64 (h) -12
40. (a) 40 (c) 25 (e) 28 (g) 3 (i) -17
    (b) 400 (d) 1/25 (f) 10 (h) 4 (j) 3
41. (a) $6x$ (c) $2x+6$ (e) $-3-3x$
    (b) $8y$ (d) $7-2x$ (f) $9x-6$
42. (a) -4 (c) 1/7 (e) 1/5 (g) 3/2
    (b) 7 (d) 3 (f) -3 (h) 6
43. (3) Whole numbers

CHAPTER 2

1. $q \to p$	11. (1)	21. (4)
2. $q \leftrightarrow p$	12. (2)	22. (2)
3. $\sim p \to q$	13. (1)	23. (4)
4. $\sim q \to \sim p$	14. (4)	24. (3)
5. $p \wedge \sim q$	15. (4)	25. (3)
6. (4)	16. (1)	26. (4)
7. (1)	17. (3)	27. (3)
8. (3)	18. (4)	28. (b) Yes.
9. (1)	19. (3)	29. (b) Yes.
10. (3)	20. (3)	(c) (1)

30. (b) The last column of the truth table shows the statement is always true.
(c) (1)
31. (a) I am happy.
(b) $7 - x = 5$
(c) Elaine will get an A.
(d) I will stay home.
(e) The winds are not above 20 knots.

CHAPTER 3

1. $x = 11$
2. $a = 1.6$
3. $x = 3$
4. 9
5. $x = 1200$
6. $z = -2$
7. 7%
8. $y = 0.5$
9. $x = 1$
10. 7
11. $x = 1$
12. 3.5 centimeters
13. $a = 18$

14. 240
15. $y = 475$
16. $x = 2$
17. $y = 24$
18. $y = 3$
19. 120 centimeters
20. width $= 7$
length $= 24$
21. $x = -9$
22. 29, 30, and 31
23. 13/18
24. 6

25. 40
26. 2 and 3
27. (2)
28. (1)
29. (3)
30. (3)
31. (3)
32. (4)
33. (3)
34. (3)
35. (3)

CHAPTER 4

1. $y = \dfrac{bx + 2}{a}$
2. $E = IR$
3. $A = 56$
4. $\{-2, 0, 2\}$
5. $B = 3V/h$
6. $A = 10$
7. (a) $x \geq -3$
8. (1)

9. (4)
10. (1)
11. (3)
12. (3)
13. (3)
14. (1)
15. (1)
16. (4)

17. $L = 19$, $W = 11$
18. 2 and 8
19. 26, 27, and 28
20. 8 and 19
21. $-1 \leq x < 2$
22. $106 < x < 286$
23. $-3 \leq x < 3$
24. $-n + 1$

CHAPTER 5

1. $7a - 3b - 3c$
2. $2x^2 + x + 3$
3. $6x^3 + 5x - 2$
4. $3x^2 + 5x - 2$
5. $3x^2 + 5x - 10$
6. $2h$
7. $2x^2 + 7x + 6$
8. $-5x$
9. $6x - 1$
10. $5x$
11. $24y^9$

12. $a^2 - 4ab + 4b^2$
13. $3x^2 + 7x - 4$
14. $-6x$
15. 5
16. $2x^4 - x^3 - 6x^2 + 13x - 5$
17. $4x - 4$
18. $2x^2 - 6x - 5$
19. $-3x^2 - 5x + 7$
20. $7x^2 - 8x + 2$
21. (2)
22. (4)

23. (3)
24. (1)
25. (3)
26. (3)
27. (3)
28. (2)
29. (4)
30. (1)
31. (4)
32. (3)
33. (4)

CHAPTER 6

1. $x - 7$
2. $(x + 5)(x - 3)$
3. $(x + 6)(x - 5)$
4. $(x + 6)(x - 6)$
5. x
6. $x = 3$
7. $(x - 5)(x - 2)$
8. $2(x + 5)(x - 5)$
9. $(3x + 1)(3x - 1)$
10. $x(x + 4)(x - 14)$
11. $rs(r + s)(r - s)$
12. $(3x + 5)(x - 1)$
13. $(x + y)(x - y)$
14. 8, 10, and 12
15. 6
16. 5
17. $\{-2, 3\}$
18. (2)
19. (4)
20. (2)
21. (2)
22. (2)
23. 2 and 9

CHAPTER 7

1. $x + 2$
2. $\dfrac{b^2 - 1}{8b}$
3. $1/2$
4. $\dfrac{3(x - 1)}{4(x - 2)}$
5. $\dfrac{-x + 18}{12}$
6. $\dfrac{5a - 6}{6}$
7. $5(x - 1)$
8. $\dfrac{3x}{x + 3}$
9. $\dfrac{2(a + 1)}{a - 1}$
10. $-3(x + y)$
11. $\dfrac{3a(x - 8)}{(x - 9)b^2}$
12. $x - 3$
13. $t = 48$
14. $r = 3$
15. $x = 1/4$
16. $y = -1$
17. $x = 1/8$
18. $a = 8$
19. $x = 7$ or -1
20. $n = 4$ or -3

CHAPTER 8

1. $\sqrt{53}$
2. 4.8
3. $8\sqrt{2}$
4. $-12\sqrt{15}$
5. $11/30$
6. 0
7. (4)
8. (3)
9. (2)
10. (4)
11. (3)
12. (4)

13. 5 and 12
14. (a) If triangle ABC is a right triangle, then the square of the hypotenuse is equal to the sum of the squares of the legs.
(b) If the square of the hypotenuse is not equal to the sum of the squares of the legs, then triangle ABC is not a right triangle.
(c) No.
(d) True.
(e) True.

CUMULATIVE REVIEW FOR CHAPTERS 1–8

1. $x = 18$
2. $(x - 4)(x + 3)$
3. $x = 2$
4. $x = 38$
5. $y = -5$
6. $x^2 - 2x + 1$
7. $x < 3$
8. $a = 18$
9. $2x - 2$
10. $2x^2 - x - 21$
11. 40%
12. $p = \dfrac{t - s}{r}$
13. $\sim p \to q$

14. $(2x + 3)(2x - 3)$
15. 40
16. $3x$
17. $x = -2$
18. $2x + 5$
19. 10
20. 6.6
21. $5/12$
22. $x = 3$
23. $87/198$
24. 6
25. 2 and 6
26. (3)

27. (1)
28. (3)
29. (3)
30. (1)
31. (2)
32. (1)
33. (2)
34. $5, 7,$ and 9
35. 8
36. 5
37. 5 and 16

38. (a) (1) 7 is an even number or 25 is a perfect square. True.
    (2) If 25 is a perfect square then 9 is a prime number. False.
    (3) 7 is not an even number and 9 is not a prime number. True
    (b) (1) $r \leftrightarrow p$ False.
    (2) $\sim q \vee \sim p$ True.
39. (b) Yes.
    (c) Statement is always true.

40. $2ab^2(c + 2)$
41. $\dfrac{y(y + 6)}{6(y + 2)}$
42. $\dfrac{4x + 7}{6x}$
43. $x = 3$

44. $-1 < x < 6$
45. $\{\ \}$
46. $x = -4, 4,$ or 2
47. $x = 3$

48. $x = 12$
49. $x = 1$
50. $x = 8, -8,$ or -6

CHAPTER 9

1. 40
2. 90
3. 30
4. 20
5. 5
6. 54
7. 100

8. 45
9. 30
10. 10
11. (3)
12. $x = 25$
13. $x = 188$
14. $x = 48$

15. $x = 130$
16. 40
17. (2)
18. (3)
19. (4)
20. (2)

CHAPTER 10

1. $10x$
2. 18
3. 49π
4. 4
5. 24
6. 8
7. $\angle SRT$
8. 5
9. 110
10. 24
11. (1)
12. (2)
13. (1)
14. (a) $4\sqrt{2}$
    (b) 8
    (c) 24
    (d) 16

15. (a) 25π
    (b) 6
    (c) 24
    (d) 48
    (e) $25\pi - 48$
16. (a) $2x$
    (b) 36
    (c) 72
    (d) 108
    (e) 36
17. (a) 4
    (b) 10
    (c) 3
    (d) 24
    (e) 18

18. (a) 12
    (b) 16
    (c) 25
    (d) 54
    (e) 300
    (f) 246
19. (a) 12
    (b) 6
    (c) 10
    (d) 48
    (e) 168
20. (a) 8
    (b) 24
    (c) 9π
    (d) 96
    (e) $120 - 9\pi$

CHAPTER 11

1. (1)
2. (2)
3. (3)
4. (2)
5. (4)
6. (1)
7. (1)
8. (3)

9. (4)
10. (2)
11. (1)
12. 10
13. -2
14. $(1, 4)$
15. $A'(-7, 0)$, $B'(0, 8)$, and $C'(0, 0)$

16. (a) (3)
    (b) (1)
    (c) (1)
    (d) (3)
17. (1)
18. (1)
19. (3)
20. (3)

CHAPTER 12

1. $x = 1$
2. $y = 5$
3. $x = 1$
4. (1)
5. (2)
6. (3)
7. $c = 2, d = 5$
8. $x = 3, y = 5$
9. $x = 2, y = -2$

10. $x = 4, y = -3$
11. $(1, -4)$
12. (b) $(2, -2)$
13. (b) $(0, 8)$
14. (b) $x = 2, y = 3$
15. 98
16. 20 2¢ and 30 22¢ stamps

17. (4)
18. (a) (4)
    (b) (2)
    (c) (1)
    (d) (1)

CHAPTER 13

1. 2/5
2. 0.4
3. 2/7
4. 5/12
5. 24
6. 18
7. 12
8. 1/26
9. 4
10. 3/4

11. 1/3
12. 24
13. (b) (1) 1/10
    (2) 3/10
    (3) 4/10
14. (b) 1/4
  (c) 7/16
  (d) 1/8
15. (b) 1/12
  (c) 1/2
  (d) 1/2

16. (b) 1/6
  (c) 1/3
  (d) 2/3
17. (a) (1) 1/3
    (2) 2/3
  (b) (1) 2/9
    (2) 4/9
    (3) 1/9
    (4) 5/9

CHAPTER 14

1. 70
2. 167
3. $4x - 2$
4. 88
5. 12
6. $2x - 2$
7. 5
8. (2)

9. (3)
10. (1)
11. (2)
12. (3)
13. (a) 4/9
  (b) 1/3
  (c) 0

14. 14
15. (b) 62
  (c) 61
  (d) 60

16. (a)

Interval	Frequency
91–100	5
81–90	6
71–80	2
61–70	2
51–60	1

  (c) 81–90
  (d) 91–100

17. (a)

Scores	Frequency	Cumulative Frequency
51–60	4	4
61–70	9	13
71–80	6	19
81–90	5	24
91–100	6	30

  (b) 30
  (c) 81–90
  (d) 11

18. (b) 70–79
  (c) 80–89
  (d) 60–69

REGENTS EXAMINATIONS

Examination June 1991

Three-Year Sequence for High School Mathematics—Course I

Part I

Answer 30 questions from this part. Each correct answer will receive 2 credits. No partial credit will be allowed. Write your answers in the spaces provided on the separate answer sheet. Where applicable, answers may be left in terms of π or in radical form. [60]

1 The mean of a set of 5 numbers is 10. If all the numbers are doubled, what is the mean of this new set of numbers?

2 Solve for x: $0.3x + 1.7 = 2$

3 Find the value of $a^2 - b$ if $a = 3$ and $b = -4$.

4 Solve for x in terms of a and b:

$$2x + a = b$$

5 In the accompanying diagram, $\overleftrightarrow{AB}$ and $\overleftrightarrow{CD}$ intersect at E. If $m\angle AEC = 3x - 40$ and $m\angle BED = 2x + 10$, find the value of x.

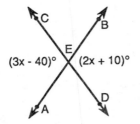

6 If the measures of the angles of a triangle are in the ratio 1:2:3, find the number of degrees in the *smallest* angle.

7 If x varies directly as y and $x = 60$ when $y = 5$, find the value of y when $x = 36$.

8 In the accompanying diagram, $\overleftrightarrow{AOB}$ is a straight line, $m\angle AOD = 3x - 8$, and $m\angle BOD = x$. Find x.

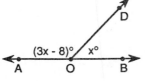

9 Write, in symbolic form, the inverse of $p \rightarrow \sim q$.

10 Find the area of the triangle whose vertices have coordinates $(8,0)$, $(0,10)$, and $(0,0)$.

11 Solve for x: $\frac{2}{3}x - 2 = 10$

12 Express $\frac{5a}{6} - \frac{4a}{9}$ as a single fraction in simplest form.

13 In the accompanying diagram, $ABCD$ is a rectangle. If $DB = 26$ and $DC = 24$, find BC.

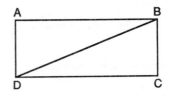

14 Solve for the positive value of x:
$$x^2 - 5x - 24 = 0$$

15 Express $2x^2 - x - 3$ as the product of two binomials.

16 From $5x^2 + 3x - 6$ subtract $4x^2 - 5x + 6$.

17 Evaluate: $_7P_3$

18 The cumulative frequency table below shows the distribution of scores on a math test. How many scores were greater than 90?

Interval	Cumulative Frequency
61–70	4
61–80	10
61–90	12
61–100	16

19 A rotation of a figure can be considered
(1) a turning of the figure about some fixed point
(2) a slide of the figure
(3) an enlargement or a reduction of the figure
(4) a mirror image of the figure

20 A tree 24 feet tall casts a shadow 16 feet long at the same time a man 6 feet tall casts a shadow x feet long. What is the length of the man's shadow?
(1) 6   (3) 3
(2) 5   (4) 4

21 If a letter is chosen at random from the word "BASEBALL," what is the probability that the letter chosen is *not* an "L"?

(1) $\frac{1}{8}$ (3) $\frac{6}{8}$

(2) $\frac{2}{8}$ (4) $\frac{7}{8}$

22 Which inequality is represented by the graph below?

(1) $-4 \leq x \leq 6$ (3) $-4 \leq x < 6$
(2) $-4 < x < 6$ (4) $-4 < x \leq 6$

23 The quotient of $\dfrac{14x^6y}{2x^2y}$, $x \neq 0$, $y \neq 0$, is

(1) $7x^3$ (3) $7x^3y$
(2) $7x^4$ (4) $7x^4y$

24 The expression $\dfrac{5}{2x - 10}$ is undefined when x is equal to
(1) 0   (3) 5
(2) –5   (4) 10

25 A quadrilateral with exactly one pair of parallel sides is a
(1) rhombus   (3) square
(2) rectangle   (4) trapezoid

26 When drawn on the same set of axes, the graph of the equations $y = x + 1$ and $y + x = 3$ intersect at the point whose coordinates are
(1) (2,1)   (3) (2,3)
(2) (1,2)   (4) (–1,4)

27 If the radius of a circle is doubled, then the circumference of the circle is multiplied by

(1) $\frac{1}{2}$ (3) 16

(2) 2   (4) 4

28 The number of feet in c inches is

(1) $\dfrac{c}{12}$ (3) $\dfrac{12}{c}$

(2) $\dfrac{c}{36}$ (4) $12c$

29 Triangle $A'B'C'$ is the image of $\triangle ABC$ under a dilation such that $A'B' = \frac{1}{2}AB$. Triangles ABC and $A'B'C'$ are
(1) congruent but not similar
(2) similar but not congruent
(3) both congruent and similar
(4) neither congruent nor similar

30 The perimeter of a square is $4a$. What is the area of the square?
(1) a^2 (3) 16
(2) $4a^2$ (4) 4

31 Let p represent "$x > 10$" and let q represent "x is a multiple of 5." Which is true if $x = 26$?
(1) $p \lor q$ (3) $p \land q$
(2) $p \to q$ (4) $p \leftrightarrow q$

32 The sum of $\sqrt{50}$ and $\sqrt{2}$ is
(1) $\sqrt{52}$ (3) $6\sqrt{2}$
(2) 10   (4) 12

33 Which ordered pair is in the solution set of the system of inequalities shown in the graph below?

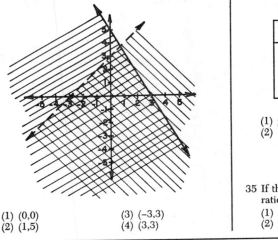

(1) (0,0)　　　　(3) (−3,3)
(2) (1,5)　　　　(4) (3,3)

34 Which statement would be a correct heading for column 3 in the table below?

Column 1	Column 2	Column 3
p	q	?
T	T	F
T	F	T
F	T	T
F	F	T

(1) $p \leftrightarrow q$　　　　(3) $\sim p \rightarrow q$
(2) $\sim (p \vee q)$　　　　(4) $\sim (p \wedge q)$

35 If the ratio of the edges of two cubes is 2:3, the ratio of the two volumes is
(1) 2:3　　　　(3) 8:27
(2) 4:9　　　　(4) 2:5

Answers to the following questions are to be written on paper provided by the school.

Part II

Answer four questions from this part. All work, including calculations, must be shown on your answer paper.　　[40]

36 *a* On the same set of coordinate axes, graph the following system of inequalities:

$$\begin{array}{c} y \geq -3 \\ 2y - x < 6 \end{array} \quad [8]$$

b Write the coordinates of a point in the solution set of the system of inequalities graphed in part *a*.　　[2]

37 If 3 is added to twice the square of an integer, the result is equal to seven times the integer. Find the integer. [*Only an algebraic solution will be accepted*.]　　[4,6]

38 The table shows the results of a math test given to a number of students.

Interval	Frequency
96–100	9
91–95	7
86–90	9
81–85	8
76–80	6
71–75	5

a Draw a frequency histogram based on the data.　　[4]

b In which interval is the median score?　　[2]

c How many students scored at or below the 25th percentile?　　[2]

d To get an A on this test, a student had to have a score greater than 90. What is the probability that a student selected at random from this distribution got an A on the test?　　[2]

39 One black marble and two red marbles are in a bag. Erika picks a marble from the bag at random. She looks at it, returns it, and makes a second random selection.

a Draw a tree diagram or list the sample space showing all possible outcomes. [2]

b What is the probability that two red marbles were selected? [2]

c What is the probability that two black marbles were selected? [2]

d What is the probability that one black and one red marble were selected? [2]

e What is the probability that *at most* one black marble was selected? [2]

40 In the accompanying diagram, *ABCD* is an isosceles trapezoid with altitude $\overline{BE}$, *AB* = 10, *AD* = 15, and *BE* = 12.

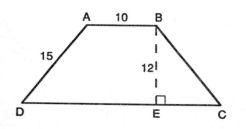

a Find *EC*. [2]

b Find the area of
   (1) triangle *BEC* [2]
   (2) trapezoid *ABCD* [3]
   (3) trapezoid *ABED* [1]

c If diagonal $\overline{DB}$ is drawn, find the area of △*ABD*. [2]

41 Use any method [algebraic, trial and error, making a table, etc.] to solve this problem. A written explanation of how you arrived at your answer is also acceptable. Show all work.

There are two pairs of integers that satisfy both of these conditions:

   The larger integer is 9 more than the smaller integer.
   The sum of the squares of the integers is 41.

a Find the two pairs of integers. [8]

b Show that one pair of integers found in part *a* satisfies both given conditions. [2]

42 Solve the following system of equations algebraically and check:

$$4x + 3y = 25$$
$$5x + 2y = 33$$
[8,2]

REGENTS EXAMINATIONS

Examination January 1992

Three-Year Sequence for High School Mathematics—Course I

Part I

Answer 30 questions from this part. Each correct answer will receive 2 credits. No partial credit will be allowed. Write your answers in the spaces provided on the separate answer sheet. Where applicable, answers may be left in terms of π or in radical form. [60]

1 Thirteen students took a math test. The number of errors was 3, 7, 4, 0, 4, 1, 5, 4, 7, 3, 4, 5, and 7. What is the mode of this distribution?

2 Express the sum of $4x^2 - 7x + 6$ and $-3x^2 + 9x - 11$ as a trinomial.

3 The circumference of a circle is 12π. What is the radius of the circle?

4 In the diagram below, m$\angle BCD = 140$ and m$\angle BAC = 80$. Find m$\angle ABC$.

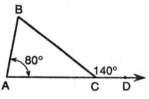

5 In the accompanying diagram, transversal $\overleftrightarrow{EF}$ intersects parallel lines $\overleftrightarrow{AB}$ and $\overleftrightarrow{CD}$ at G and H, respectively. If m$\angle AGH = 3x + 40$ and m$\angle GHD = 6x - 17$, what is the value of x?

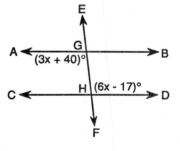

6 Solve for x: $8x - 5(x - 1) = 20$

7 If 340,000 is expressed in the form 3.4×10^n, what is the value of n?

8 If $m = 3$ and $v = -4$, find the value of $\frac{1}{2}mv^2$.

9 Two angles are supplementary, and the measure of one angle is three times the measure of the other. Find the measure of the *smaller* angle.

10 Solve for x: $\dfrac{x - 3}{4} = \dfrac{x}{10}$

11 A school menu lists two soups, three main dishes, three desserts, and four drinks. How many different meals consisting of one soup, one main dish, one dessert, and one drink are possible?

12 If a number is picked at random from the set $\{-4,-3,-2,-1,0,1,2,3,4\}$, what is the probability that the number satisfies the equation $x^2 - 9 = 0$?

13 If $(2x + 3)(x - 2)$ is written in the form $ax^2 + bx + c$, what is the value of c?

14 The number of chirps made by a cricket varies directly as the temperature. If at 12° a cricket chirps 30 times per minute, how many times per minute will the cricket chirp at 20°?

15 A rectangular floor uses 50 tiles for its length and 20 tiles for its width. Ten of the tiles in this floor are cracked. In an inspection, one tile is selected at random. What is the probability that this tile is cracked?

16 The perimeter of a square is $4a + 12$. Express the length of a side of the square in terms of a.

17 Express as a single fraction in simplest form:

$$\frac{5x + 2}{6} + \frac{2x - 3}{3}$$

Directions (18–35): For *each* question chosen, write on the separate answer sheet the *numeral* preceding the word or expression that best completes the statement or answers the question.

18 If p represents "It will rain" and q represents "We go to the movies," the statement "If we do not go to the movies, then it will rain" can be expressed by
(1) $p \rightarrow q$
(2) $q \rightarrow {\sim}p$
(3) ${\sim}q \rightarrow p$
(4) ${\sim}p \rightarrow {\sim}q$

19 Let p represent "x is an odd integer," and let q represent "x is a multiple of 3." For which value of x will $p \wedge q$ be true?
(1) 1
(2) 6
(3) 9
(4) 12

20 The product of $-4a^2b^3$ and $5ab^4$ is
(1) a^2b^{12}
(2) $-20a^2b^7$
(3) $-20a^2b^{12}$
(4) $-20a^3b^7$

21 Maria is twice as old as Sue. If x represents Sue's age, which expression represents how old Maria will be in three years?
(1) $2x$
(2) $x + 3$
(3) $\frac{1}{2}x - 3$
(4) $2x + 3$

22 Which measure is *always* the same as the 50th percentile?
(1) mean
(2) median
(3) mode
(4) lower quartile

23 Which statement represents the inverse of the statement "If I do not study, then I will fail"?
(1) If I study, then I will not fail.
(2) If I fail, then I did not study.
(3) If I study, then I will fail.
(4) If I do not fail, then I did study.

24 The width and length of a rectangle are represented by x and $3x + 5$, respectively. If the area of the rectangle is 24, which equation can be used to find the dimensions of the rectangle?
(1) $x(3x + 5) = 24$
(2) $2x(3x + 5) = 24$
(3) $x + (3x + 5) = 24$
(4) $2x + 2(3x + 5) = 24$

25 In which graph is the slope of line ℓ negative?

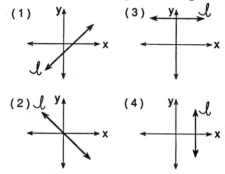

26 Which figure has one and only one line of symmetry?
(1) rhombus
(2) circle
(3) square
(4) isosceles triangle

27 What are the coordinates of the point where the graph of the equation $x + 2y = 8$ crosses the y-axis?
(1) (0,8)
(2) (8,0)
(3) (0,4)
(4) (4,0)

28 Which inequality is equivalent to $2x + 6 > 2$?
(1) $x > -2$
(2) $x < -2$
(3) $x > 2$
(4) $x < 2$

29 If the legs of a right triangle are 4 and 7, the length of the hypotenuse is
(1) $\sqrt{3}$
(2) $\sqrt{11}$
(3) $\sqrt{33}$
(4) $\sqrt{65}$

30 Which is the additive inverse of $-\frac{a}{3}$?
(1) $\frac{a}{3}$
(2) $\frac{3}{a}$
(3) $-\frac{3}{a}$
(4) 0

31 Which is the solution set of the equation $2x^2 + 3x - 2 = 0$?
(1) $\left\{ -\frac{1}{2}, 2 \right\}$
(2) $\left\{ \frac{1}{2}, -2 \right\}$
(3) $\left\{ \frac{1}{2}, 2 \right\}$
(4) $\left\{ -\frac{1}{2}, -2 \right\}$

32 In the accompanying diagram, square ABCD has vertices A(0,0), B(a,0), C(a,a), and D(0,a).

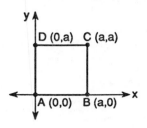

What is the area of square ABCD?

(1) 4a   (3) a^2

(2) 2a   (4) $a\sqrt{2}$

33 Which property is *not* common to all parallelograms?
   (1) Opposite sides are parallel.
   (2) Opposite angles are congruent.
   (3) Consecutive angles are supplementary.
   (4) Diagonals are congruent.

34 Which expression could be used to change 8 kilometers per hour to meters per minute?

(1) $\dfrac{8 \text{ km}}{\text{hr}} \cdot \dfrac{\text{km}}{1000 \text{ m}} \cdot \dfrac{\text{hr}}{60 \text{ min}}$

(2) $\dfrac{8 \text{ km}}{\text{hr}} \cdot \dfrac{1000 \text{ m}}{\text{km}} \cdot \dfrac{60 \text{ min}}{\text{hr}}$

(3) $\dfrac{8 \text{ km}}{\text{hr}} \cdot \dfrac{1000 \text{ m}}{\text{km}} \cdot \dfrac{\text{hr}}{60 \text{ min}}$

(4) $\dfrac{8 \text{ km}}{\text{hr}} \cdot \dfrac{\text{km}}{1000 \text{ m}} \cdot \dfrac{60 \text{ min}}{\text{hr}}$

35 The value of 5^{-2} is

(1) $-\dfrac{1}{25}$ (3) –10

(2) $\dfrac{1}{25}$ (4) –25

Answers to the following questions are to be written on paper provided by the school.

Part II

Answer four questions from this part. All work, including calculations, must be shown on your answer paper.   [40]

36 Solve the following system of equations graphically and check:

$$y = -x + 2$$
$$3y - 2x = -9 \qquad [8,2]$$

37 A jar contains one dime, two quarters, and three nickels. Without looking, Andrew picks one coin from the jar. Without replacing this coin, he picks another coin.

   a Draw a tree diagram or list the sample space of all possible outcomes.   [3]

   b What is the probability Andrew picked a dime first and then a nickel?   [2]

   c What is the probability he picked two dimes from the jar?   [2]

   d What is the probability he picked two coins such that the sum of their values is greater than or equal to 35 cents?   [3]

38 In the accompanying diagram, right triangle DEF is similar to right triangle ABC. The measure of $\overline{AC}$ is 2 more than the measure of $\overline{BC}$, the measure of $\overline{EF}$ is 3 less than the measure of $\overline{BC}$, and $DF = 4$.

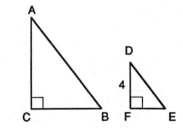

   a Find the measure of $\overline{BC}$.   [6]

   b Find the measure of $\overline{AB}$.   [2]

   c What is the ratio of the area of $\triangle ABC$ to the area of $\triangle DEF$?   [2]

39 Brian has $78 and wants to purchase tapes through a music club. Each tape costs $7.50. The music club will add a total postage and handling charge of $3.50 to his order. What is the greatest number of tapes he can purchase? [*Only an algebraic solution will be accepted.*]   [5,5]

40 The table below shows the distribution of scores that 20 math students received on a classroom test.

Interval	Frequency
90–99	3
80–89	8
70–79	6
60–69	2
50–59	1

a In which interval does the median lie?   [2]
b In which interval is the upper quartile?   [2]
c *On your answer paper*, copy and complete the cumulative frequency table below, using the data given in the frequency table.   [2]

Interval	Cumulative Frequency
50–99	
50–89	
50–79	
50–69	
50–59	1

d Construct a cumulative frequency histogram using the table completed in part *c*.   [4]

41 Each part below consists of a set of three statements. The truth values for two statements in each set are given. Based on this information, determine the truth value of the remaining statement. *On your answer paper*, write the letters *a* through *e*, and next to each letter, write the missing truth value (TRUE or FALSE). If the truth value cannot be determined from the information given, write "CANNOT BE DETERMINED."

	Statements	Truth Value	
a	(1) $p \lor q$ (2) q (3) p	TRUE ? FALSE	[2]
b	(1) p (2) q (3) $p \leftrightarrow q$	? FALSE TRUE	[2]
c	(1) $p \land q$ (2) p (3) q	FALSE FALSE ?	[2]
d	(1) $q \rightarrow p$ (2) p (3) $\sim q$	TRUE FALSE ?	[2]
e	(1) $p \lor q$ (2) $p \rightarrow q$ (3) q	TRUE TRUE ?	[2]

42 Answer *both a* and *b*.

a The measure of the vertex angle of an isosceles triangle exceeds 3 times the measure of a base angle by 20. Write an equation or system of equations that could be used to find the measure of *each* angle of the triangle. State what the variable(s) represents. [*Solution of the equation(s) is not required.*]   [5]

b Write an equation that could be used to find three consecutive positive even integers such that the product of the first and third is six more than nine times the second. State what the variable represents. [*Solution of the equation is not required.*]   [5]

REGENTS EXAMINATIONS

Examination June 1992

Three-Year Sequence for High School Mathematics—Course I

Part I

Answer 30 questions from this part. Each correct answer will receive 2 credits. No partial credit will be allowed. Write your answers in the spaces provided on the separate answer sheet. Where applicable, answers may be left in terms of π or in radical form. [60]

1 A letter is chosen at random from the word "REGENTS." Find the probability that the letter chosen is an E.

2 Let p represent the statement "The triangle is isosceles," and let q represent the statement "The triangle is scalene." Write in symbolic form: "If the triangle is isosceles, then the triangle is *not* scalene."

3 Solve for x: $3(2x - 1) = x + 2$

4 In a basketball game, the number of points scored by five members of the team were 28, 20, 16, 15, and 8. How many players scored fewer than the mean number of points?

5 Solve for x: $0.5x - 12 = 3.5$

6 If $x = 5$ and $y = -2$, what is the value of $\dfrac{2x - y}{3}$?

7 The histogram below shows the distribution of temperatures for ten days. Which temperature is the mode?

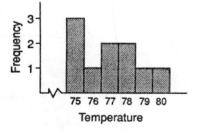

Temperature

8 A rectangle has an area of 20. If the length of the rectangle is doubled and the width remains the same, what is the area of the new rectangle?

9 Solve for y: $\dfrac{3}{4}y - 8 = 1$

10 In the accompanying diagram, $m\angle A = 2x - 30$, $m\angle B = x$, and $m\angle C = x + 10$. Find the number of degrees in $\angle B$.

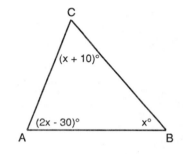

11 If $x = 4y$, what is the value of $\dfrac{x}{y}$, $y \neq 0$?

12 What is the inverse of $\sim s \rightarrow t$?

13 The sides of a triangle measure 6, 11, and 15. If the smallest side of a similar triangle measures 4, find the length of its longest side.

14 In the accompanying diagram, $\overleftrightarrow{AB}$ is parallel to $\overleftrightarrow{CD}$ and transversal $\overleftrightarrow{EF}$ intersects $\overleftrightarrow{AB}$ and $\overleftrightarrow{CD}$ at G and H, respectively. If $m\angle DHG : m\angle BGH = 1:2$, find $m\angle DHG$.

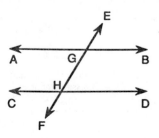

15 The length of a rectangular solid is 3.0 meters, the width is 0.6 meter, and the height is 0.4 meter. Find, to the *nearest tenth*, the number of cubic meters in the volume of the solid.

16 If the coordinates of the vertices of $\triangle ABC$ are $A(-5,0)$, $B(5,0)$, and $C(0,8)$, what is the area of the triangle?

17 Which value for n makes this sentence true?

$$0.00045 = 4.5 \times 10^n$$

18 The area of a circle is 49π. Find, in terms of π, the circumference of the circle.

19 If x varies directly as y and $x = 3$ when $y = 4$, find x when $y = 20$.

Directions (20–35): For *each* question chosen, write on the separate answer sheet the *numeral* preceding the word or expression that best completes the statement or answers the question.

20 If $n + 7$ represents an even number, the next larger even number is represented by
(1) $n + 8$ (3) $10n + 7$
(2) $n + 9$ (4) $2n + 7$

21 What is the total number of lines of symmetry in a square?
(1) 1   (3) 0
(2) 2   (4) 4

22 If $3x + c = 4$, then x equals
(1) $4 - c$ (3) $\dfrac{c - 4}{3}$

(2) $\dfrac{4 - c}{3}$ (4) $c - 4$

23 If $-21a^6b$ is divided by $-3a^2b$, the quotient is
(1) $7a^4$ (3) $7a^3b$
(2) $-7a^3$ (4) $7a^4b$

24 Which is the greatest integer that makes the inequality $3 - 2x > 9$ a true statement?
(1) -2 (3) 5
(2) 2   (4) -4

25 Let p represent "x is prime," and let q represent "x is even." Which statement is true if $x = 2$?
(1) $\sim p \wedge q$ (3) $p \wedge q$
(2) $\sim q \wedge p$ (4) $\sim (p \wedge q)$

26 A line is represented by the equation $y = 3x - 7$. Which statement about the line is true?

(1) The slope of the line is $\frac{1}{3}$.

(2) The y-intercept is -7.

(3) Point $(1,4)$ lies on the line.

(4) This line is parallel to the line whose equation is $y = 2x - 7$.

27 Which graph shows the solution set of $-2 \leq x < 4$?

(1)

-4 -3 -2 -1 0 1 2 3 4 5

(2)

-4 -3 -2 -1 0 1 2 3 4 5

(3)

-4 -3 -2 -1 0 1 2 3 4 5

(4)

-4 -3 -2 -1 0 1 2 3 4 5

28 The expression $\sqrt{500}$ is equivalent to
(1) $5\sqrt{10}$ (3) $500\sqrt{2}$
(2) $10\sqrt{5}$ (4) $5\sqrt{100}$

29 If the length and width of a rectangle are 8 and 5, the length of a diagonal is
(1) 89   (3) $\sqrt{89}$
(2) $\sqrt{39}$ (4) $\sqrt{13}$

30 Which inequality is illustrated in the accompanying graph?

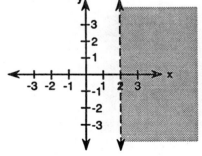

(1) $x > 2$ (3) $y > 2$
(2) $x < 2$ (4) $y < 2$

31 The perimeter of a rectangle is $12x + 4$. If the width is $2x$, the length of the rectangle is
(1) $6x + 2$ (3) $4x + 2$
(2) $6x - 2$ (4) $4x - 2$

32 The solution set for $2x^2 - 7x - 4 = 0$ is

(1) $\{2,-1\}$ (3) $\{-2,1\}$

(2) $\left\{-\frac{1}{2},4\right\}$ (4) $\left\{\frac{1}{2}, -4\right\}$

33 In parallelogram $ABCD$, $m\angle A = 2x + 50$ and $m\angle C = 3x + 40$. The measure of $\angle A$ is
(1) $18°$ (3) $70°$
(2) $20°$ (4) $86°$

34 In the accompanying diagram, the faces are congruent.

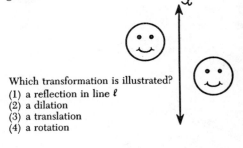

Which transformation is illustrated?
(1) a reflection in line ℓ
(2) a dilation
(3) a translation
(4) a rotation

35 If the probability that an event will occur is p, what is the probability that the event will *not* occur?

(1) $1 - p$ (3) p

(2) $p - 1$ (4) $\dfrac{1}{p}$

Answers to the following questions are to be written on paper provided by the school.

Part II

Answer four questions from this part. Clearly indicate the necessary steps, including appropriate formula substitutions, diagrams, graphs, charts, etc. Calculations that may be obtained by mental arithmetic or the calculator do not need to be shown.   [40]

36 The cumulative frequency histogram below shows the number of mistakes 28 students in a French language class made on a test.

   a *On your answer paper,* copy and complete the frequency table below using the data shown in the cumulative frequency histogram.   [4]

   b If the number of mistakes John made is included in the interval that contains the median, what is the maximum number of mistakes that John could have made?   [2]

   c What percent of the French class made fewer than 11 mistakes?   [2]

   d What is the probability that a student selected at random made *at least* 16 mistakes?   [2]

Frequency Table

Number of Mistakes	Number of Students
0–5	
6–10	
11–15	
16–20	
21–25	

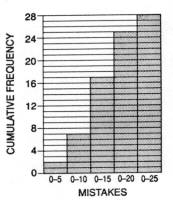

37 Find three positive consecutive integers such that the product of the first and second is two more than three times the third. [*Only an algebraic solution will be accepted.*] [5,5]

38 *a* *On your answer paper*, construct and complete a truth table for the statement $(p \longleftrightarrow q) \rightarrow (\sim p \lor q)$. [9]

   b From the truth table constructed in part *a*, is the statement $(p \longleftrightarrow q) \rightarrow (\sim p \lor q)$ a tautology? [1]

39 In the accompanying diagram, *ABCD* is an isosceles trapezoid with bases $\overline{AB}$ and $\overline{DC}$, $DA = .13$, *CDEF* is a square, and circle *O* has a diameter of 12. The length of a side of the square is equal to the diameter of the circle.

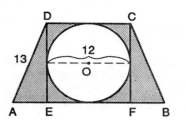

   a Find the measure of
   (1) $\overline{AE}$ [2]
   (2) $\overline{AB}$ [1]
   b Find the area of trapezoid *ABCD*. [2]
   c Find the area of the circle in terms of π. [2]
   d Using $\pi = 3.14$, find, to the *nearest integer*, the area of the shaded region. [3]

40 The width of a rectangle is two more than a side of a square. The length of the rectangle is one less than twice the side of the square. If the area of the rectangle is 68 more than the area of the square, find the measure of a side of the square. [*Show or explain the procedure used to obtain your answer.*] [10]

41 *a* On the same set of coordinate axes, graph the following system of inequalities. Label the region that represents the solution set S.

$$y - 2x \geq 0$$
$$x + y < 6$$ [8]

   b Write the coordinates of a point that does *not* satisfy either inequality graphed in part *a*. [2]

42 The letters **M**, **A**, **T**, and **H** are put in a jar.
   a One letter is drawn at random from the jar, not replaced, and then a second letter is drawn.
      (1) Draw a tree diagram or list the sample space showing all possible outcomes. [4]
      (2) Find the probability that one of the two letters selected has both horizontal and vertical line symmetry. [2]
      (3) Find the probability that both letters selected have at least one line of symmetry. [2]
   b Using all the letters **M**, **A**, **T**, and **H**, how many different four-letter arrangements can be made? [2]

INDEX

Cumulative frequency
  histogram, 399-402
  polygon, 403
Cumulative relative frequency, 403
Cylinder, right circular, 280-281

D

Data, 385
Decimals
  in equations, 66-67
  nonrepeating, 168
  repeating vs. terminating, 163
Degree
  of an angle, 196
  of a polynomial, 108
Denominator
  lowest common, 12
  rationalizing, 176
Dilations, 319
Dimensional analysis, 150
Direct variation, 83-84
Disjunction, 30-31
Distributive property, 21
Divide-and-average method, 170
Divisibility, 8
Division
  by 0, 8
  in solving inequalities, 93
  in solving linear equations, 61
  of polynomials by monomials, 117
  of powers, 16
  of radicals, 175-176
  of signed numbers, 10, 12
Division (and multiplication) property
  of equality, 61
  of inequality, 93
Domain, 25

E

Element of a set, 2
Empty set, 2
Equation of a line, 301
  direct variation, 313-314
  general forms, 306
  slope-intercept form, 302
  writing, 304-305
Equations, 2
  checking, 61-62
  equivalent, 59
  first degree, 59
  graphing, 310-313
  literal equations, 88
  of lines, 301, 306
  open sentence, 25
  quadratic, 135-138
  solution set, 25
  solving linear equations, 59-65
  systems of linear equations, 330-331,
    338-341, 343-347
  translating words into, 57
  using equations to solve problems, 62, 70,
    75-76, 81-82, 140-142
  using systems of equations to solve
    problems, 349-353
Equilateral triangle, 203, 244
Equivalent
  equations, 59
  ratios, 81
Even integers, 8
Event, 358

Experiment, 358
Exponents, 15
  dividing powers, 16
  multiplying powers, 16
  negative and zero exponents, 17
  power law, 110
Extremes of a proportion, 82

F

Faces, 275-276
Factor, 15
Factorial of a number, 378
Factoring,
  completely, 134
  difference of two squares, 128-129
  greatest common factor (GCF), 124
  polynomials, 125-126
  prime factorization, 15
  quadratic trinomials, 130-133
  solving higher degree equations by, 138-139
  solving quadratic equations by, 135-138
FOIL, 119
Formulas
  area, 262
  slope, 294
  solving for a given variable, 89
  volume, 283
Fractions,
  addition and subtraction, 151-152, 154-155
  dividing, 149-150
  equations, 159
  finding the LCD, 154
  multiplying, 148-149, 151-152
  simplifying, 145-147
Frequency, 389
  cumulative, 398-402
  histograms, 391-394
  tables, 390

G

Geometry,
  angle, 192
  area, 251
  collinear points, 192
  complementary angles, 206
  congruent triangles, 236-238
  coordinate geometry, 289-315, 330-336
  line, 191
  line segment, 192
  parallel lines, 210, 212-215
  perimeter, 58, 89, 113, 247
  perpendicular lines, 197
  plane, 191
  polygons, 201-202
  postulates, 193-194
  ray, 192
  similar triangles, 246-248
  simple closed curves, 201
  supplementary angles, 205
  transformational geometry, 315-320
  undefined terms, 191
  vertical angles, 207
Graphs
  cumulative frequency histograms, 399
  frequency histograms, 390
  number line, 4
  of linear equations, 301-302
  of linear inequalities, 92, 333-334
  of systems of equations, 330-332
  of systems of inequalities, 334-336
Greatest common factor, 124

H

Half-plane, 333
Hexagon, 202
Histogram, 389
  cumulative frequency, 398-402
  frequency, 390-392
Hypotenuse, 181
Hypothesis, 35

I

Identity elements, 5
Image, 315
Implication, 37
Index, 167
Inequalities, 2
  compound, 95-96
  extended, 98
  graphs of, 92-93, 333-334
  negating, 28
  properties of, 91- 93
  word problems, 100-102
  systems of inequalities, 334-336
Integers,
  consecutive, 75
  signed, 4
Inscribed polygon, 267
Intersection
  of lines, 330
  of sets, 3
Inverse
  elements, 5
  of a conditional statement, 38-39
Irrational number, 5, 168
Isosceles triangle, 203, 242-243

L

Lateral faces, 276
Laws of exponents, 16-17
Least common multiple (LCM), 9
Like terms, 21
Line(s)
  equation of, 301-302, 304
  graphing, 310-313
  oblique, 296
  of symmetry, 315
  parallel, 210
  perpendicular, 197
  slope of, 293
  x-intercept of, 311
  y-intercept of, 311
Line segments, 192
  horizontal and vertical, 290
  measuring, 195
Linear equations
  graphing, 301, 310-313
  in one variable, 59-72
  in two variables, 301
  systems of, 330-332, 338-347
  writing, 304-306
Linear inequalities
  in one variable, 91-94, 333-334
  in two variables, 334-336
Logic
  biconditional, 44-45
  compound statement, 32-33
  conclusion (consequent), 35
  conditional statement, 35
  conjunction, 29-30
  contradiction, 43
  contrapositive, 38-39

converse, 38-39
disjunction, 30-31
drawing conclusions, 48-50
equivalence, 40
hypothesis (antecedent), 35
inverse, 38-39
negation of a statement, 27
open sentence, 25
statement, 25
tautology, 43
truth table, 27, 32-33
truth value, 25
Logically equivalent, 40
Lowest common denominator, 12, 154

M

Mean, 385
Means of a proportion, 82
Measure of a(n)
  angle, 195
  line segment, 195
Measures of central tendency, 385-386
Median, 386
Midpoint, 198
Mode, 386
Monomial(s), 106
  coefficient, 106
  division, 111
  like, 107
  multiplication, 110
Multiplication
  in solving inequalities, 93
  in solving linear equations, 61
  in solving systems of linear equations, 345-347
  of algebraic fractions, 148-149
  of conjugate binomials 128-129
  of polynomials, 110, 116-117
  of powers, 16
  of radicals, 175
  of signed numbers, 10, 12
  property of inequalities, 93
  properties of 0 and 1, 5
  using FOIL, 119
  zero product rule, 135
Multiplicative inverse, 5

N

Negation
  of a statement, 27
  of an inequality, 28
Nonrepeating decimals, 163
Null set, 2
Number line, 4
Number systems, 4-5, 163, 168
Numerals, 1

O

Oblique line, 296
Obtuse
  angle, 197
  triangle, 203
Odd integers, 8
Open sentence, 25
Ordered pairs, 289
Order of operations, 20
Ordinate, 289
Origin, 289
Outcomes, 358, 362-364

P

Parallel lines, 210
  properties of, 212-214
  proving lines are, 215
  slope of, 297
Parallelograms, 228
  area of, 253
  properties of, 229, 239
Percent problems, 78-79
Percentiles, 403
Perfect squares, 167
Perimeter, 58, 89, 113, 247
Permutation, 378
Perpendicular lines, 197
Pi (π), 168, 265
Plane, 191, 193
Points, 191-192
Point symmetry, 324
Polygons, 201
  classifying, 202
  congruent vs. similar, 246
  cumulative frequency, 403
  inscribed and circumscribed, 267
  regular, 202
Polyhedron, 275
Polynomials, 106
  addition and subtraction, 113-114
  classifying, 106
  degree, 108
  divided by a monomial, 111, 117
  factoring, 125-126
  multiplying, 110, 116, 119
  quadratic form, 130
  simplifying, 108-109
  standard form, 108
Postulate, 193
Powers, 15-16, 20, 110
Prime
  factorization, 15
  number, 8
Principal square root, 166
Prisms, 275-276
Probability, 358
  counting principle, 365
  involving AND, 369
  involving OR, 370
  joint, 373-374
  of a certainty, 360
  of an event, 359
  of an event *not* occurring, 360
  of an impossiblity, 360
  outcomes, 358, 362-364
  permutations, 378
  range of values, 360
  sample space, 358
  successful (favorable) outcomes, 358
  tree diagrams, 363-364
Proportions, 81-83
Protractor, 196
Pyramid, 277
Pythagorean Theorem, 181-182
  converse of, 184-185
Pythagorean triples, 183

Q

Quadrants, 290
Quadratic equations, 135-138
Quadratic trinomials, 135-138

Quadrilaterals,
  angles of, 227
  special types, 202, 230
Quartiles, 387-388
Quotients
  of polynomials, 111, 117
  of powers, 16
  of radicals, 175-176
  of signed numbers, 10-12

R

Radical(s),
  addition and subtraction, 178-180
  index, 167
  like, 178
  multiplication and division, 175-176
  radicand, 166
  rationalizing denominators, 176
  squaring, 175
  sign, 166
  simplifying, 172-173, 176
Radical sign, 166
Radicand, 166
Radius, 264
Rationalizing denominators, 176
Rational numbers, 5, 163
Ratios, 81
Ray, 192
Real numbers, 168
Reciprocal, 5
Rectangles, 230
  area of, 252
Rectangular solid, 276
Regular polygons, 202
Repeating decimals, 163-165
Repetend, 164
Replacement set, 25
Rhombus, 230
Right angle, 197
Right triangles, 181, 203
Root
  of an equation, 61
  square, 166
Rotations, 318

S

Sample space, 358
SAS, 237
Scalene triangle, 203
Scientific notation, 18
Semicircle, 265
Sets 2-3, 25
  empty, 2
  intersection, 3
  notation, 2
  replacement (domain), 25
  sample space, 358
  solution, 25
  subset, 3
  union, 3
Set-builder notation, 4
Similar
  polygons, 240-246
  triangles, 248-249
Simple closed curves, 201
Simplifying
  algebraic fractions, 145-147